The Witch's House
The Diary of Ellen

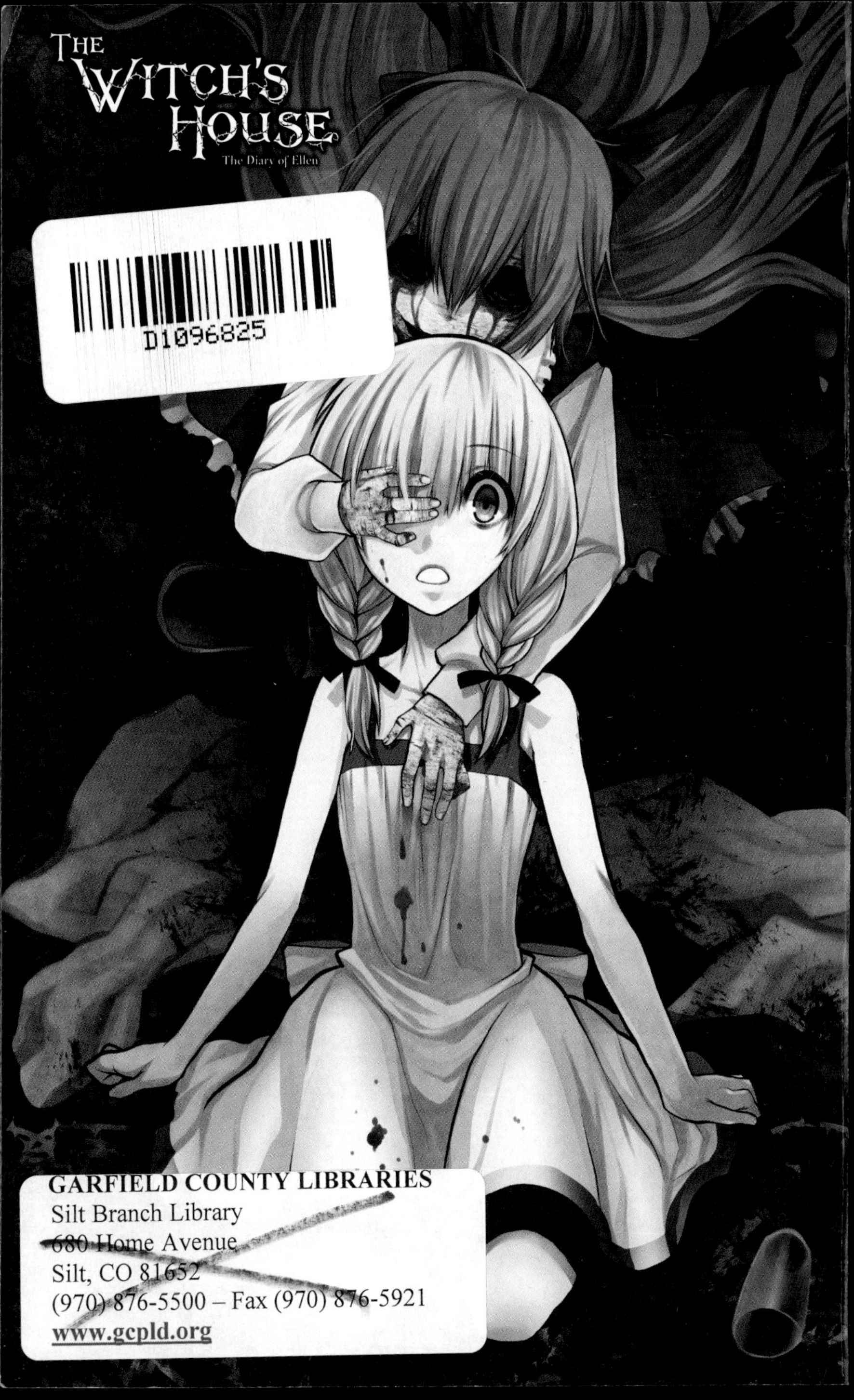

The Witch's House

The Diary of Ellen

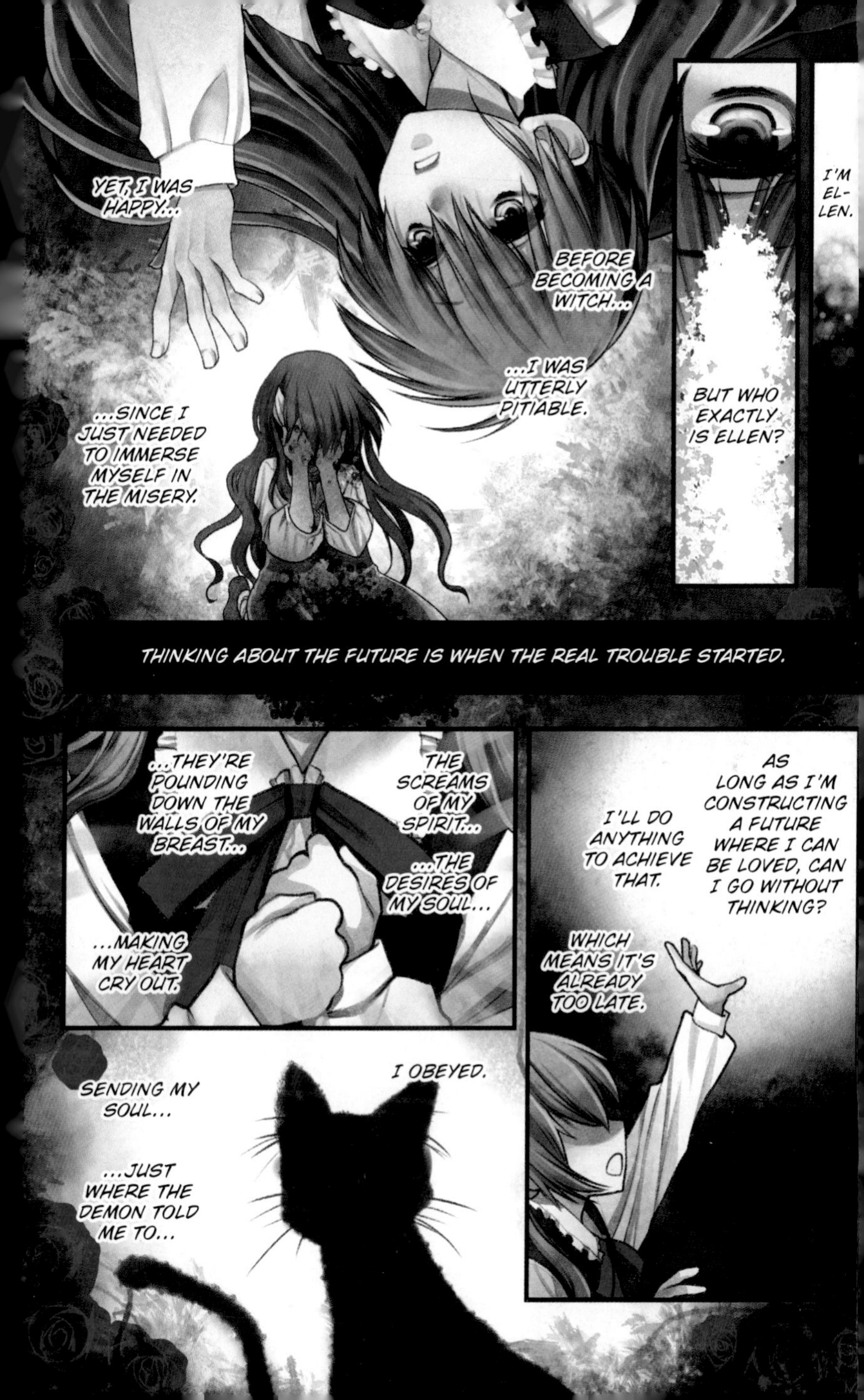
I'M EL-LEN.
BUT WHO EXACTLY IS ELLEN?
BEFORE BECOMING A WITCH...
...I WAS UTTERLY PITIABLE.
YET, I WAS HAPPY...
...SINCE I JUST NEEDED TO IMMERSE MYSELF IN THE MISERY.
THINKING ABOUT THE FUTURE IS WHEN THE REAL TROUBLE STARTED.
AS LONG AS I'M CONSTRUCTING A FUTURE WHERE I CAN BE LOVED, CAN I GO WITHOUT THINKING?
I'LL DO ANYTHING TO ACHIEVE THAT.
WHICH MEANS IT'S ALREADY TOO LATE.
THE SCREAMS OF MY SPIRIT...
...THE DESIRES OF MY SOUL...
...THEY'RE POUNDING DOWN THE WALLS OF MY BREAST...
...MAKING MY HEART CRY OUT.
I OBEYED.
SENDING MY SOUL...
...JUST WHERE THE DEMON TOLD ME TO...

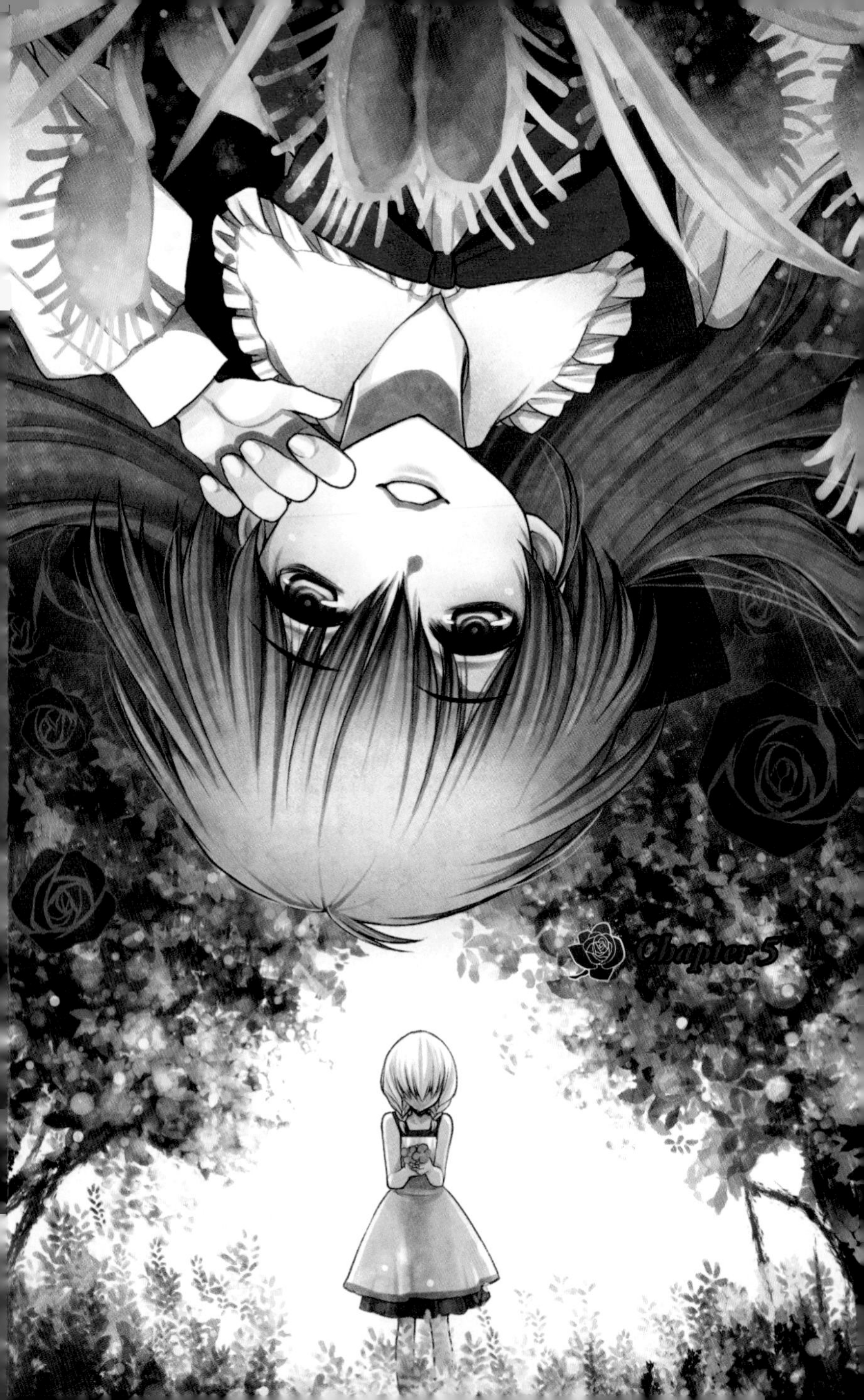
Chapter 5

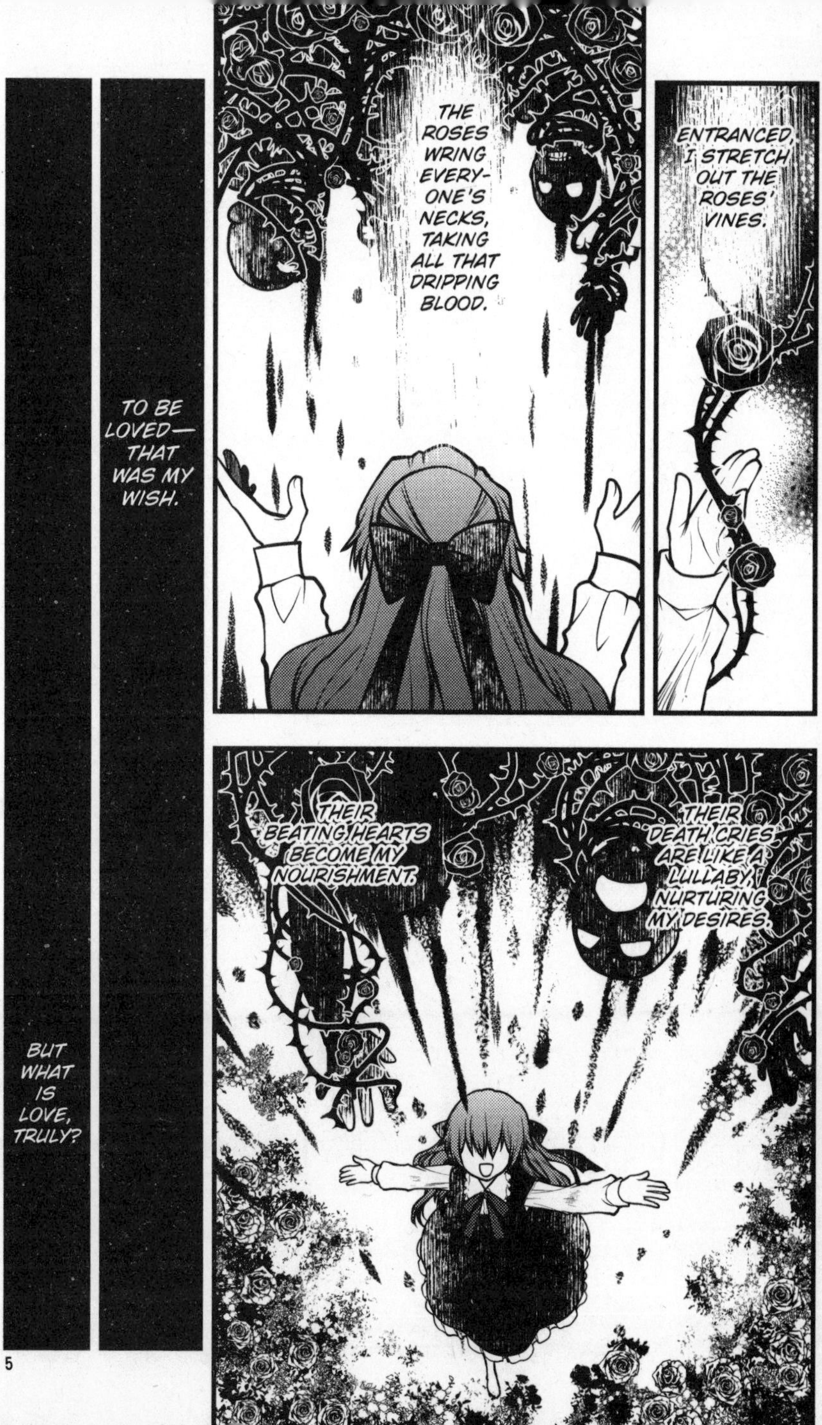

ENTRANCED, I STRETCH OUT THE ROSES' VINES.
THE ROSES WRING EVERY-ONE'S NECKS, TAKING ALL THAT DRIPPING BLOOD.
THEIR DEATH CRIES ARE LIKE A LULLABY, NURTURING MY DESIRES.
THEIR BEATING HEARTS BECOME MY NOURISHMENT.
TO BE LOVED—THAT WAS MY WISH.
BUT WHAT IS LOVE, TRULY?

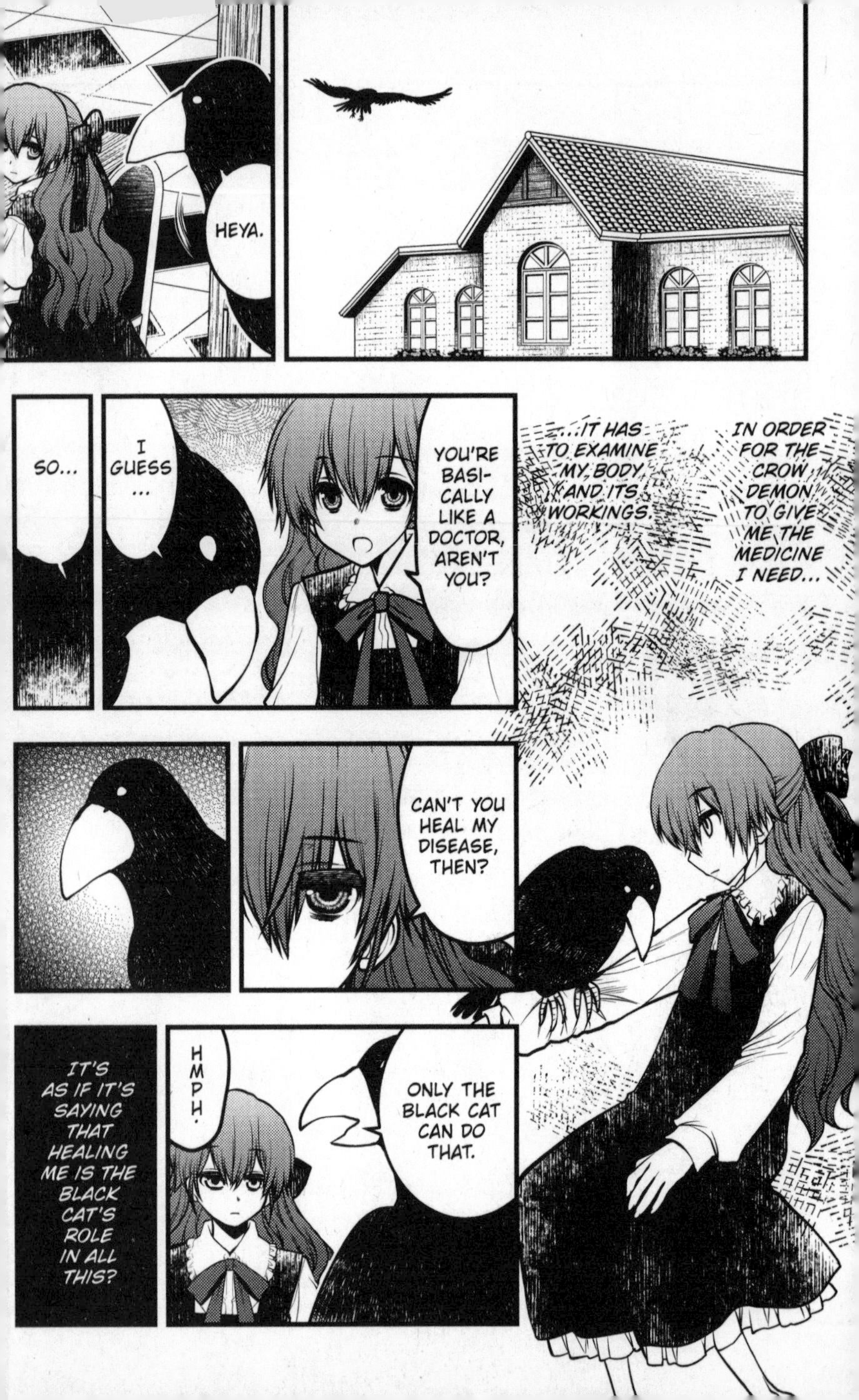
HEYA.
IN ORDER FOR THE CROW DEMON TO GIVE ME THE MEDICINE I NEED...
...IT HAS TO EXAMINE MY BODY AND ITS WORKINGS.
YOU'RE BASICALLY LIKE A DOCTOR, AREN'T YOU?
I GUESS...
SO...
CAN'T YOU HEAL MY DISEASE, THEN?
ONLY THE BLACK CAT CAN DO THAT.
HMPH.
IT'S AS IF IT'S SAYING THAT HEALING ME IS THE BLACK CAT'S ROLE IN ALL THIS?

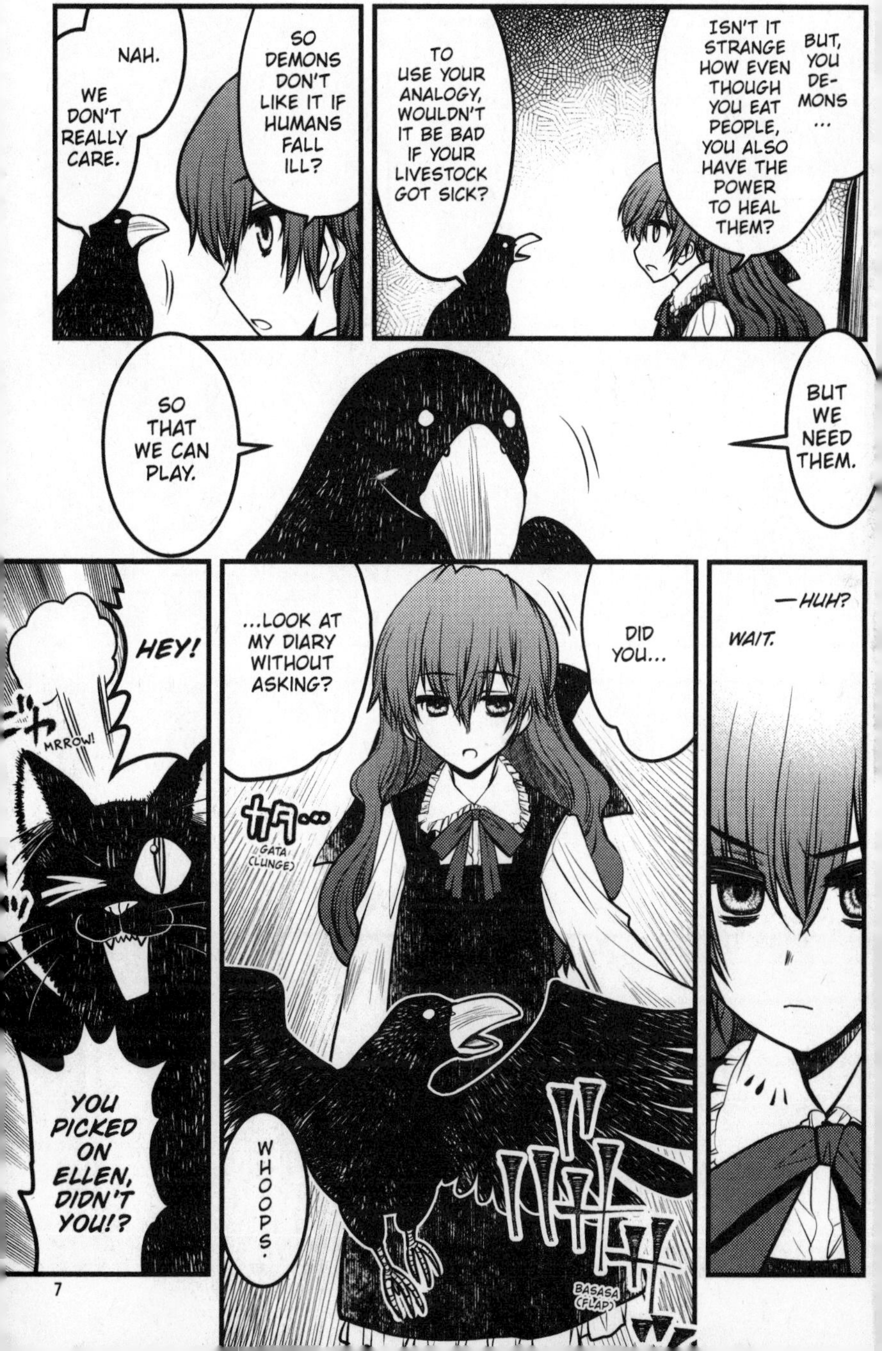
BUT, YOU DE-MONS...
ISN'T IT STRANGE HOW EVEN THOUGH YOU EAT PEOPLE, YOU ALSO HAVE THE POWER TO HEAL THEM?
TO USE YOUR ANALOGY, WOULDN'T IT BE BAD IF YOUR LIVESTOCK GOT SICK?
SO DEMONS DON'T LIKE IT IF HUMANS FALL ILL?
NAH.
WE DON'T REALLY CARE.
BUT WE NEED THEM.
SO THAT WE CAN PLAY.
—HUH?
WAIT.
DID YOU...
...LOOK AT MY DIARY WITHOUT ASKING?
カタ…
GATA (LUNGE)
WHOOPS.
BASASA (FLAP)
HEY!
ニャ
MRROW!
YOU PICKED ON ELLEN, DIDN'T YOU!?

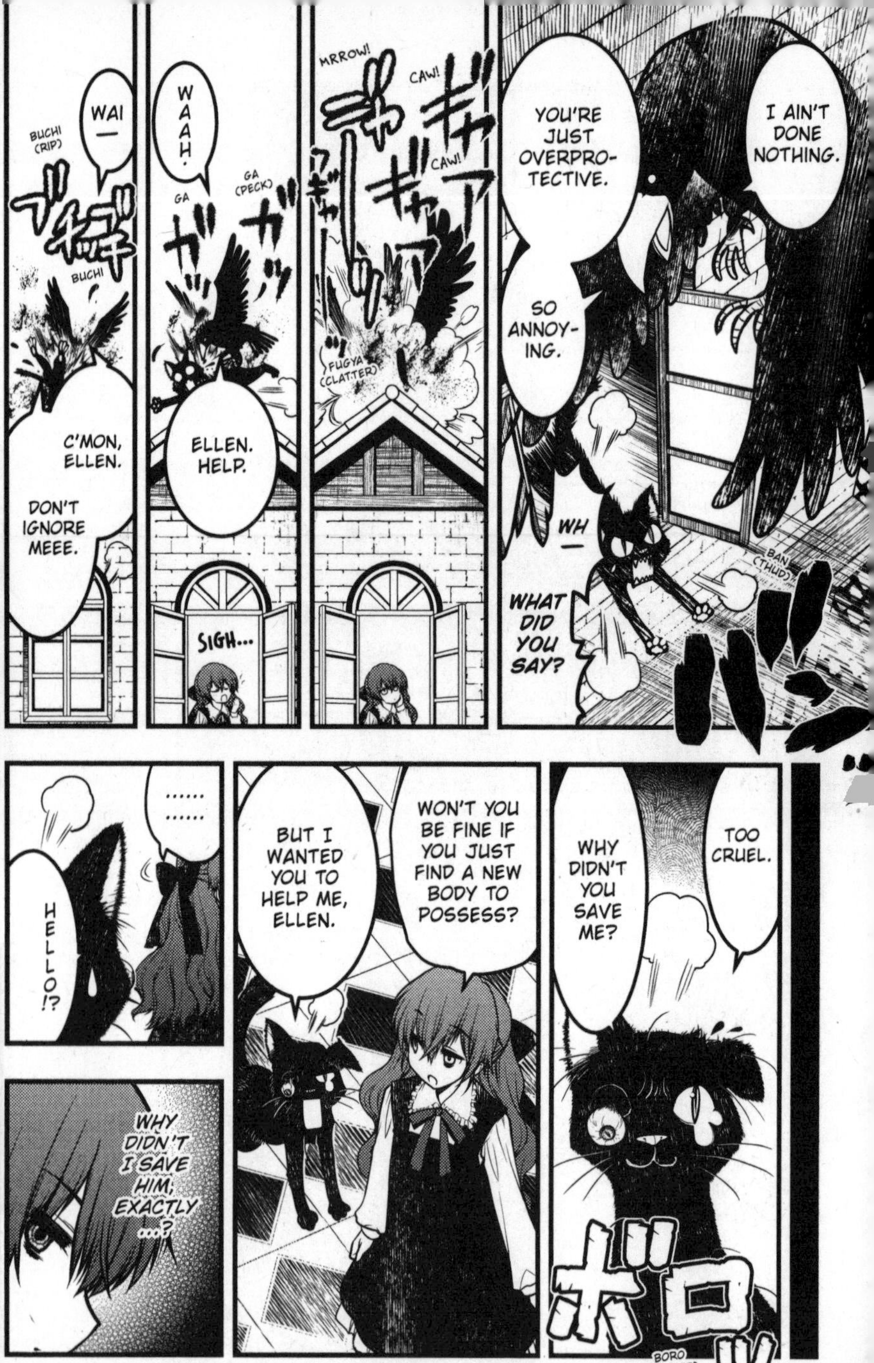
I AIN'T DONE NOTHING.
YOU'RE JUST OVERPROTECTIVE.
SO ANNOYING.
WH—
WHAT DID YOU SAY?
BAN (THUD)
MRROW!
CAW!
CAW!
FUGYA (CLATTER)
WAAH.
GA (PECK)
GA
ELLEN. HELP.
SIGH...
WAI—
BUCHI (RIP)
BUCHI
C'MON, ELLEN.
DON'T IGNORE MEEE.
TOO CRUEL.
WHY DIDN'T YOU SAVE ME?
BORO (RAGGED)
WON'T YOU BE FINE IF YOU JUST FIND A NEW BODY TO POSSESS?
BUT I WANTED YOU TO HELP ME, ELLEN.
......
......
HELLO!?
WHY DIDN'T I SAVE HIM, EXACTLY...?

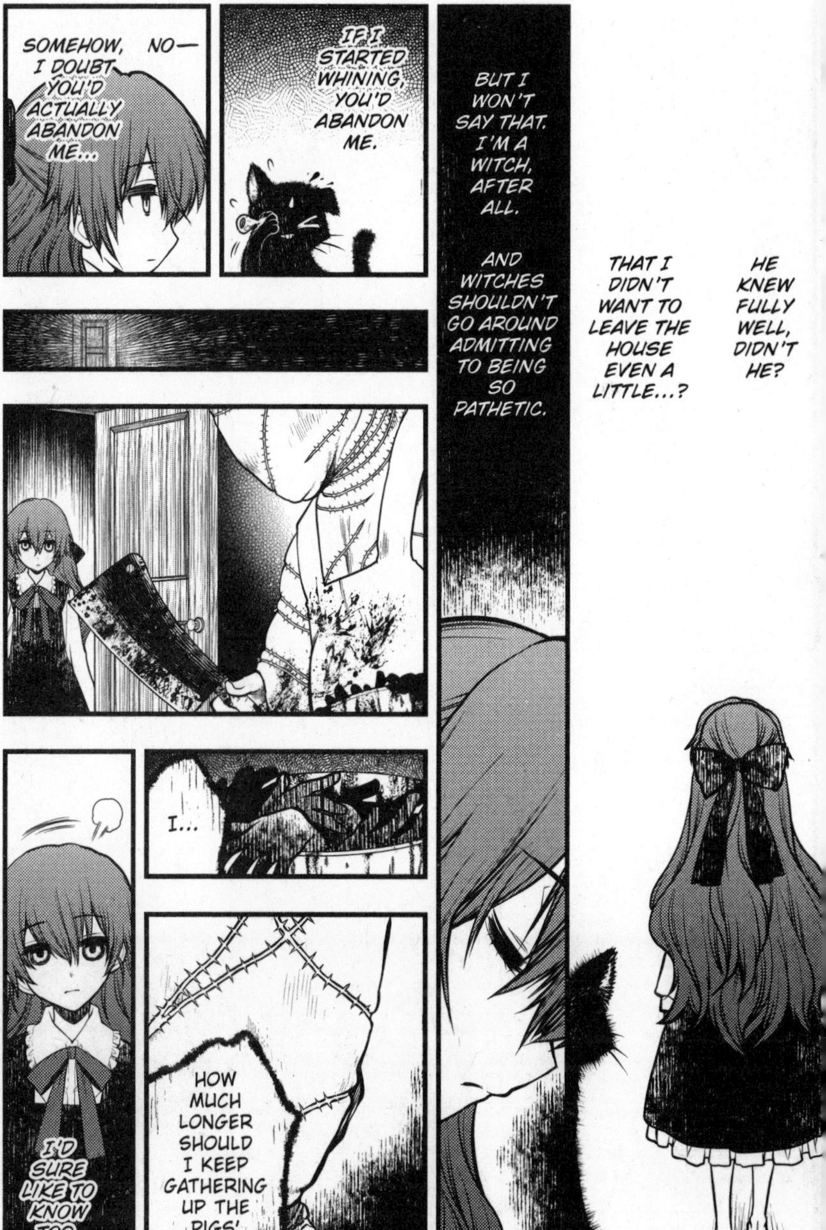
HE KNEW FULLY WELL, DIDN'T HE?
THAT I DIDN'T WANT TO LEAVE THE HOUSE EVEN A LITTLE...?
BUT I WON'T SAY THAT. I'M A WITCH, AFTER ALL.
AND WITCHES SHOULDN'T GO AROUND ADMITTING TO BEING SO PATHETIC.
IF I STARTED WHINING, YOU'D ABANDON ME.
NO—
SOMEHOW, I DOUBT YOU'D ACTUALLY ABANDON ME...
I...
HOW MUCH LONGER SHOULD I KEEP GATHERING UP THE PIGS' HANDS?
I'D SURE LIKE TO KNOW TOO.

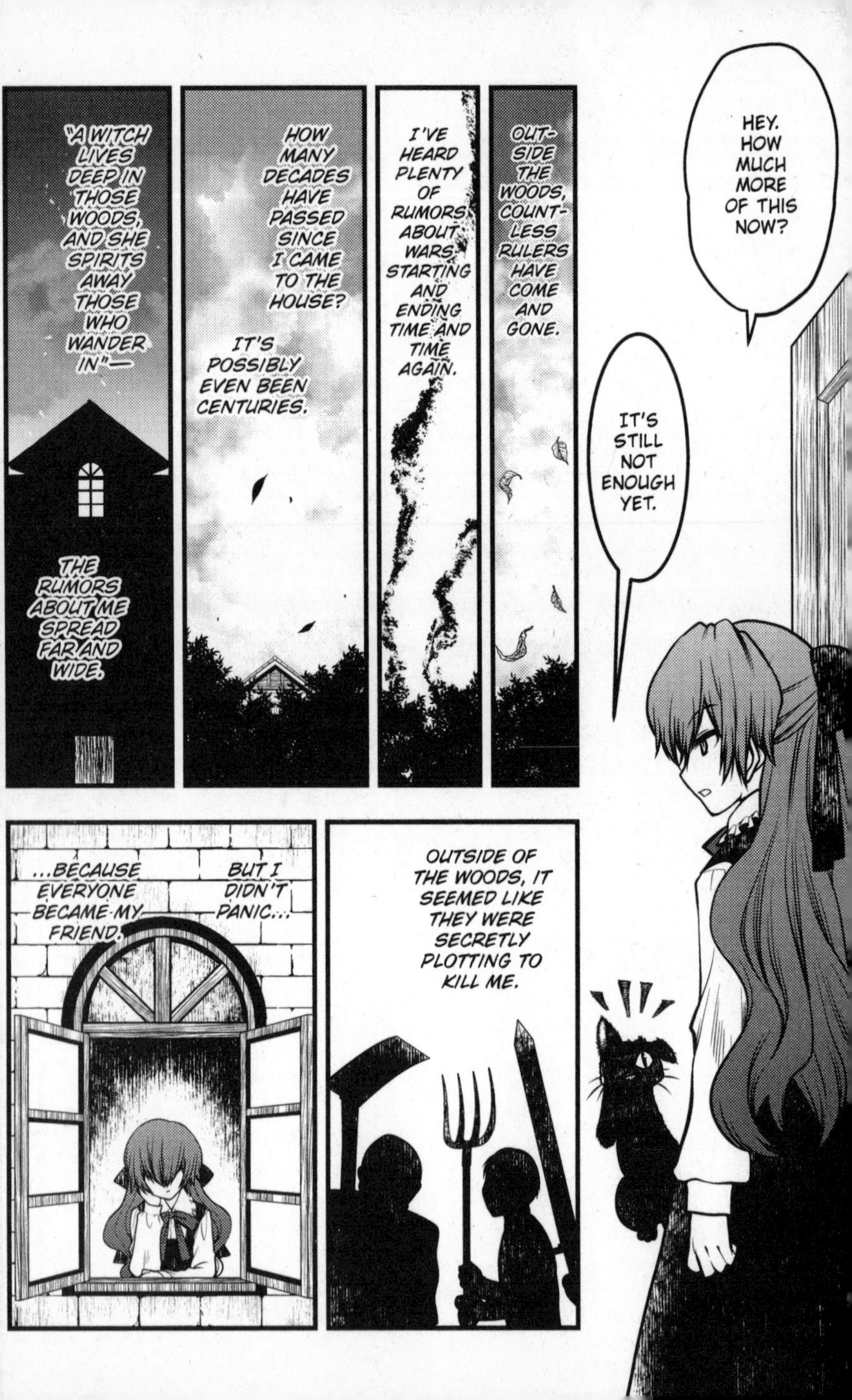
HEY. HOW MUCH MORE OF THIS NOW?
IT'S STILL NOT ENOUGH YET.
OUT-SIDE THE WOODS, COUNT-LESS RULERS HAVE COME AND GONE.
I'VE HEARD PLENTY OF RUMORS ABOUT WARS STARTING AND ENDING TIME AND TIME AGAIN.
HOW MANY DECADES HAVE PASSED SINCE I CAME TO THE HOUSE?
IT'S POSSIBLY EVEN BEEN CENTURIES.
"A WITCH LIVES DEEP IN THOSE WOODS, AND SHE SPIRITS AWAY THOSE WHO WANDER IN"—
THE RUMORS ABOUT ME SPREAD FAR AND WIDE.
OUTSIDE OF THE WOODS, IT SEEMED LIKE THEY WERE SECRETLY PLOTTING TO KILL ME.
BUT I DIDN'T PANIC...
...BECAUSE EVERYONE BECAME MY FRIEND.

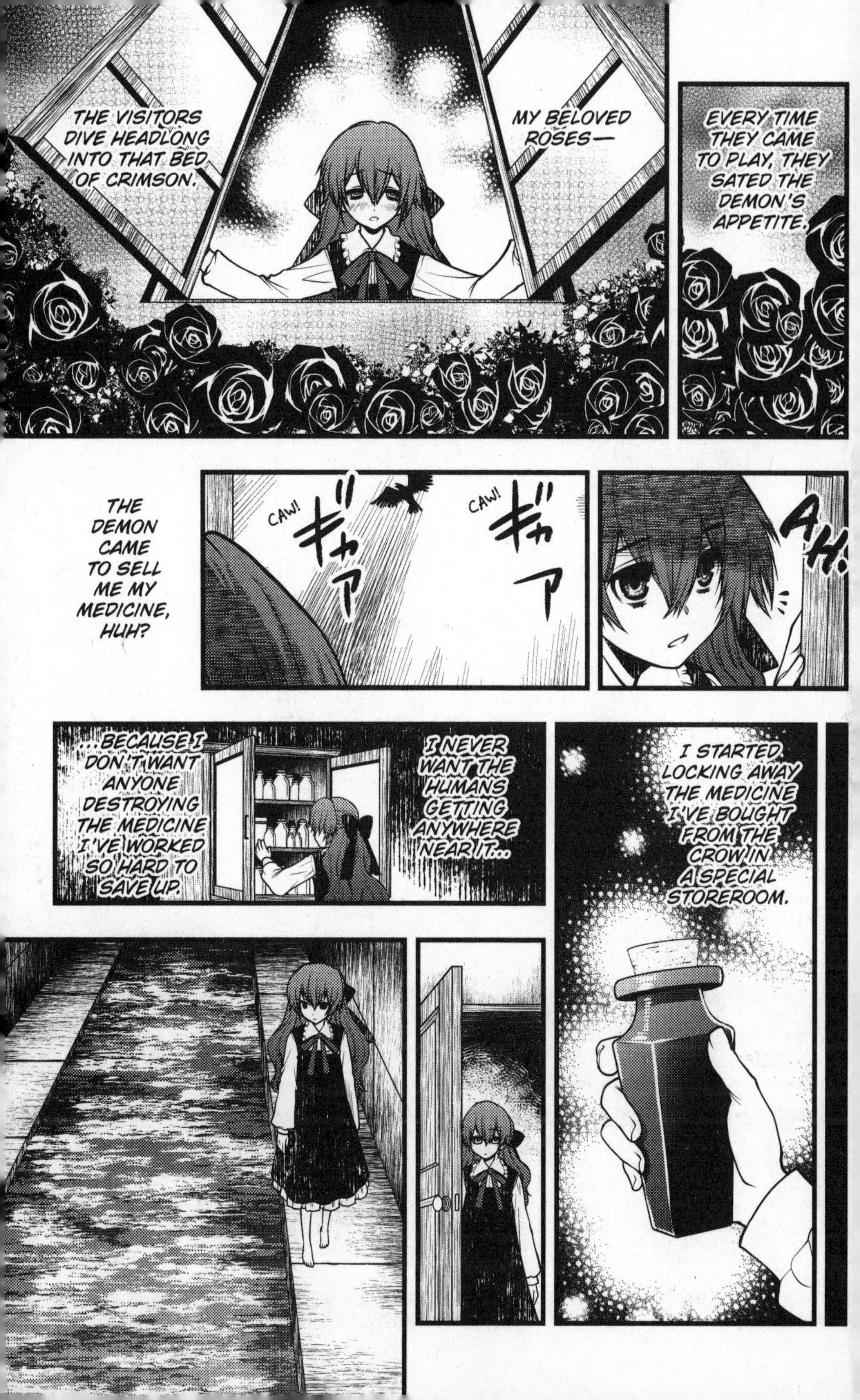
EVERY TIME THEY CAME TO PLAY, THEY SATED THE DEMON'S APPETITE.
MY BELOVED ROSES—
THE VISITORS DIVE HEADLONG INTO THAT BED OF CRIMSON.
AH!
CAW!
ギャア
CAW!
ギャア
THE DEMON CAME TO SELL ME MY MEDICINE, HUH?
I STARTED LOCKING AWAY THE MEDICINE I'VE BOUGHT FROM THE CROW IN A SPECIAL STOREROOM.
I NEVER WANT THE HUMANS GETTING ANYWHERE NEAR IT...
...BECAUSE I DON'T WANT ANYONE DESTROYING THE MEDICINE I'VE WORKED SO HARD TO SAVE UP.

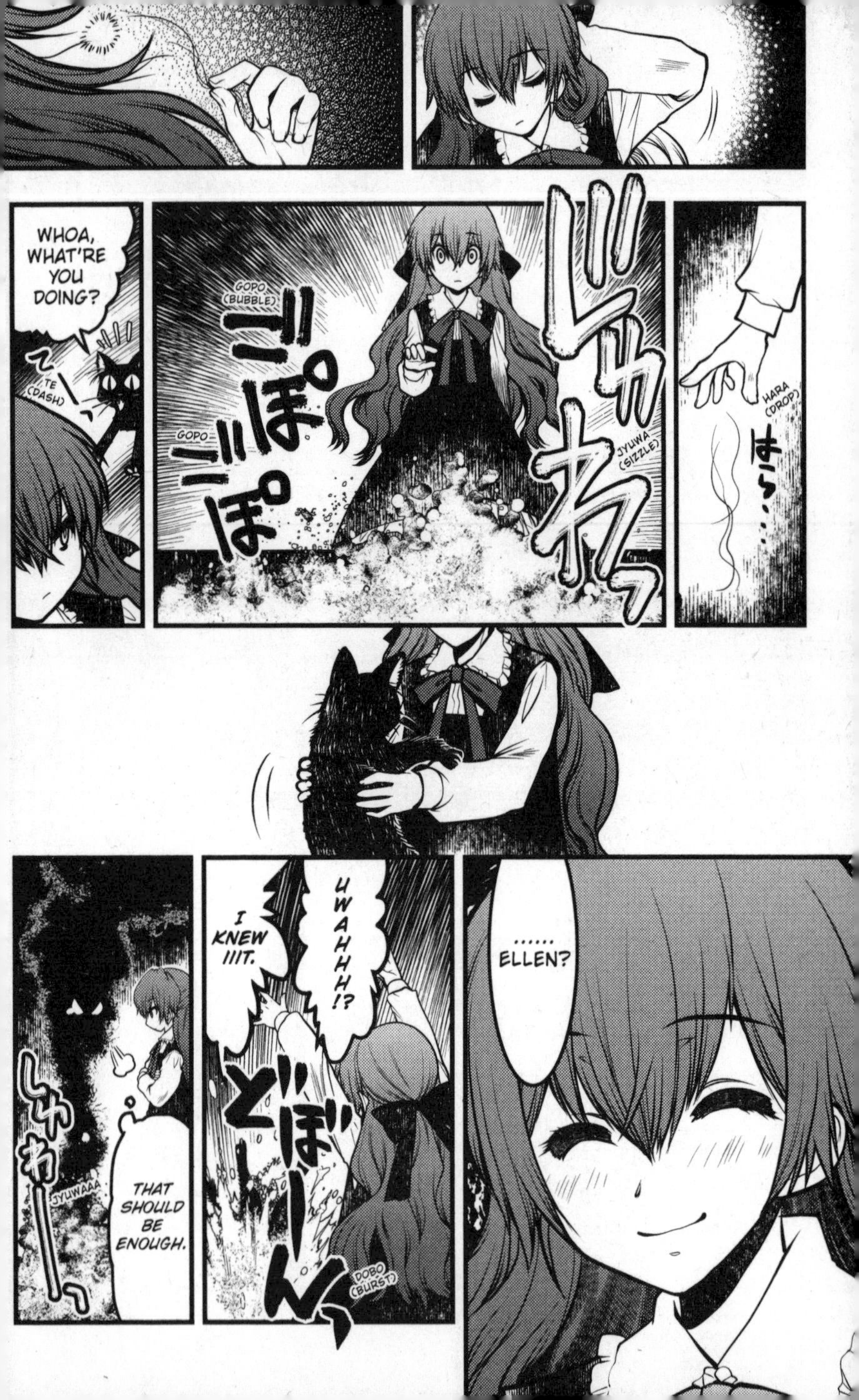
はら…
HARA (DROP)
じゅわっ
JYUWA (SIZZLE)
ごぽごぽ
GOPO (BUBBLE)
GOPO
WHOA, WHAT'RE YOU DOING?
TE (DASH)
……ELLEN?
UWAHHH!?
I KNEW IIIT.
どぼーん
DOBO (BURST)
THAT SHOULD BE ENOUGH.
しゅわーっ
JYUWAAA

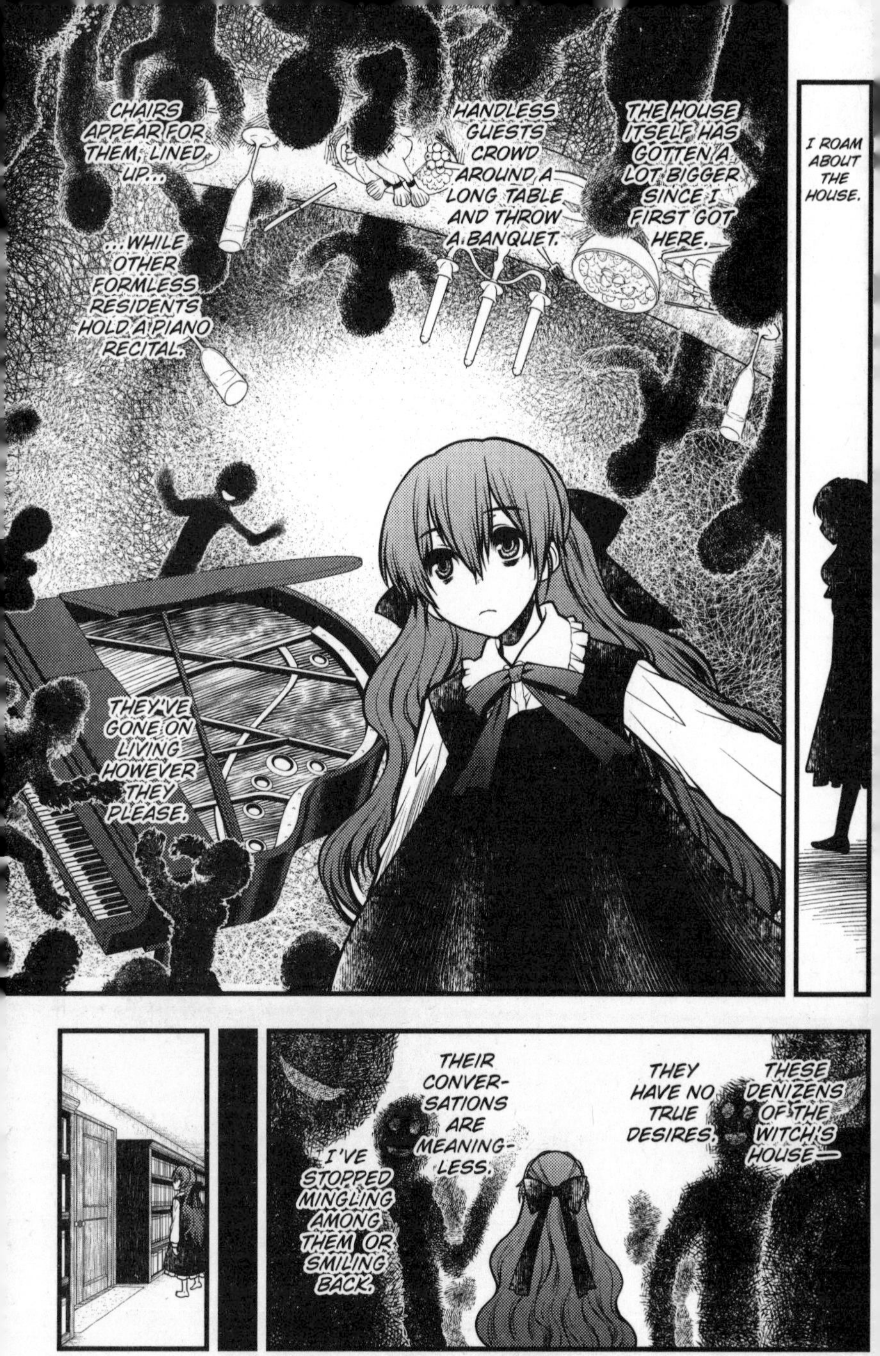
I ROAM ABOUT THE HOUSE.
THE HOUSE ITSELF HAS GOTTEN A LOT BIGGER SINCE I FIRST GOT HERE.
HANDLESS GUESTS CROWD AROUND A LONG TABLE AND THROW A BANQUET.
CHAIRS APPEAR FOR THEM, LINED UP...
...WHILE OTHER FORMLESS RESIDENTS HOLD A PIANO RECITAL.
THEY'VE GONE ON LIVING HOWEVER THEY PLEASE.
THESE DENIZENS OF THE WITCH'S HOUSE—
THEY HAVE NO TRUE DESIRES.
THEIR CONVER-SATIONS ARE MEANING-LESS.
I'VE STOPPED MINGLING AMONG THEM OR SMILING BACK.

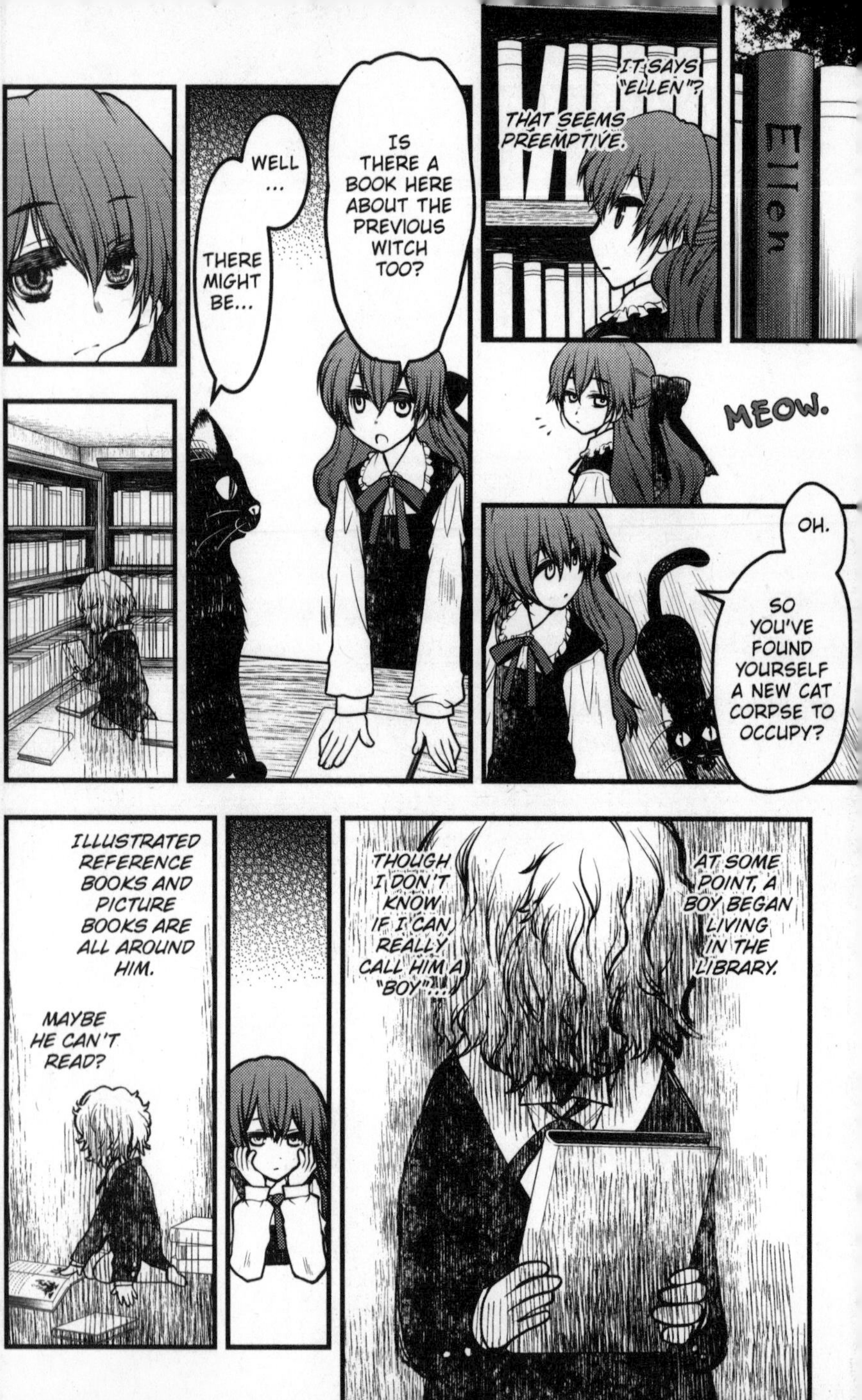
IT SAYS "ELLEN"?
THAT SEEMS PREEMPTIVE.
Ellen
MEOW.
OH.
SO YOU'VE FOUND YOURSELF A NEW CAT CORPSE TO OCCUPY?
IS THERE A BOOK HERE ABOUT THE PREVIOUS WITCH TOO?
WELL ...
THERE MIGHT BE...
AT SOME POINT, A BOY BEGAN LIVING IN THE LIBRARY.
THOUGH I DON'T KNOW IF I CAN REALLY CALL HIM A "BOY"...
ILLUSTRATED REFERENCE BOOKS AND PICTURE BOOKS ARE ALL AROUND HIM.
MAYBE HE CAN'T READ?

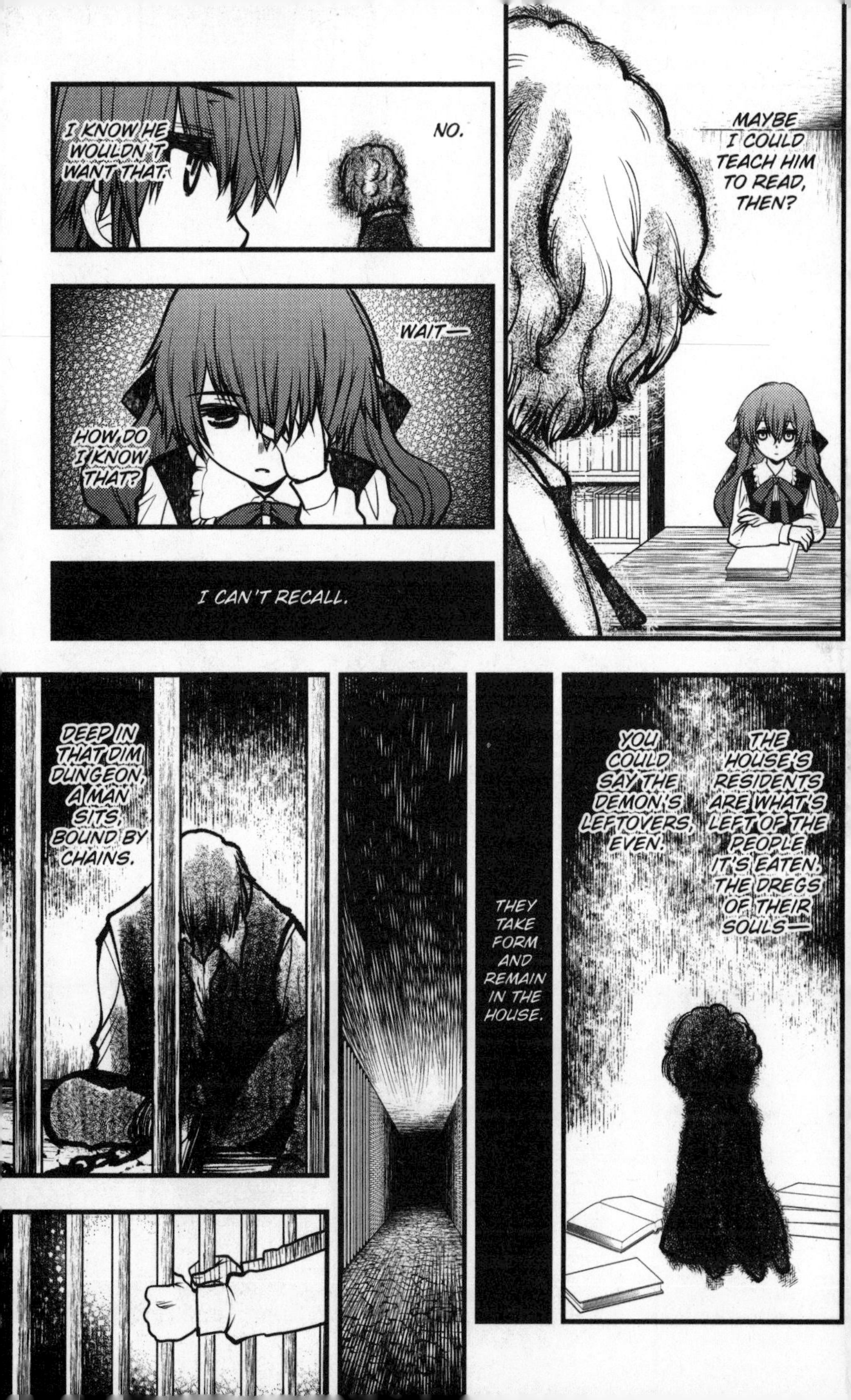
MAYBE I COULD TEACH HIM TO READ, THEN?
NO.
I KNOW HE WOULDN'T WANT THAT.
WAIT—
HOW DO I KNOW THAT?
I CAN'T RECALL.
THE HOUSE'S RESIDENTS ARE WHAT'S LEFT OF THE PEOPLE IT'S EATEN. THE DREGS OF THEIR SOULS—
YOU COULD SAY THE DEMON'S LEFTOVERS, EVEN.
THEY TAKE FORM AND REMAIN IN THE HOUSE.
DEEP IN THAT DIM DUNGEON, A MAN SITS, BOUND BY CHAINS.

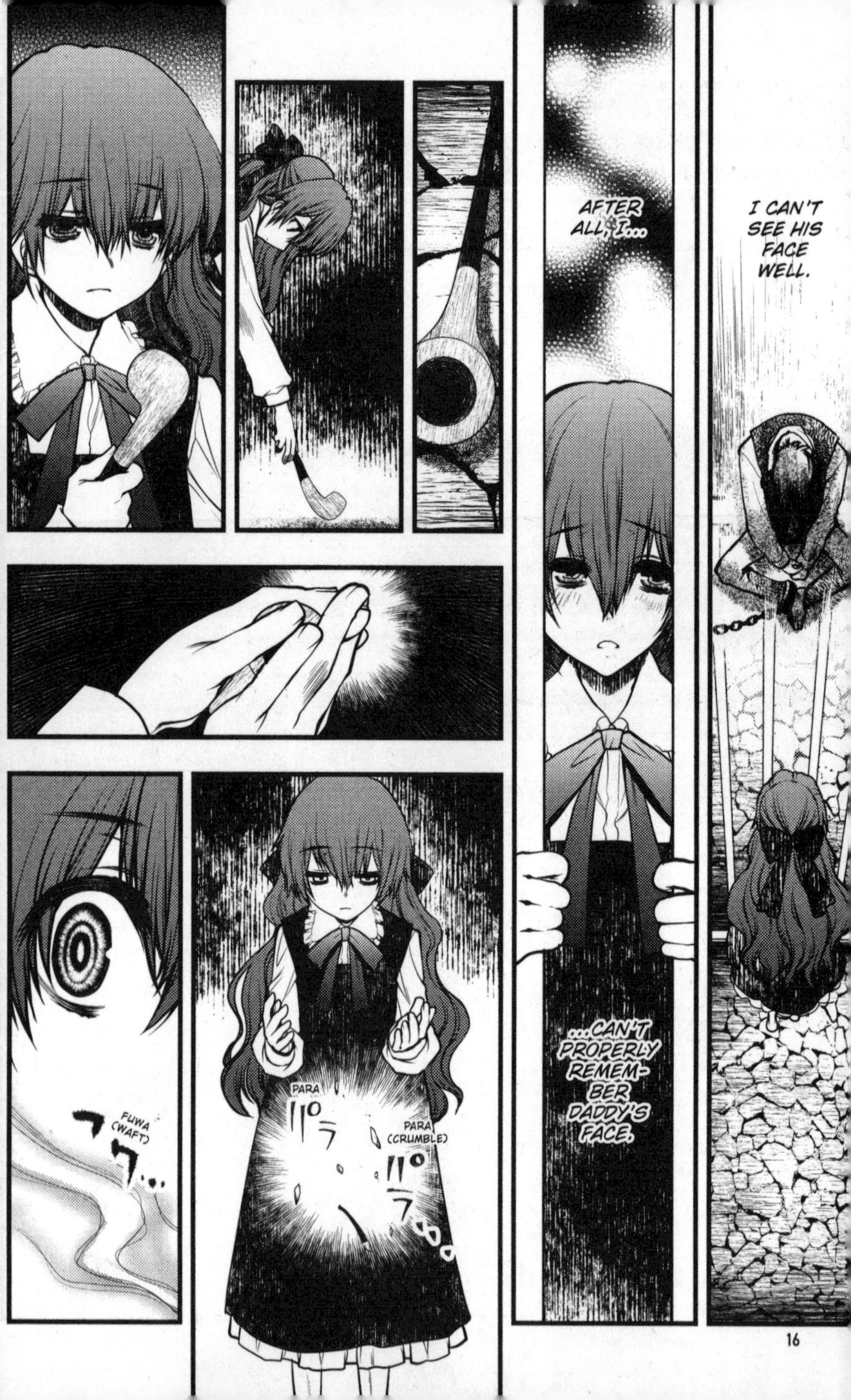
I CAN'T SEE HIS FACE WELL.
AFTER ALL, I...
...CAN'T PROPERLY REMEM-BER DADDY'S FACE.
PARA
PARA (CRUMBLE)
FUWA (WAFT)

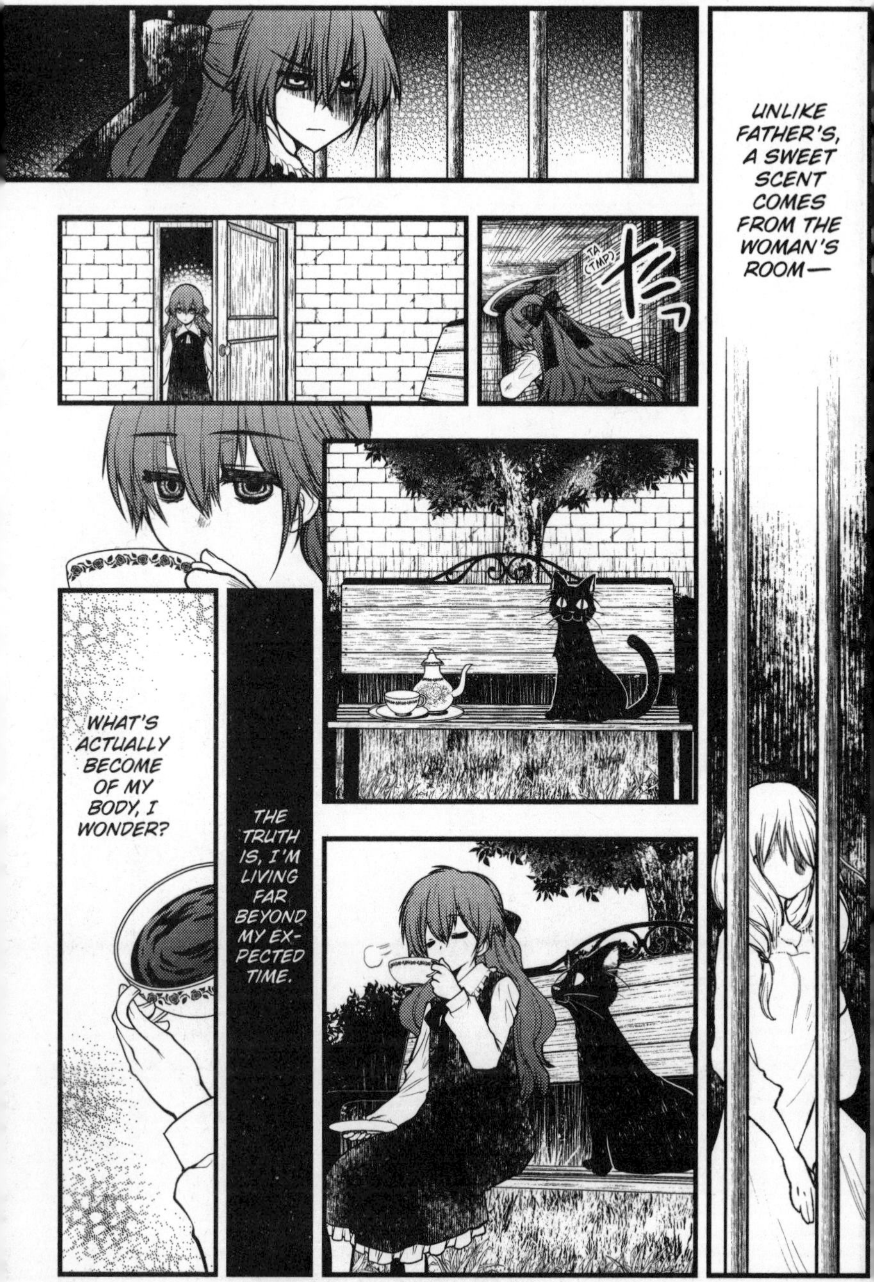
UNLIKE FATHER'S, A SWEET SCENT COMES FROM THE WOMAN'S ROOM—
TA (TMP)
THE TRUTH IS, I'M LIVING FAR BEYOND MY EX-PECTED TIME.
WHAT'S ACTUALLY BECOME OF MY BODY, I WONDER?

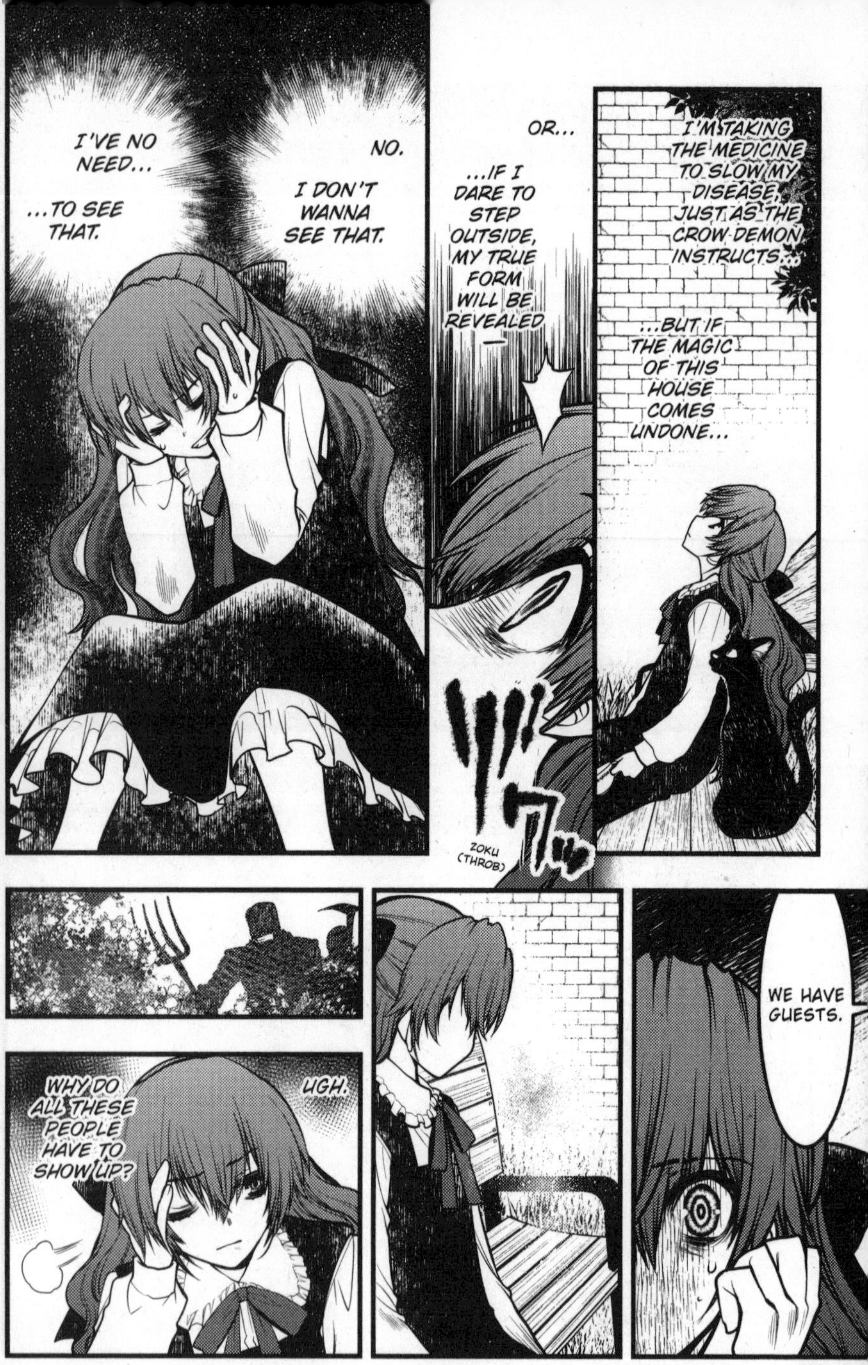
I'M TAKING THE MEDICINE TO SLOW MY DISEASE, JUST AS THE CROW DEMON INSTRUCTS...
...BUT IF THE MAGIC OF THIS HOUSE COMES UNDONE...
OR...
...IF I DARE TO STEP OUTSIDE, MY TRUE FORM WILL BE REVEALED—
ZOKU (THROB)
NO.
I DON'T WANNA SEE THAT.
I'VE NO NEED...
...TO SEE THAT.
WE HAVE GUESTS.
UGH.
WHY DO ALL THESE PEOPLE HAVE TO SHOW UP?

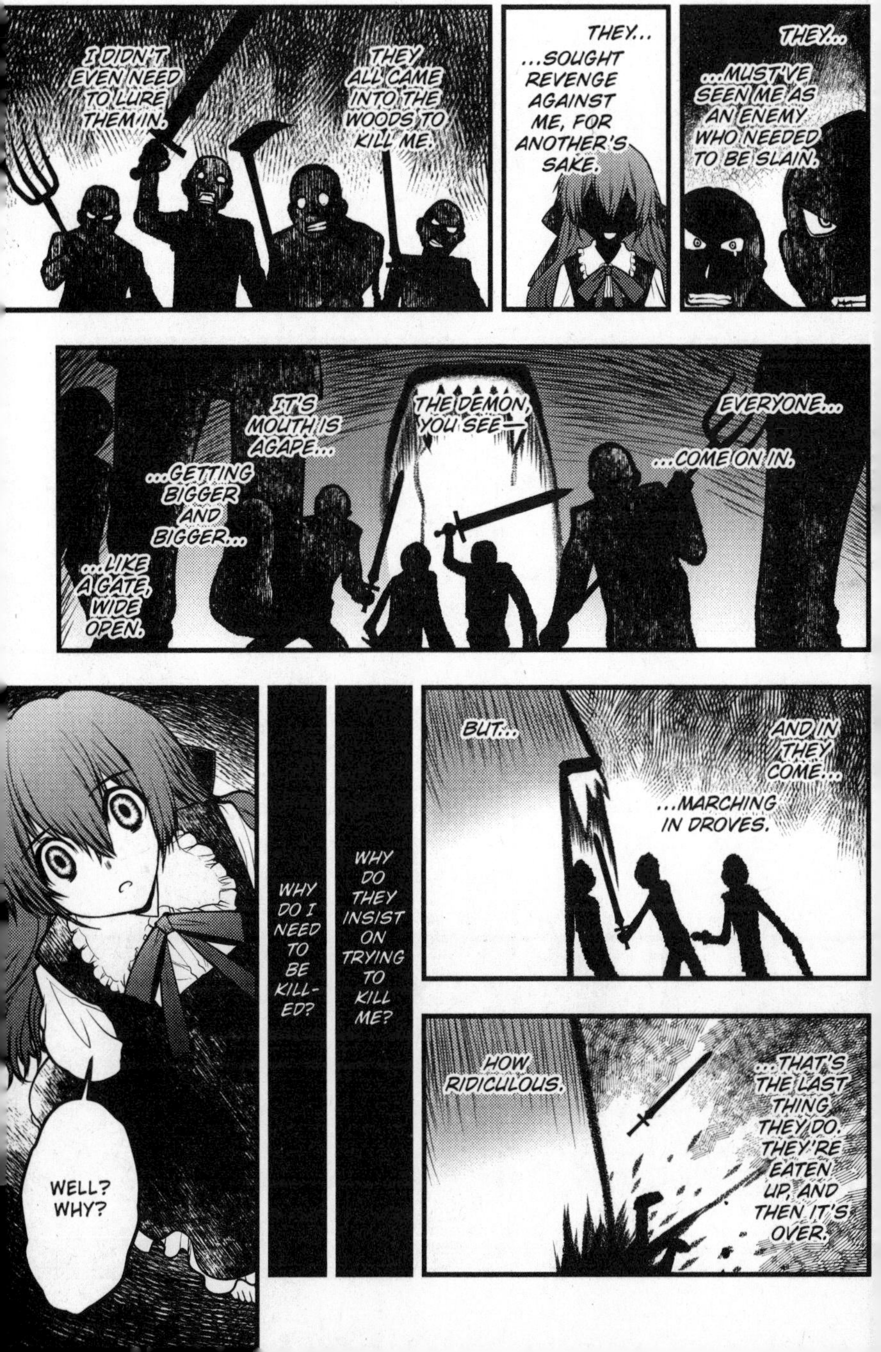
THEY...
...MUST'VE SEEN ME AS AN ENEMY WHO NEEDED TO BE SLAIN.
THEY...
...SOUGHT REVENGE AGAINST ME, FOR ANOTHER'S SAKE.
THEY ALL CAME INTO THE WOODS TO KILL ME.
I DIDN'T EVEN NEED TO LURE THEM IN.
EVERYONE...
...COME ON IN.
THE DEMON, YOU SEE—
IT'S MOUTH IS AGAPE...
...GETTING BIGGER AND BIGGER...
...LIKE A GATE, WIDE OPEN.
AND IN THEY COME...
...MARCHING IN DROVES.
BUT...
...THAT'S THE LAST THING THEY DO. THEY'RE EATEN UP, AND THEN IT'S OVER.
HOW RIDICULOUS.
WHY DO THEY INSIST ON TRYING TO KILL ME?
WHY DO I NEED TO BE KILL-ED?
WELL? WHY?

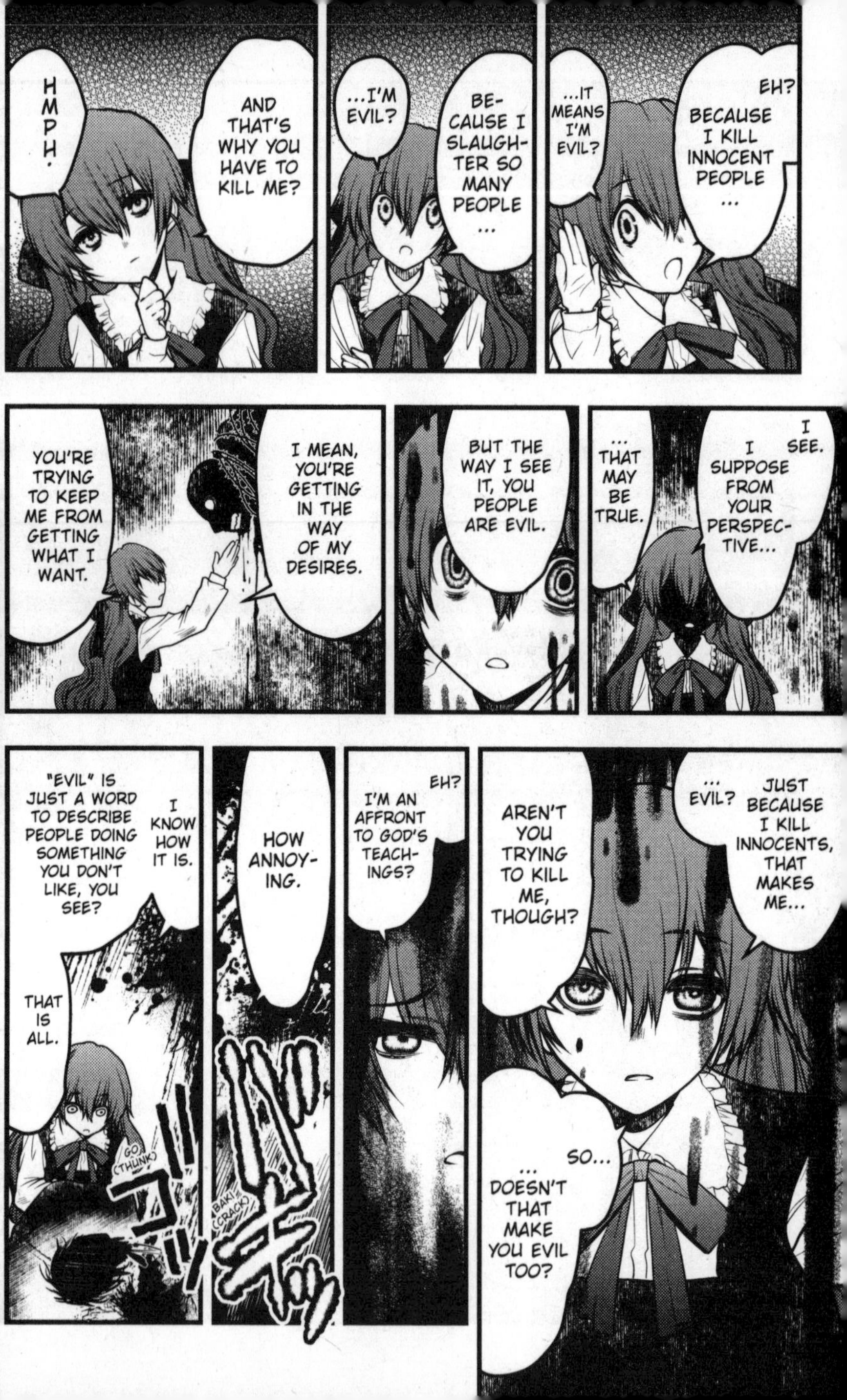
EH?
BECAUSE I KILL INNOCENT PEOPLE ...
...IT MEANS I'M EVIL?
BECAUSE I SLAUGHTER SO MANY PEOPLE ...
...I'M EVIL?
AND THAT'S WHY YOU HAVE TO KILL ME?
HMPH.
I SEE.
I SUPPOSE FROM YOUR PERSPECTIVE...
... THAT MAY BE TRUE.
BUT THE WAY I SEE IT, YOU PEOPLE ARE EVIL.
I MEAN, YOU'RE GETTING IN THE WAY OF MY DESIRES.
YOU'RE TRYING TO KEEP ME FROM GETTING WHAT I WANT.
JUST BECAUSE I KILL INNOCENTS, THAT MAKES ME...
... EVIL?
AREN'T YOU TRYING TO KILL ME, THOUGH?
SO...
... DOESN'T THAT MAKE YOU EVIL TOO?
EH?
I'M AN AFFRONT TO GOD'S TEACHINGS?
HOW ANNOYING.
I KNOW HOW IT IS.
"EVIL" IS JUST A WORD TO DESCRIBE PEOPLE DOING SOMETHING YOU DON'T LIKE, YOU SEE?
THAT IS ALL.
BAKI (CRACK)
GO (THUNK)

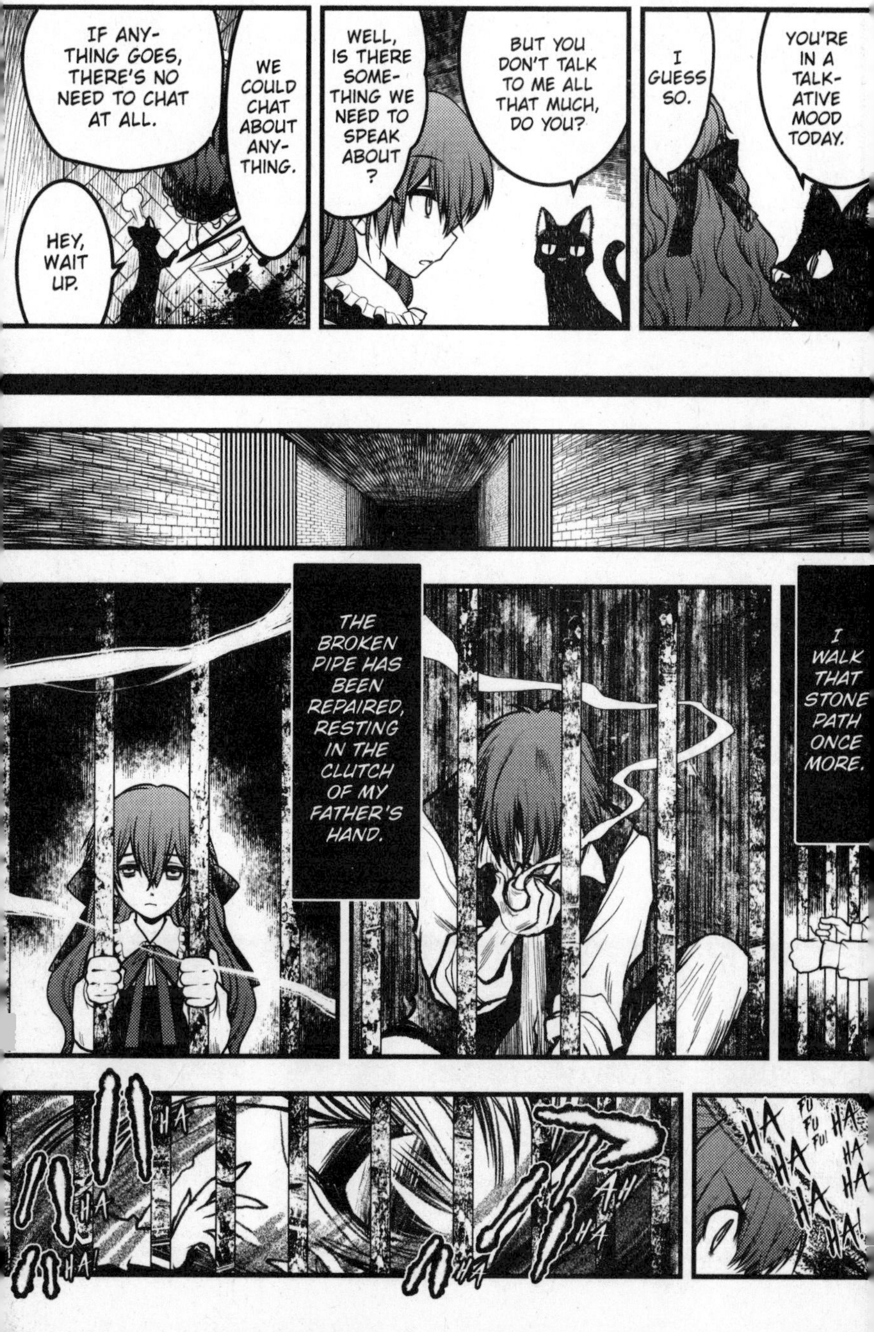
YOU'RE IN A TALK-ATIVE MOOD TODAY.
I GUESS SO.
BUT YOU DON'T TALK TO ME ALL THAT MUCH, DO YOU?
WELL, IS THERE SOME-THING WE NEED TO SPEAK ABOUT?
WE COULD CHAT ABOUT ANY-THING.
IF ANY-THING GOES, THERE'S NO NEED TO CHAT AT ALL.
HEY, WAIT UP.
I WALK THAT STONE PATH ONCE MORE.
THE BROKEN PIPE HAS BEEN REPAIRED, RESTING IN THE CLUTCH OF MY FATHER'S HAND.
HA HA HA HA HA!
FU FU FU!
HA HA HA HA!
AH HA HA
HA
HA HA HA!

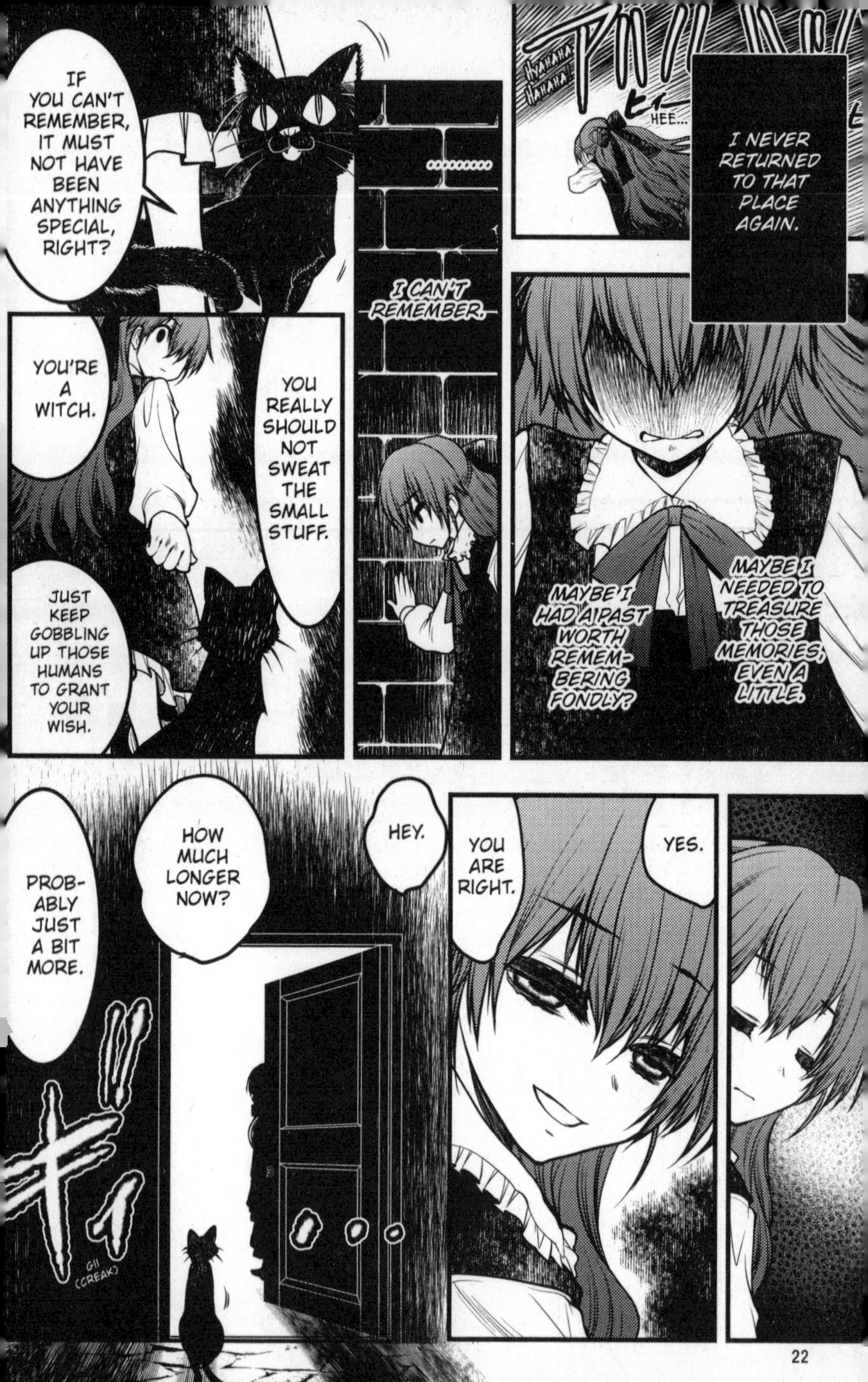
HYAHAHA HAHAHA!
HEE...
I NEVER RETURNED TO THAT PLACE AGAIN.
MAYBE I NEEDED TO TREASURE THOSE MEMORIES, EVEN A LITTLE.
MAYBE I HAD A PAST WORTH REMEMBERING FONDLY?
....
I CAN'T REMEMBER.
IF YOU CAN'T REMEMBER, IT MUST NOT HAVE BEEN ANYTHING SPECIAL, RIGHT?
YOU REALLY SHOULD NOT SWEAT THE SMALL STUFF.
YOU'RE A WITCH.
JUST KEEP GOBBLING UP THOSE HUMANS TO GRANT YOUR WISH.
YES.
YOU ARE RIGHT.
HEY.
HOW MUCH LONGER NOW?
PROBABLY JUST A BIT MORE.
GII (CREAK)

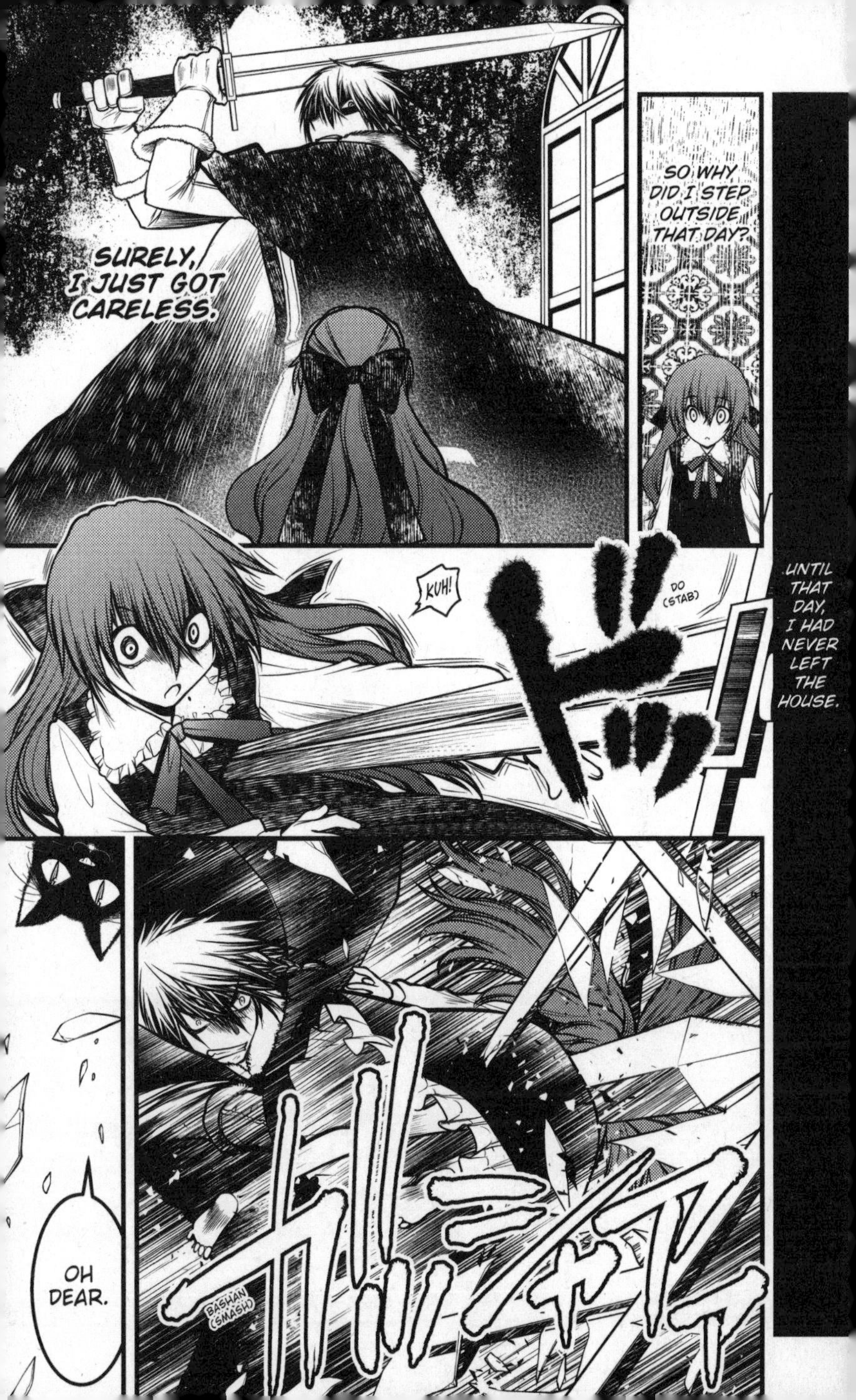
UNTIL THAT DAY, I HAD NEVER LEFT THE HOUSE.
SO WHY DID I STEP OUTSIDE THAT DAY?
SURELY, I JUST GOT CARELESS.
DO (STAB)
KUH!
BASHAN (SMASH)
OH DEAR.

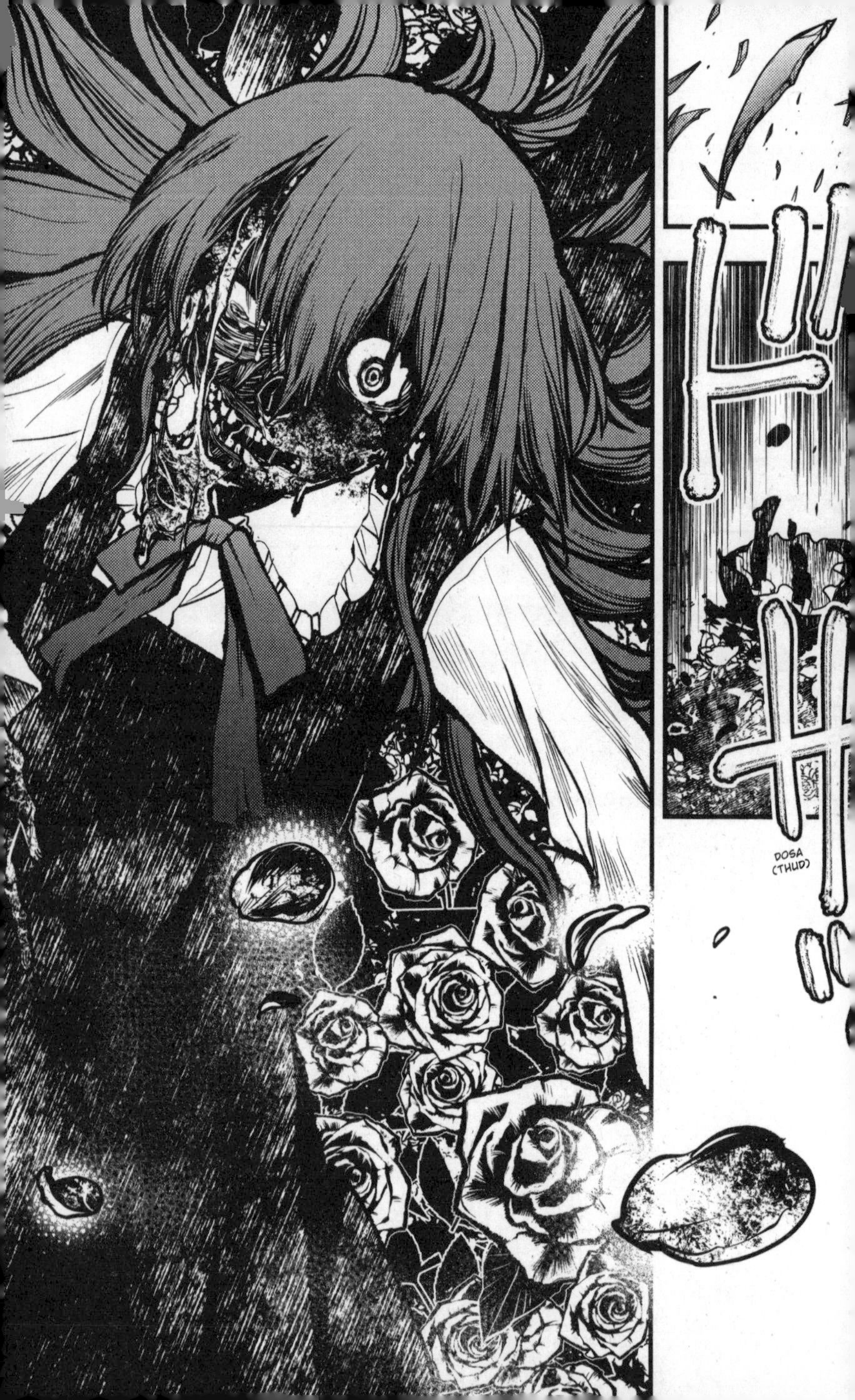
DOSA
(THUD)

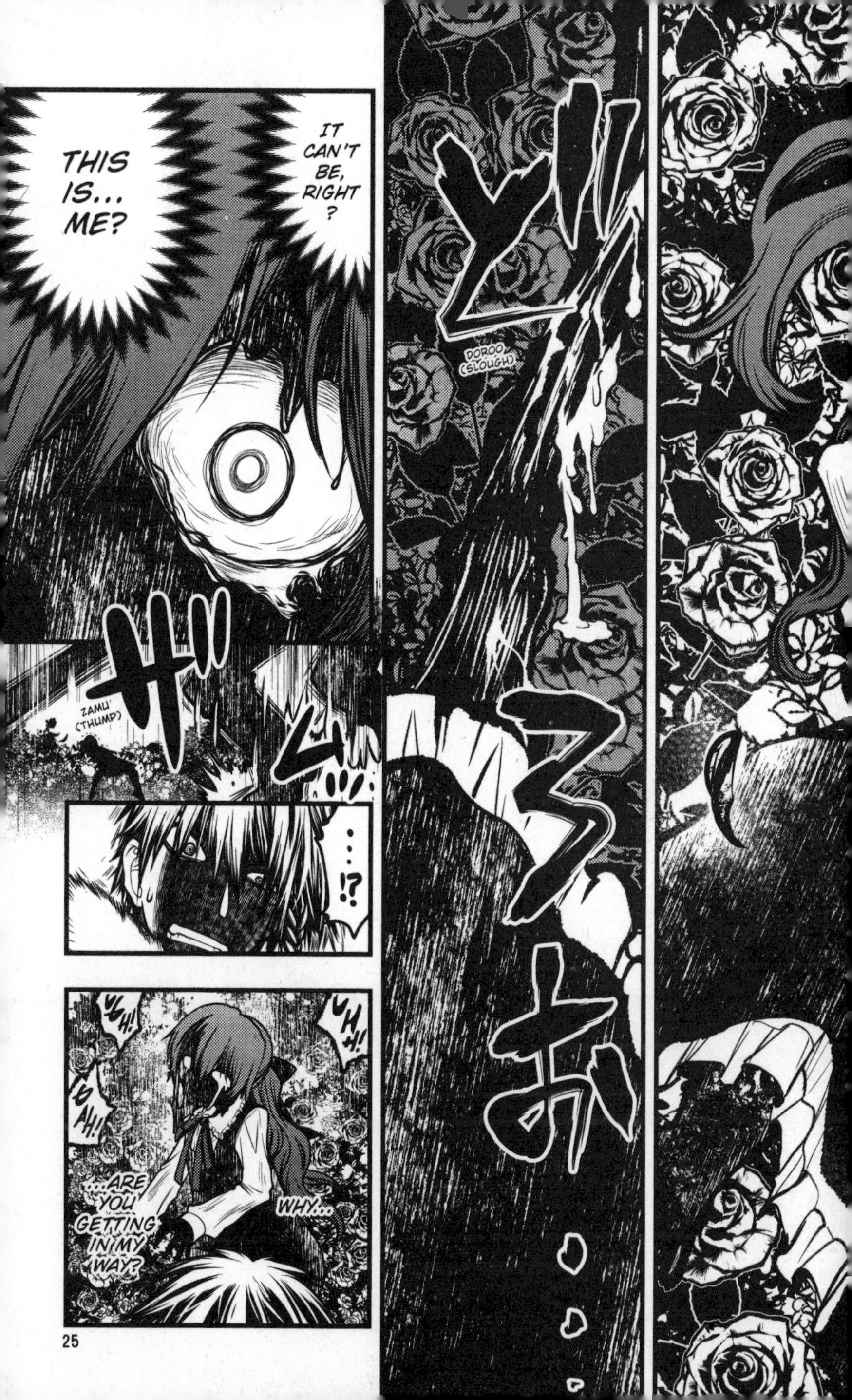
DOROO (SLOUGH)
IT CAN'T BE, RIGHT?
THIS IS... ME?
ZAMU' (THUMP)
...!?
WHY...
...ARE YOU GETTING IN MY WAY?

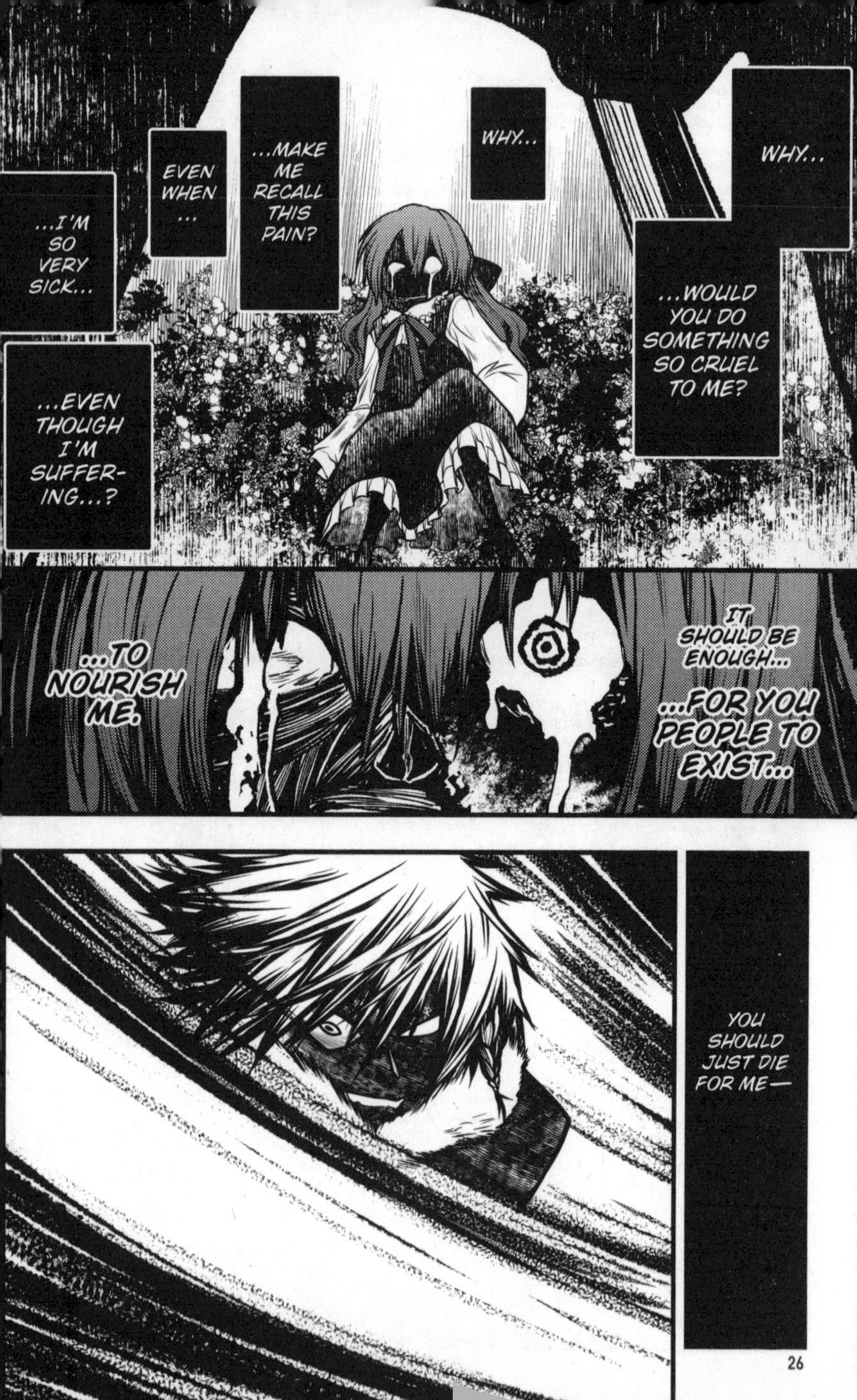
WHY...
WHY...
...WOULD YOU DO SOMETHING SO CRUEL TO ME?
...MAKE ME RECALL THIS PAIN?
EVEN WHEN...
...I'M SO VERY SICK...
...EVEN THOUGH I'M SUFFER-ING...?
IT SHOULD BE ENOUGH...
...FOR YOU PEOPLE TO EXIST...
...TO NOURISH ME.
YOU SHOULD JUST DIE FOR ME—

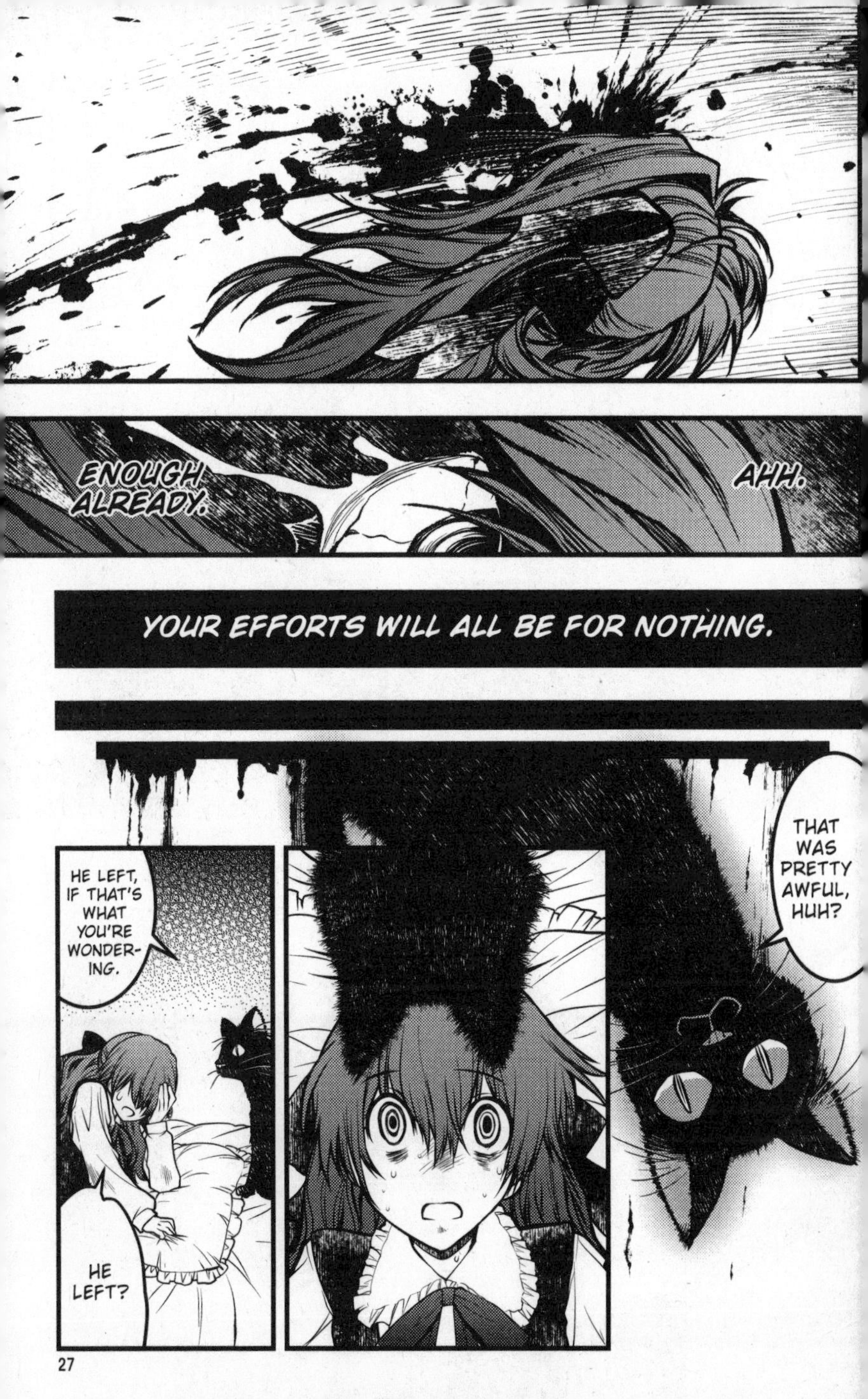
AHH.
ENOUGH ALREADY.
YOUR EFFORTS WILL ALL BE FOR NOTHING.
THAT WAS PRETTY AWFUL, HUH?
HE LEFT, IF THAT'S WHAT YOU'RE WONDERING.
HE LEFT?

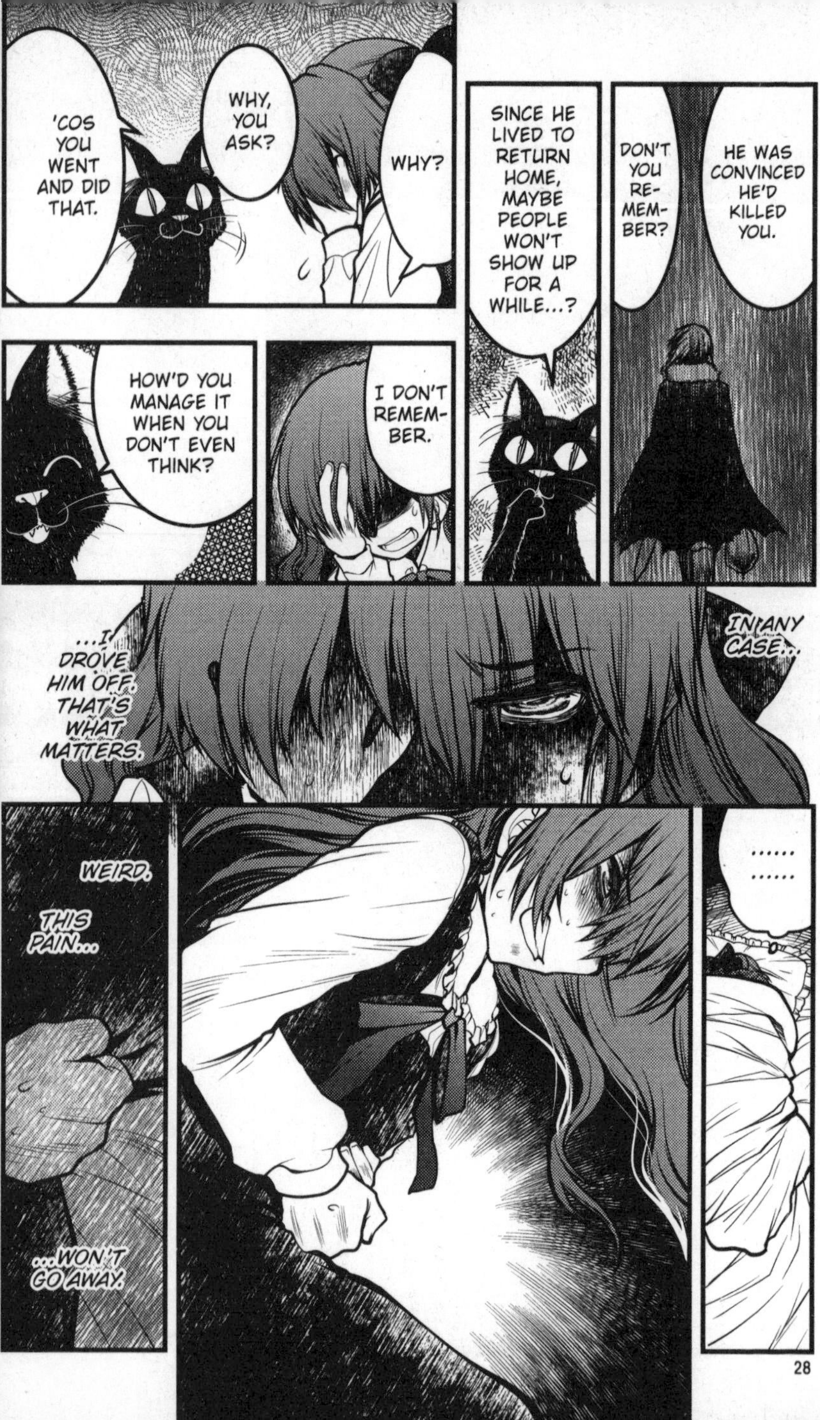

HE WAS CONVINCED HE'D KILLED YOU.
DON'T YOU RE-MEMBER?
SINCE HE LIVED TO RETURN HOME, MAYBE PEOPLE WON'T SHOW UP FOR A WHILE...?
WHY?
WHY, YOU ASK?
'COS YOU WENT AND DID THAT.
I DON'T REMEM-BER.
HOW'D YOU MANAGE IT WHEN YOU DON'T EVEN THINK?
IN ANY CASE...
...I DROVE HIM OFF. THAT'S WHAT MATTERS.
......
......
WEIRD.
THIS PAIN...
...WON'T GO AWAY.

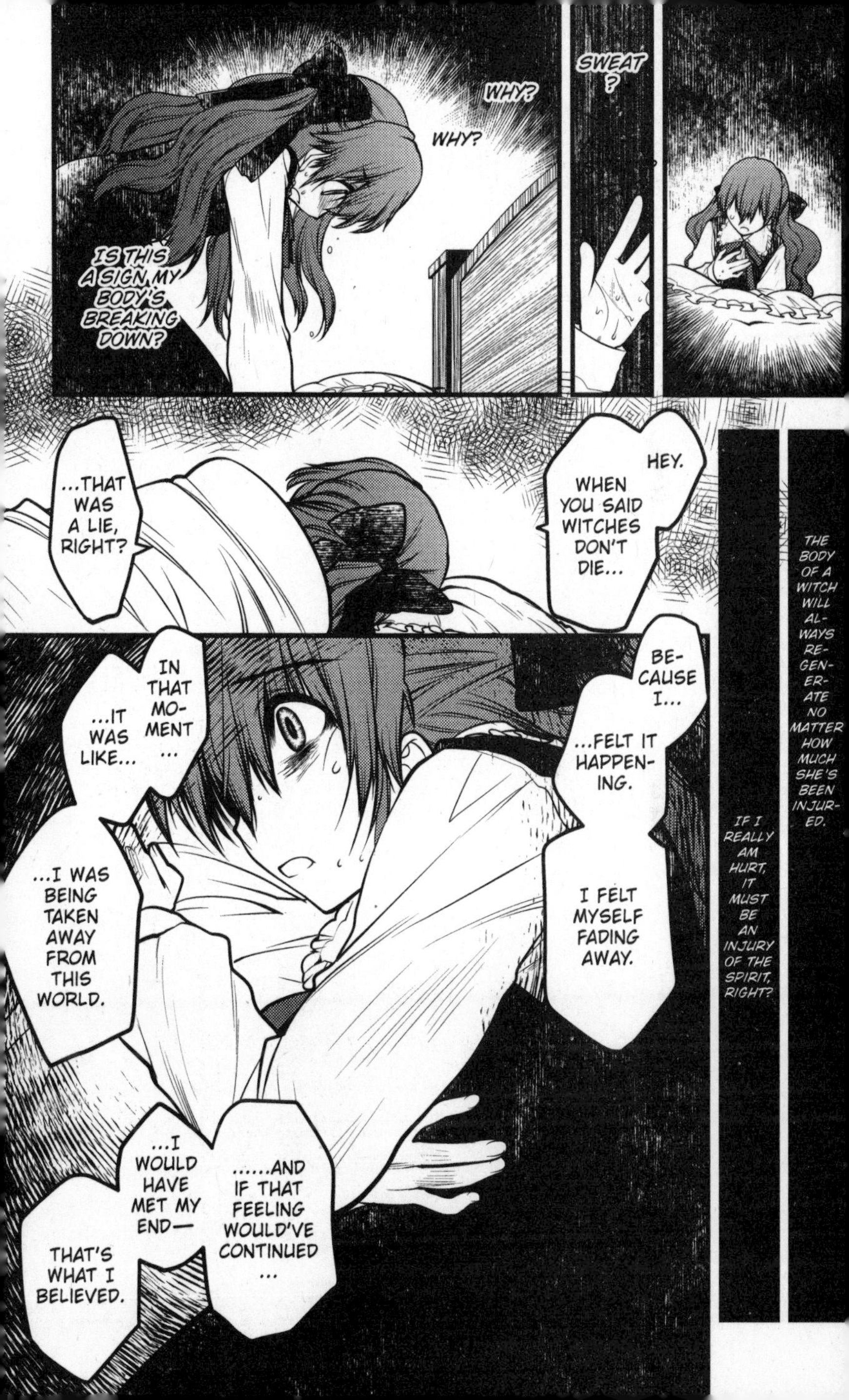
SWEAT?
WHY?
WHY?
IS THIS A SIGN MY BODY'S BREAKING DOWN?
THE BODY OF A WITCH WILL ALWAYS REGENERATE NO MATTER HOW MUCH SHE'S BEEN INJURED.
IF I REALLY AM HURT, IT MUST BE AN INJURY OF THE SPIRIT, RIGHT?
HEY. WHEN YOU SAID WITCHES DON'T DIE...
...THAT WAS A LIE, RIGHT?
BECAUSE I...
...FELT IT HAPPENING.
I FELT MYSELF FADING AWAY.
IN THAT MOMENT...
...IT WAS LIKE...
...I WAS BEING TAKEN AWAY FROM THIS WORLD.
......AND IF THAT FEELING WOULD'VE CONTINUED...
...I WOULD HAVE MET MY END—
THAT'S WHAT I BELIEVED.

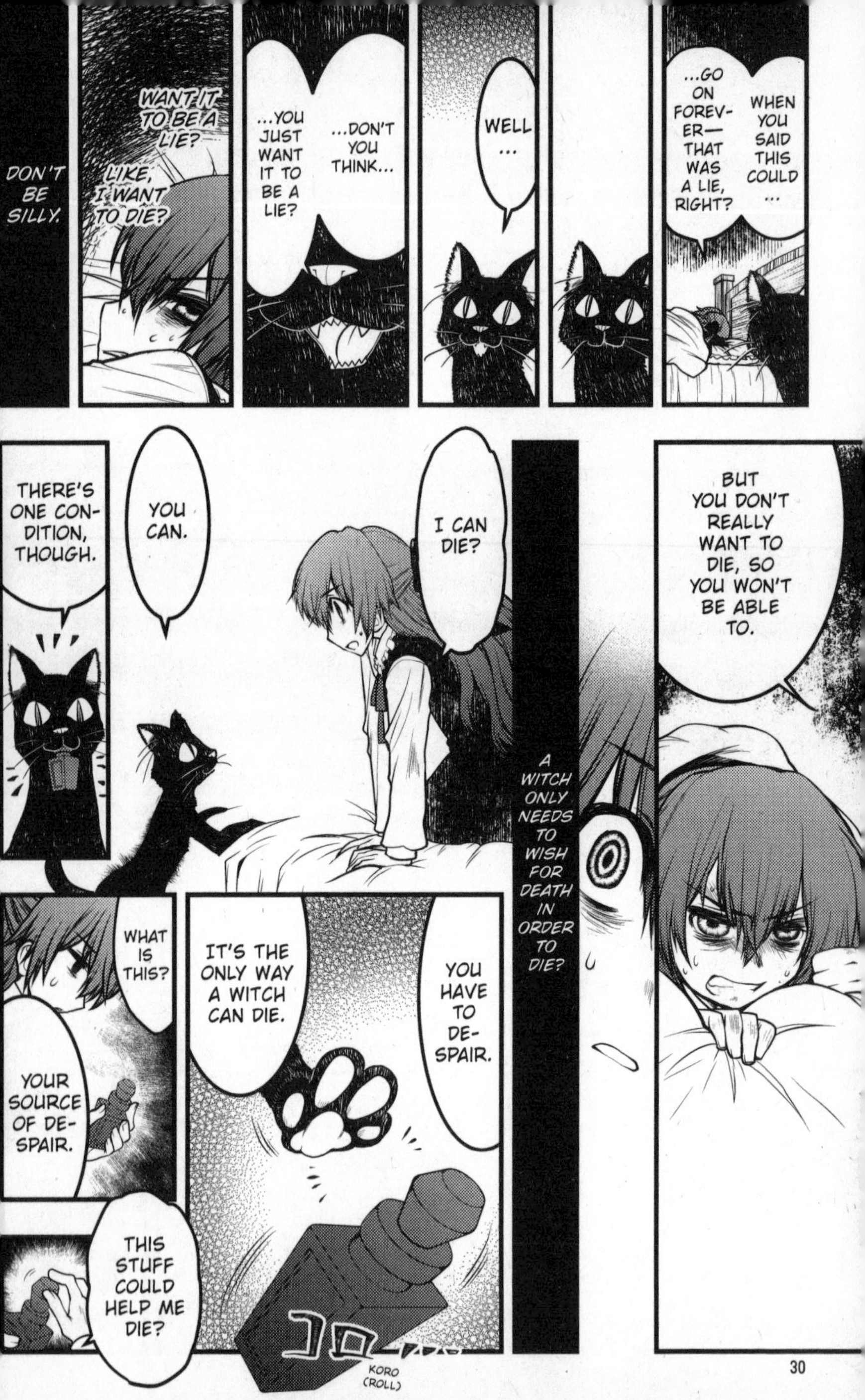
WHEN YOU SAID THIS COULD...
...GO ON FOREVER—THAT WAS A LIE, RIGHT?
WELL...
...DON'T YOU THINK...
...YOU JUST WANT IT TO BE A LIE?
WANT IT TO BE A LIE?
LIKE, I WANT TO DIE?
DON'T BE SILLY.
BUT YOU DON'T REALLY WANT TO DIE, SO YOU WON'T BE ABLE TO.
A WITCH ONLY NEEDS TO WISH FOR DEATH IN ORDER TO DIE?
I CAN DIE?
YOU CAN.
THERE'S ONE CONDITION, THOUGH.
YOU HAVE TO DESPAIR.
IT'S THE ONLY WAY A WITCH CAN DIE.
KORO (ROLL)
WHAT IS THIS?
YOUR SOURCE OF DESPAIR.
THIS STUFF COULD HELP ME DIE?

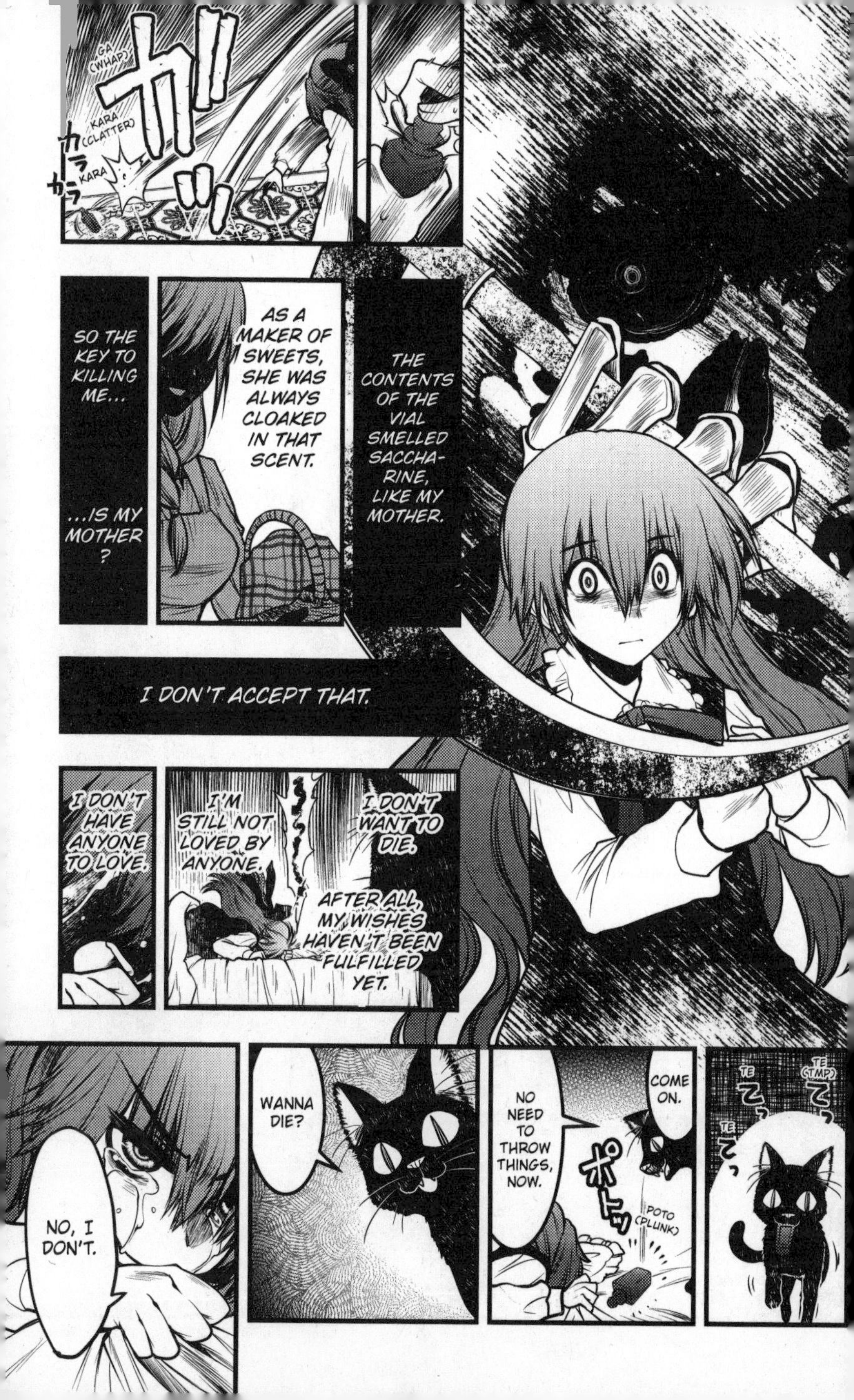
GA (WHAP)
KARA (CLATTER)
KARA
THE CONTENTS OF THE VIAL SMELLED SACCHARINE, LIKE MY MOTHER.
AS A MAKER OF SWEETS, SHE WAS ALWAYS CLOAKED IN THAT SCENT.
SO THE KEY TO KILLING ME...
...IS MY MOTHER?
I DON'T ACCEPT THAT.
I DON'T WANT TO DIE.
AFTER ALL, MY WISHES HAVEN'T BEEN FULFILLED YET.
I'M STILL NOT LOVED BY ANYONE.
I DON'T HAVE ANYONE TO LOVE.
TE (TMP)
TE
TE
COME ON.
NO NEED TO THROW THINGS, NOW.
POTO (PLUNK)
WANNA DIE?
NO, I DON'T.

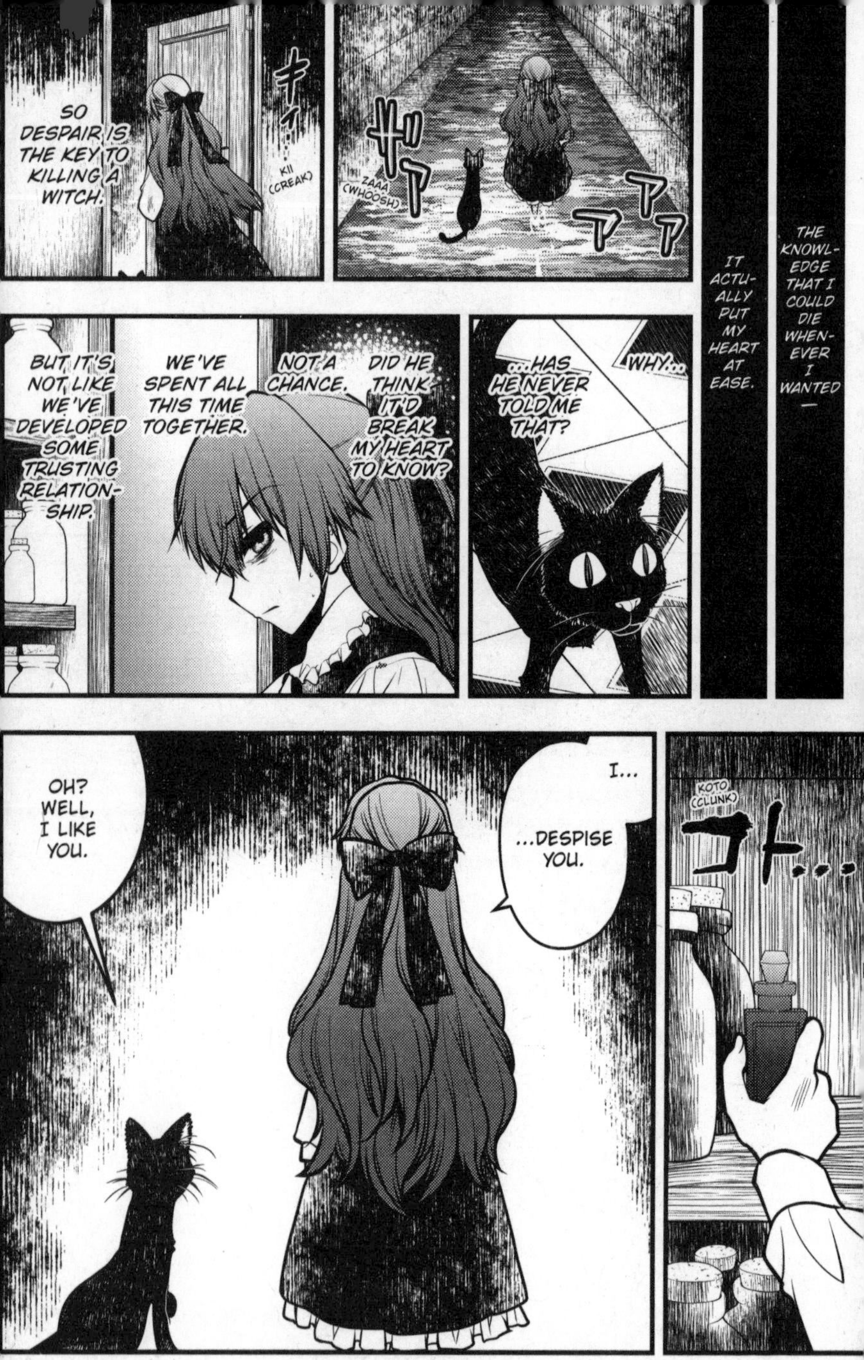
THE KNOWLEDGE THAT I COULD DIE WHENEVER I WANTED—
IT ACTUALLY PUT MY HEART AT EASE.
ザアアア
ZAAA (WHOOSH)
キィ
KII (CREAK)
SO DESPAIR IS THE KEY TO KILLING A WITCH.
WHY...
...HAS HE NEVER TOLD ME THAT?
DID HE THINK IT'D BREAK MY HEART TO KNOW?
NOT A CHANCE.
WE'VE SPENT ALL THIS TIME TOGETHER.
BUT IT'S NOT LIKE WE'VE DEVELOPED SOME TRUSTING RELATIONSHIP.
KOTO (CLUNK)
コト...
I...
...DESPISE YOU.
OH? WELL, I LIKE YOU.

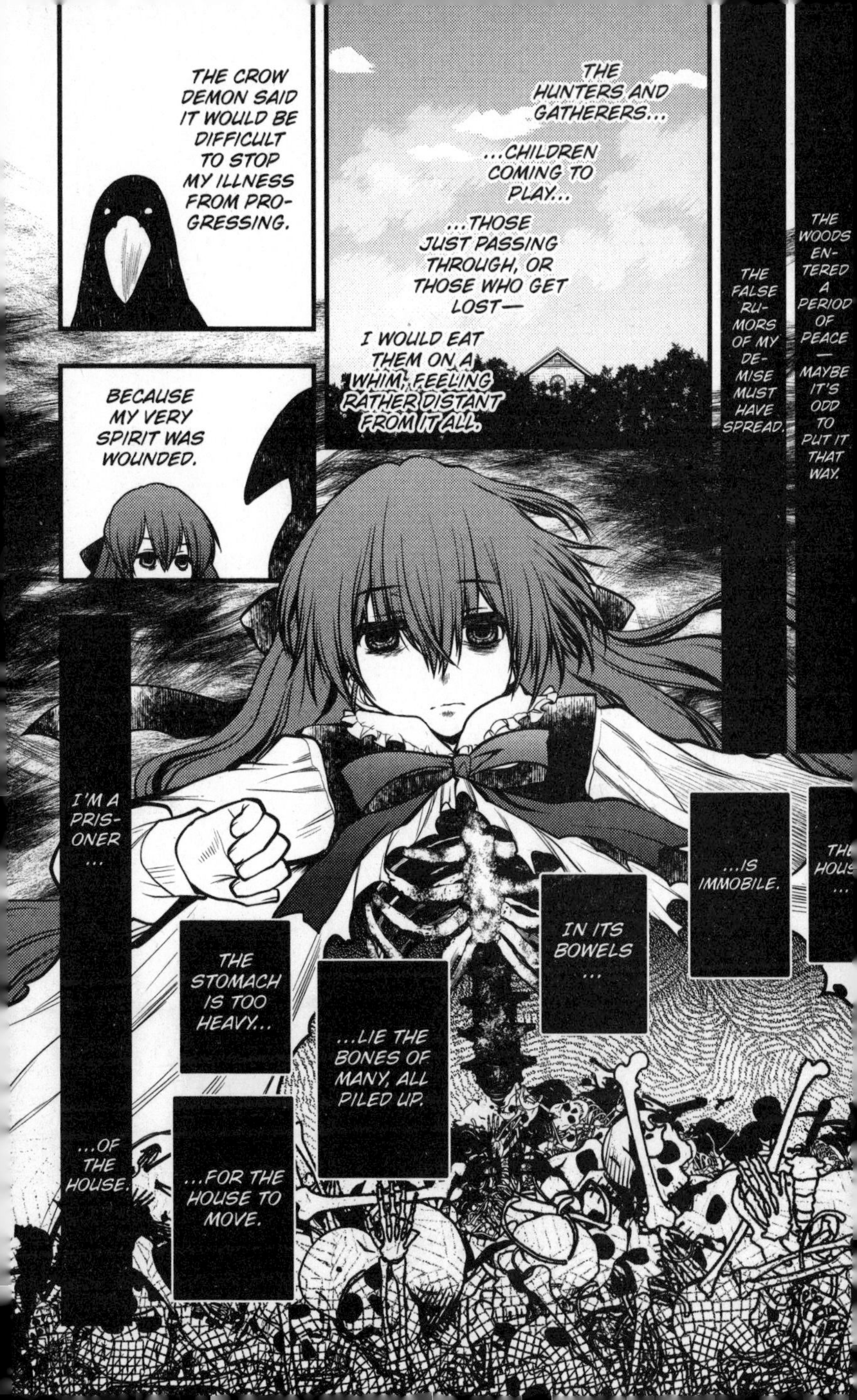
THE WOODS ENTERED A PERIOD OF PEACE—MAYBE IT'S ODD TO PUT IT THAT WAY.
THE FALSE RUMORS OF MY DEMISE MUST HAVE SPREAD.
THE HUNTERS AND GATHERERS...
...CHILDREN COMING TO PLAY...
...THOSE JUST PASSING THROUGH, OR THOSE WHO GET LOST—
I WOULD EAT THEM ON A WHIM, FEELING RATHER DISTANT FROM IT ALL.
THE CROW DEMON SAID IT WOULD BE DIFFICULT TO STOP MY ILLNESS FROM PROGRESSING.
BECAUSE MY VERY SPIRIT WAS WOUNDED.
THE HOUS...
...IS IMMOBILE.
IN ITS BOWELS...
...LIE THE BONES OF MANY, ALL PILED UP.
THE STOMACH IS TOO HEAVY...
...FOR THE HOUSE TO MOVE.
I'M A PRISONER...
...OF THE HOUSE.

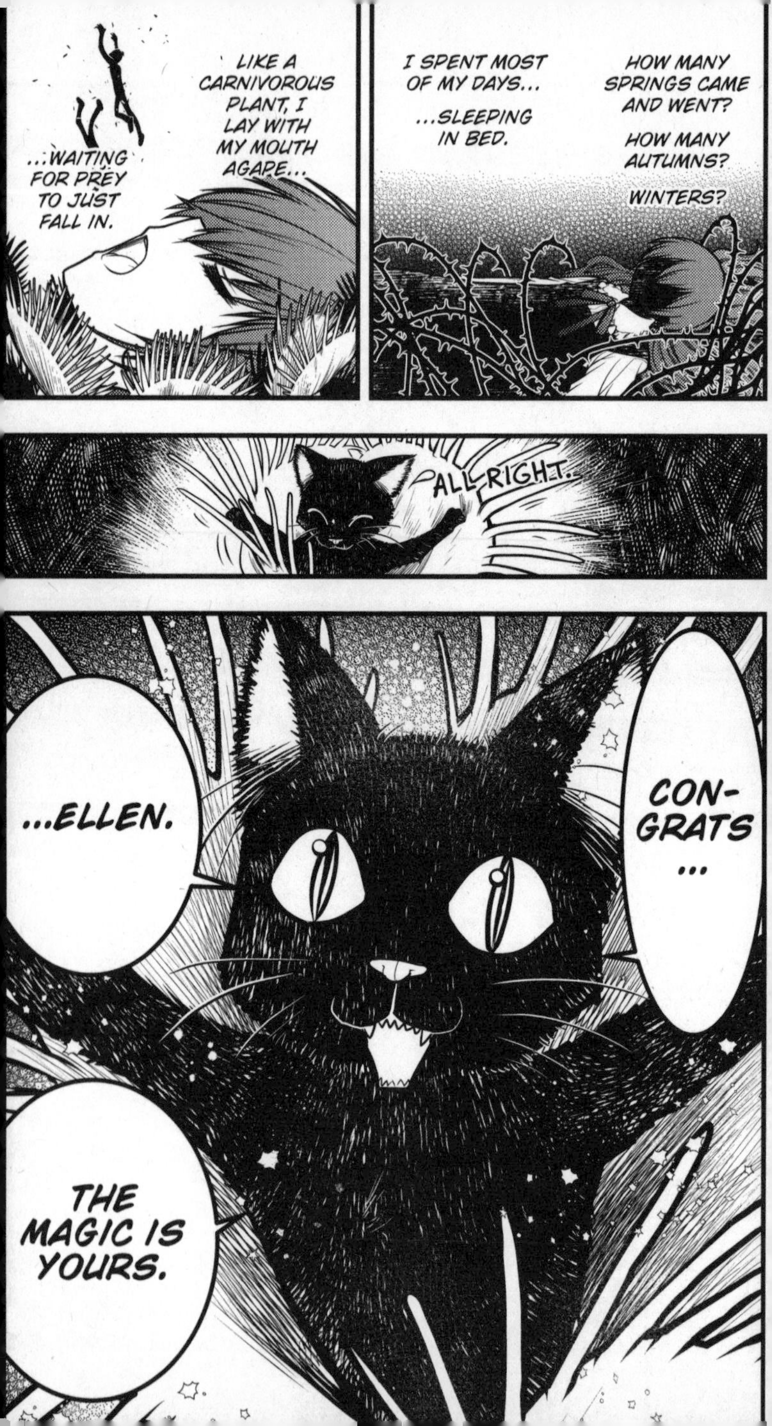
HOW MANY SPRINGS CAME AND WENT?
HOW MANY AUTUMNS?
WINTERS?
I SPENT MOST OF MY DAYS...
...SLEEPING IN BED.
LIKE A CARNIVOROUS PLANT, I LAY WITH MY MOUTH AGAPE...
...WAITING FOR PREY TO JUST FALL IN.
ALL RIGHT.
CON-GRATS...
...ELLEN.
THE MAGIC IS YOURS.

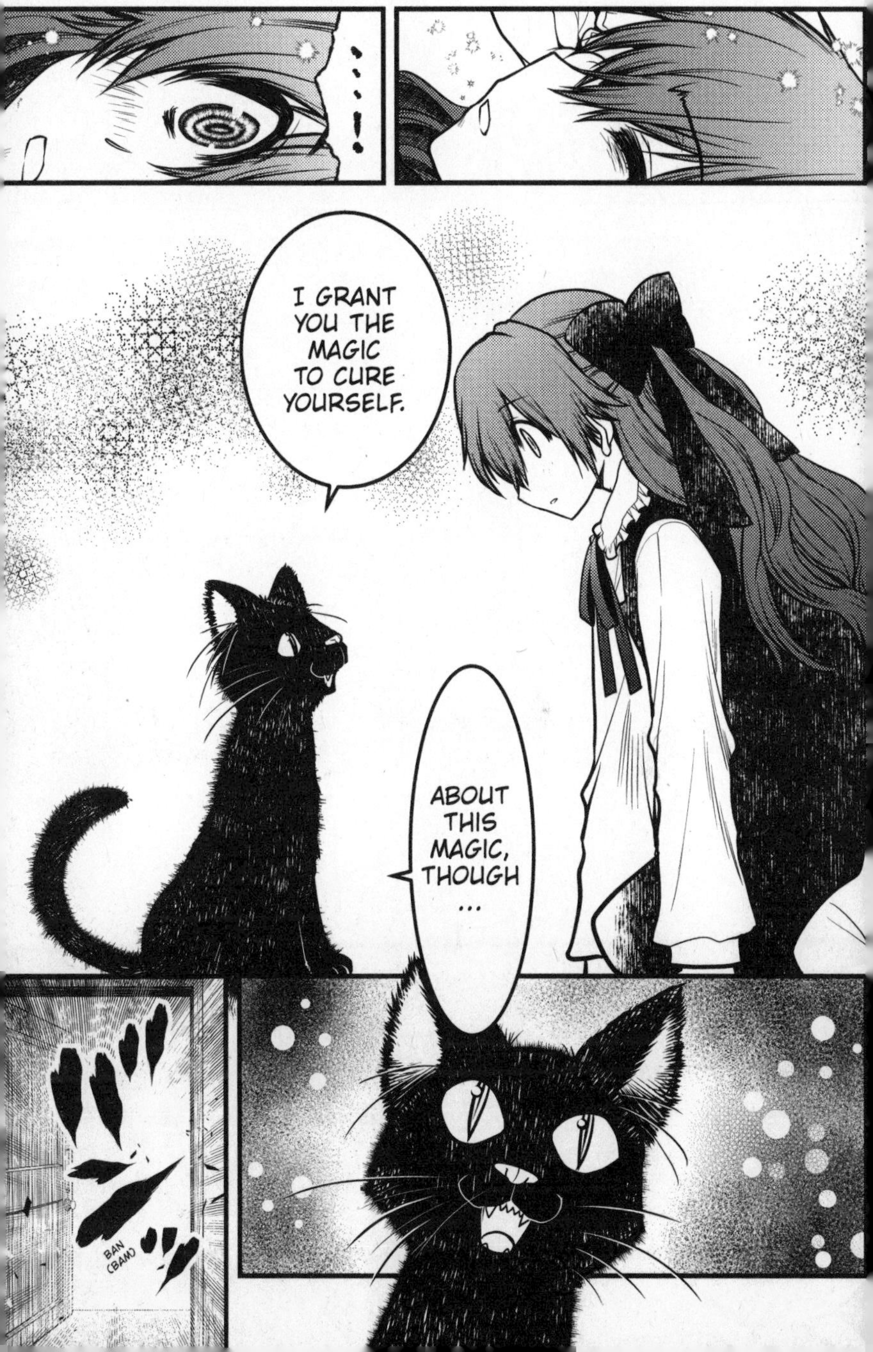
...!
I GRANT YOU THE MAGIC TO CURE YOURSELF.
ABOUT THIS MAGIC, THOUGH ...
BAN (BAM)

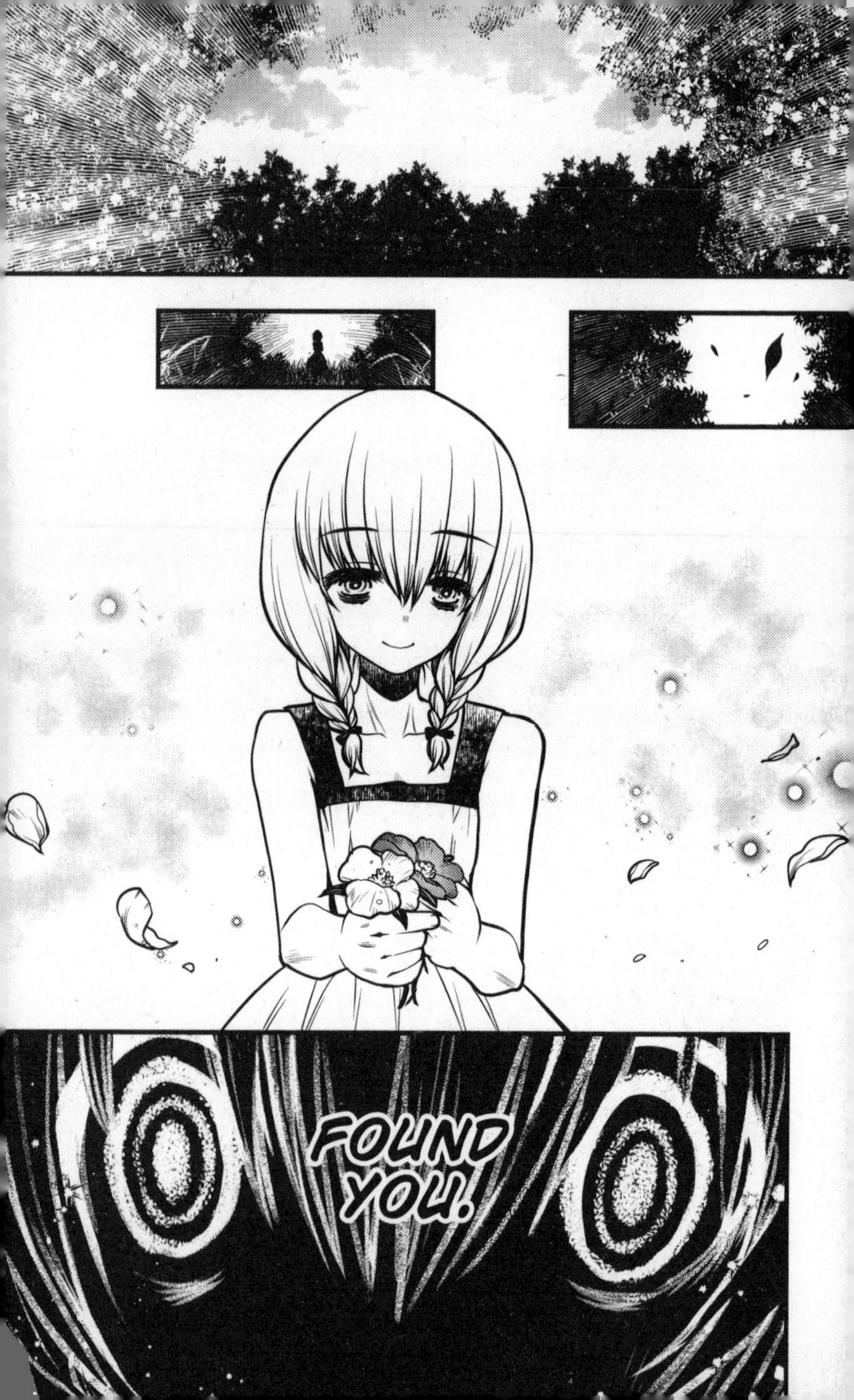
FOUND YOU.

THE WITCH'S HOUSE

HOUSE

The Diary of Ellen

THE
WITCH'S
HOUSE

The Diary of Ellen

Chapter 6

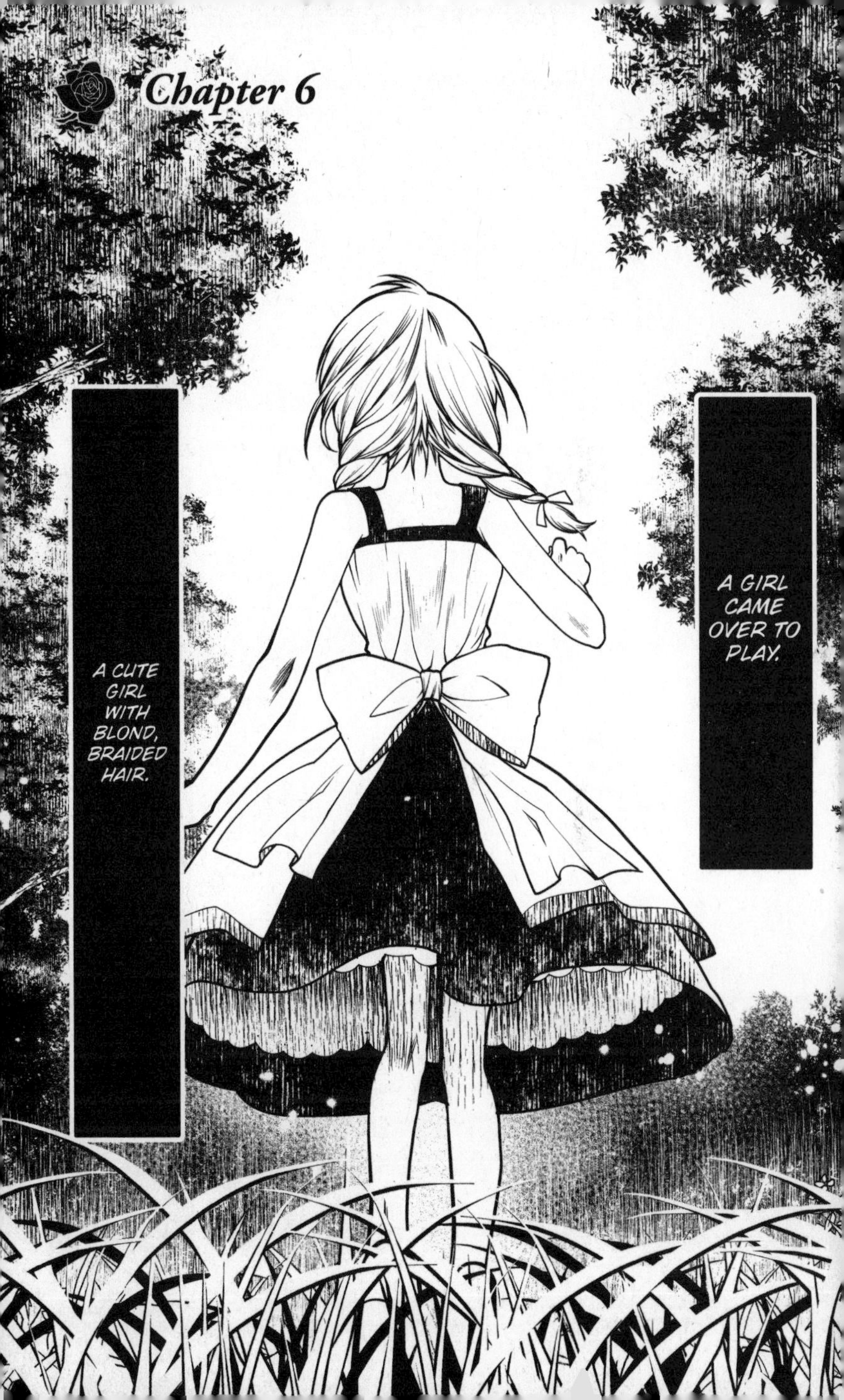
A GIRL CAME OVER TO PLAY.
A CUTE GIRL WITH BLOND, BRAIDED HAIR.

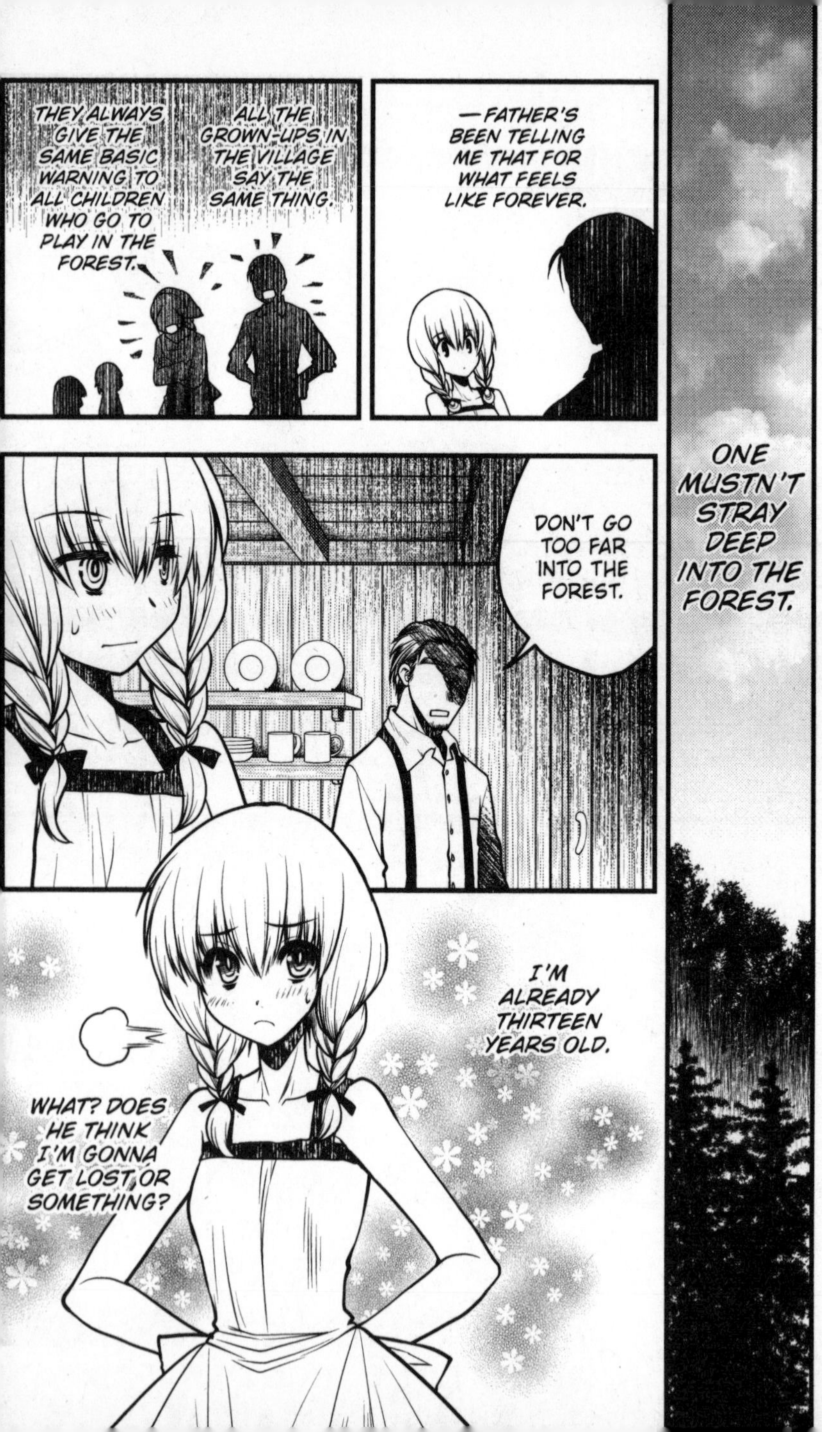
ONE MUSTN'T STRAY DEEP INTO THE FOREST.
—FATHER'S BEEN TELLING ME THAT FOR WHAT FEELS LIKE FOREVER.
ALL THE GROWN-UPS IN THE VILLAGE SAY THE SAME THING.
THEY ALWAYS GIVE THE SAME BASIC WARNING TO ALL CHILDREN WHO GO TO PLAY IN THE FOREST.
DON'T GO TOO FAR INTO THE FOREST.
I'M ALREADY THIRTEEN YEARS OLD.
WHAT? DOES HE THINK I'M GONNA GET LOST OR SOMETHING?

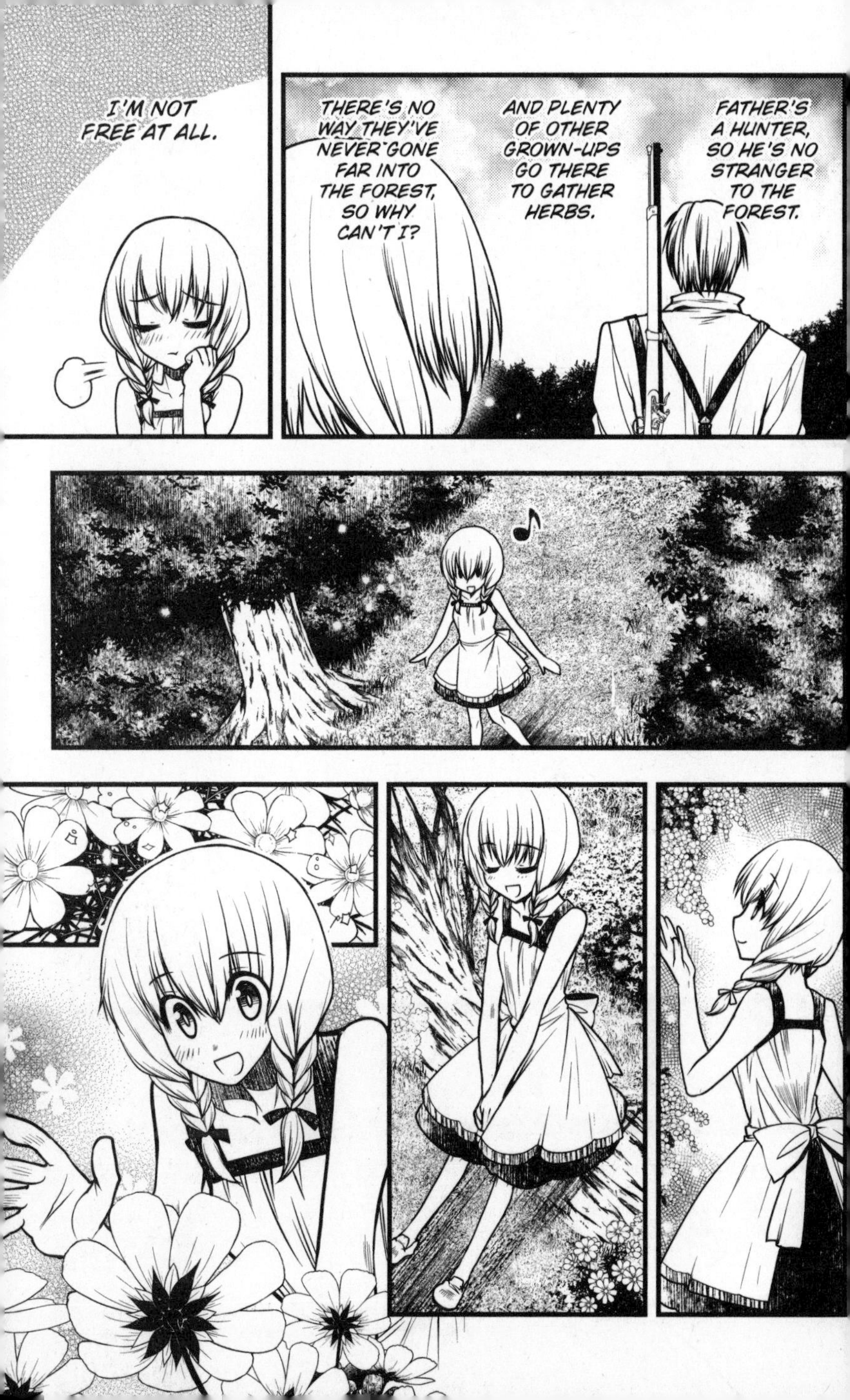
FATHER'S A HUNTER, SO HE'S NO STRANGER TO THE FOREST.
AND PLENTY OF OTHER GROWN-UPS GO THERE TO GATHER HERBS.
THERE'S NO WAY THEY'VE NEVER GONE FAR INTO THE FOREST, SO WHY CAN'T I?
I'M NOT FREE AT ALL.

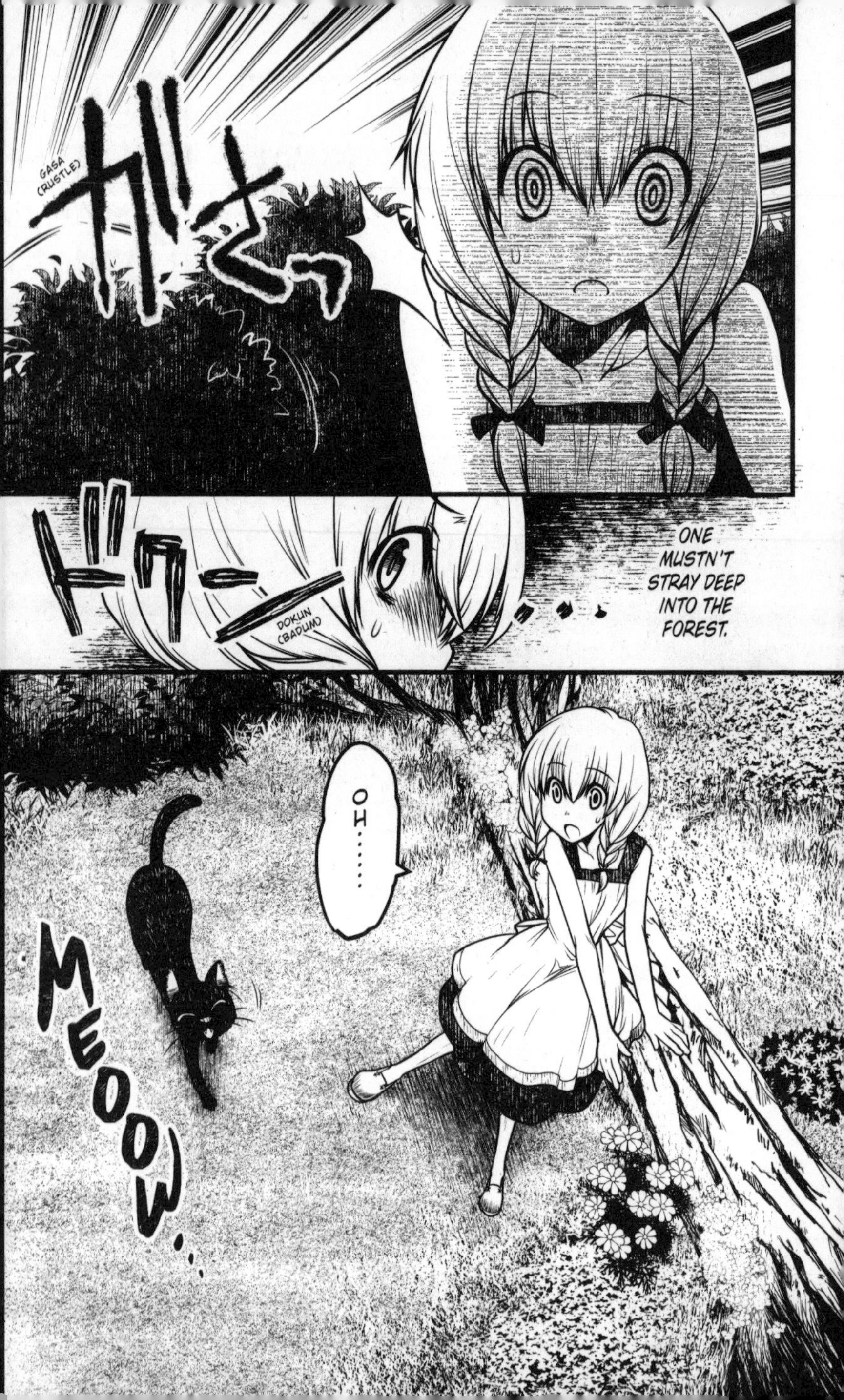

ガさっ
GASA (RUSTLE)
ONE MUSTN'T STRAY DEEP INTO THE FOREST.
ドクー
DOKUN (BADUM)
OH.....
MEOOW...

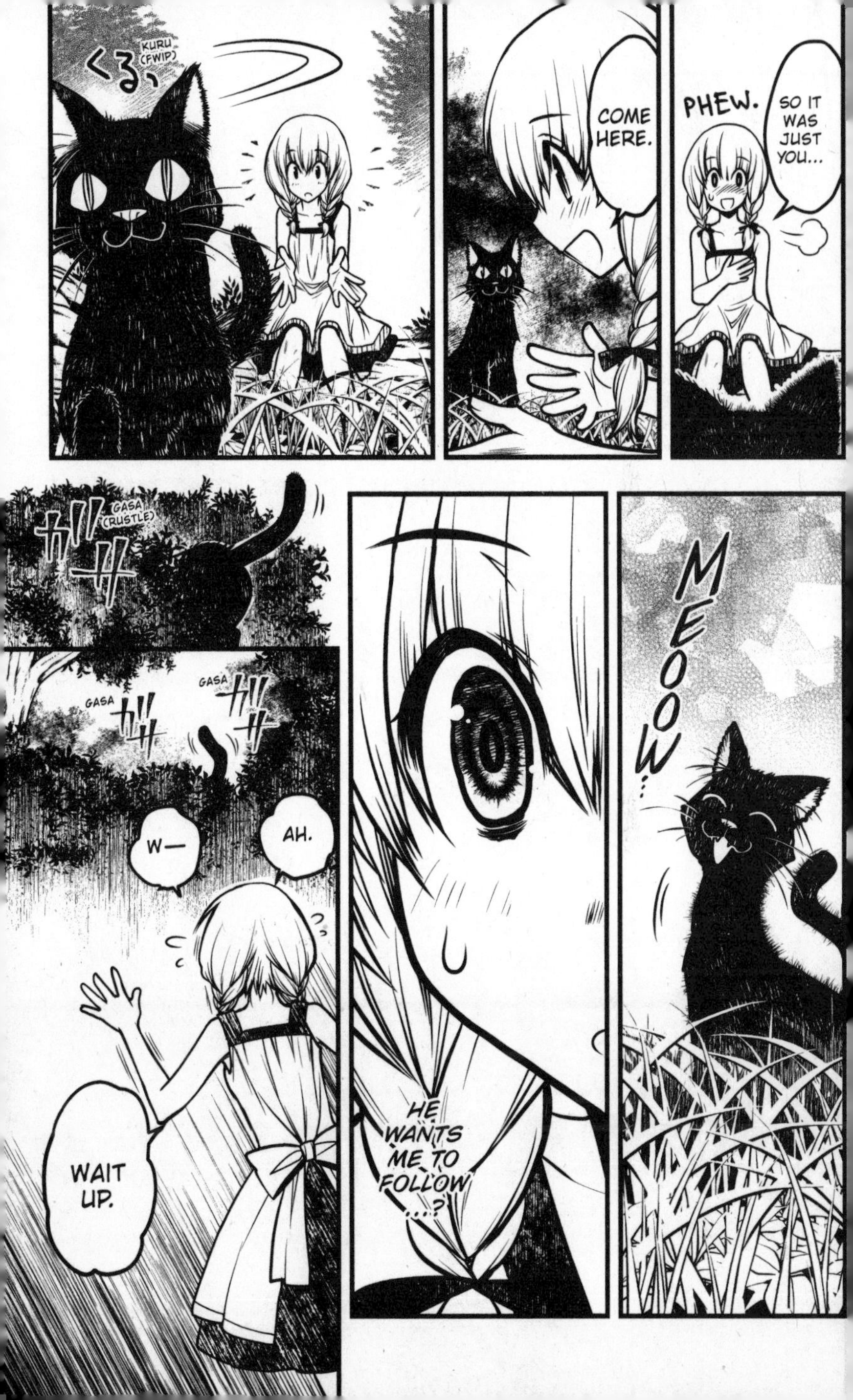
PHEW.
SO IT WAS JUST YOU...
COME HERE.
くる、
KURU (FWIP)
MEOOOW...
HE WANTS ME TO FOLLOW...?
ガサ
GASA (RUSTLE)
ガサ
GASA
ガサ
GASA
AH.
W—
WAIT UP.

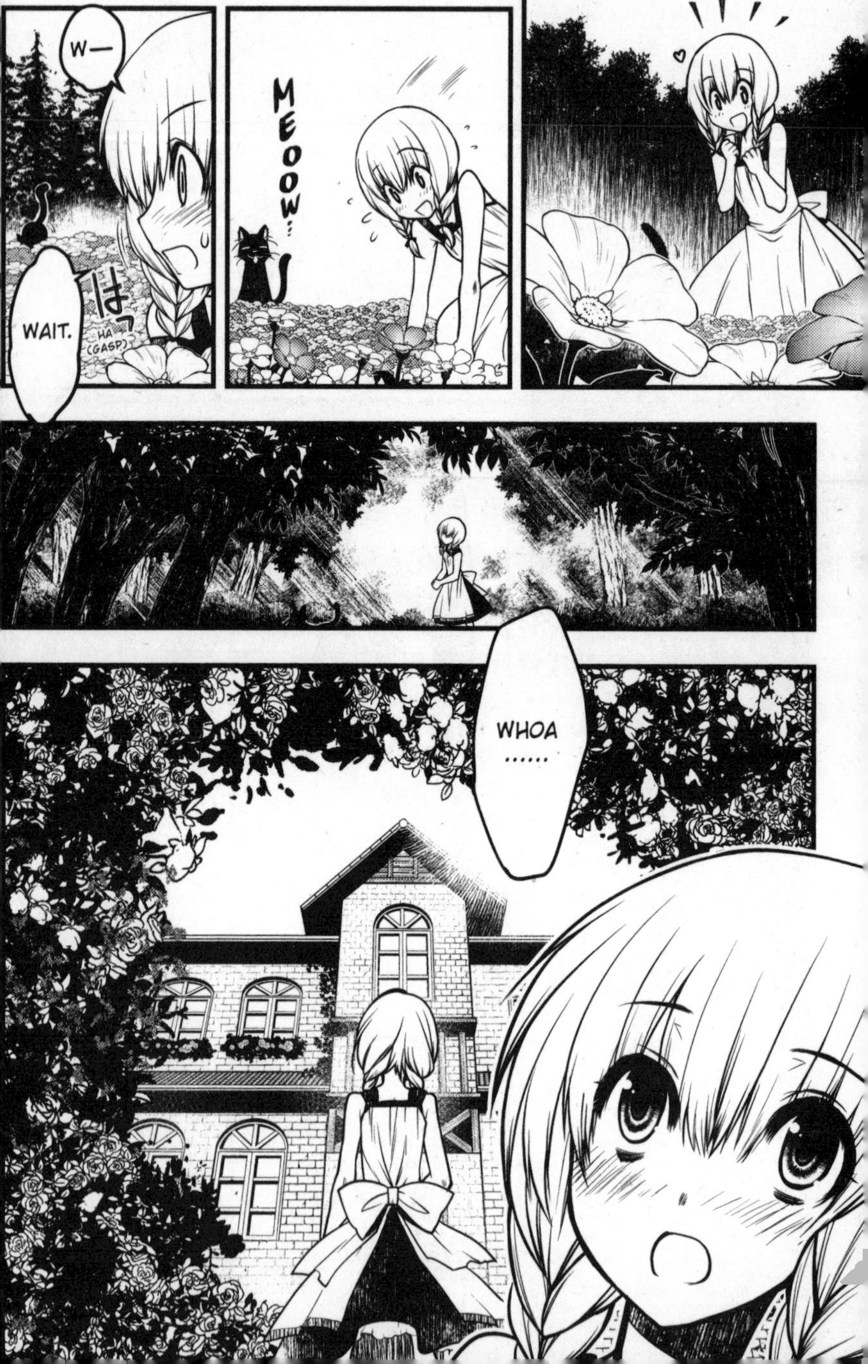
MEOOW...
W—
はっ
HA (GASP)
WAIT.
WHOA ......

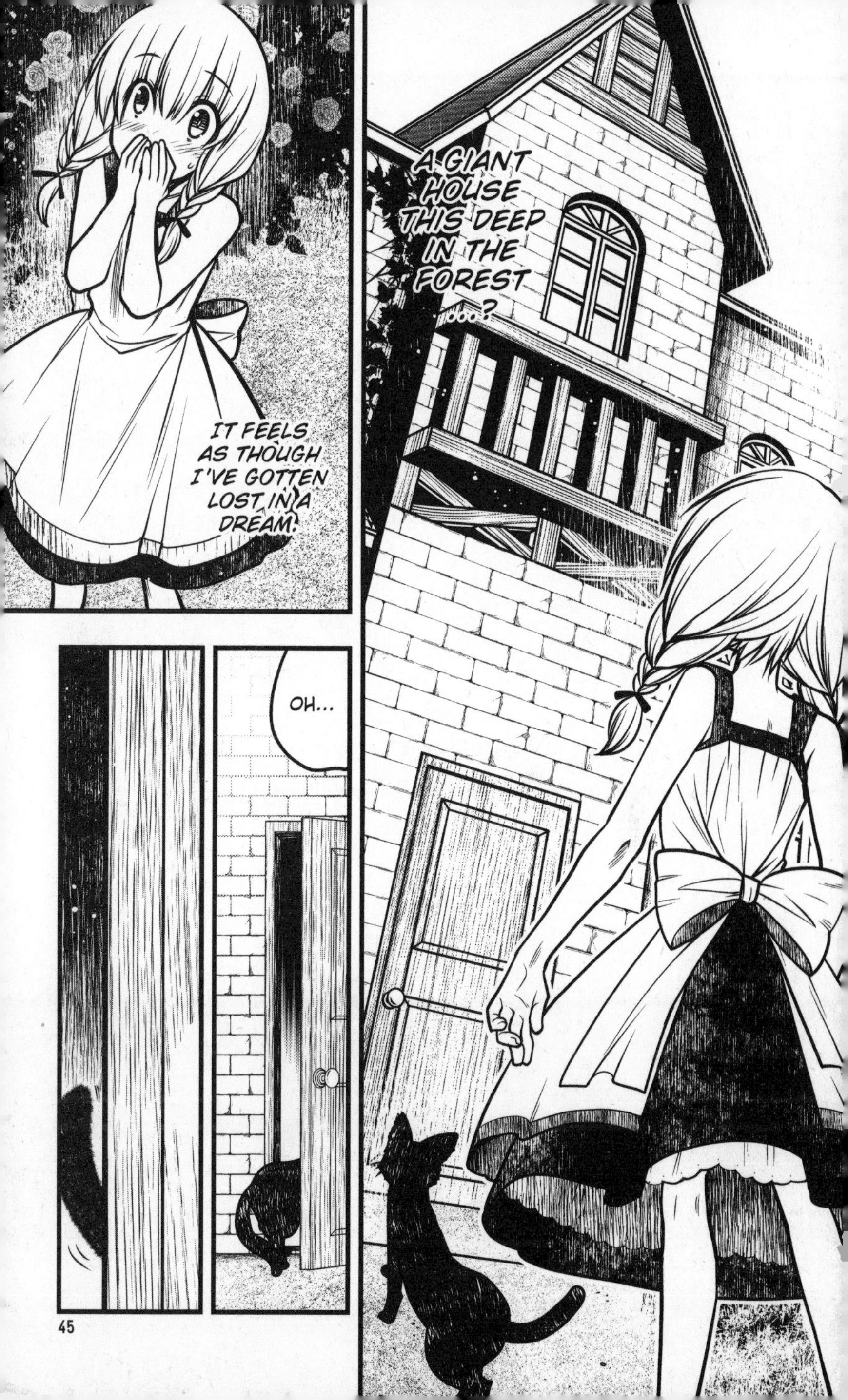
A GIANT HOUSE THIS DEEP IN THE FOREST ...?
IT FEELS AS THOUGH I'VE GOTTEN LOST IN A DREAM.
OH...

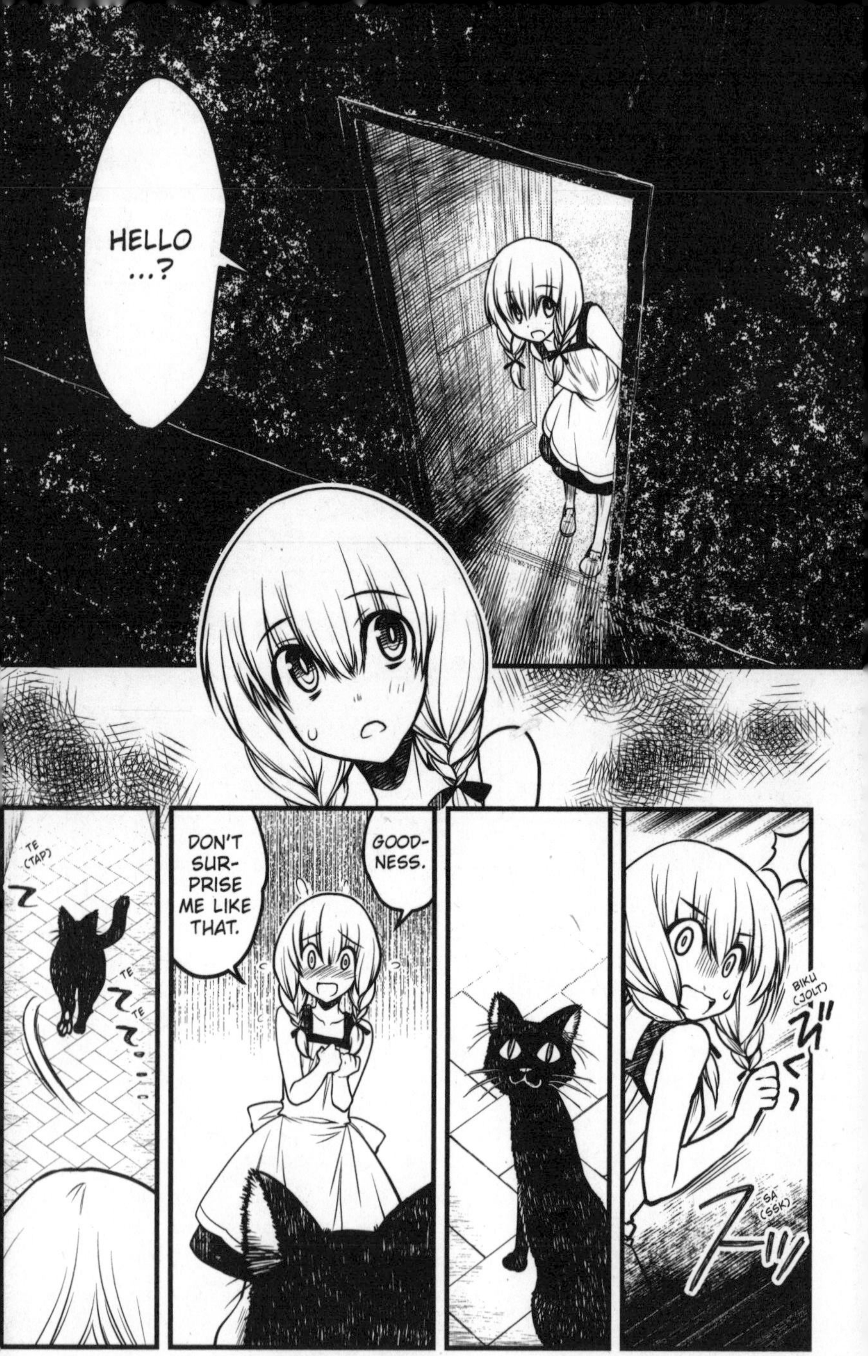
HELLO ...?
BIKU (JOLT)
SA (SSK)
GOOD-NESS.
DON'T SUR-PRISE ME LIKE THAT.
TE (TAP)
TE
TE

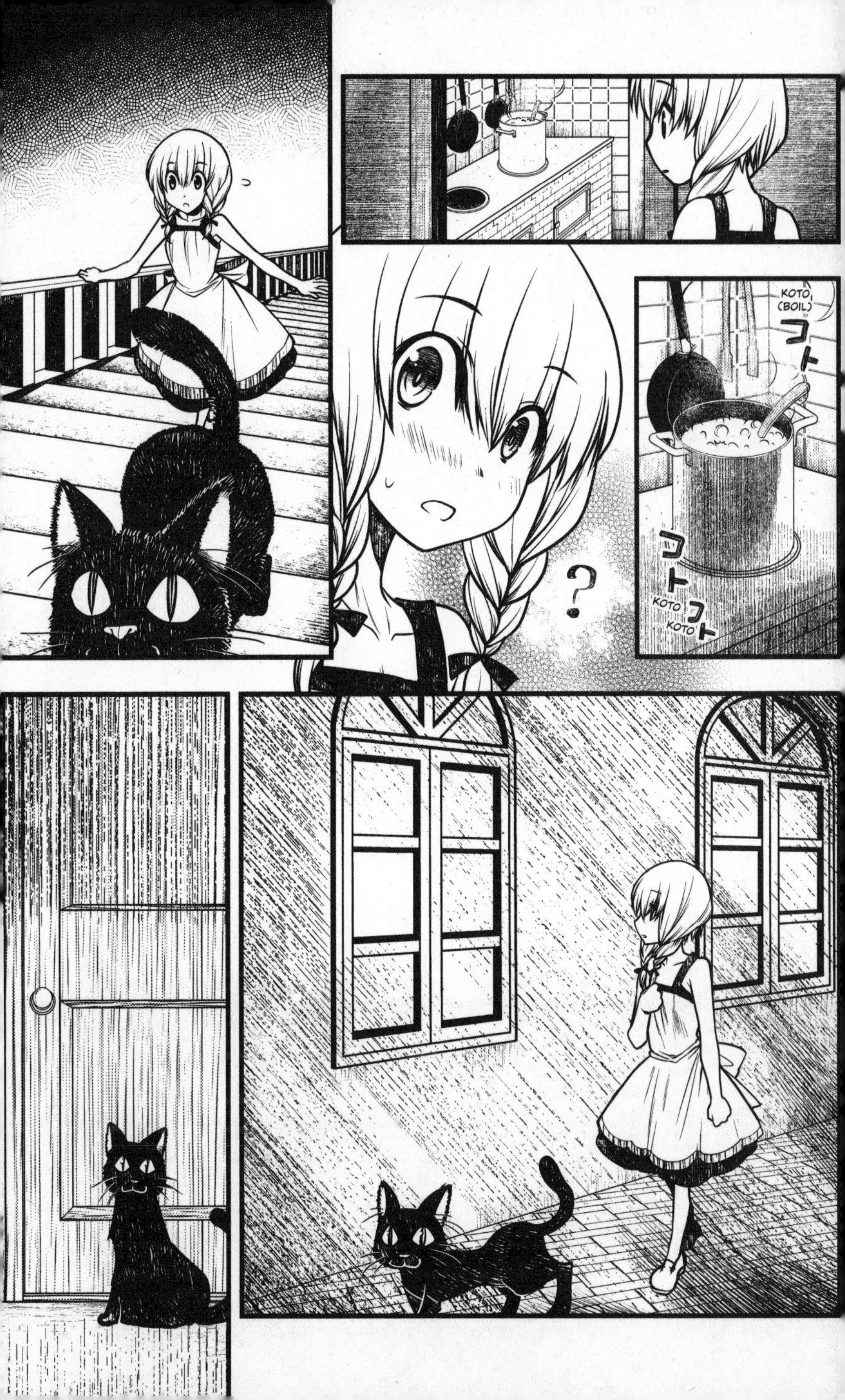
KOTO (BOIL)
コト
KOTO
コト
KOTO
コト
?

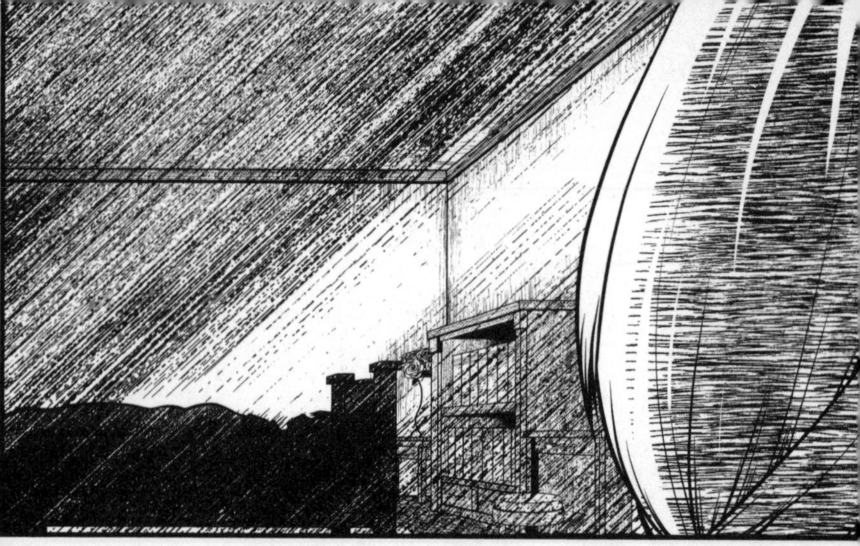
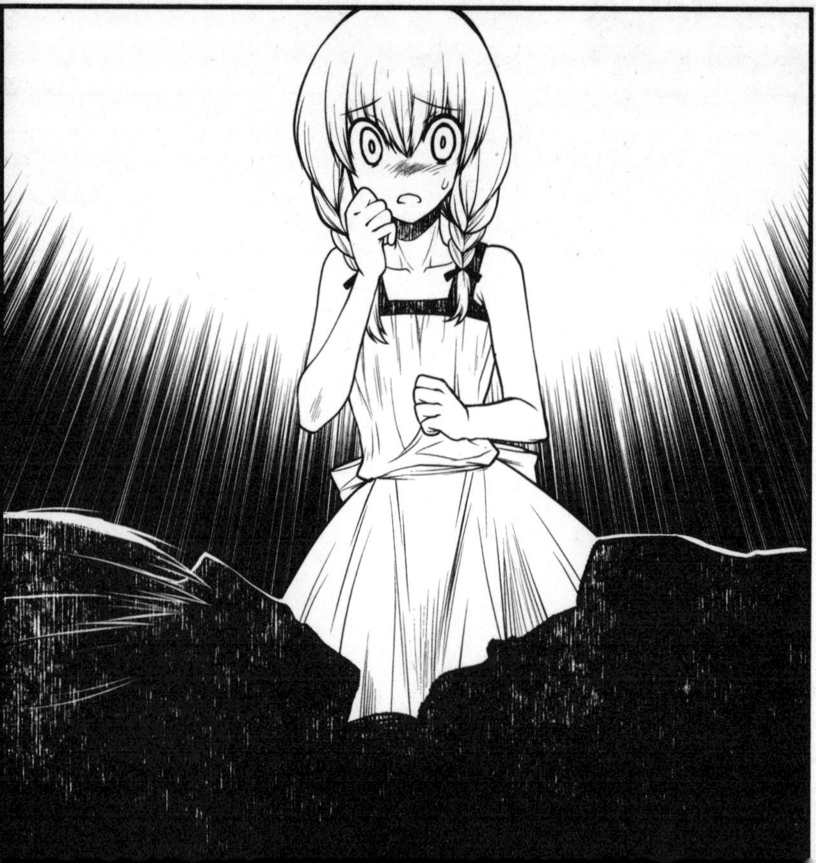

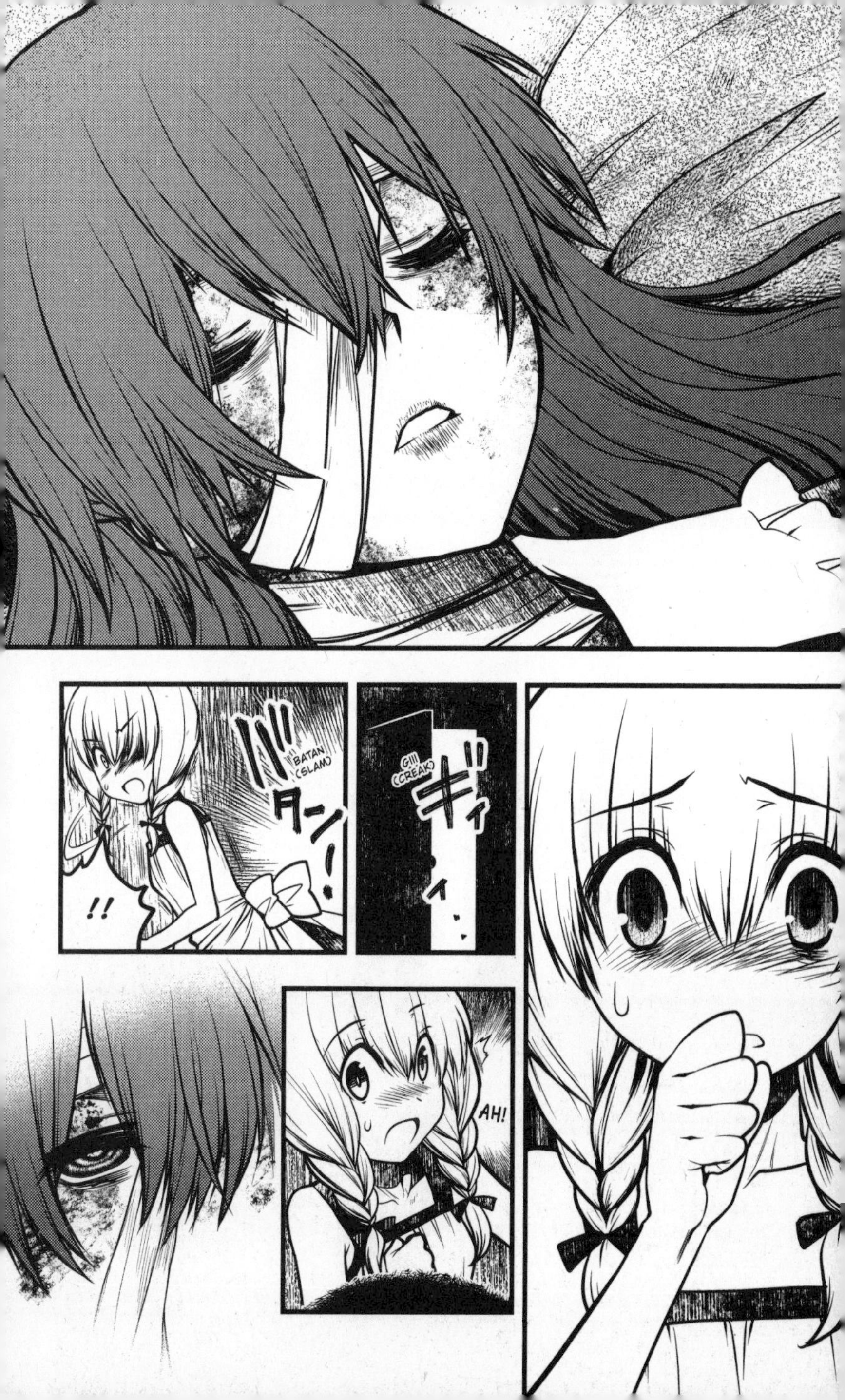
GIII (CREAK)
BATAN (SLAM)
!!
AH!

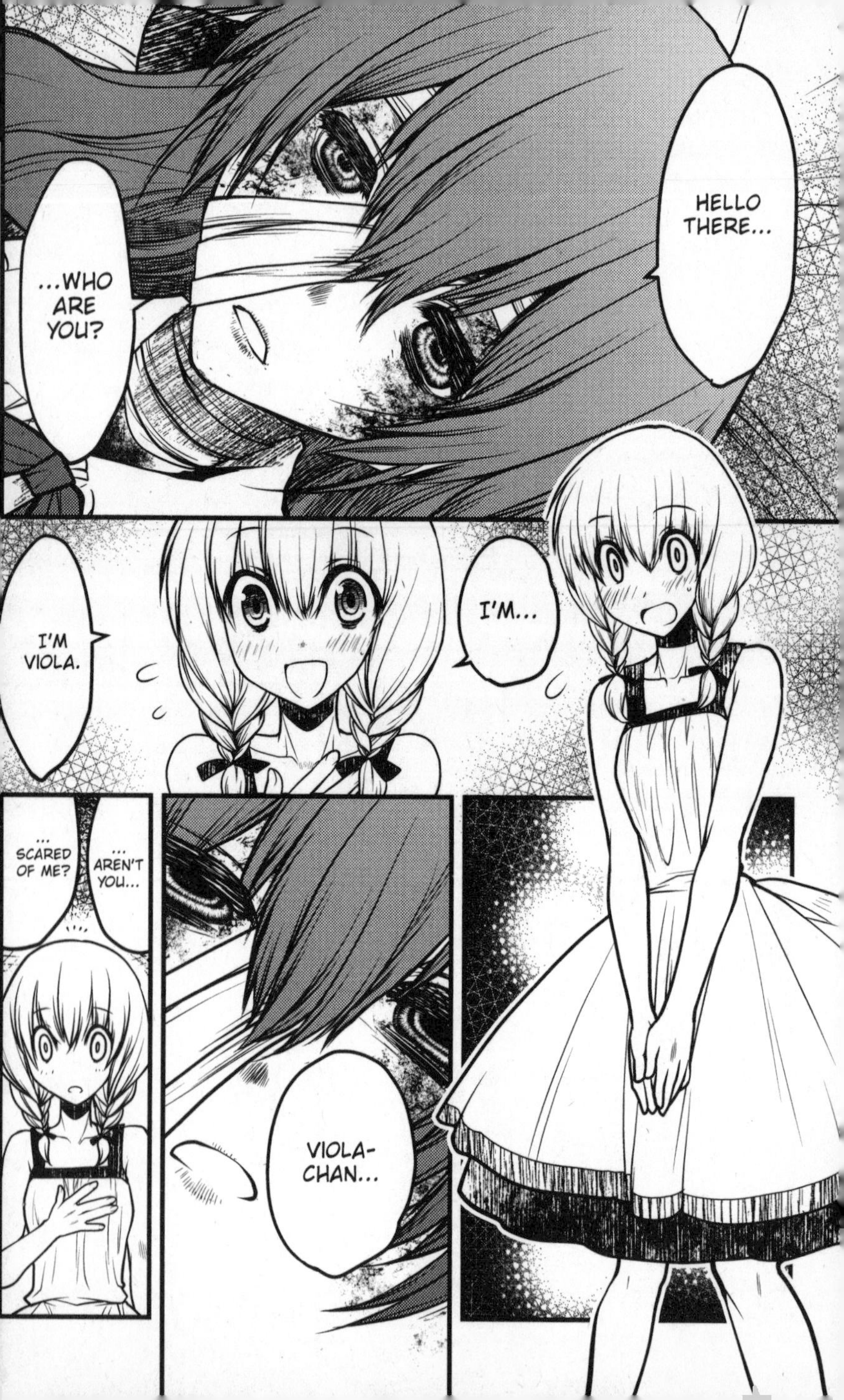
HELLO THERE...
...WHO ARE YOU?
I'M...
I'M VIOLA.
VIOLA-CHAN...
...AREN'T YOU...
...SCARED OF ME?

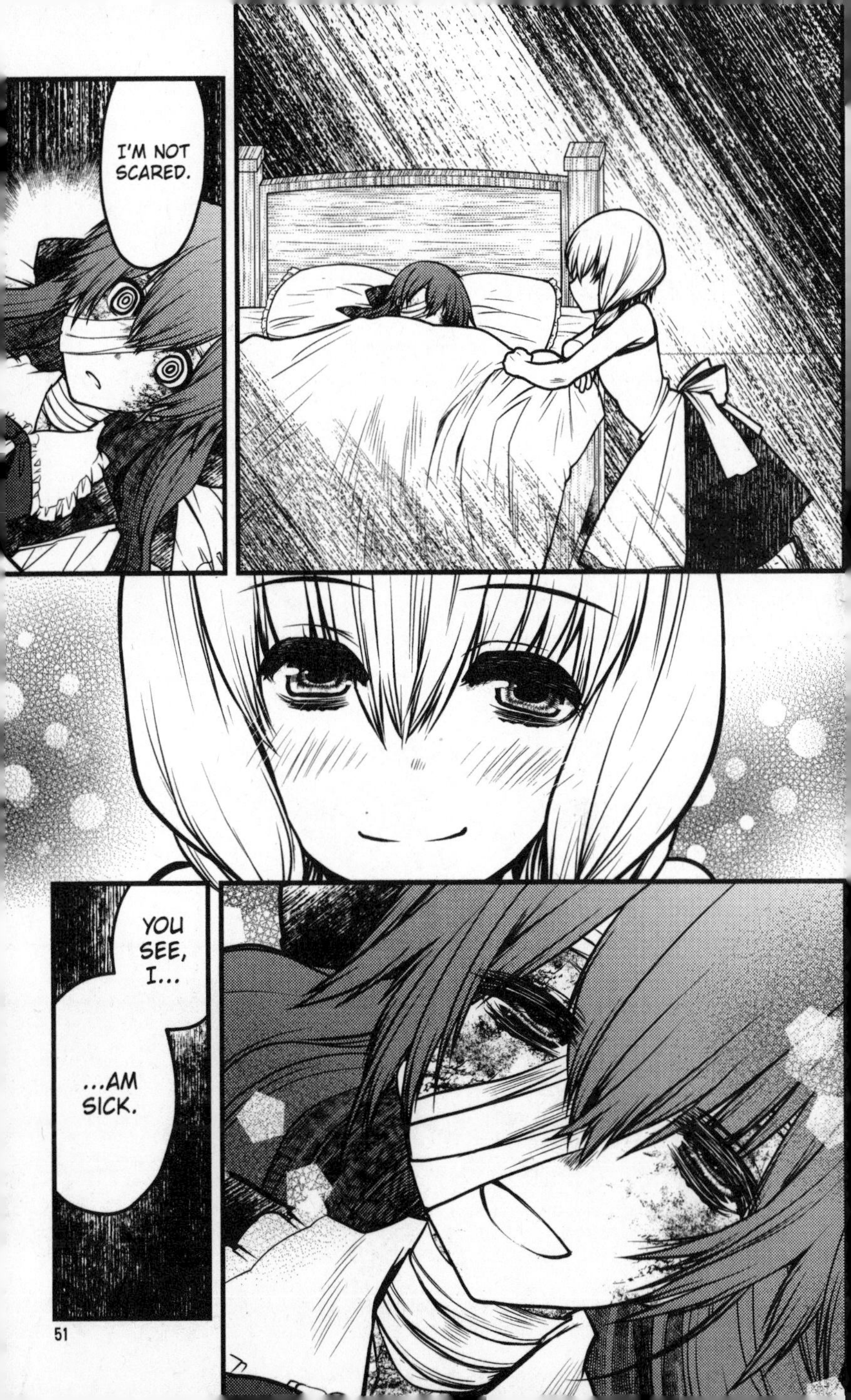
I'M NOT SCARED.
YOU SEE, I...
...AM SICK.

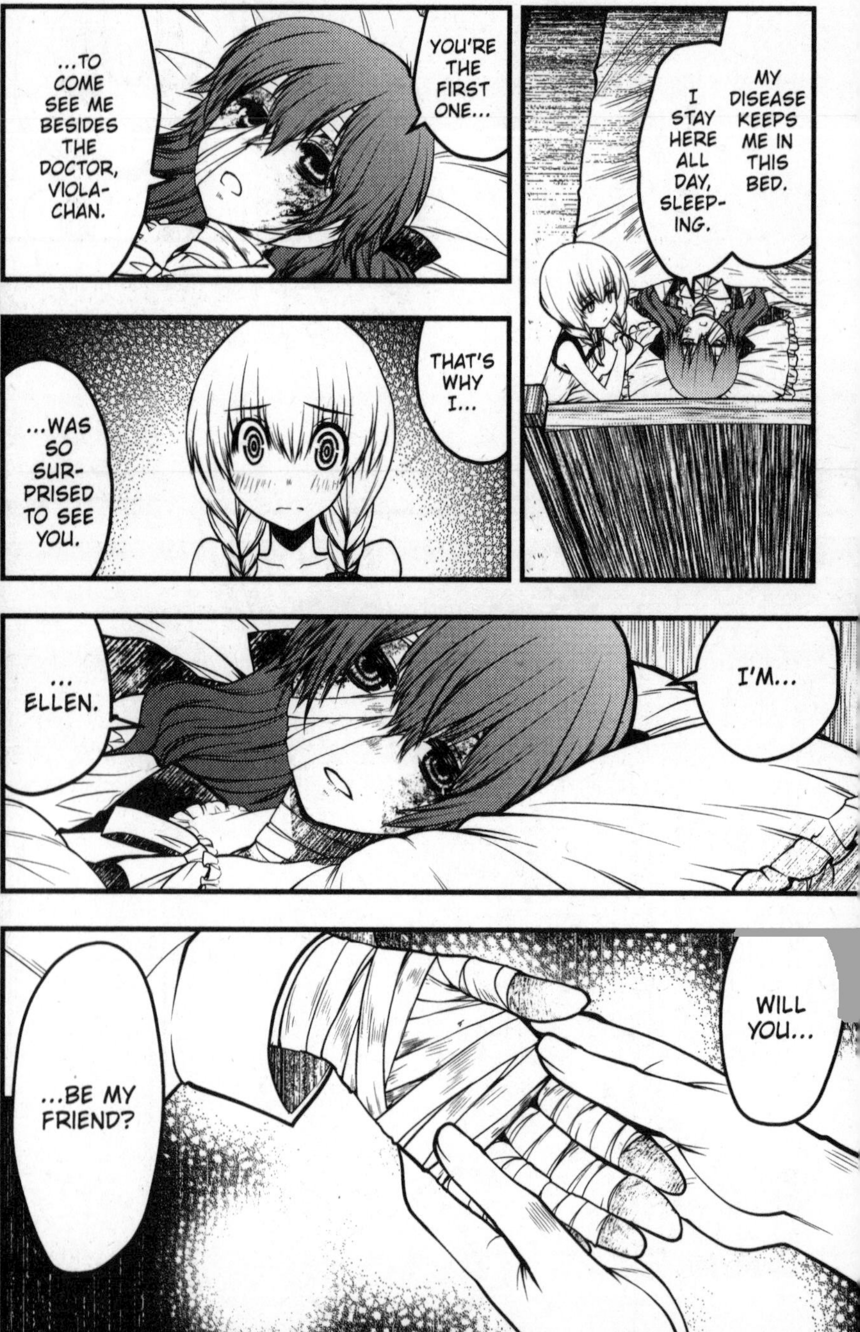
MY DISEASE KEEPS ME IN THIS BED.
I STAY HERE ALL DAY, SLEEPING.
YOU'RE THE FIRST ONE...
...TO COME SEE ME BESIDES THE DOCTOR, VIOLA-CHAN.
THAT'S WHY I...
...WAS SO SURPRISED TO SEE YOU.
I'M...
...ELLEN.
WILL YOU...
...BE MY FRIEND?

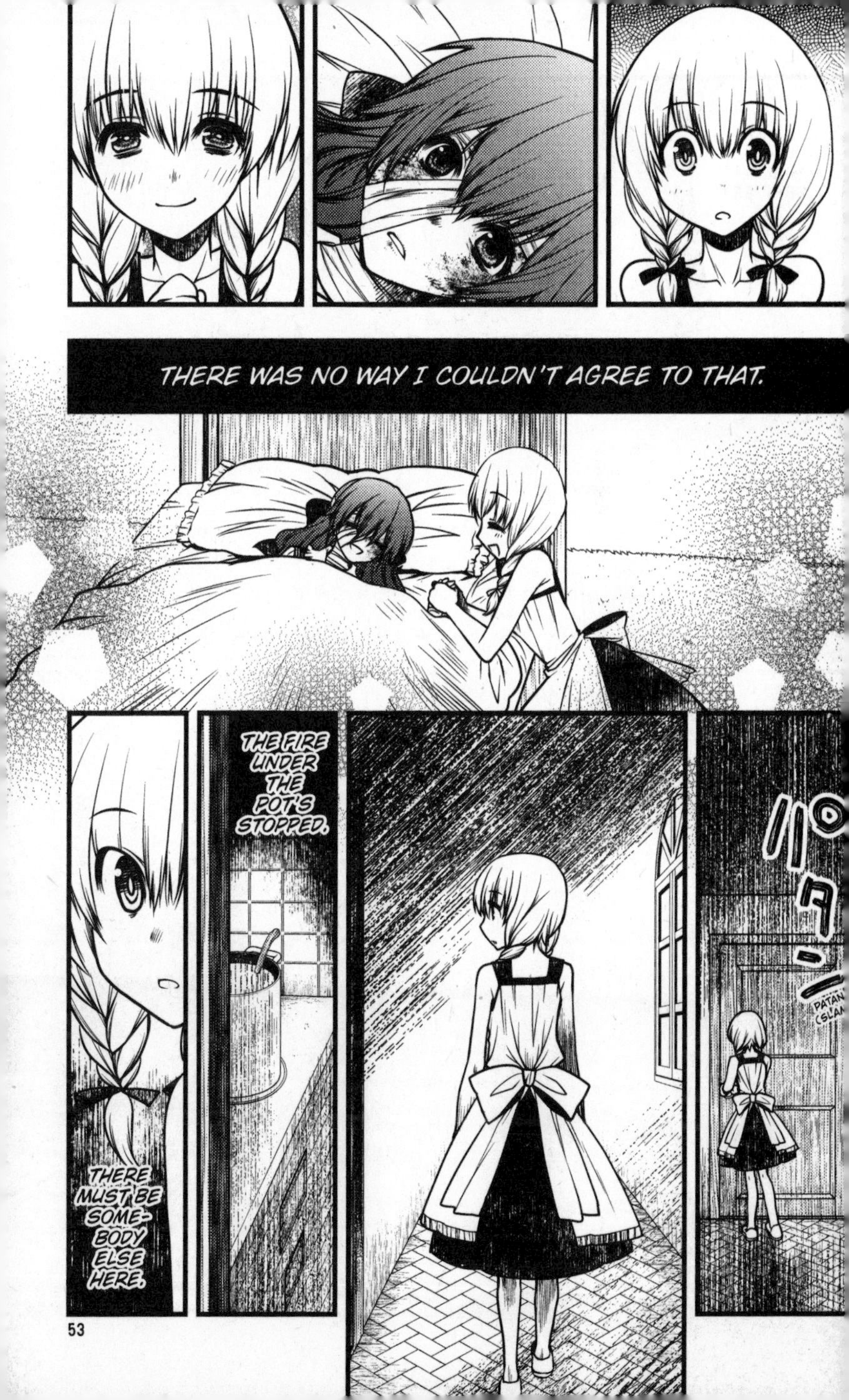
THERE WAS NO WAY I COULDN'T AGREE TO THAT.
パタン
PATAN (SLAM
THE FIRE UNDER THE POT'S STOPPED.
THERE MUST BE SOME-BODY ELSE HERE.

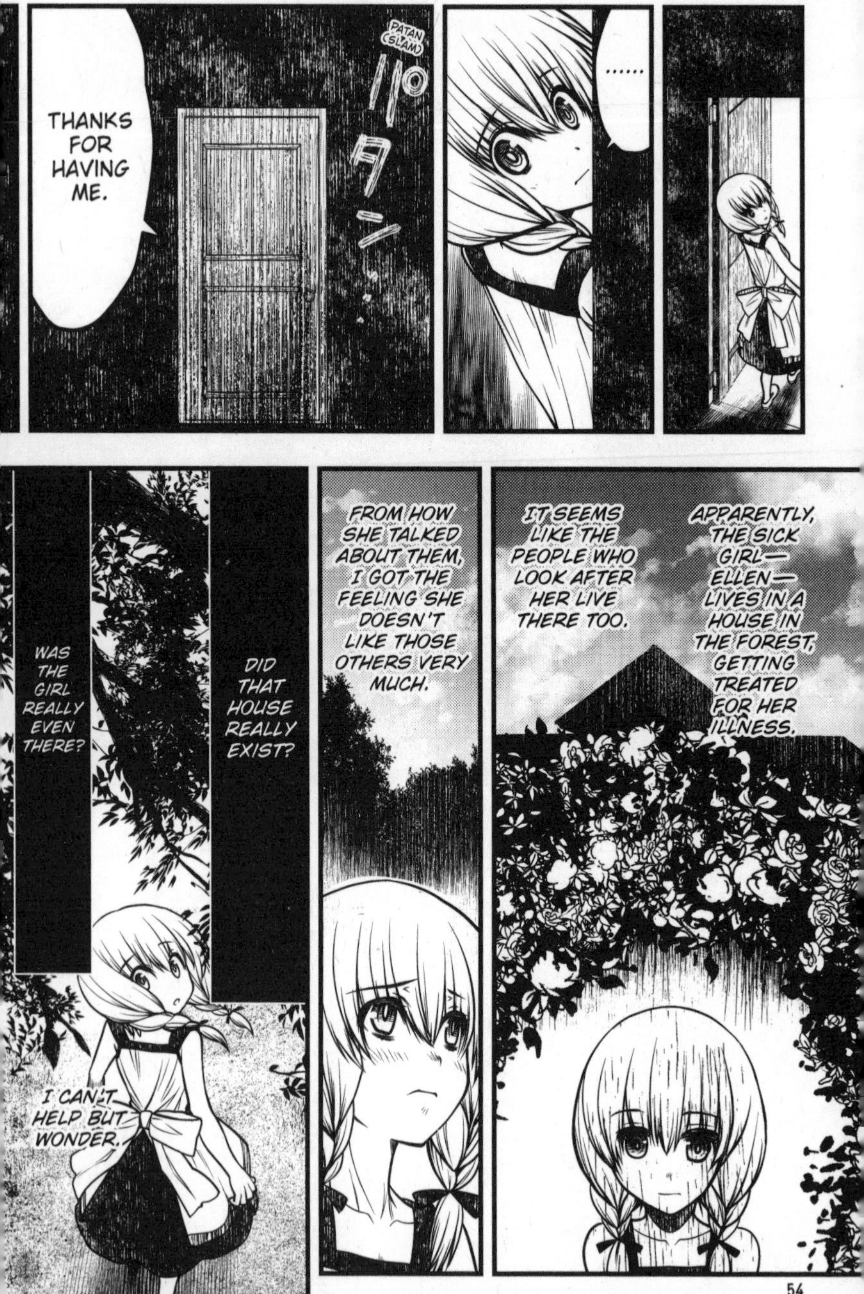
......
THANKS FOR HAVING ME.
PATAN (SLAM)
パタン
APPARENTLY, THE SICK GIRL—ELLEN—LIVES IN A HOUSE IN THE FOREST, GETTING TREATED FOR HER ILLNESS.
IT SEEMS LIKE THE PEOPLE WHO LOOK AFTER HER LIVE THERE TOO.
FROM HOW SHE TALKED ABOUT THEM, I GOT THE FEELING SHE DOESN'T LIKE THOSE OTHERS VERY MUCH.
DID THAT HOUSE REALLY EXIST?
WAS THE GIRL REALLY EVEN THERE?
I CAN'T HELP BUT WONDER.

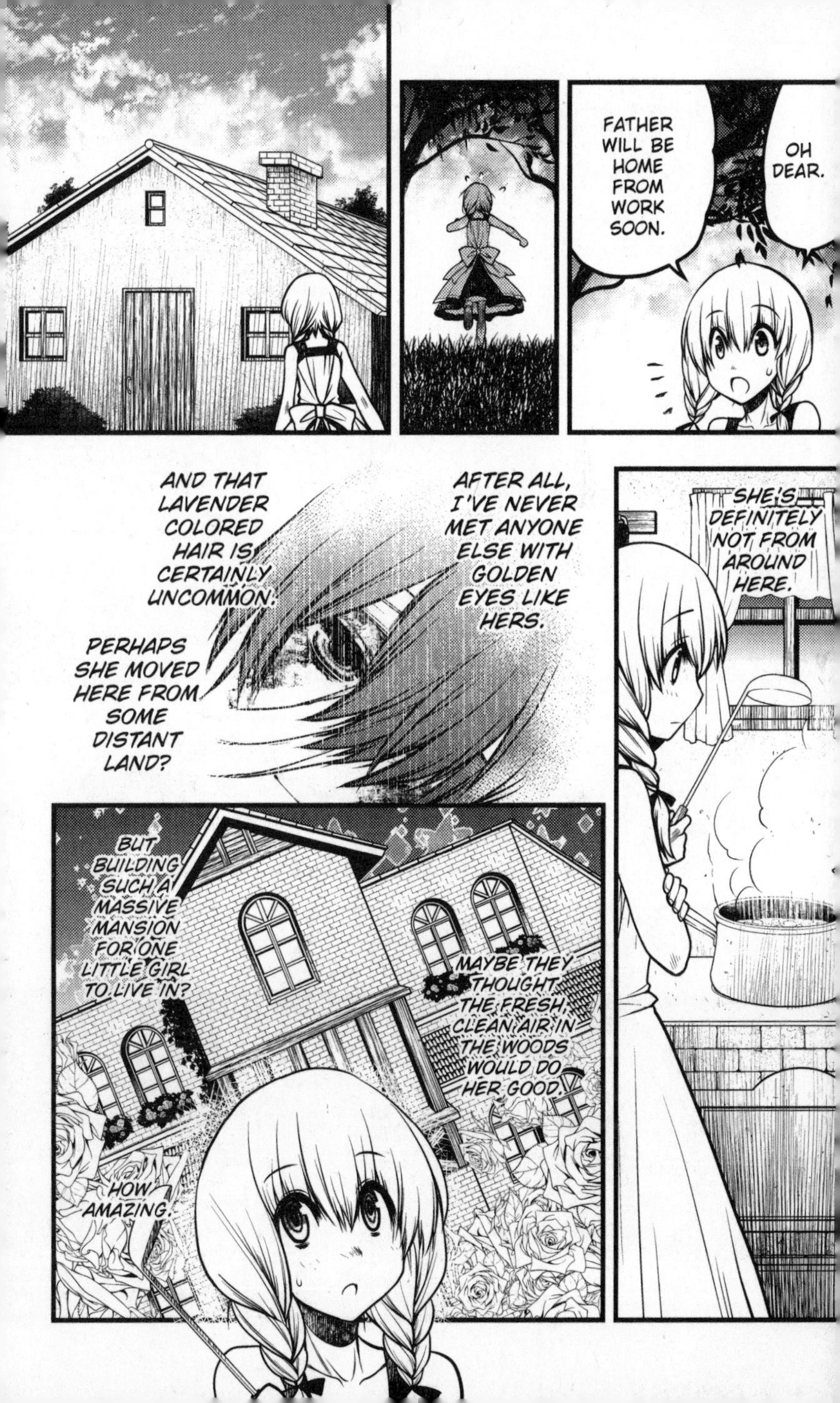
OH DEAR.
FATHER WILL BE HOME FROM WORK SOON.
SHE'S DEFINITELY NOT FROM AROUND HERE.
AFTER ALL, I'VE NEVER MET ANYONE ELSE WITH GOLDEN EYES LIKE HERS.
AND THAT LAVENDER COLORED HAIR IS CERTAINLY UNCOMMON.
PERHAPS SHE MOVED HERE FROM SOME DISTANT LAND?
BUT BUILDING SUCH A MASSIVE MANSION FOR ONE LITTLE GIRL TO LIVE IN?
MAYBE THEY THOUGHT THE FRESH, CLEAN AIR IN THE WOODS WOULD DO HER GOOD.
HOW AMAZING.

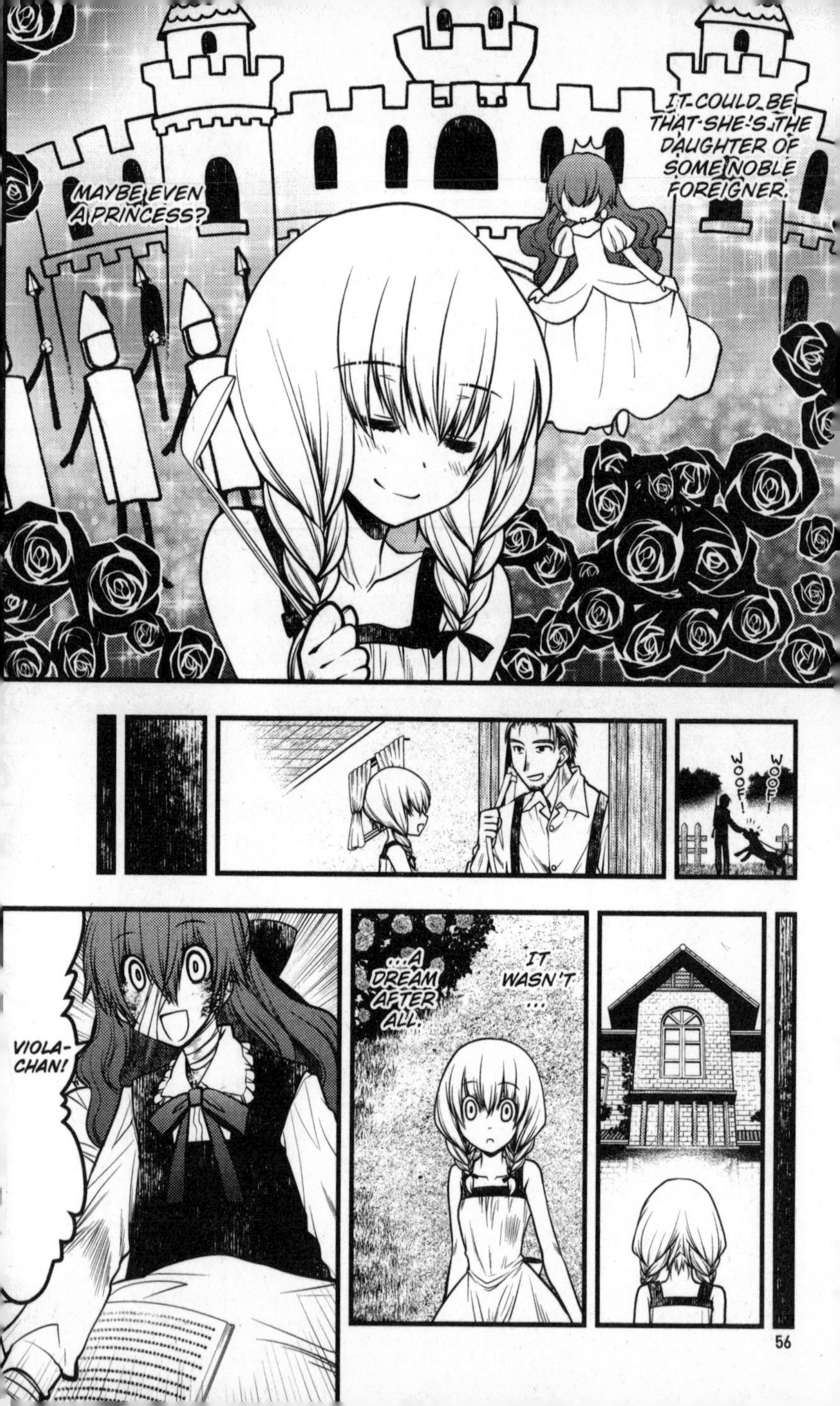
IT COULD BE THAT SHE'S THE DAUGHTER OF SOME NOBLE FOREIGNER.
MAYBE EVEN A PRINCESS?
WOOF!
WOOF!
IT WASN'T ...
...A DREAM AFTER ALL.
VIOLA-CHAN!

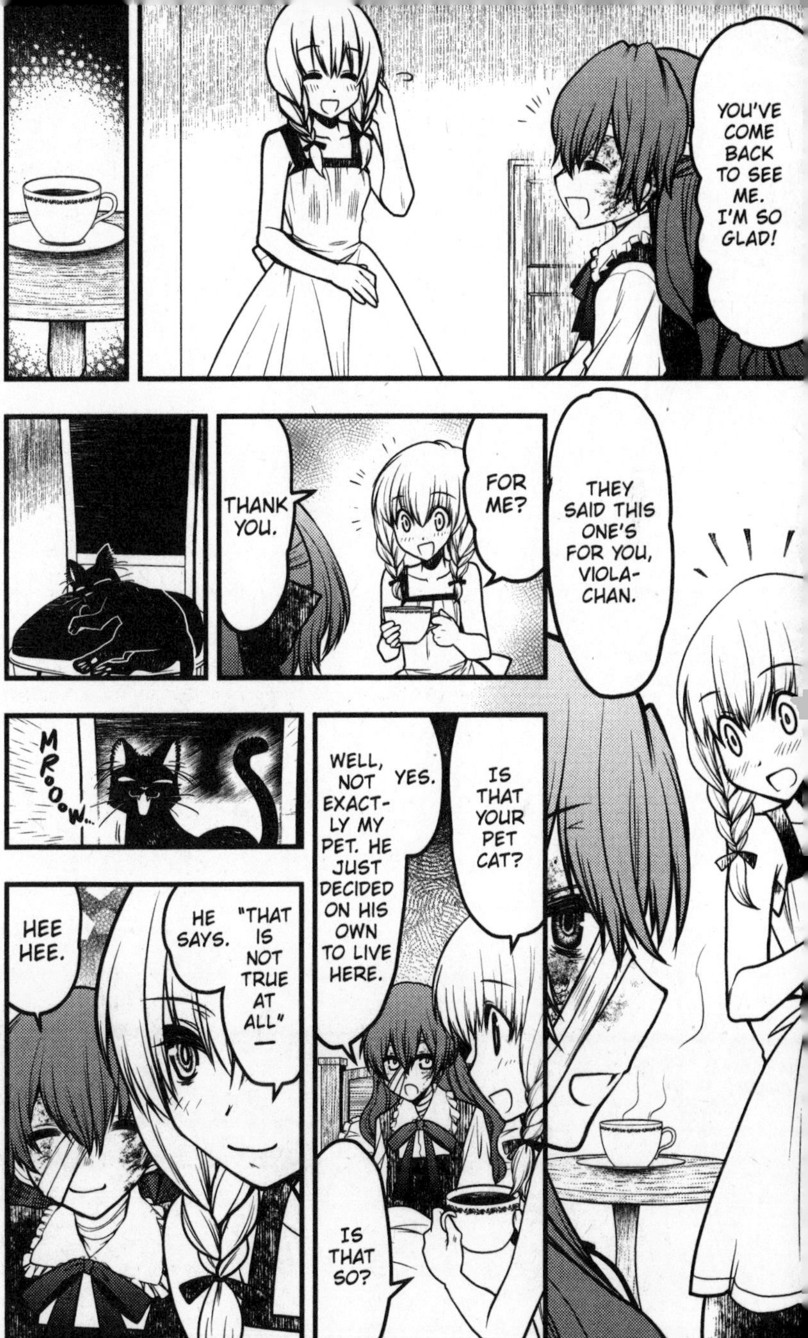

YOU'VE COME BACK TO SEE ME. I'M SO GLAD!
THEY SAID THIS ONE'S FOR YOU, VIOLA-CHAN.
FOR ME?
THANK YOU.
IS THAT YOUR PET CAT?
YES.
WELL, NOT EXACTLY MY PET. HE JUST DECIDED ON HIS OWN TO LIVE HERE.
IS THAT SO?
MROOOW...
"THAT IS NOT TRUE AT ALL"—
HE SAYS.
HEE HEE.

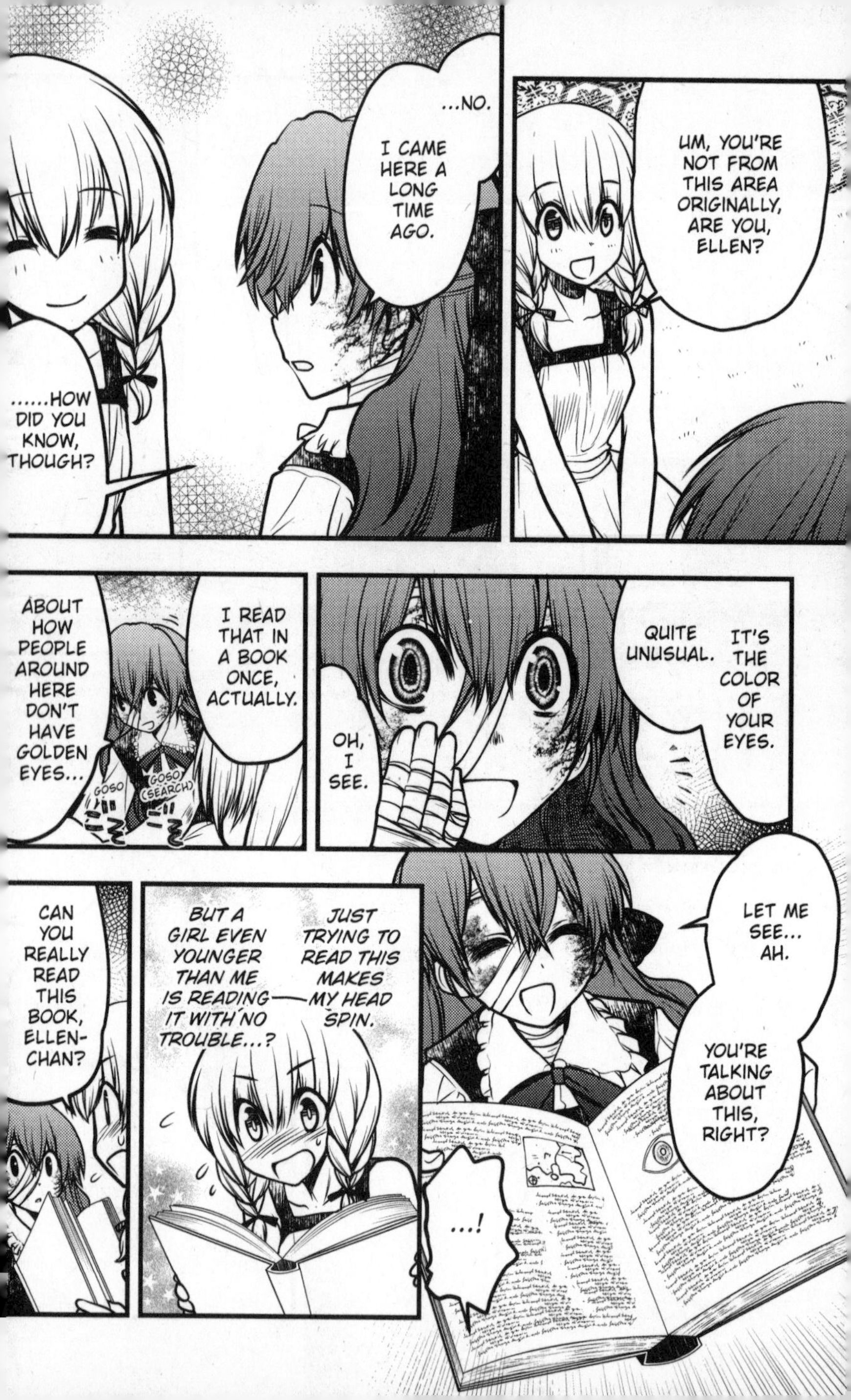
UM, YOU'RE NOT FROM THIS AREA ORIGINALLY, ARE YOU, ELLEN?
...NO.
I CAME HERE A LONG TIME AGO.
......HOW DID YOU KNOW, THOUGH?
IT'S THE COLOR OF YOUR EYES.
QUITE UNUSUAL.
OH, I SEE.
I READ THAT IN A BOOK ONCE, ACTUALLY.
ABOUT HOW PEOPLE AROUND HERE DON'T HAVE GOLDEN EYES...
GOSO (SEARCH)
GOSO
LET ME SEE... AH.
YOU'RE TALKING ABOUT THIS, RIGHT?
...!
JUST TRYING TO READ THIS MAKES MY HEAD SPIN.
BUT A GIRL EVEN YOUNGER THAN ME IS READING IT WITH NO TROUBLE...?
CAN YOU REALLY READ THIS BOOK, ELLEN-CHAN?

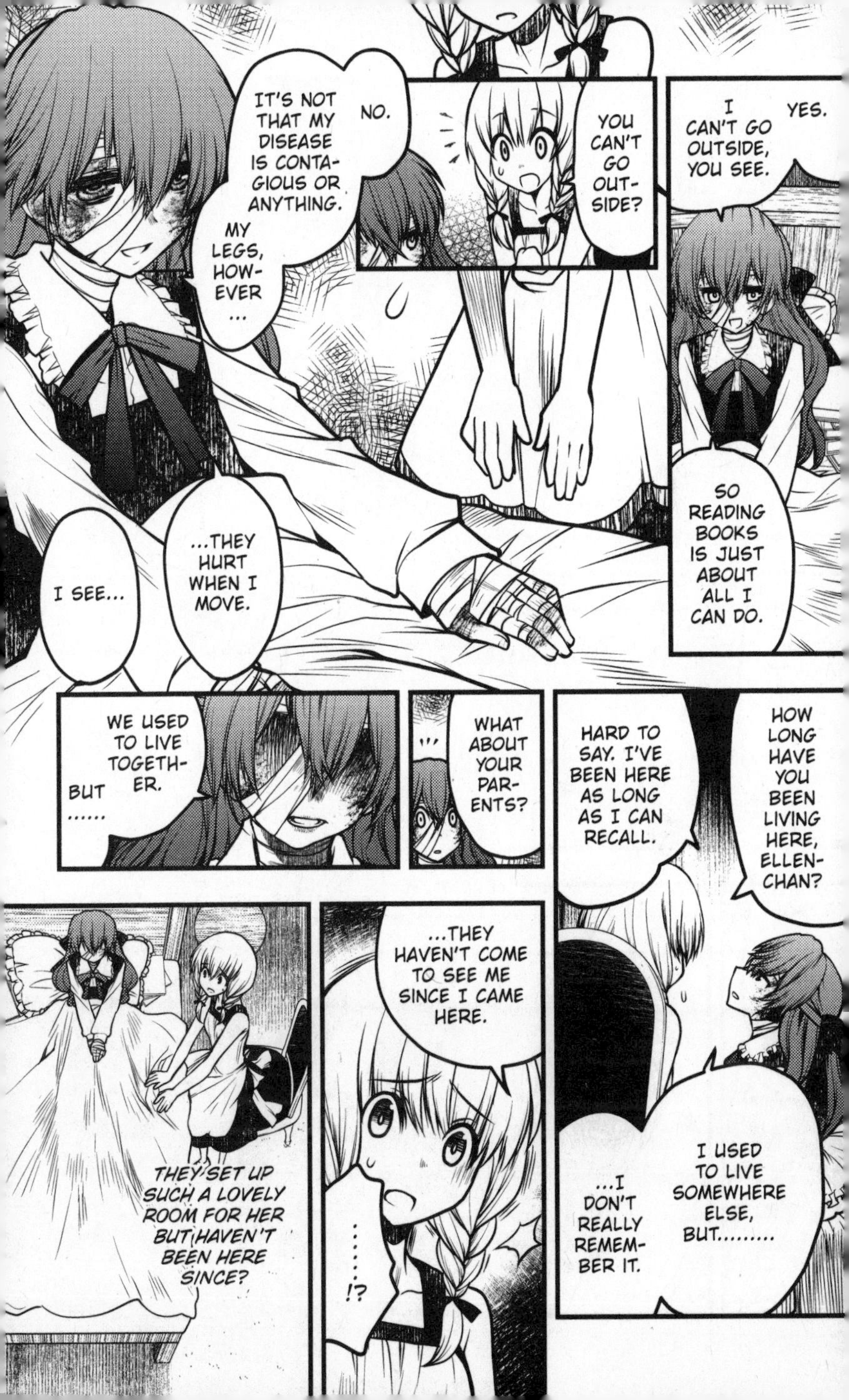
YES.
I CAN'T GO OUTSIDE, YOU SEE.
SO READING BOOKS IS JUST ABOUT ALL I CAN DO.
YOU CAN'T GO OUT-SIDE?
NO.
IT'S NOT THAT MY DISEASE IS CONTA-GIOUS OR ANYTHING.
MY LEGS, HOW-EVER ...
...THEY HURT WHEN I MOVE.
I SEE...
HOW LONG HAVE YOU BEEN LIVING HERE, ELLEN-CHAN?
HARD TO SAY. I'VE BEEN HERE AS LONG AS I CAN RECALL.
WHAT ABOUT YOUR PAR-ENTS?
WE USED TO LIVE TOGETH-ER.
BUT ......
I USED TO LIVE SOMEWHERE ELSE, BUT.........
...I DON'T REALLY REMEM-BER IT.
...THEY HAVEN'T COME TO SEE ME SINCE I CAME HERE.
......!?
THEY SET UP SUCH A LOVELY ROOM FOR HER BUT HAVEN'T BEEN HERE SINCE?

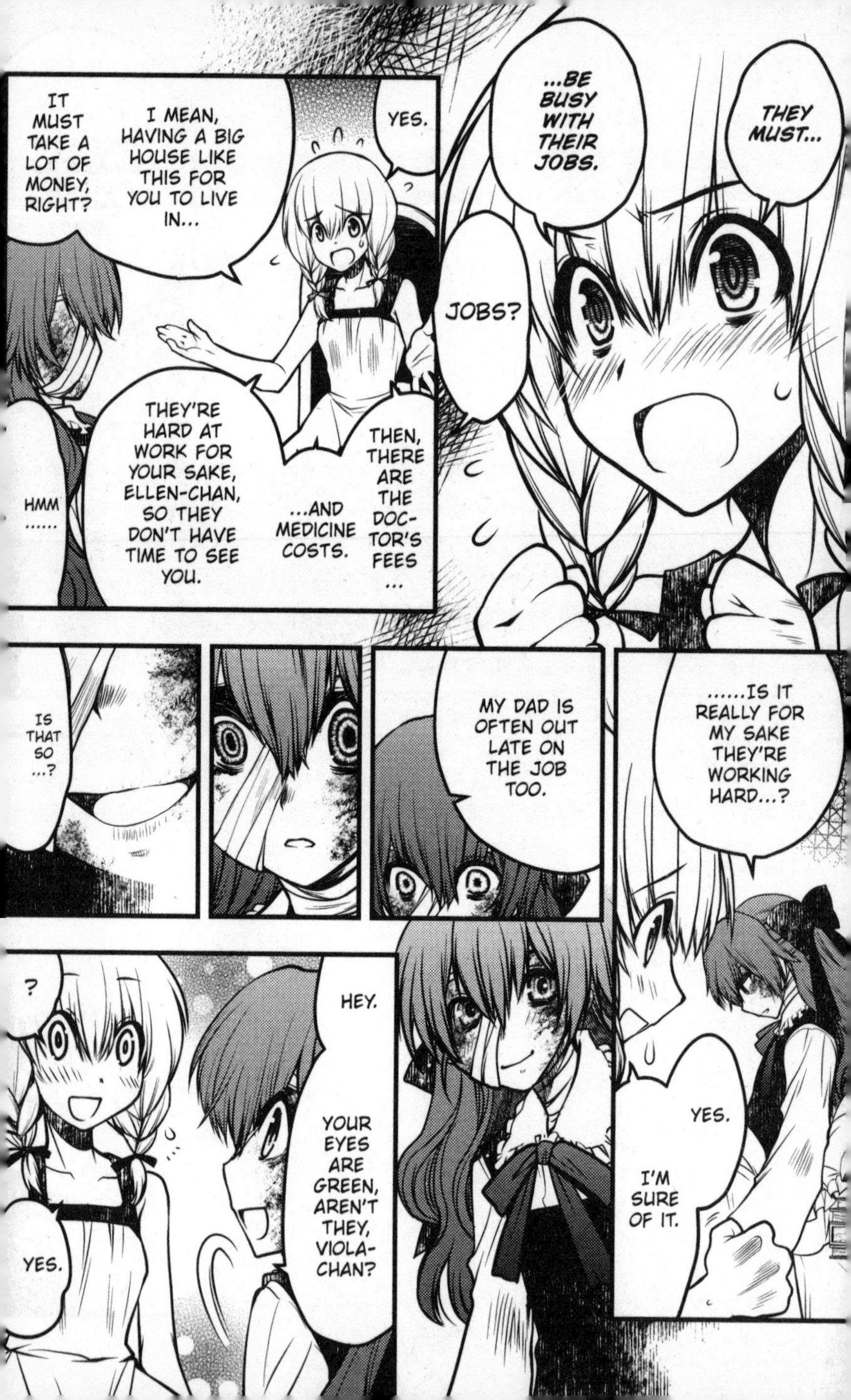
THEY MUST...
...BE BUSY WITH THEIR JOBS.
JOBS?
YES.
I MEAN, HAVING A BIG HOUSE LIKE THIS FOR YOU TO LIVE IN...
IT MUST TAKE A LOT OF MONEY, RIGHT?
THEN, THERE ARE THE DOC-TOR'S FEES...
...AND MEDICINE COSTS.
THEY'RE HARD AT WORK FOR YOUR SAKE, ELLEN-CHAN, SO THEY DON'T HAVE TIME TO SEE YOU.
HMM......
......IS IT REALLY FOR MY SAKE THEY'RE WORKING HARD...?
MY DAD IS OFTEN OUT LATE ON THE JOB TOO.
IS THAT SO...?
YES.
I'M SURE OF IT.
HEY.
YOUR EYES ARE GREEN, AREN'T THEY, VIOLA-CHAN?
?
YES.

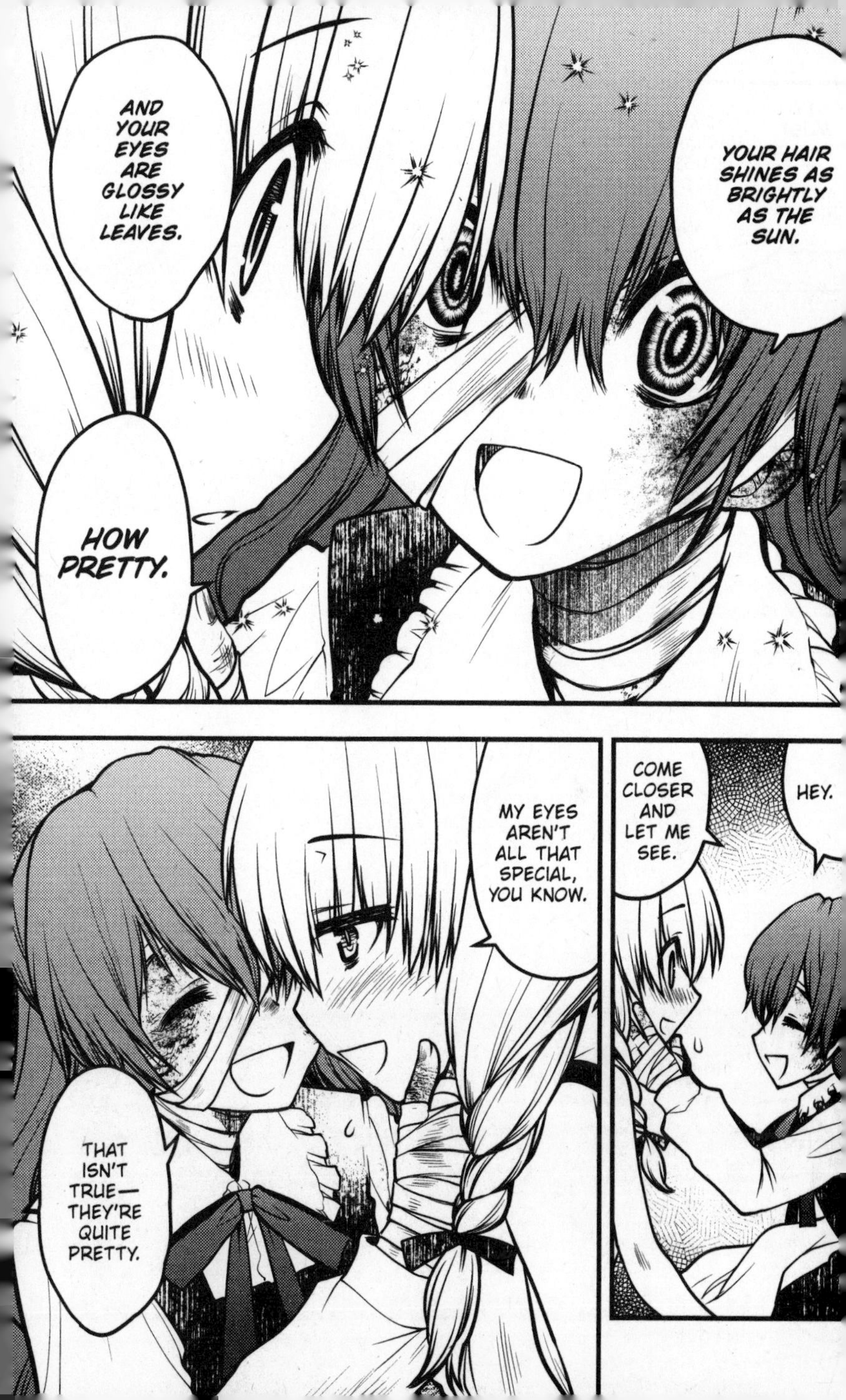
YOUR HAIR SHINES AS BRIGHTLY AS THE SUN.
AND YOUR EYES ARE GLOSSY LIKE LEAVES.
HOW PRETTY.
HEY.
COME CLOSER AND LET ME SEE.
MY EYES AREN'T ALL THAT SPECIAL, YOU KNOW.
THAT ISN'T TRUE—THEY'RE QUITE PRETTY.

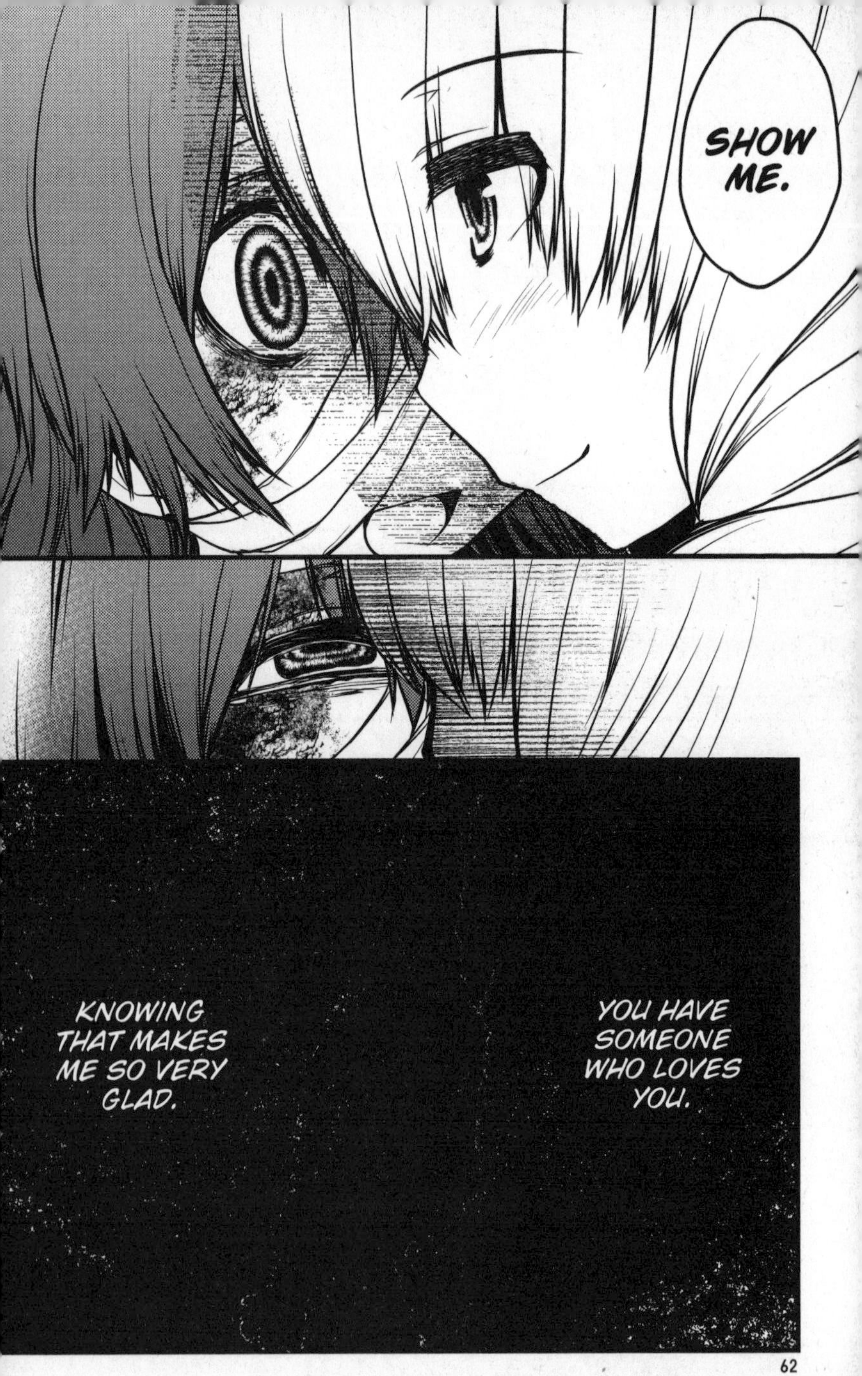
SHOW ME.
YOU HAVE SOMEONE WHO LOVES YOU.
KNOWING THAT MAKES ME SO VERY GLAD.

THE WITCH'S HOUSE

The Diary of Ellen

THE WITCH'S HOUSE

The Diary of Ellen

Chapter 7

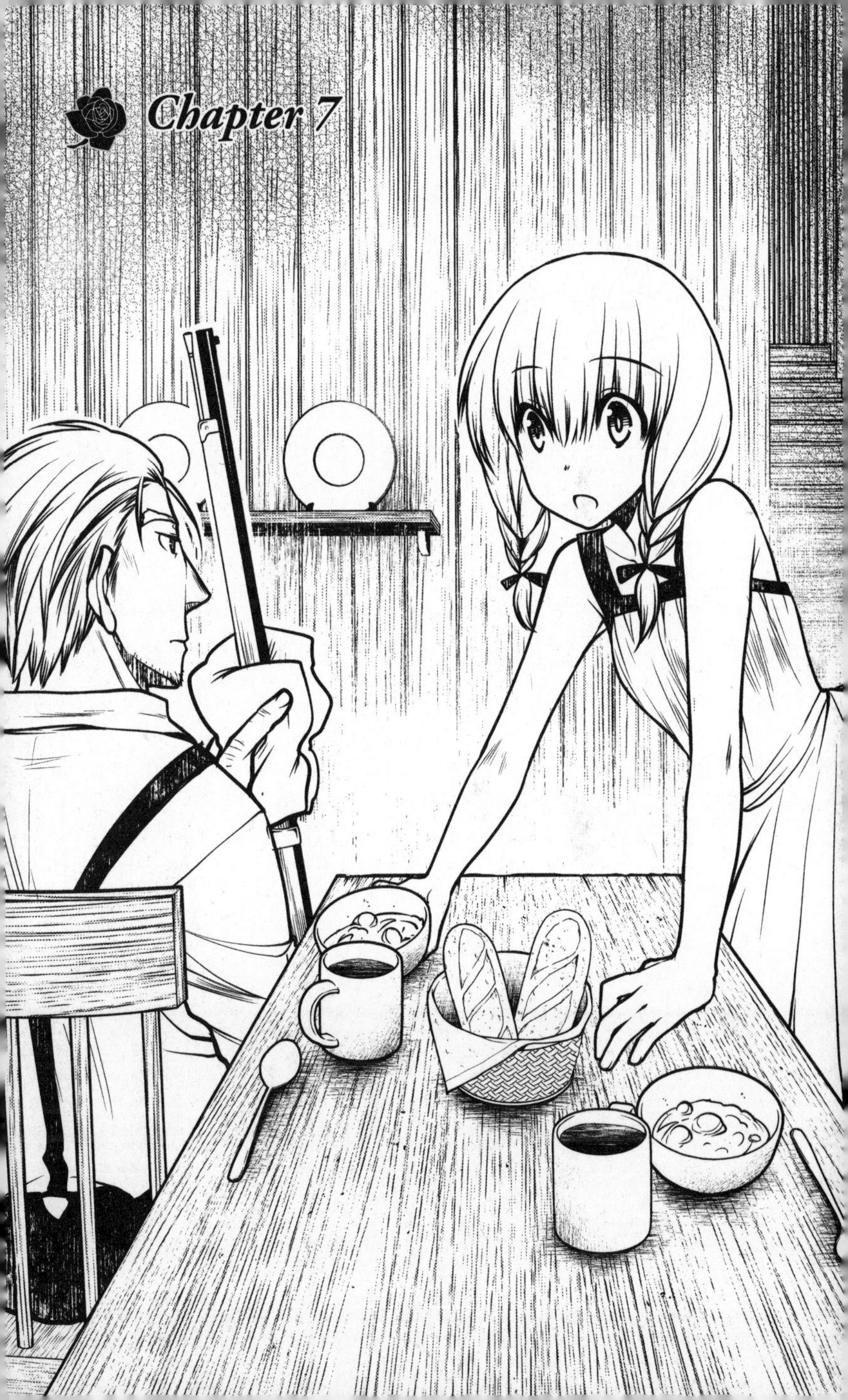

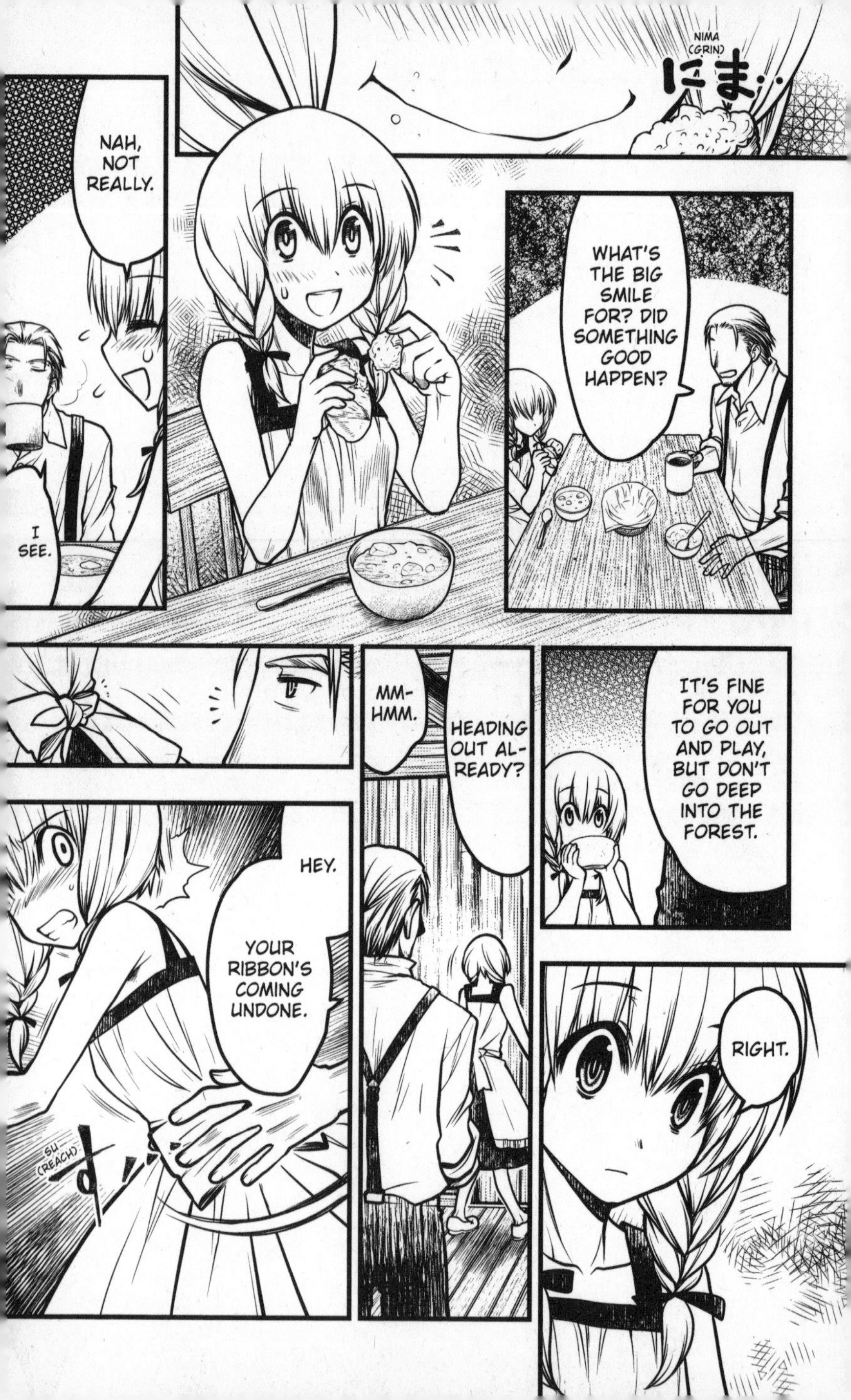
NIMA (GRIN)
にま…
WHAT'S THE BIG SMILE FOR? DID SOMETHING GOOD HAPPEN?
NAH, NOT REALLY.
I SEE.
IT'S FINE FOR YOU TO GO OUT AND PLAY, BUT DON'T GO DEEP INTO THE FOREST.
RIGHT.
HEADING OUT AL-READY?
MM-HMM.
HEY.
YOUR RIBBON'S COMING UNDONE.
SU (REACH)
す

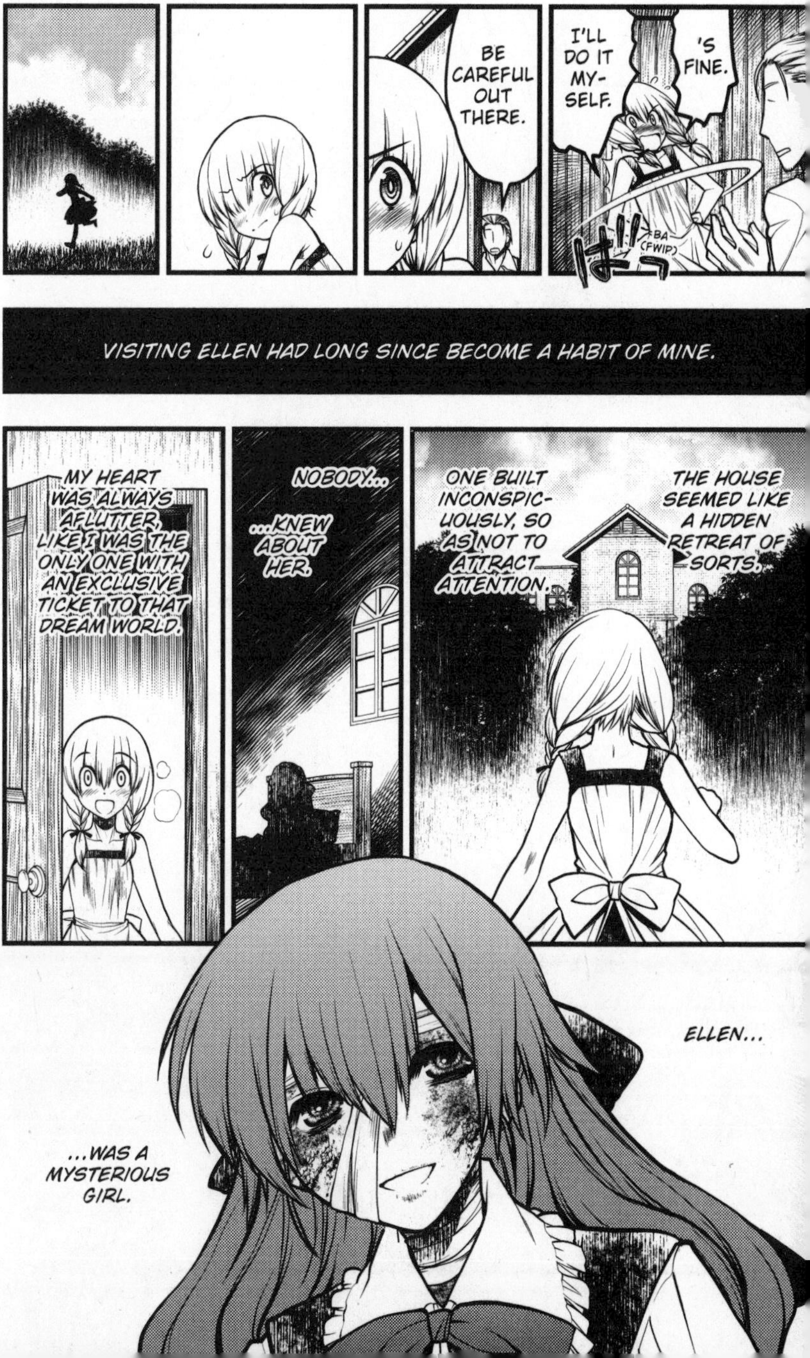
'S FINE.
I'LL DO IT MYSELF.
BA (FWIP)
はっ
BE CAREFUL OUT THERE.
VISITING ELLEN HAD LONG SINCE BECOME A HABIT OF MINE.
THE HOUSE SEEMED LIKE A HIDDEN RETREAT OF SORTS.
ONE BUILT INCONSPICUOUSLY, SO AS NOT TO ATTRACT ATTENTION.
NOBODY...
...KNEW ABOUT HER.
MY HEART WAS ALWAYS AFLUTTER, LIKE I WAS THE ONLY ONE WITH AN EXCLUSIVE TICKET TO THAT DREAM WORLD.
ELLEN...
...WAS A MYSTERIOUS GIRL.

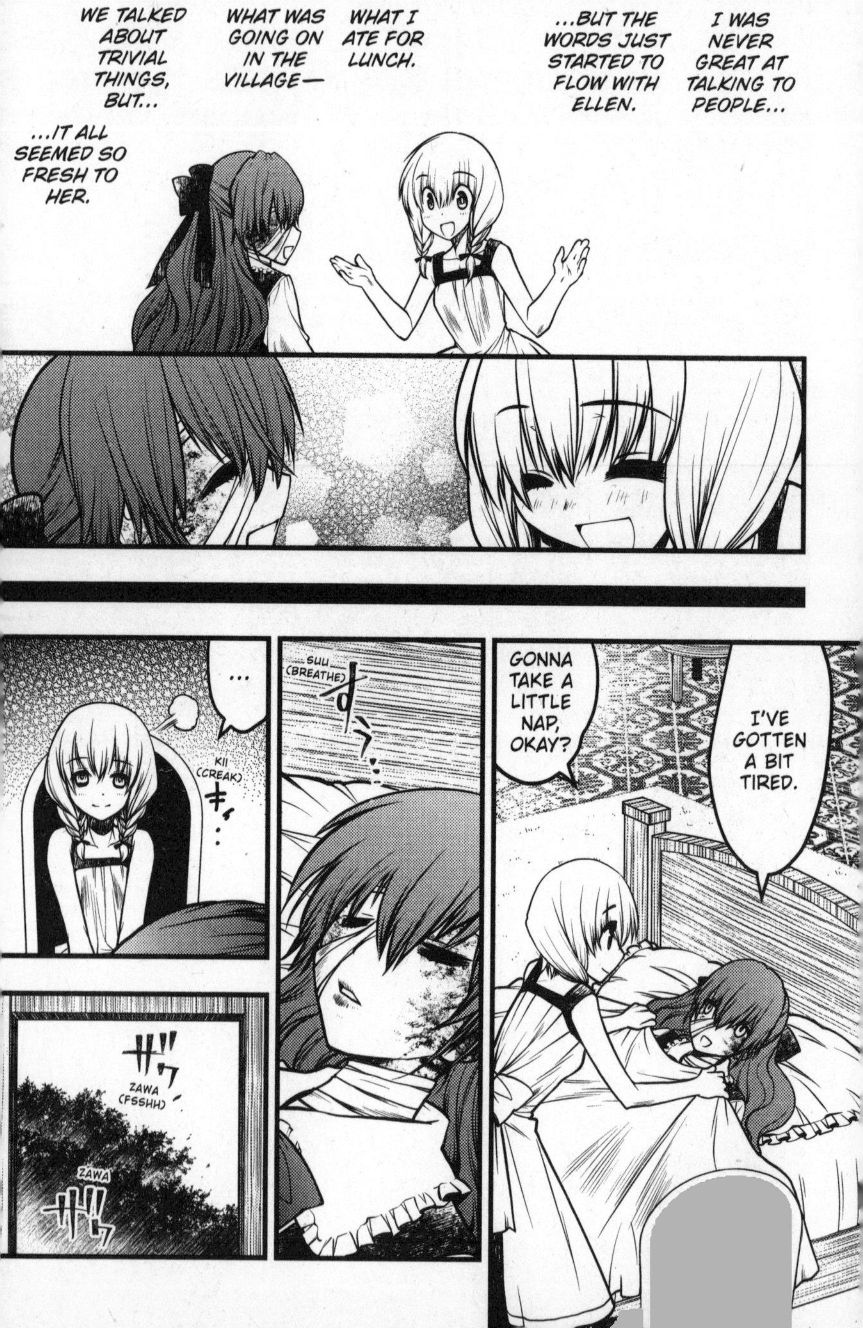
I WAS NEVER GREAT AT TALKING TO PEOPLE...
...BUT THE WORDS JUST STARTED TO FLOW WITH ELLEN.
WHAT I ATE FOR LUNCH.
WHAT WAS GOING ON IN THE VILLAGE—
WE TALKED ABOUT TRIVIAL THINGS, BUT...
...IT ALL SEEMED SO FRESH TO HER.
I'VE GOTTEN A BIT TIRED.
GONNA TAKE A LITTLE NAP, OKAY?
SUU (BREATHE)
...
KII (CREAK)
ZAWA (FSSHH)
ZAWA

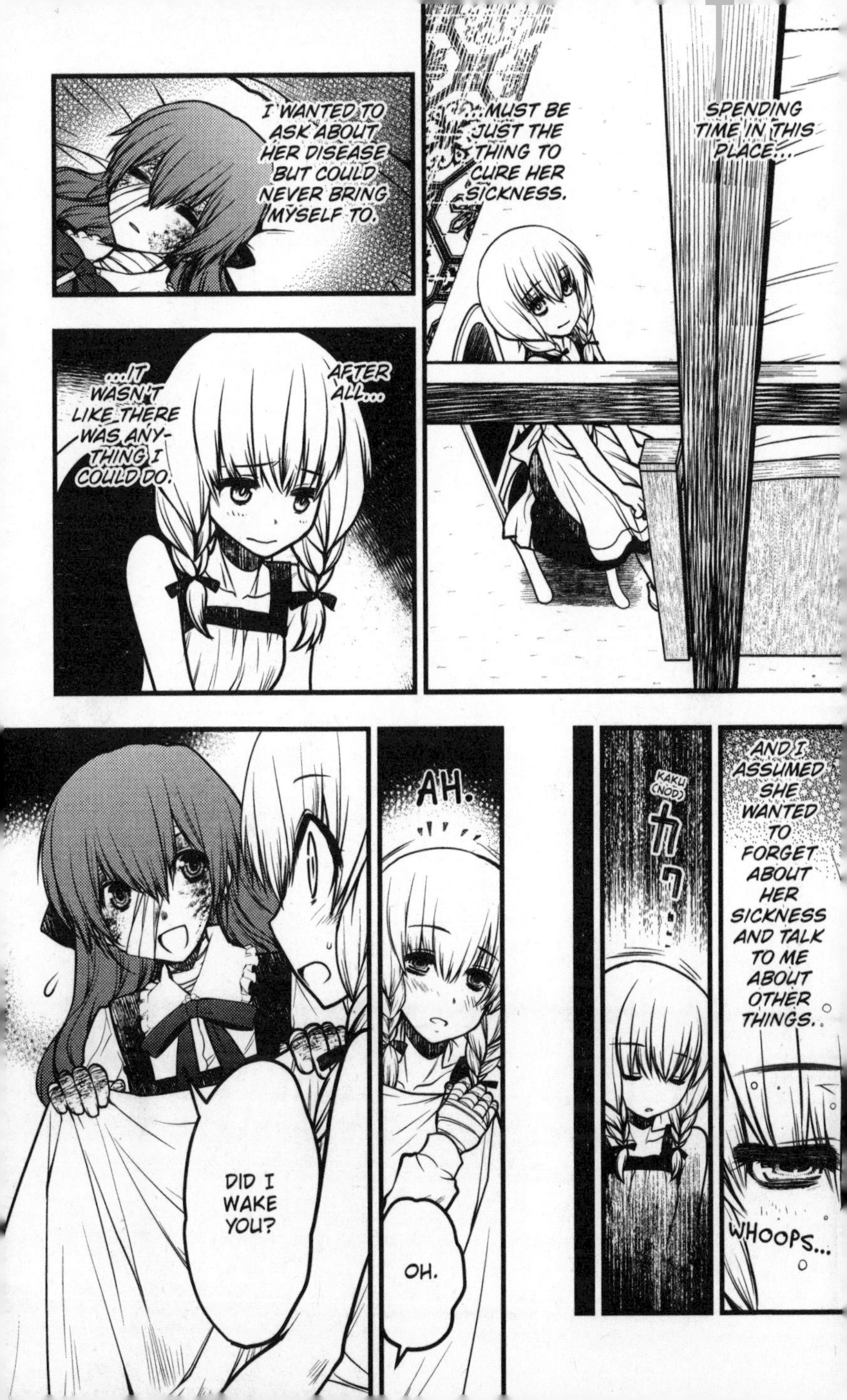
SPENDING TIME IN THIS PLACE...
...MUST BE JUST THE THING TO CURE HER SICKNESS.
I WANTED TO ASK ABOUT HER DISEASE BUT COULD NEVER BRING MYSELF TO.
AFTER ALL...
...IT WASN'T LIKE THERE WAS ANY-THING I COULD DO.
AND I ASSUMED SHE WANTED TO FORGET ABOUT HER SICKNESS AND TALK TO ME ABOUT OTHER THINGS.
WHOOPS...
KAKU (NOD)
カク…
AH.
OH.
DID I WAKE YOU?

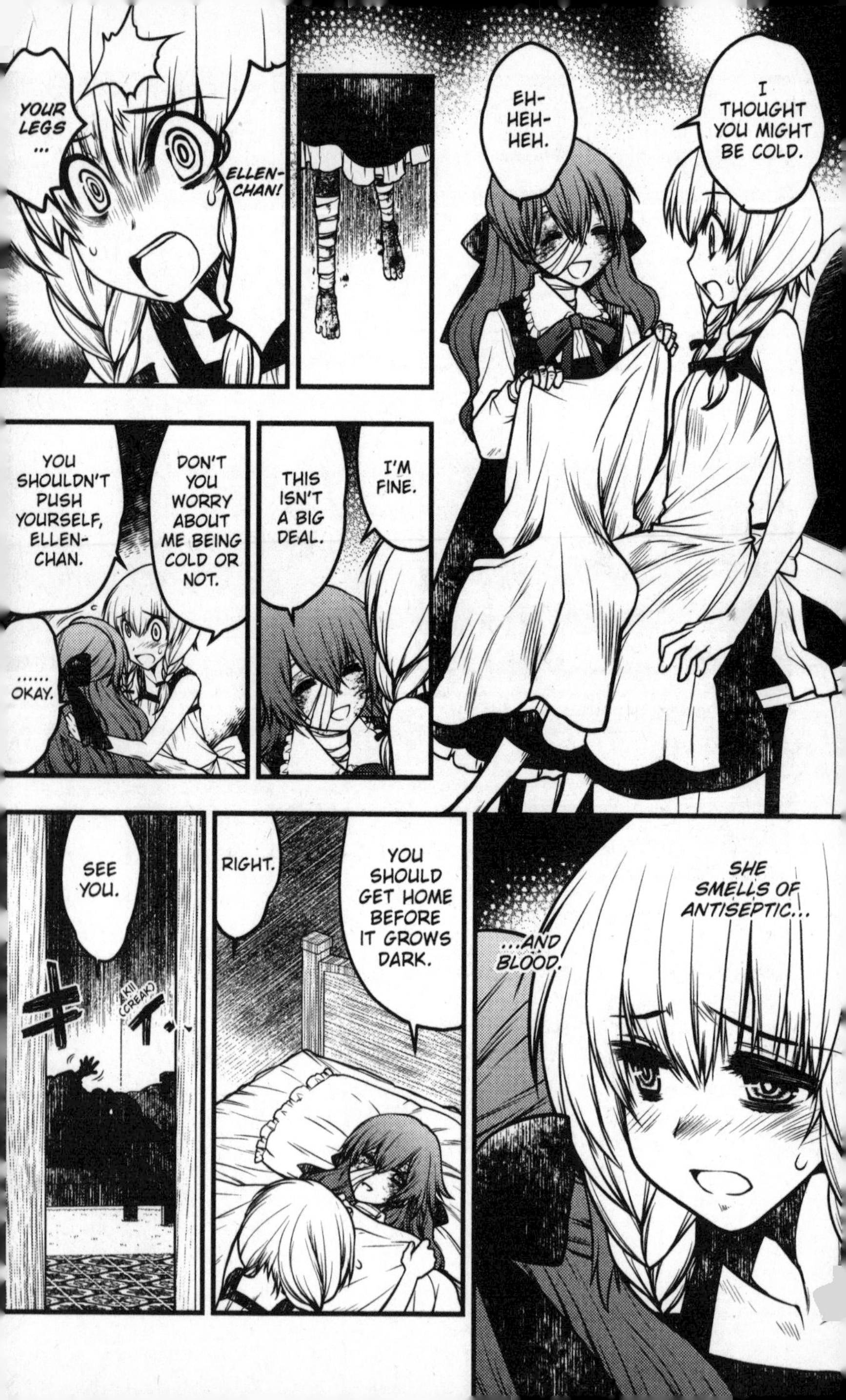
I THOUGHT YOU MIGHT BE COLD.
EH-HEH-HEH.
YOUR LEGS ...
ELLEN-CHAN!
I'M FINE.
THIS ISN'T A BIG DEAL.
DON'T YOU WORRY ABOUT ME BEING COLD OR NOT.
YOU SHOULDN'T PUSH YOURSELF, ELLEN-CHAN.
...... OKAY.
SHE SMELLS OF ANTISEPTIC...
...AND BLOOD.
YOU SHOULD GET HOME BEFORE IT GROWS DARK.
RIGHT.
SEE YOU.
KII (CREAK)

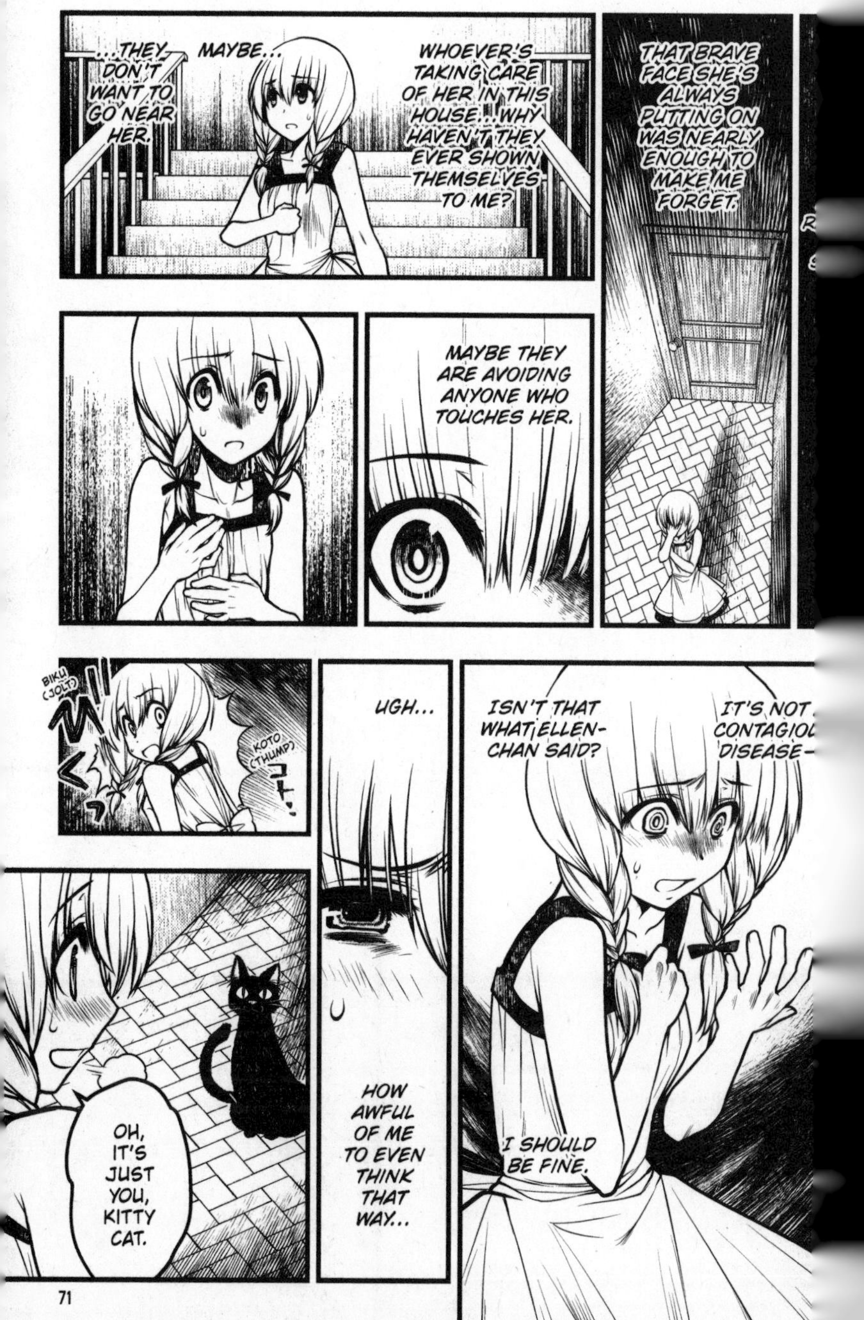
THAT BRAVE FACE SHE'S ALWAYS PUTTING ON WAS NEARLY ENOUGH TO MAKE ME FORGET.
WHOEVER'S TAKING CARE OF HER IN THIS HOUSE...WHY HAVEN'T THEY EVER SHOWN THEMSELVES TO ME?
MAYBE...
...THEY DON'T WANT TO GO NEAR HER.
MAYBE THEY ARE AVOIDING ANYONE WHO TOUCHES HER.
IT'S NOT CONTAGIOU DISEASE—
ISN'T THAT WHAT ELLEN-CHAN SAID?
I SHOULD BE FINE.
UGH...
HOW AWFUL OF ME TO EVEN THINK THAT WAY...
KOTO (THUMP)
BIKU (JOLT)
OH, IT'S JUST YOU, KITTY CAT.

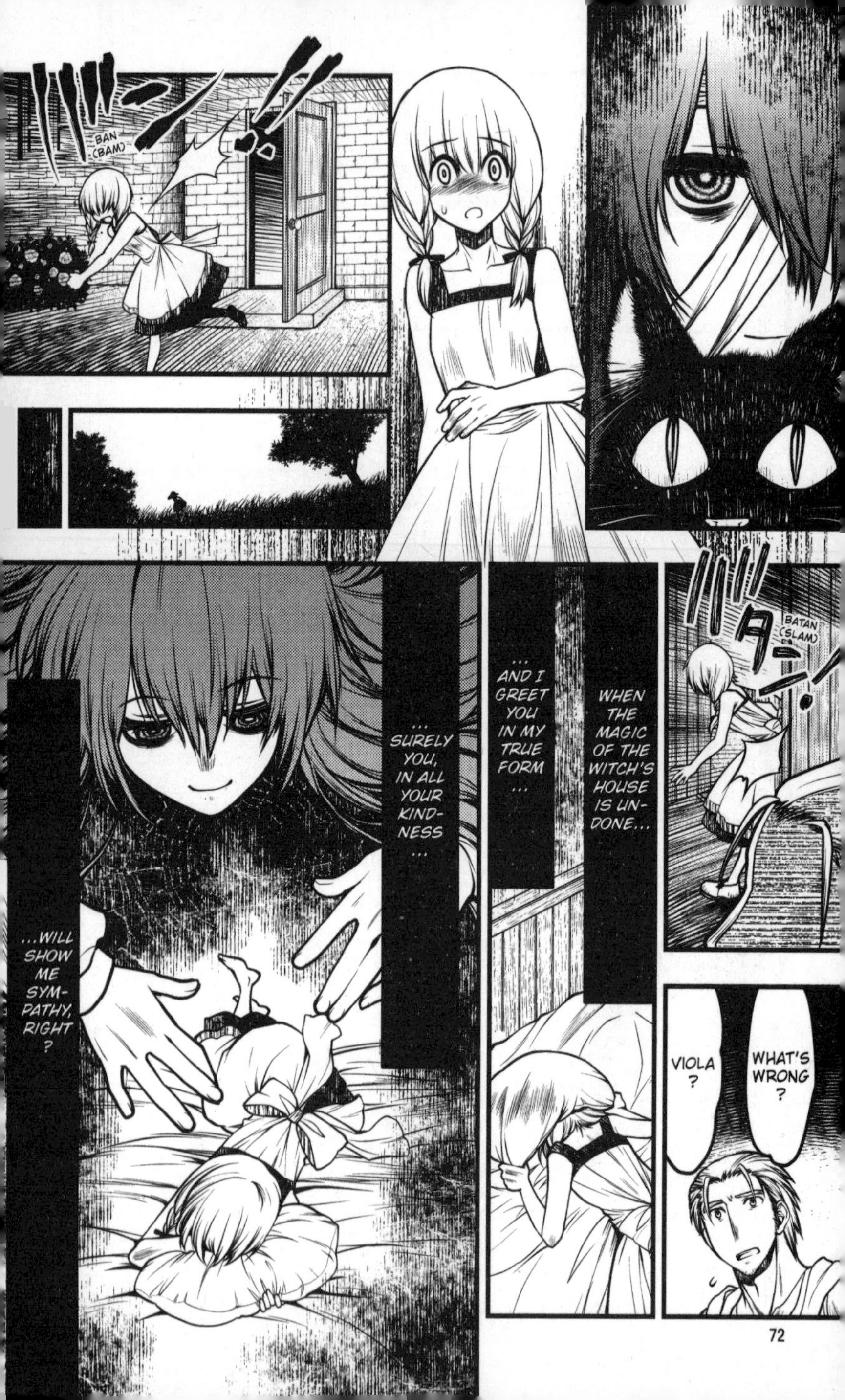
BAN (BAM)
BATAN (SLAM)
WHAT'S WRONG?
VIOLA?
WHEN THE MAGIC OF THE WITCH'S HOUSE IS UNDONE...
...AND I GREET YOU IN MY TRUE FORM...
...SURELY YOU, IN ALL YOUR KINDNESS...
...WILL SHOW ME SYMPATHY, RIGHT?

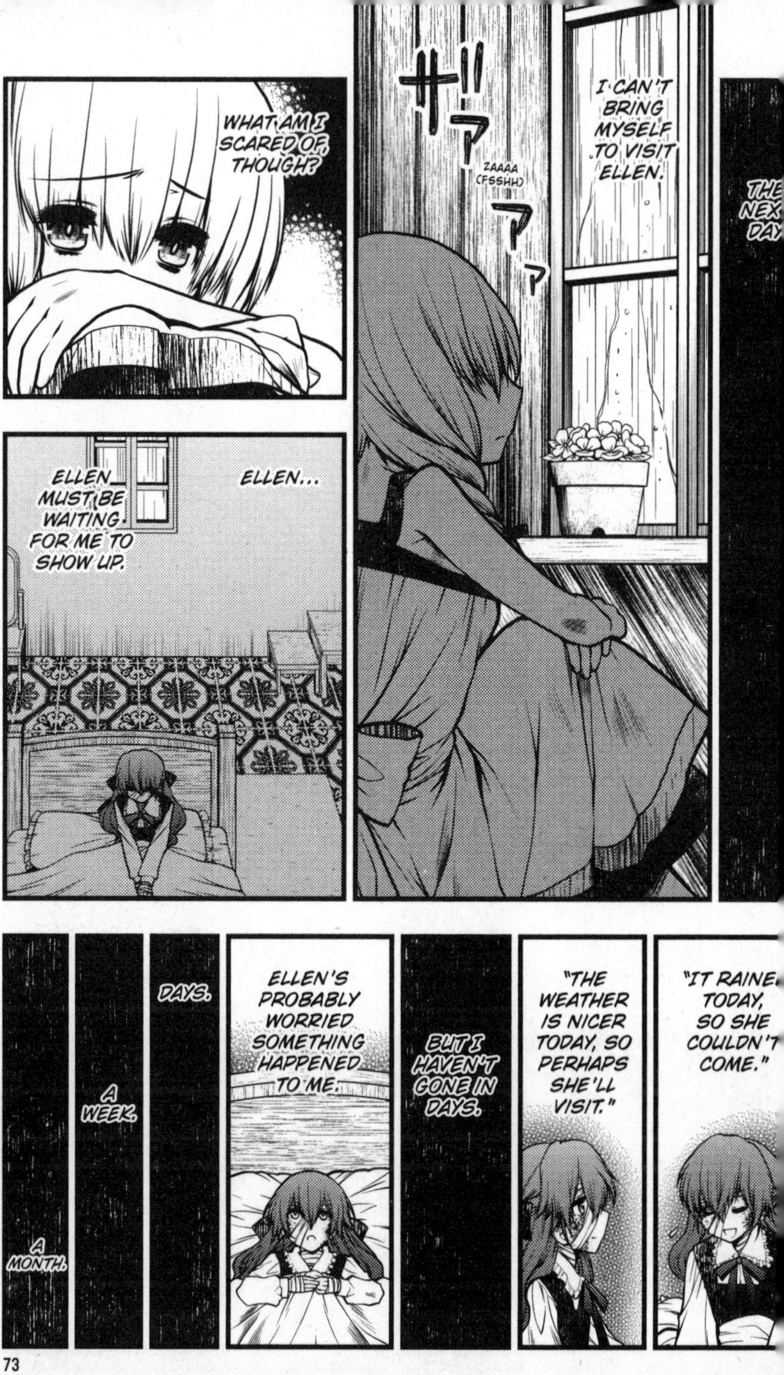
THE NEX DAY
I CAN'T BRING MYSELF TO VISIT ELLEN.
ZAAAA (FSSHH)
WHAT AM I SCARED OF, THOUGH?
ELLEN...
ELLEN MUST BE WAITING FOR ME TO SHOW UP.
"IT RAINE TODAY, SO SHE COULDN'T COME."
"THE WEATHER IS NICER TODAY, SO PERHAPS SHE'LL VISIT."
BUT I HAVEN'T GONE IN DAYS.
ELLEN'S PROBABLY WORRIED SOMETHING HAPPENED TO ME.
DAYS.
A WEEK.
A MONTH.

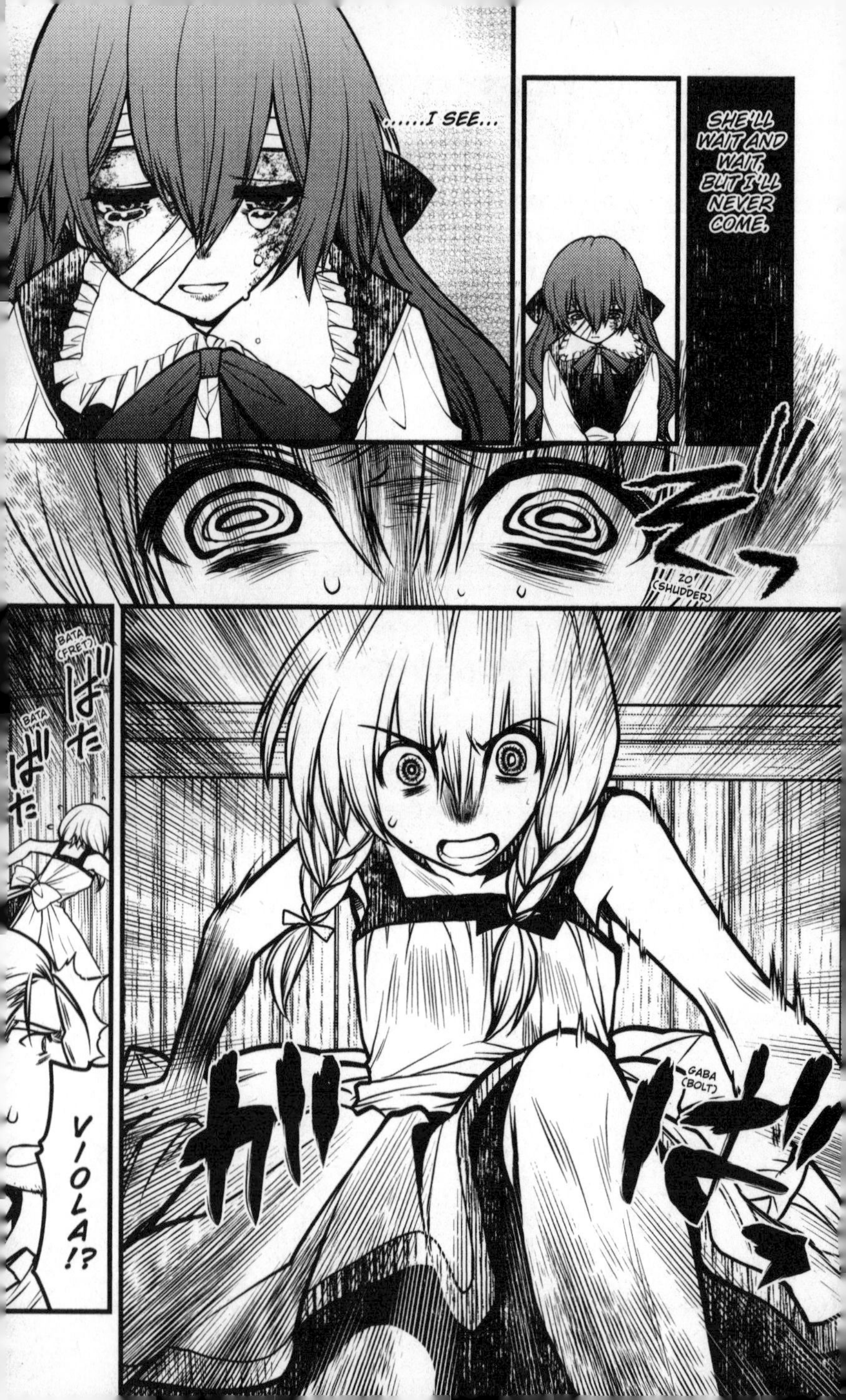
SHE'LL WAIT AND WAIT, BUT I'LL NEVER COME.
......I SEE...
ZO (SHUDDER)
GABA (BOLT)
BATA (FRET)
BATA
VIOLA!?

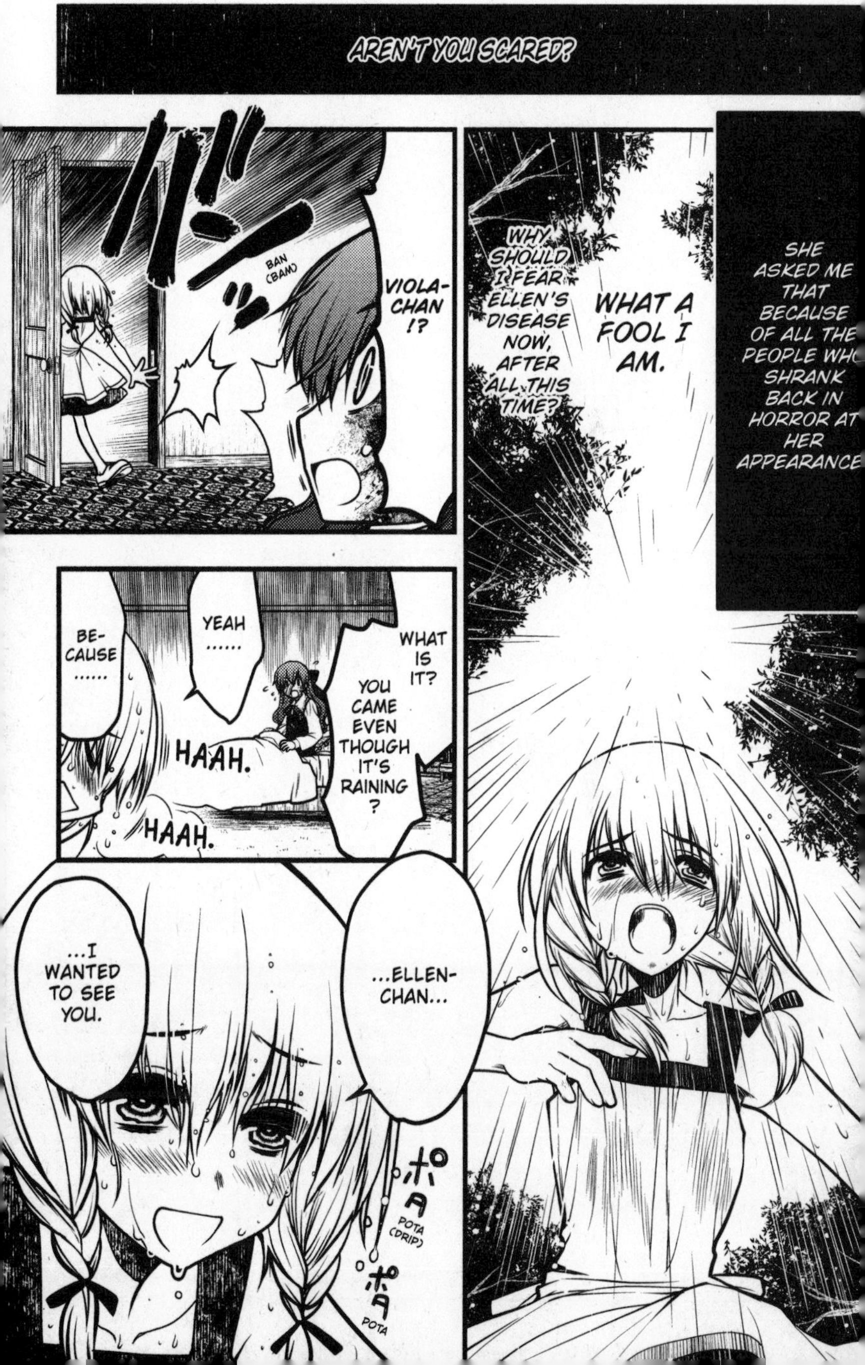
AREN'T YOU SCARED?
SHE ASKED ME THAT BECAUSE OF ALL THE PEOPLE WHO SHRANK BACK IN HORROR AT HER APPEARANCE
WHAT A FOOL I AM.
WHY SHOULD I FEAR ELLEN'S DISEASE NOW, AFTER ALL THIS TIME?
BAN (BAM)
VIOLA-CHAN!?
WHAT IS IT?
YOU CAME EVEN THOUGH IT'S RAINING?
YEAH......
BE-CAUSE......
HAAH.
HAAH.
...ELLEN-CHAN...
...I WANTED TO SEE YOU.
POTA (DRIP)
POTA

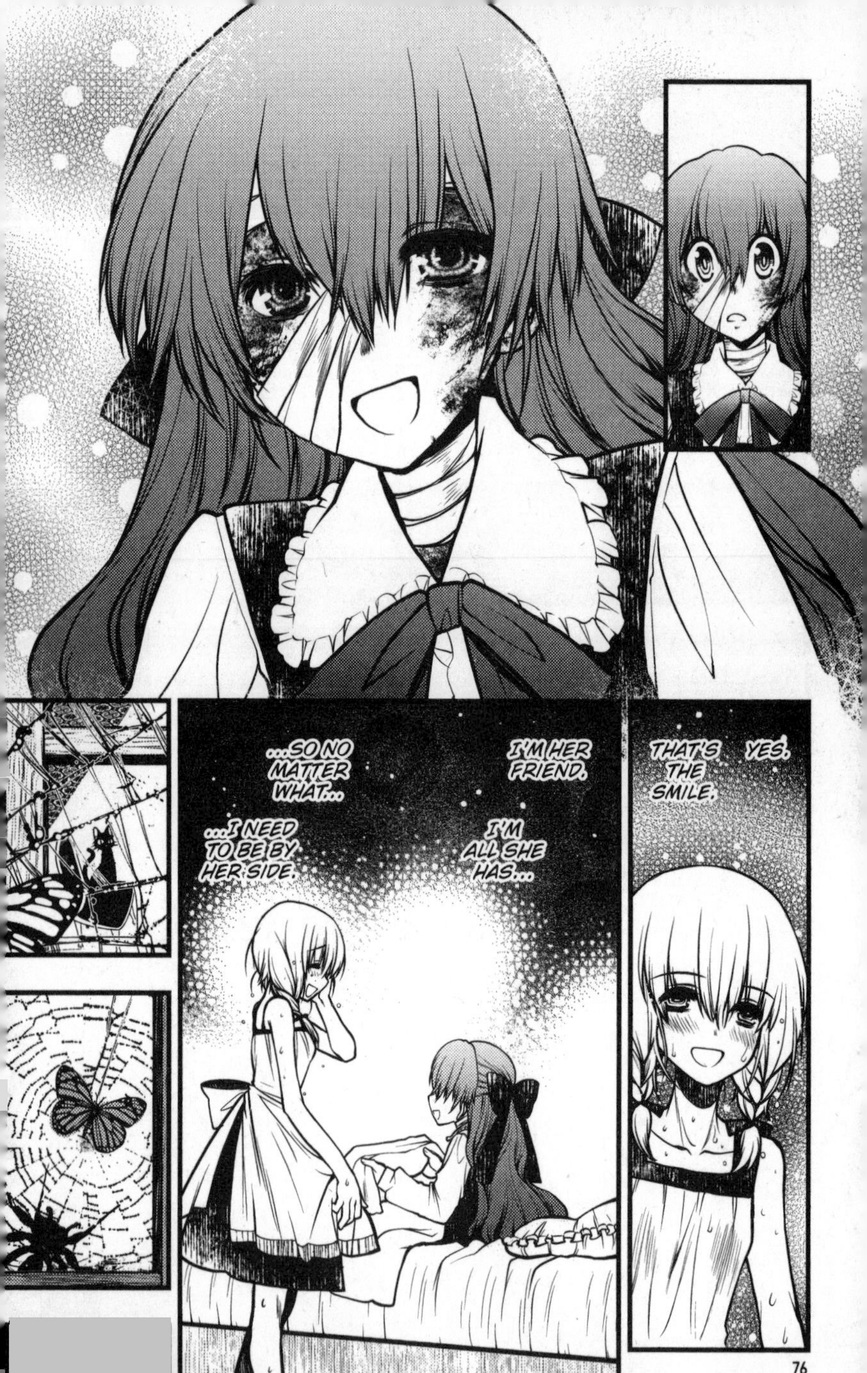
YES.
THAT'S THE SMILE.
I'M HER FRIEND.
I'M ALL SHE HAS...
...SO NO MATTER WHAT...
...I NEED TO BE BY HER SIDE.

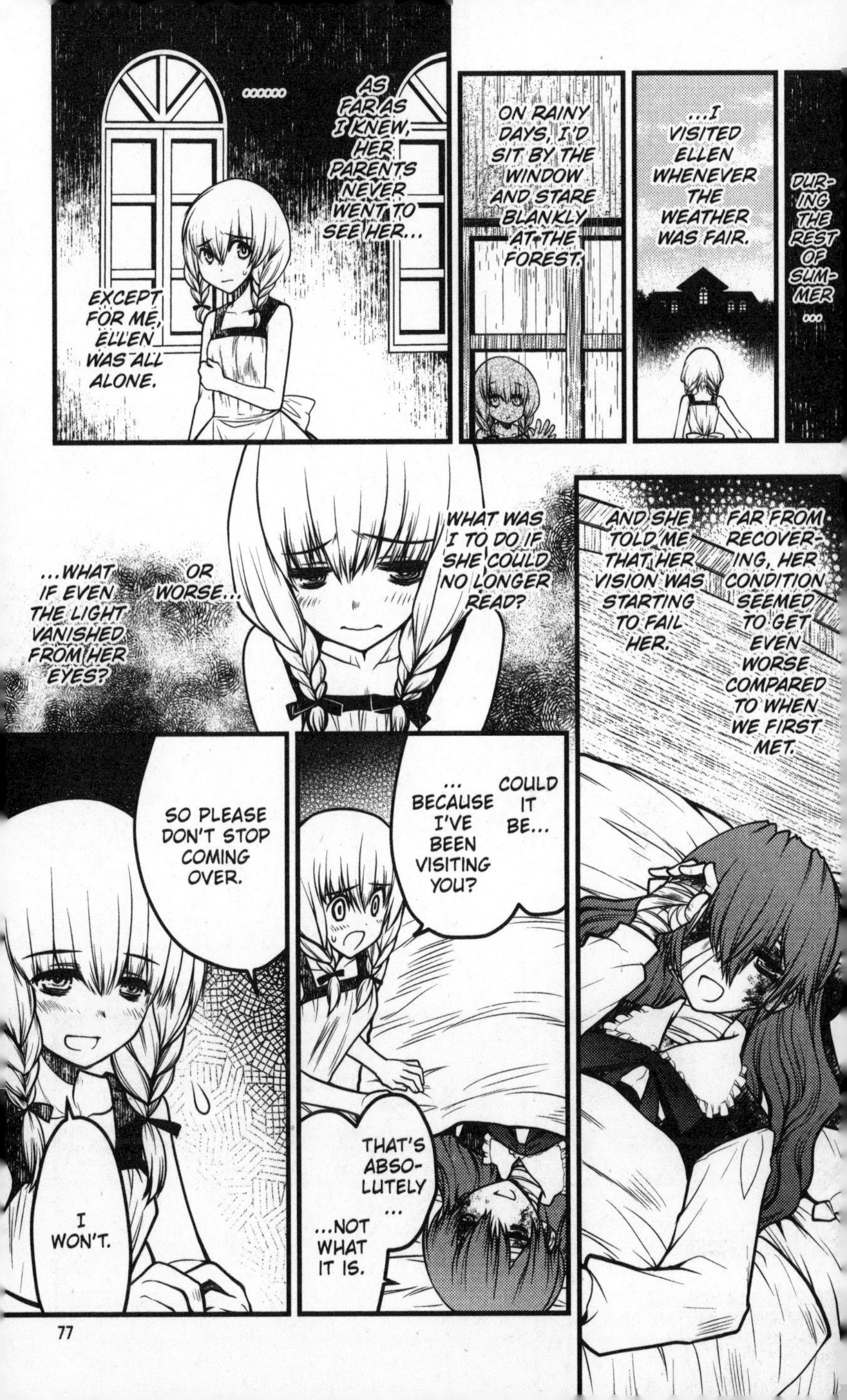
DURING THE REST OF SUMMER...
...I VISITED ELLEN WHENEVER THE WEATHER WAS FAIR.
ON RAINY DAYS, I'D SIT BY THE WINDOW AND STARE BLANKLY AT THE FOREST.
AS FAR AS I KNEW, HER PARENTS NEVER WENT TO SEE HER...
......
EXCEPT FOR ME, ELLEN WAS ALL ALONE.
FAR FROM RECOVERING, HER CONDITION SEEMED TO GET EVEN WORSE COMPARED TO WHEN WE FIRST MET.
AND SHE TOLD ME THAT HER VISION WAS STARTING TO FAIL HER.
WHAT WAS I TO DO IF SHE COULD NO LONGER READ?
OR WORSE...
...WHAT IF EVEN THE LIGHT VANISHED FROM HER EYES?
COULD IT BE...
...BECAUSE I'VE BEEN VISITING YOU?
THAT'S ABSOLUTELY...
...NOT WHAT IT IS.
SO PLEASE DON'T STOP COMING OVER.
I WON'T.

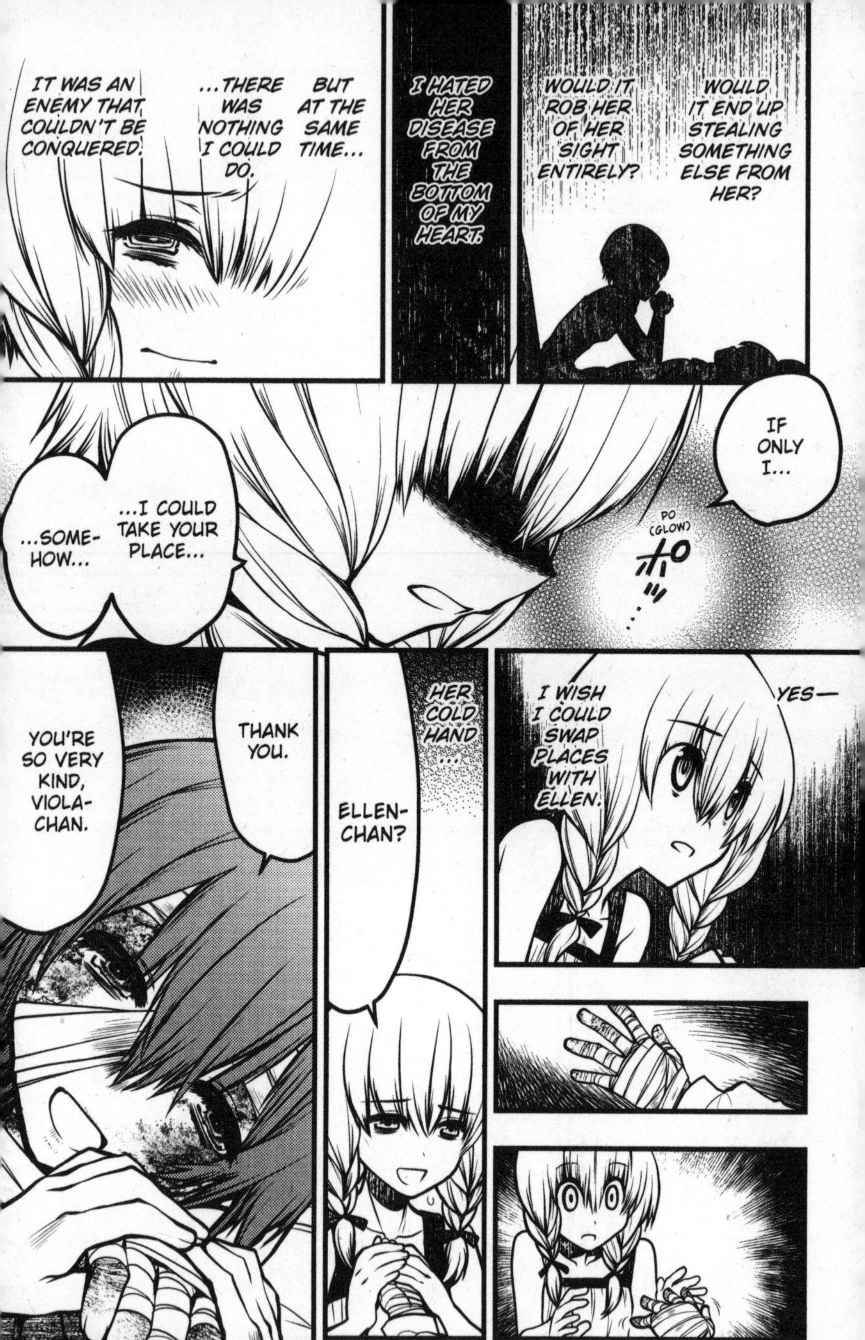
WOULD IT END UP STEALING SOMETHING ELSE FROM HER?
WOULD IT ROB HER OF HER SIGHT ENTIRELY?
I HATED HER DISEASE FROM THE BOTTOM OF MY HEART.
BUT AT THE SAME TIME...
...THERE WAS NOTHING I COULD DO.
IT WAS AN ENEMY THAT COULDN'T BE CONQUERED.
IF ONLY I...
PO (GLOW)
...I COULD TAKE YOUR PLACE...
...SOME-HOW...
YES—
I WISH I COULD SWAP PLACES WITH ELLEN.
HER COLD HAND...
ELLEN-CHAN?
THANK YOU.
YOU'RE SO VERY KIND, VIOLA-CHAN.

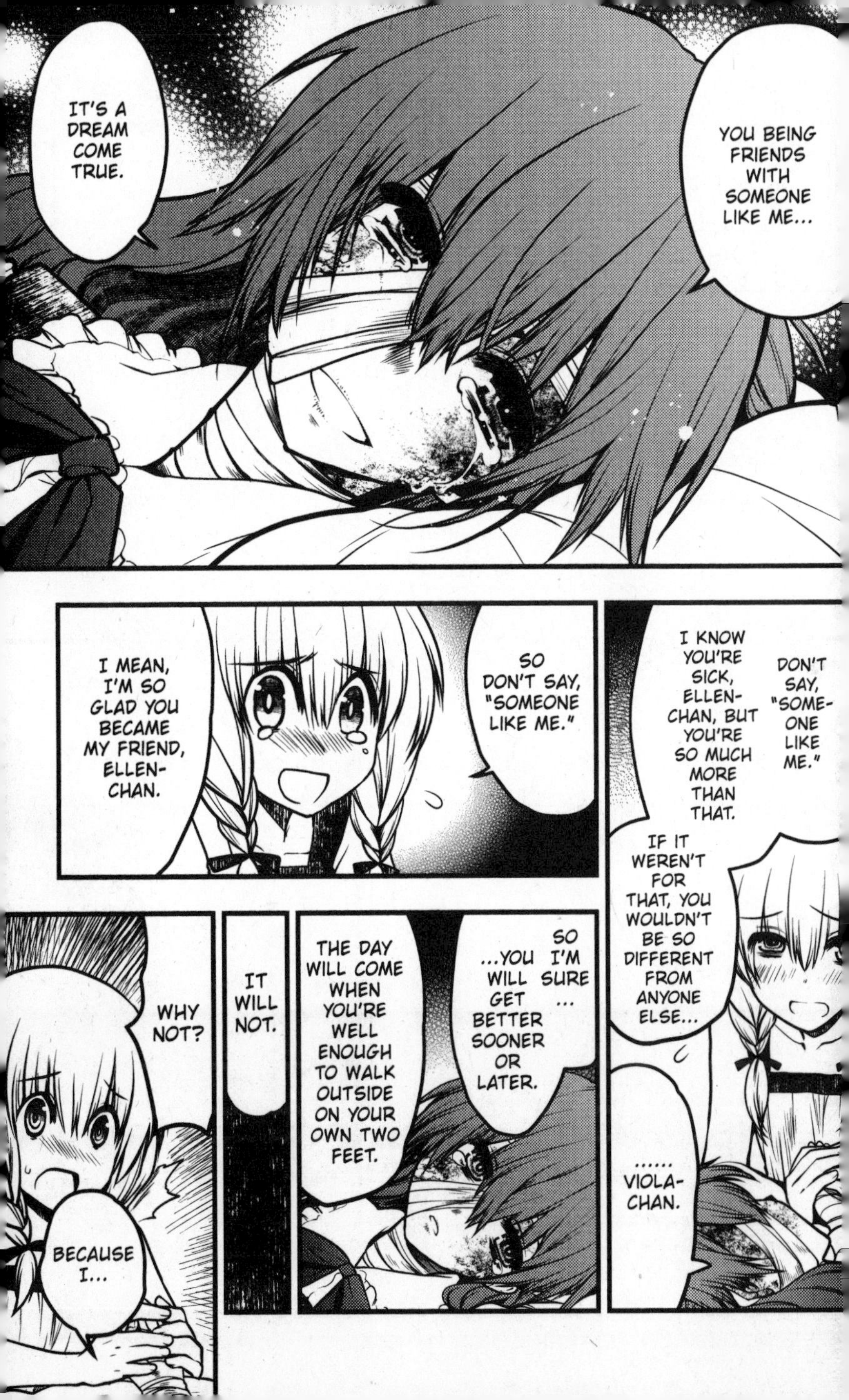
YOU BEING FRIENDS WITH SOMEONE LIKE ME...
IT'S A DREAM COME TRUE.
DON'T SAY, "SOME-ONE LIKE ME."
I KNOW YOU'RE SICK, ELLEN-CHAN, BUT YOU'RE SO MUCH MORE THAN THAT.
IF IT WEREN'T FOR THAT, YOU WOULDN'T BE SO DIFFERENT FROM ANYONE ELSE...
......VIOLA-CHAN.
SO DON'T SAY, "SOMEONE LIKE ME."
I MEAN, I'M SO GLAD YOU BECAME MY FRIEND, ELLEN-CHAN.
SO I'M SURE...
...YOU WILL GET BETTER SOONER OR LATER.
THE DAY WILL COME WHEN YOU'RE WELL ENOUGH TO WALK OUTSIDE ON YOUR OWN TWO FEET.
IT WILL NOT.
WHY NOT?
BECAUSE I...

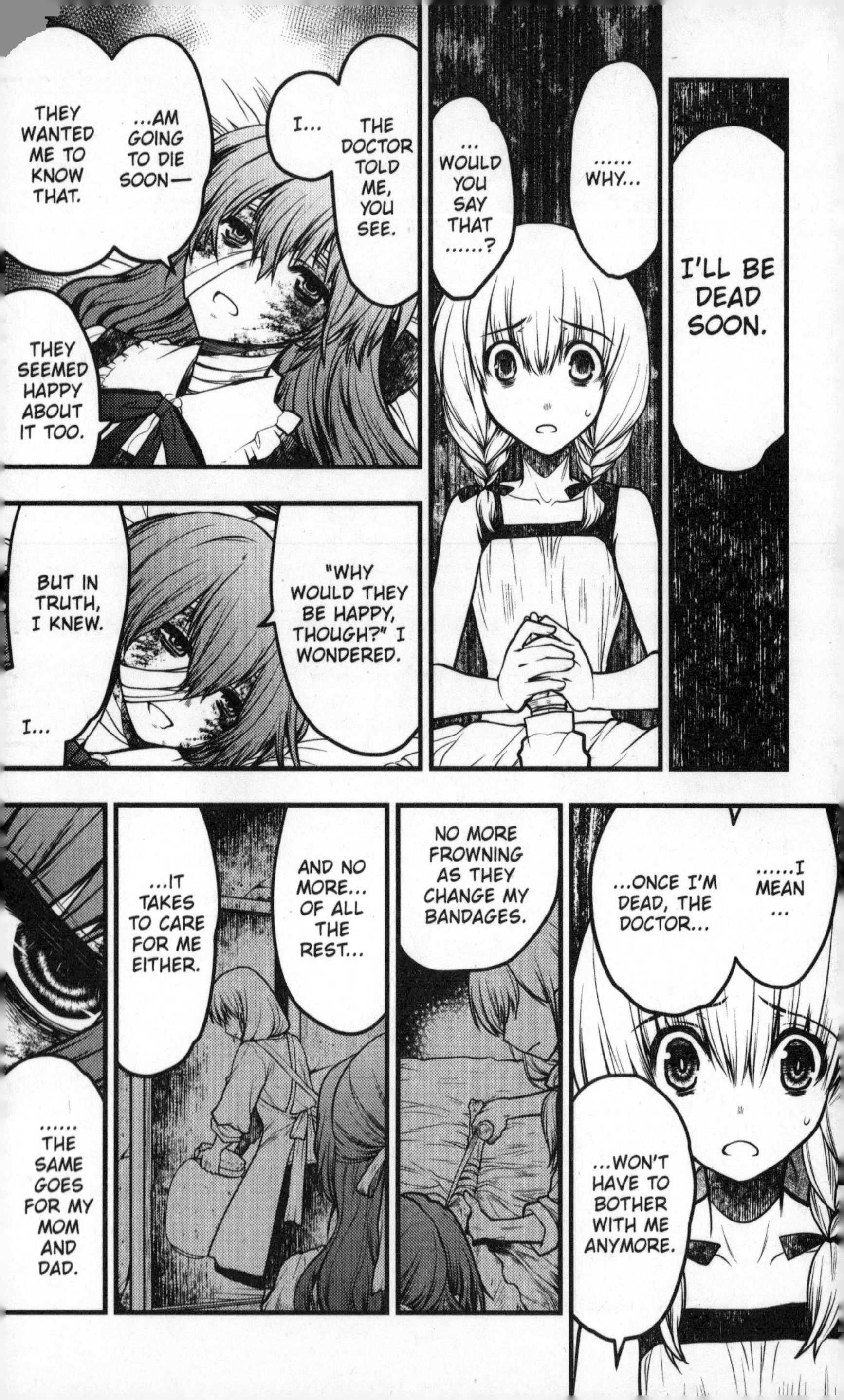
I'LL BE DEAD SOON.
......WHY...
...WOULD YOU SAY THAT ......?
THE DOCTOR TOLD ME, YOU SEE.
I...
...AM GOING TO DIE SOON—
THEY WANTED ME TO KNOW THAT.
THEY SEEMED HAPPY ABOUT IT TOO.
"WHY WOULD THEY BE HAPPY, THOUGH?" I WONDERED.
BUT IN TRUTH, I KNEW.
I...
......I MEAN ...
...ONCE I'M DEAD, THE DOCTOR...
...WON'T HAVE TO BOTHER WITH ME ANYMORE.
NO MORE FROWNING AS THEY CHANGE MY BANDAGES.
AND NO MORE... OF ALL THE REST...
...IT TAKES TO CARE FOR ME EITHER.
......THE SAME GOES FOR MY MOM AND DAD.

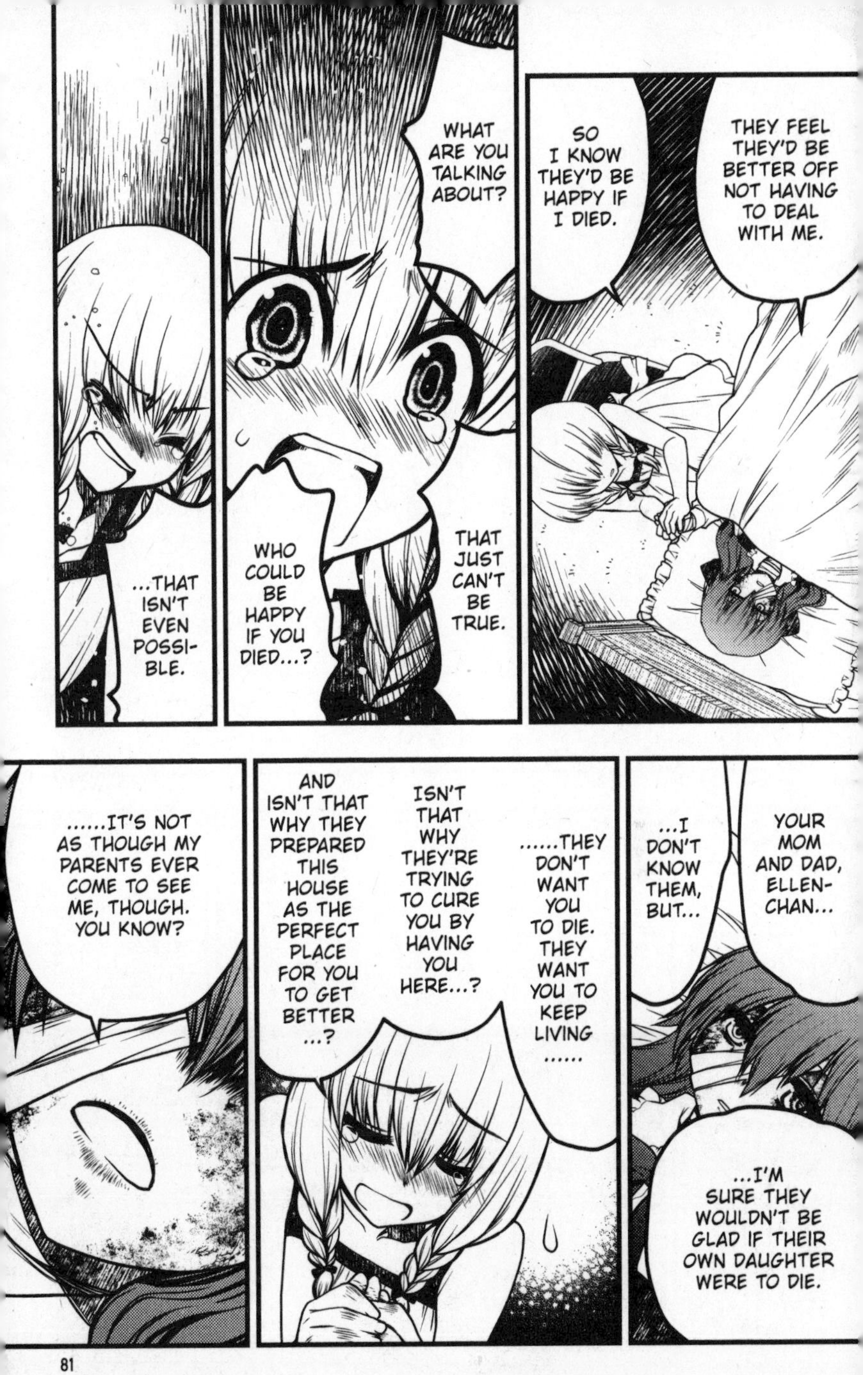
THEY FEEL THEY'D BE BETTER OFF NOT HAVING TO DEAL WITH ME.
SO I KNOW THEY'D BE HAPPY IF I DIED.
WHAT ARE YOU TALKING ABOUT?
THAT JUST CAN'T BE TRUE.
WHO COULD BE HAPPY IF YOU DIED...?
...THAT ISN'T EVEN POSSI-BLE.
YOUR MOM AND DAD, ELLEN-CHAN...
...I DON'T KNOW THEM, BUT...
...I'M SURE THEY WOULDN'T BE GLAD IF THEIR OWN DAUGHTER WERE TO DIE.
......THEY DON'T WANT YOU TO DIE. THEY WANT YOU TO KEEP LIVING......
ISN'T THAT WHY THEY'RE TRYING TO CURE YOU BY HAVING YOU HERE...?
AND ISN'T THAT WHY THEY PREPARED THIS HOUSE AS THE PERFECT PLACE FOR YOU TO GET BETTER...?
......IT'S NOT AS THOUGH MY PARENTS EVER COME TO SEE ME, THOUGH. YOU KNOW?

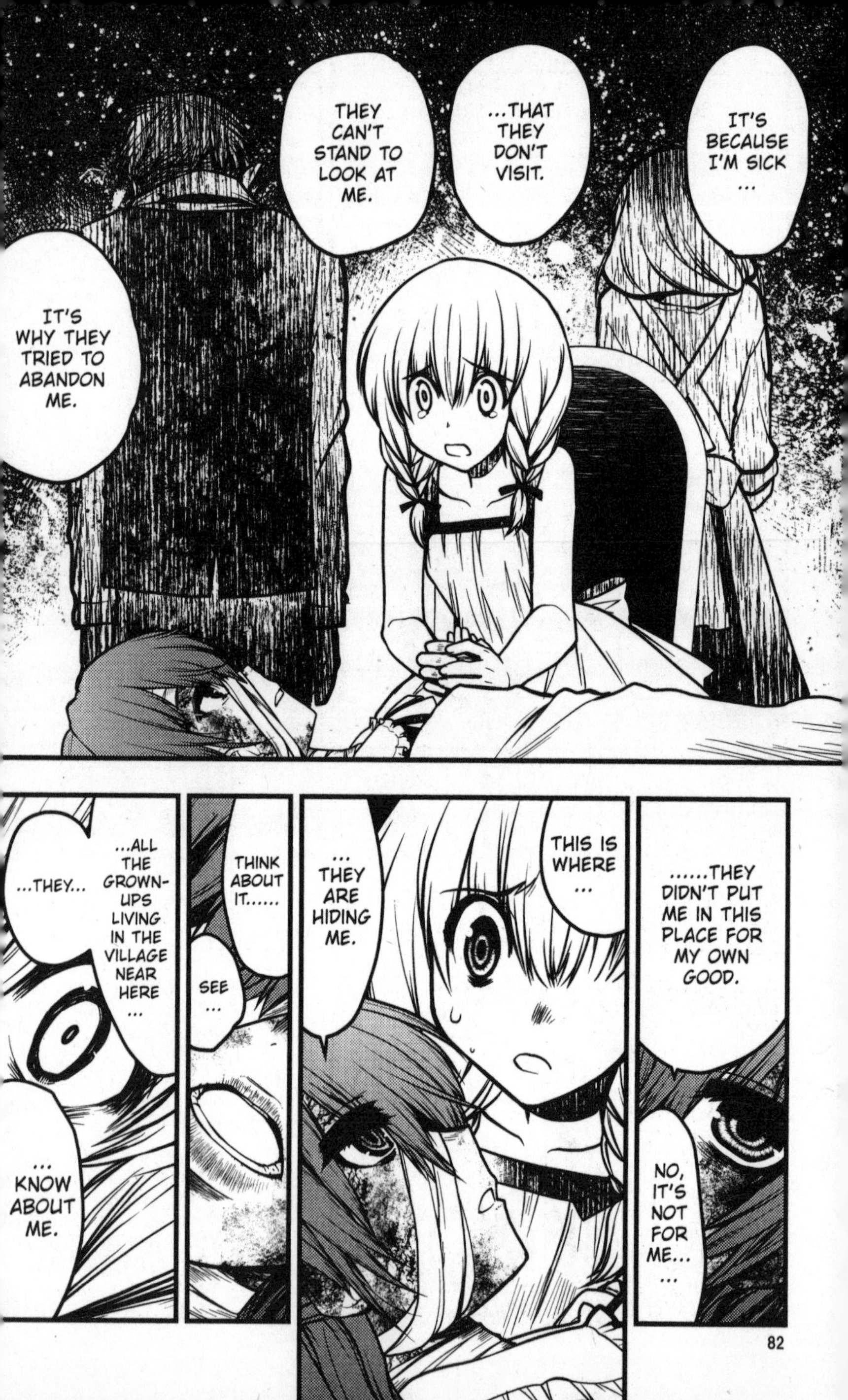
IT'S BECAUSE I'M SICK ...
...THAT THEY DON'T VISIT.
THEY CAN'T STAND TO LOOK AT ME.
IT'S WHY THEY TRIED TO ABANDON ME.
......THEY DIDN'T PUT ME IN THIS PLACE FOR MY OWN GOOD.
NO, IT'S NOT FOR ME... ...
THIS IS WHERE ...
... THEY ARE HIDING ME.
THINK ABOUT IT......
SEE ...
...ALL THE GROWN-UPS LIVING IN THE VILLAGE NEAR HERE ...
...THEY...
... KNOW ABOUT ME.

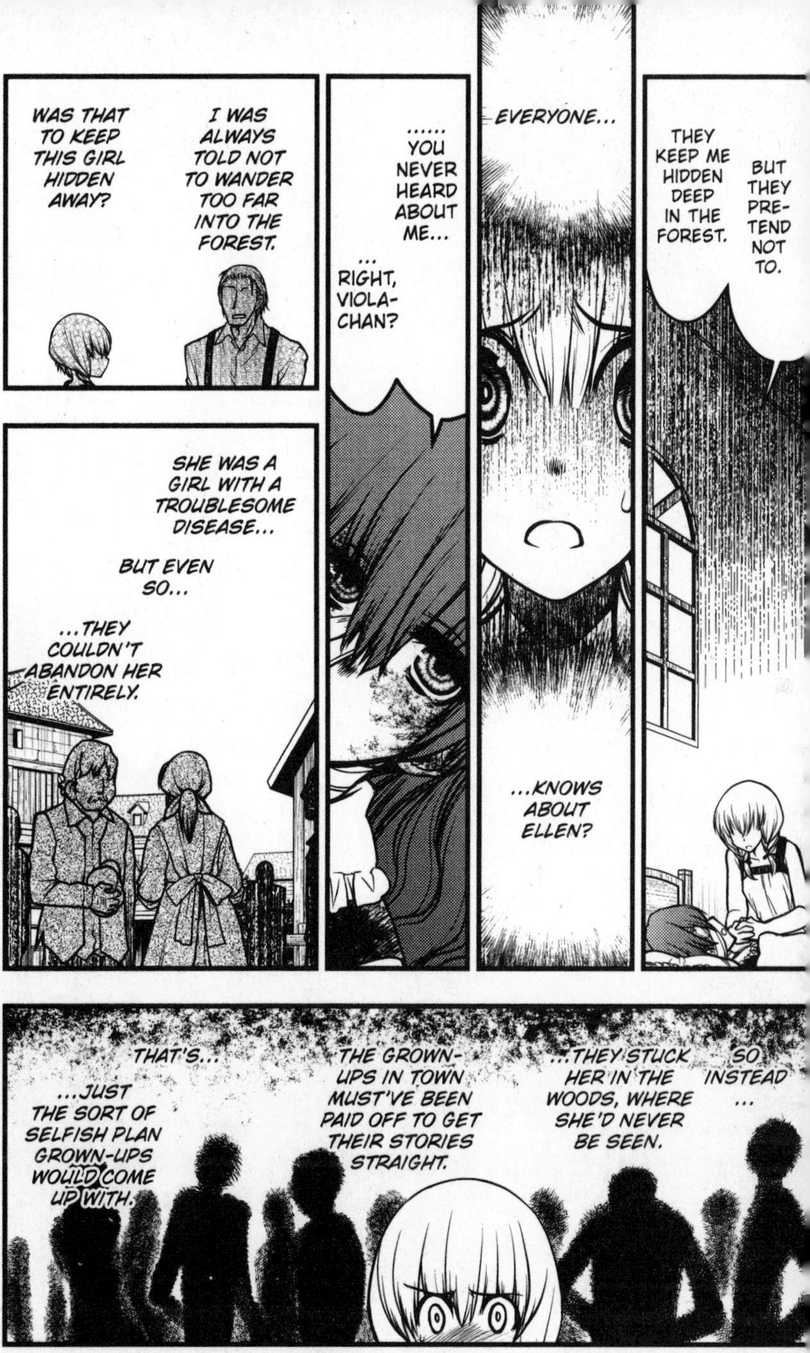
THEY KEEP ME HIDDEN DEEP IN THE FOREST.
BUT THEY PRE-TEND NOT TO.
EVERYONE...
...KNOWS ABOUT ELLEN?
......YOU NEVER HEARD ABOUT ME...
...RIGHT, VIOLA-CHAN?
I WAS ALWAYS TOLD NOT TO WANDER TOO FAR INTO THE FOREST.
WAS THAT TO KEEP THIS GIRL HIDDEN AWAY?
SHE WAS A GIRL WITH A TROUBLESOME DISEASE...
BUT EVEN SO...
...THEY COULDN'T ABANDON HER ENTIRELY.
SO INSTEAD...
...THEY STUCK HER IN THE WOODS, WHERE SHE'D NEVER BE SEEN.
THE GROWN-UPS IN TOWN MUST'VE BEEN PAID OFF TO GET THEIR STORIES STRAIGHT.
THAT'S...
...JUST THE SORT OF SELFISH PLAN GROWN-UPS WOULD COME UP WITH.

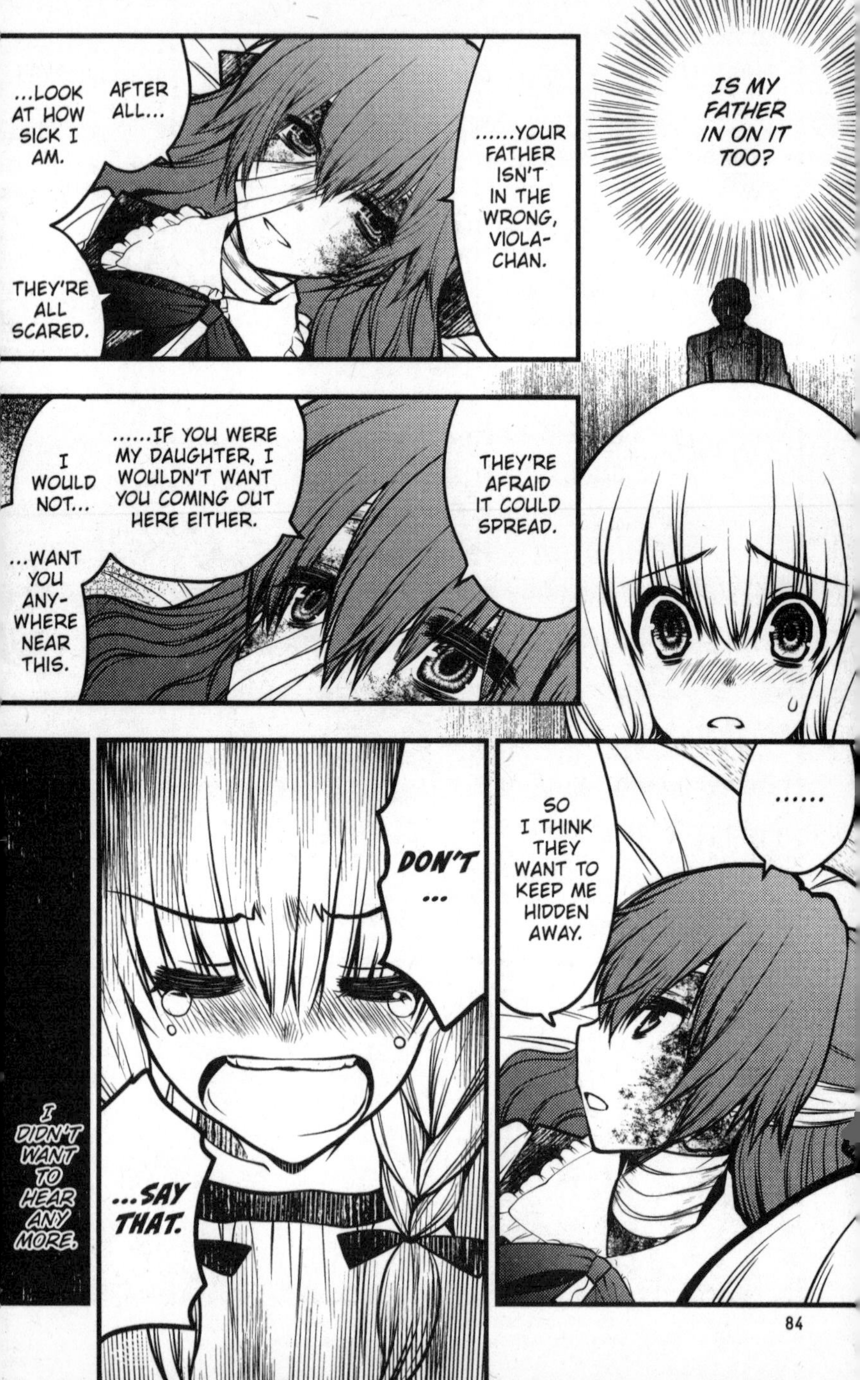
IS MY FATHER IN ON IT TOO?
......YOUR FATHER ISN'T IN THE WRONG, VIOLA-CHAN.
AFTER ALL...
...LOOK AT HOW SICK I AM.
THEY'RE ALL SCARED.
THEY'RE AFRAID IT COULD SPREAD.
......IF YOU WERE MY DAUGHTER, I WOULDN'T WANT YOU COMING OUT HERE EITHER.
I WOULD NOT...
...WANT YOU ANY-WHERE NEAR THIS.
......
SO I THINK THEY WANT TO KEEP ME HIDDEN AWAY.
DON'T ...
...SAY THAT.
I DIDN'T WANT TO HEAR ANY MORE.

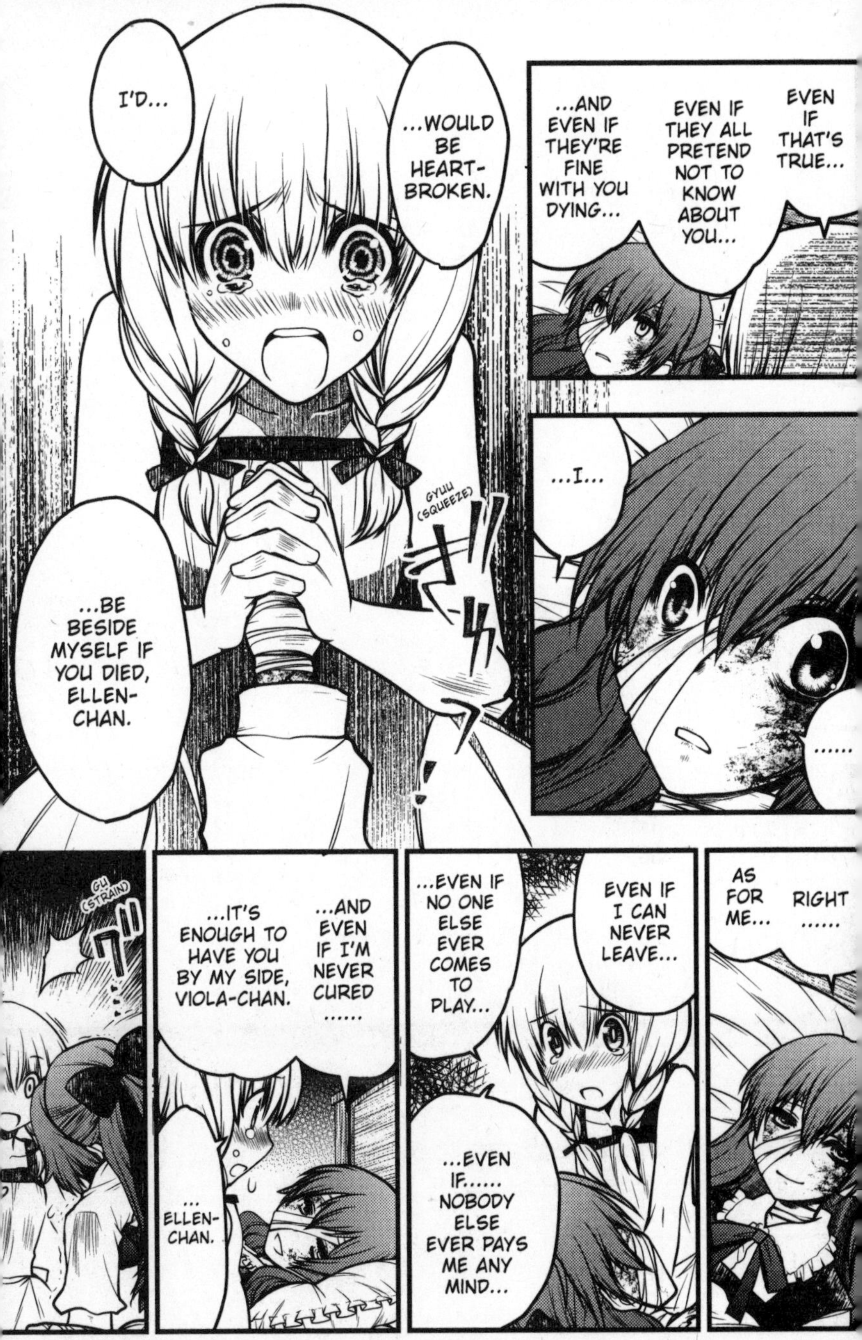
EVEN IF THAT'S TRUE...
EVEN IF THEY ALL PRETEND NOT TO KNOW ABOUT YOU...
...AND EVEN IF THEY'RE FINE WITH YOU DYING...
......
...I...
I'D...
...WOULD BE HEART-BROKEN.
GYUU (SQUEEZE)
...BE BESIDE MYSELF IF YOU DIED, ELLEN-CHAN.
RIGHT ......
AS FOR ME...
EVEN IF I CAN NEVER LEAVE...
...EVEN IF NO ONE ELSE EVER COMES TO PLAY...
...EVEN IF...... NOBODY ELSE EVER PAYS ME ANY MIND...
...AND EVEN IF I'M NEVER CURED ......
...IT'S ENOUGH TO HAVE YOU BY MY SIDE, VIOLA-CHAN.
... ELLEN-CHAN.
GU (STRAIN)

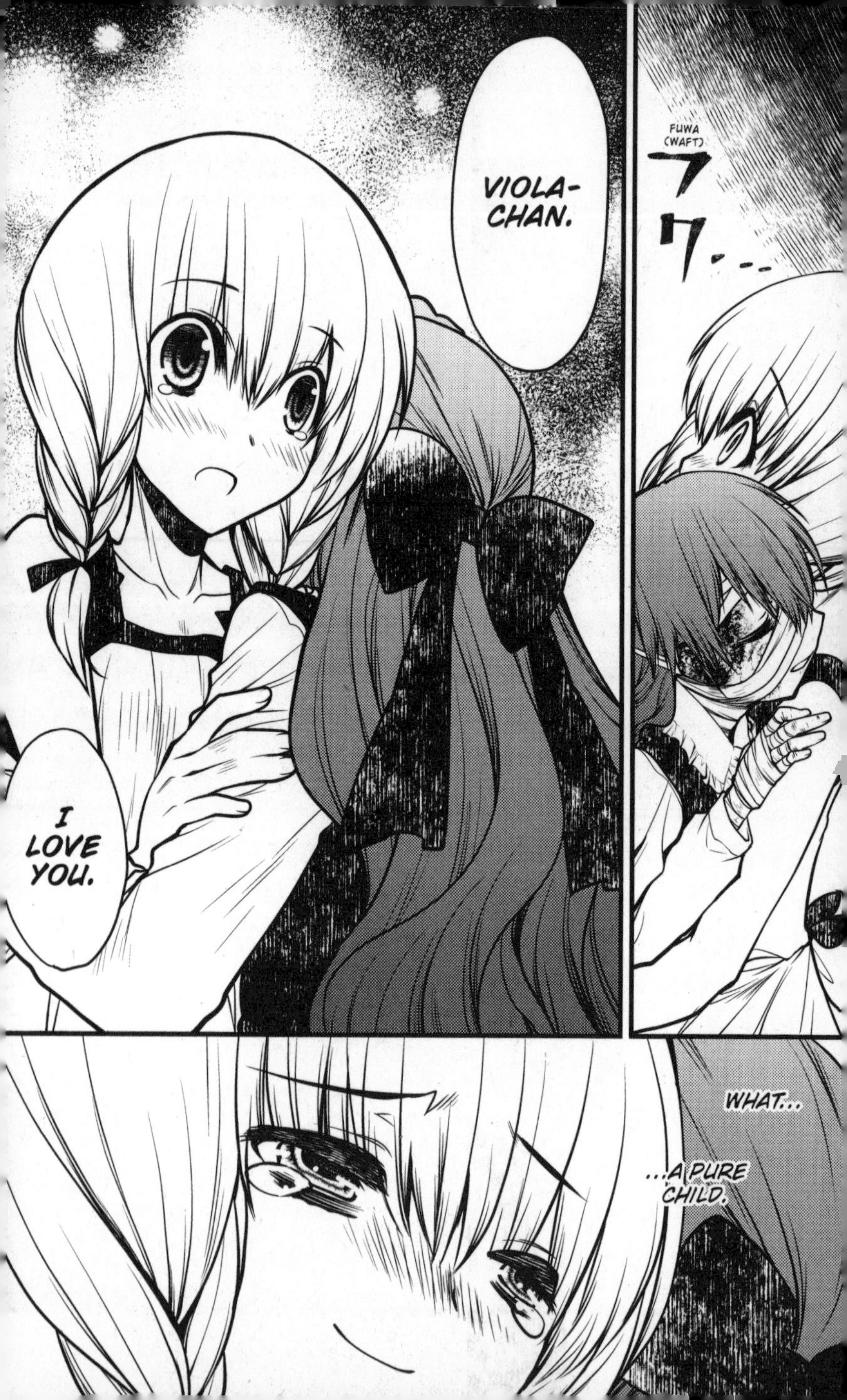
FUWA (WAFT)
VIOLA-CHAN.
I LOVE YOU.
WHAT...
...A PURE CHILD.

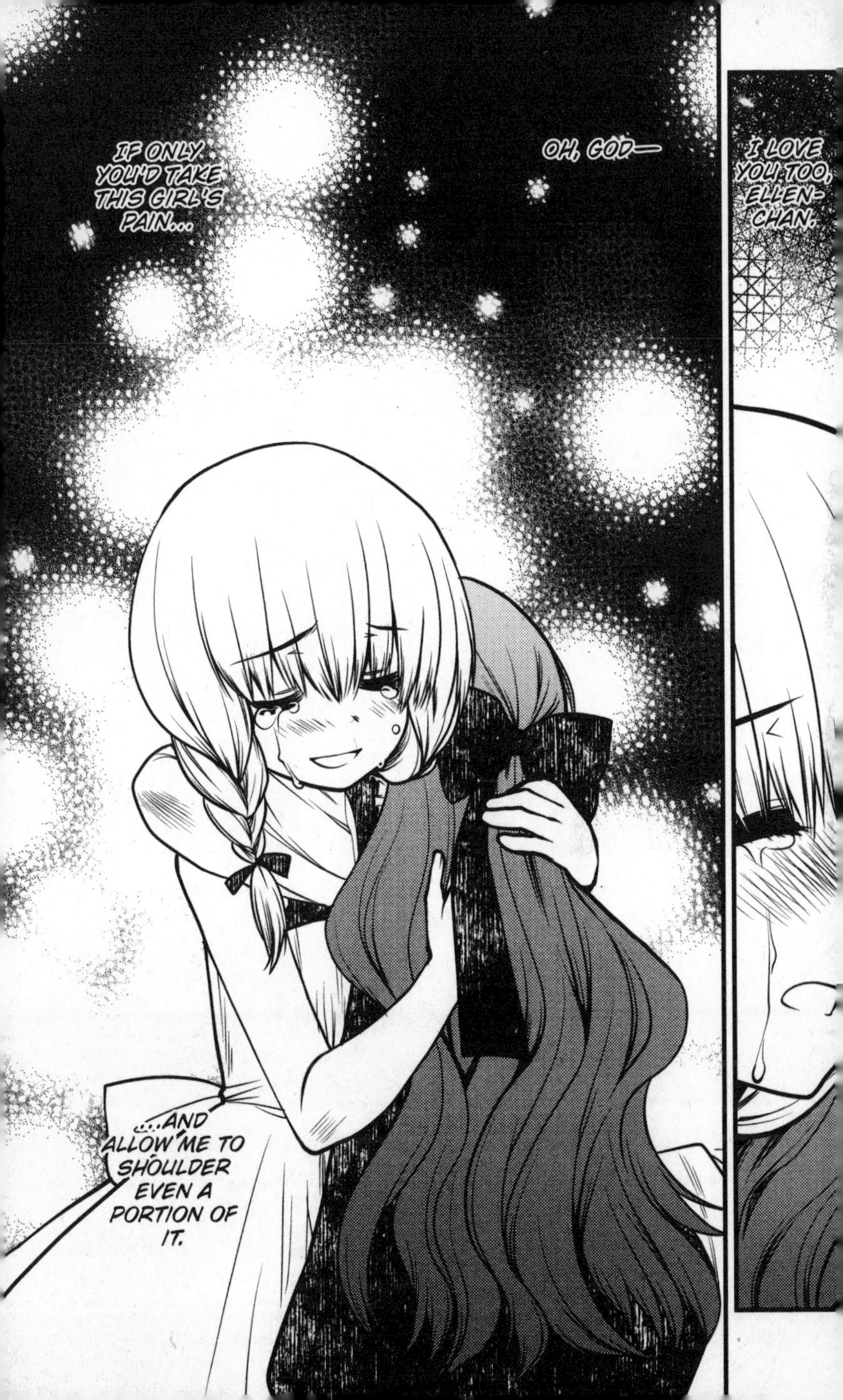
I LOVE YOU TOO, ELLEN-CHAN.
OH, GOD—
IF ONLY YOU'D TAKE THIS GIRL'S PAIN...
...AND ALLOW ME TO SHOULDER EVEN A PORTION OF IT.

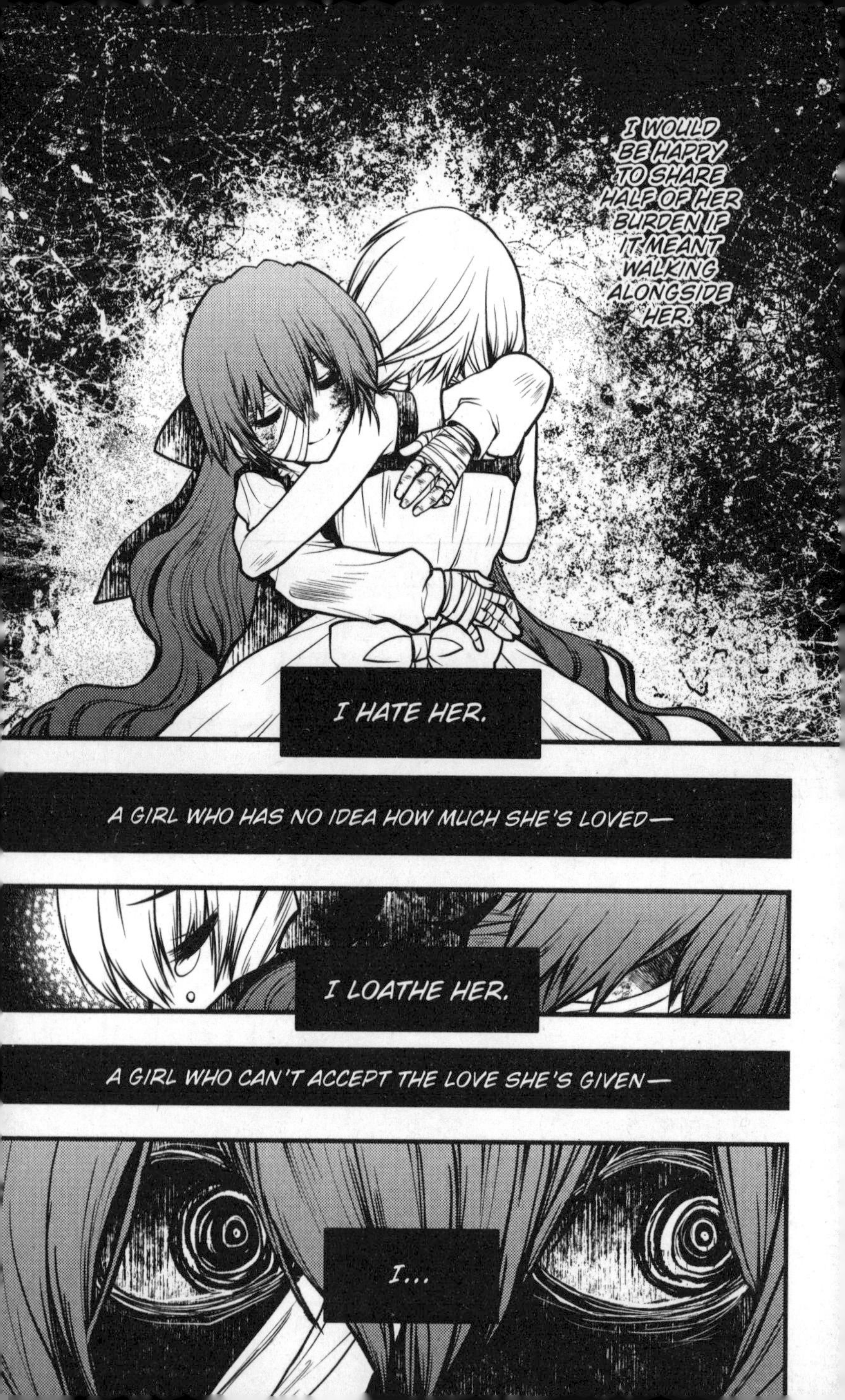
I WOULD BE HAPPY TO SHARE HALF OF HER BURDEN IF IT MEANT WALKING ALONGSIDE HER.
I HATE HER.
A GIRL WHO HAS NO IDEA HOW MUCH SHE'S LOVED—
I LOATHE HER.
A GIRL WHO CAN'T ACCEPT THE LOVE SHE'S GIVEN—
I...

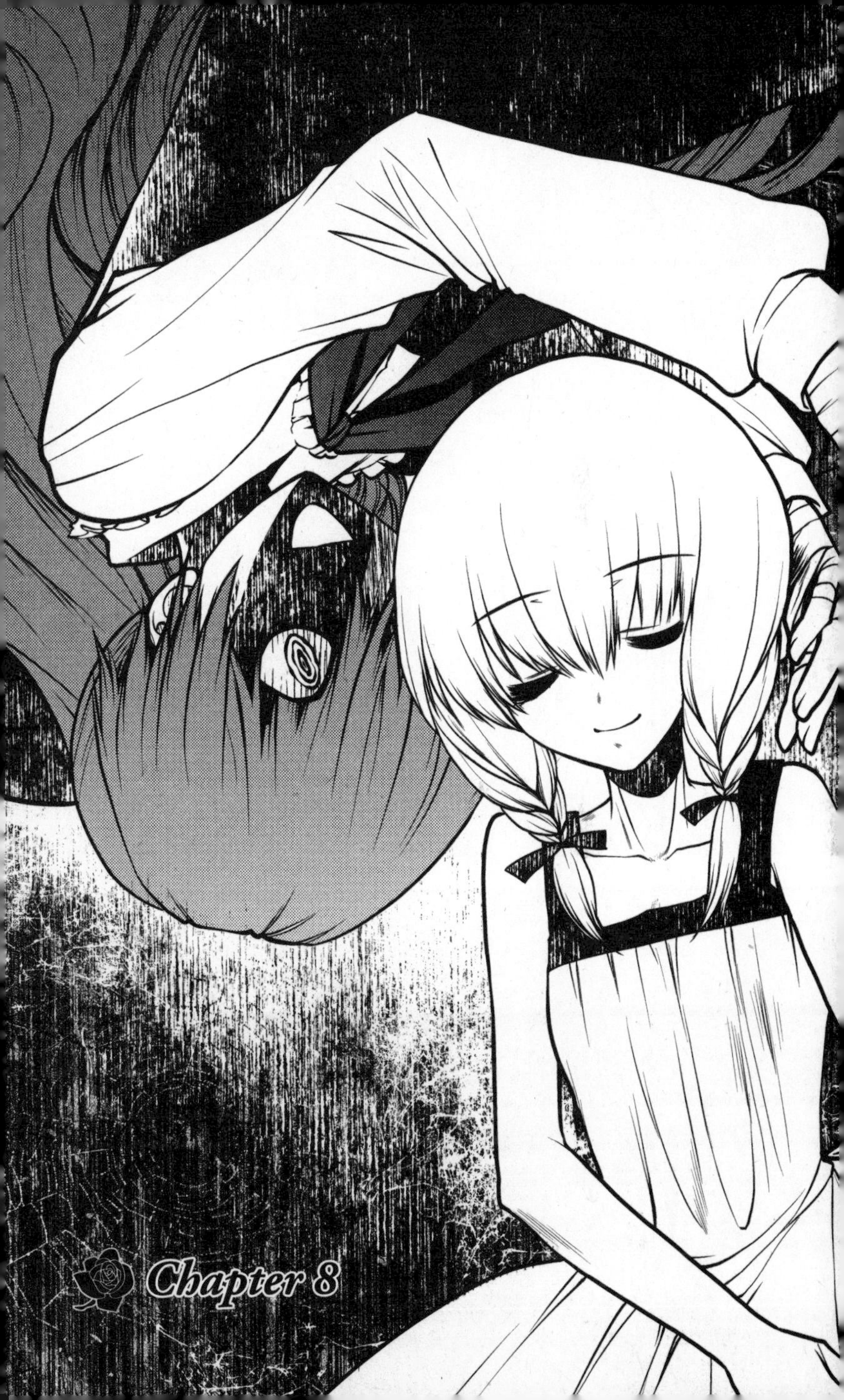
Chapter 8

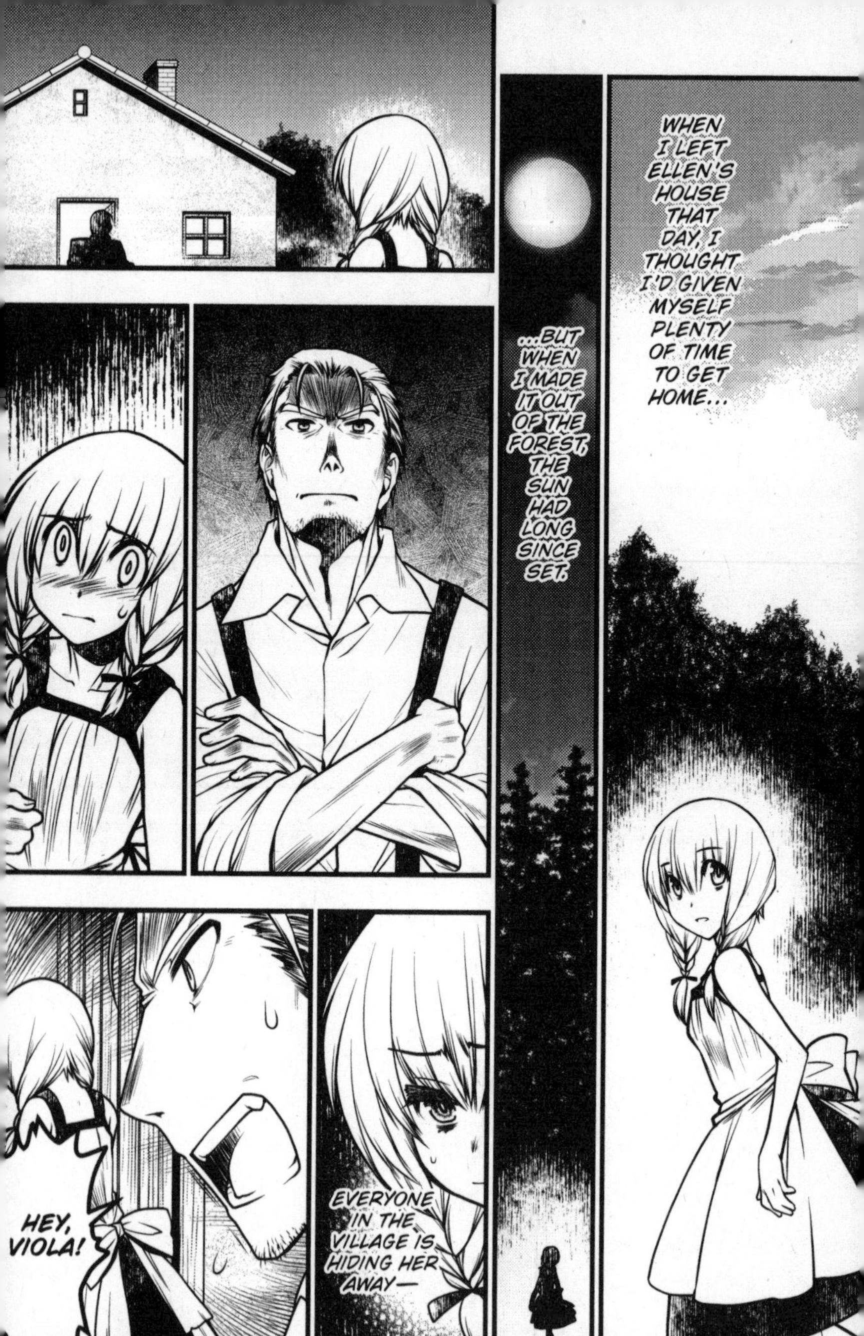
WHEN I LEFT ELLEN'S HOUSE THAT DAY, I THOUGHT I'D GIVEN MYSELF PLENTY OF TIME TO GET HOME...
...BUT WHEN I MADE IT OUT OF THE FOREST, THE SUN HAD LONG SINCE SET.
EVERYONE IN THE VILLAGE IS HIDING HER AWAY—
HEY, VIOLA!

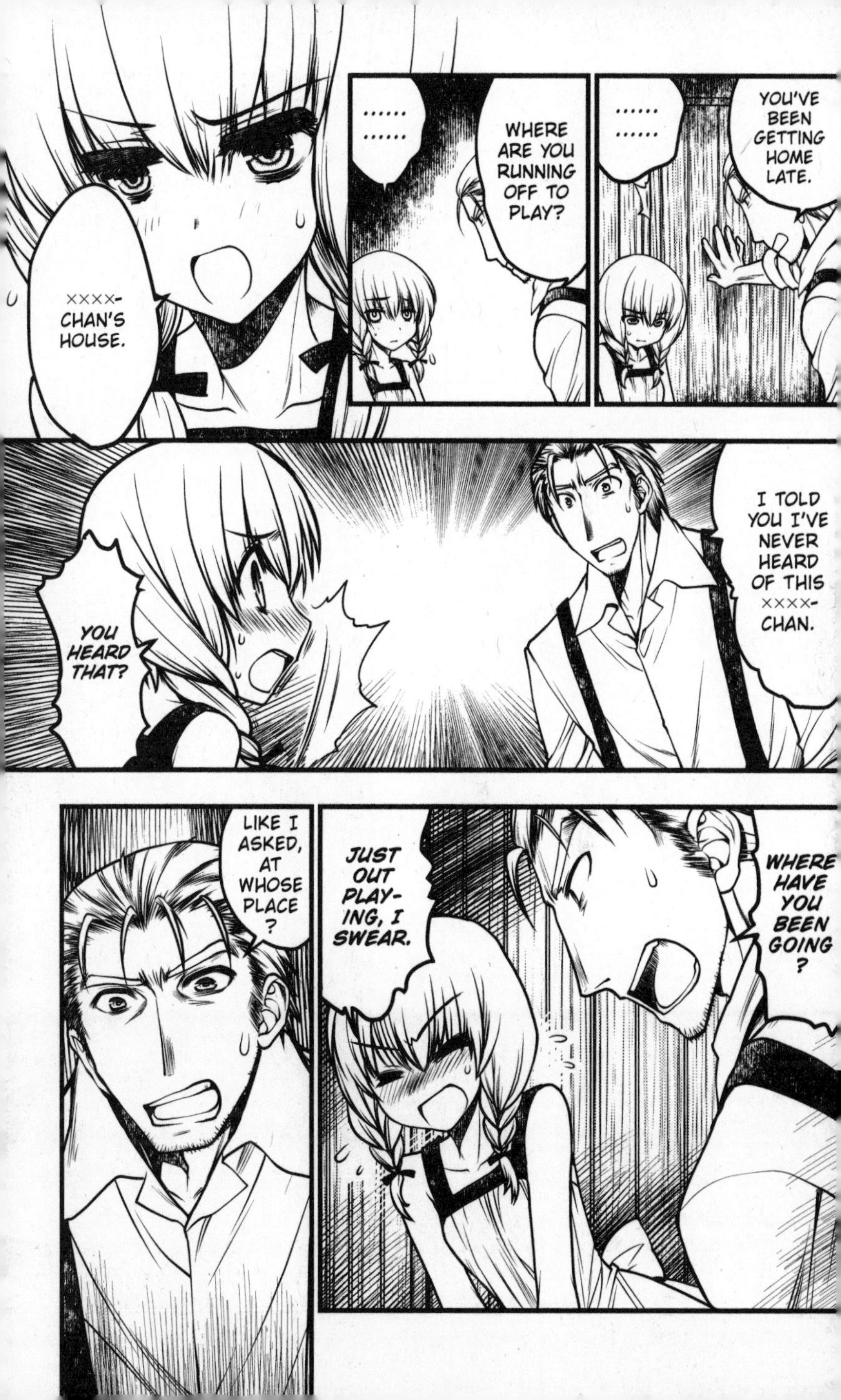
YOU'VE BEEN GETTING HOME LATE.
......
......
WHERE ARE YOU RUNNING OFF TO PLAY?
......
......
××××-CHAN'S HOUSE.
I TOLD YOU I'VE NEVER HEARD OF THIS ××××-CHAN.
YOU HEARD THAT?
WHERE HAVE YOU BEEN GOING?
JUST OUT PLAY-ING, I SWEAR.
LIKE I ASKED, AT WHOSE PLACE?

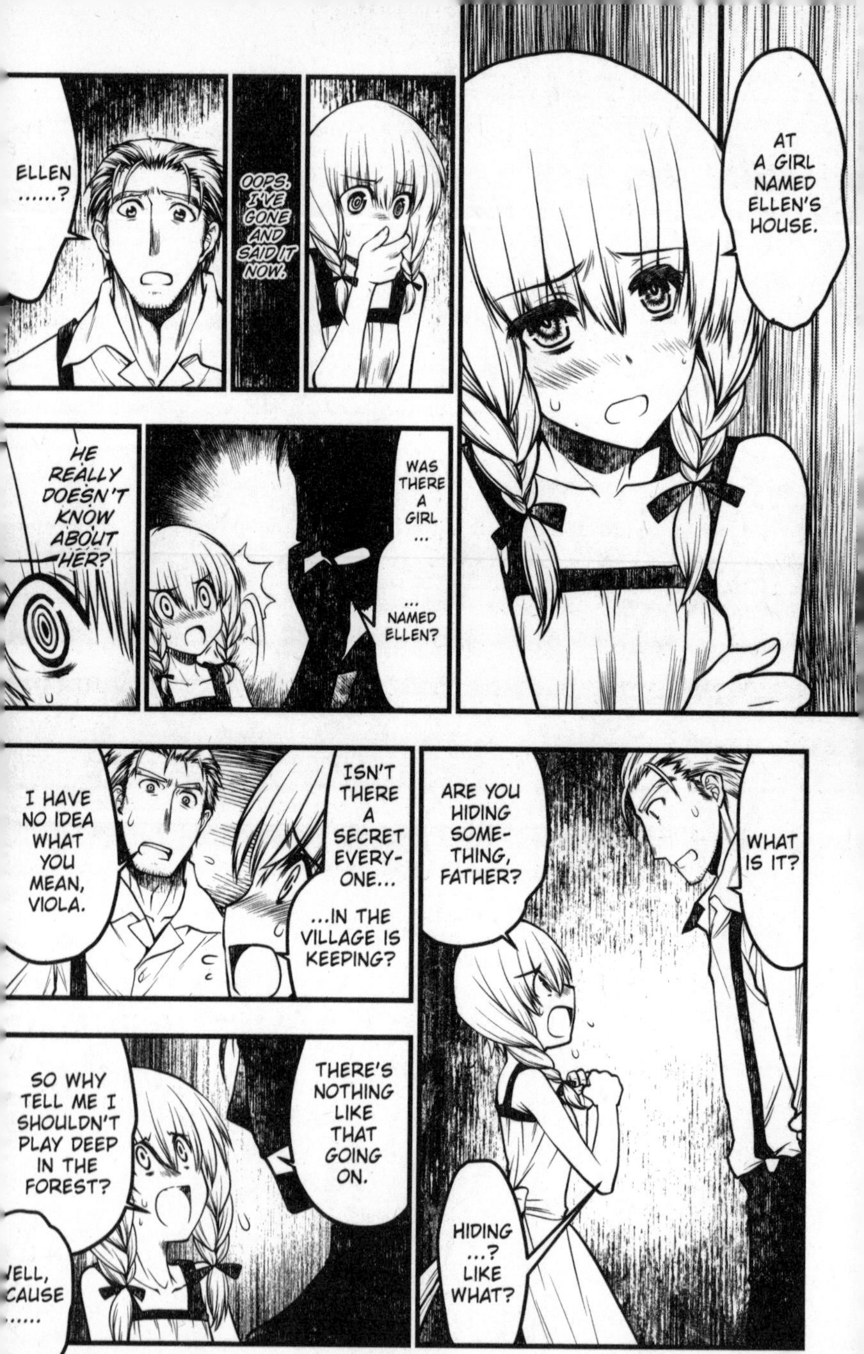
AT A GIRL NAMED ELLEN'S HOUSE.
OOPS. I'VE GONE AND SAID IT NOW.
ELLEN ......?
WAS THERE A GIRL ...
... NAMED ELLEN?
HE REALLY DOESN'T KNOW ABOUT HER?
WHAT IS IT?
ARE YOU HIDING SOME-THING, FATHER?
HIDING ...? LIKE WHAT?
ISN'T THERE A SECRET EVERY-ONE...
...IN THE VILLAGE IS KEEPING?
I HAVE NO IDEA WHAT YOU MEAN, VIOLA.
THERE'S NOTHING LIKE THAT GOING ON.
SO WHY TELL ME I SHOULDN'T PLAY DEEP IN THE FOREST?
ELL, CAUSE ......

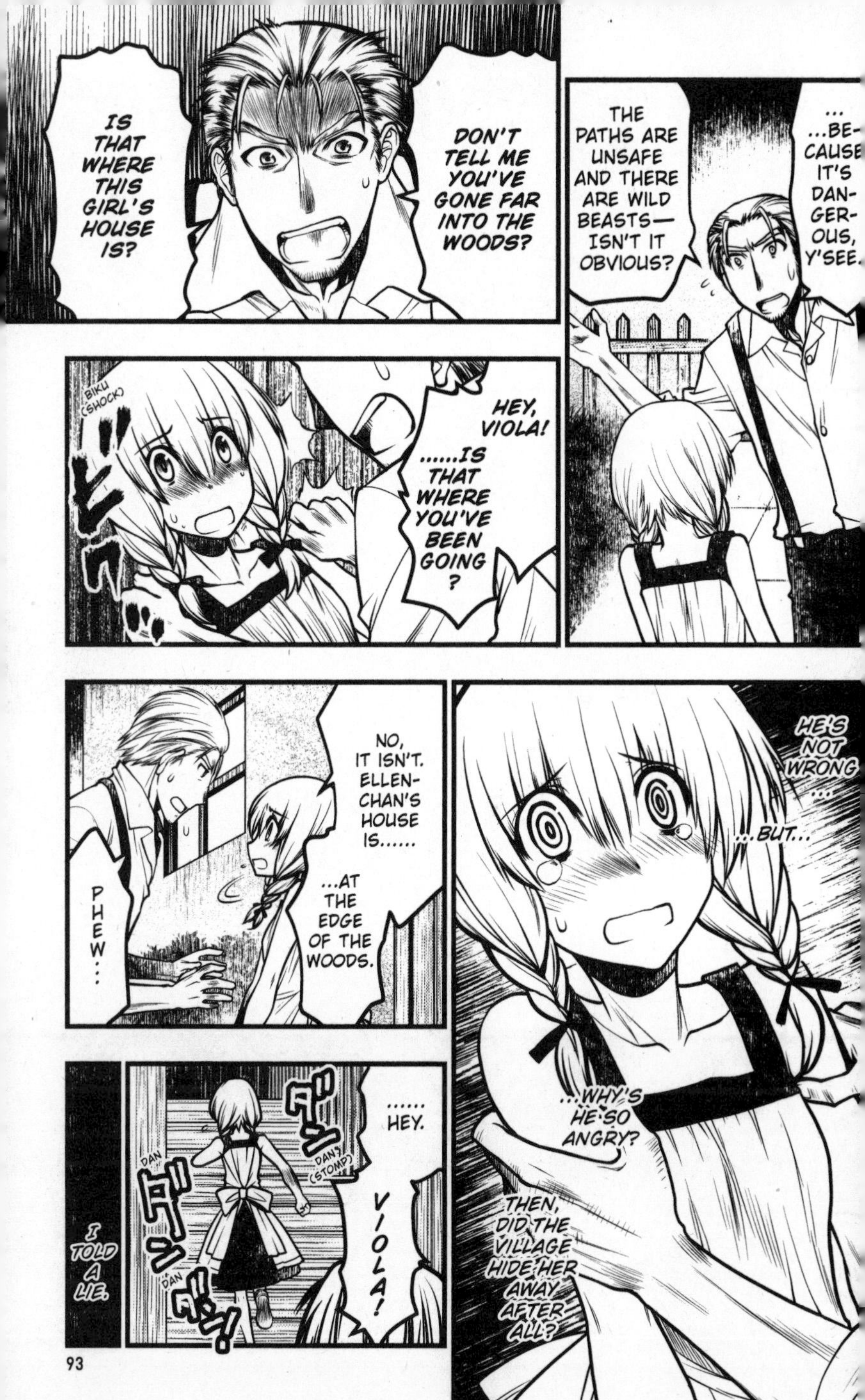

...
...BE-CAUSE IT'S DAN-GER-OUS, Y'SEE.
THE PATHS ARE UNSAFE AND THERE ARE WILD BEASTS— ISN'T IT OBVIOUS?
DON'T TELL ME YOU'VE GONE FAR INTO THE WOODS?
IS THAT WHERE THIS GIRL'S HOUSE IS?
HEY, VIOLA!
......IS THAT WHERE YOU'VE BEEN GOING?
BIKU (SHOCK)
HE'S NOT WRONG...
...BUT...
...WHY'S HE SO ANGRY?
THEN, DID THE VILLAGE HIDE HER AWAY AFTER ALL?
NO, IT ISN'T. ELLEN-CHAN'S HOUSE IS......
...AT THE EDGE OF THE WOODS.
PHEW...
...... HEY.
VIOLA!
DAN (STOMP)
DAN
DAN
I TOLD A LIE.

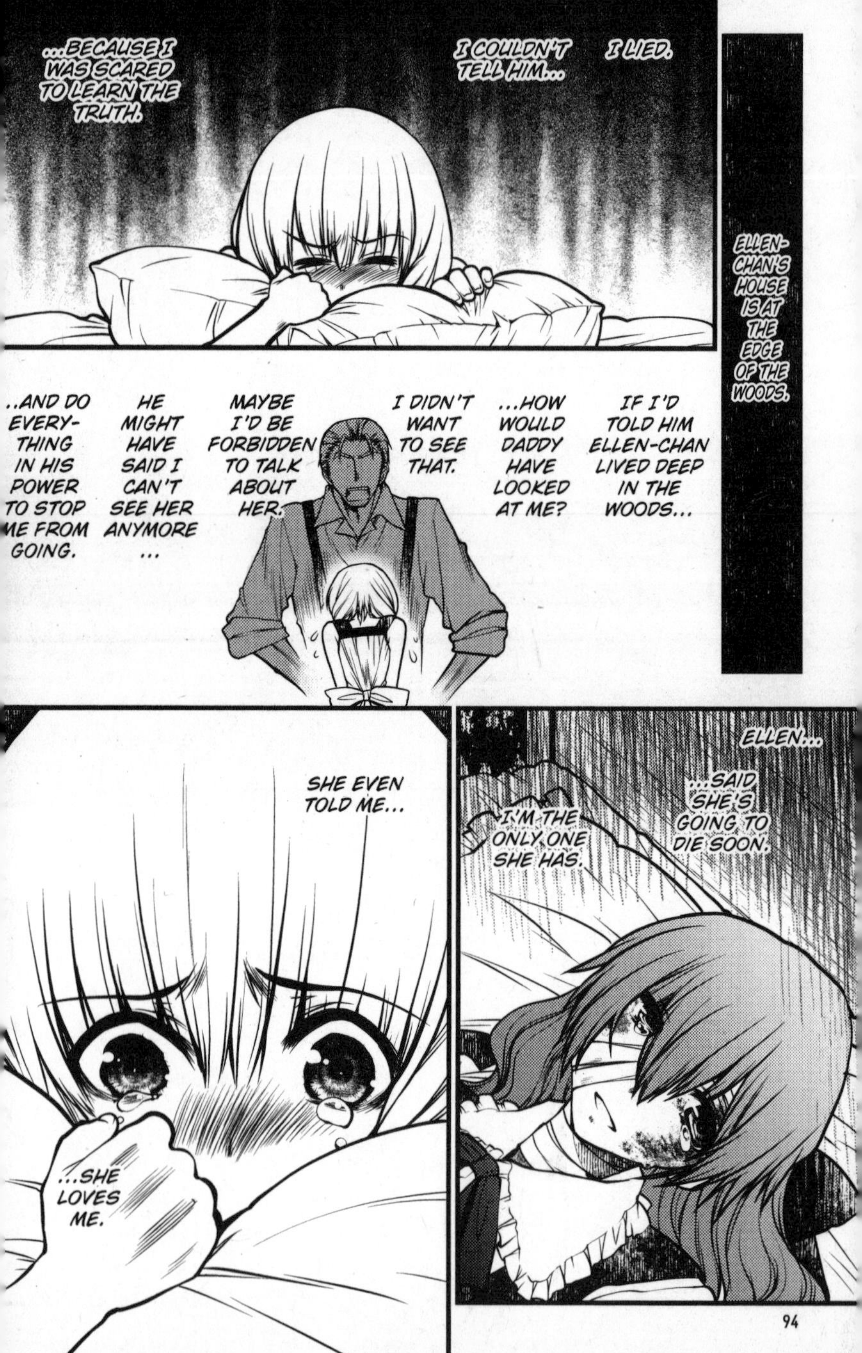
ELLEN-CHAN'S HOUSE IS AT THE EDGE OF THE WOODS.
I LIED.
I COULDN'T TELL HIM...
...BECAUSE I WAS SCARED TO LEARN THE TRUTH.
IF I'D TOLD HIM ELLEN-CHAN LIVED DEEP IN THE WOODS...
...HOW WOULD DADDY HAVE LOOKED AT ME?
I DIDN'T WANT TO SEE THAT.
MAYBE I'D BE FORBIDDEN TO TALK ABOUT HER.
HE MIGHT HAVE SAID I CAN'T SEE HER ANYMORE...
..AND DO EVERY-THING IN HIS POWER TO STOP ME FROM GOING.
ELLEN...
...SAID SHE'S GOING TO DIE SOON.
I'M THE ONLY ONE SHE HAS.
SHE EVEN TOLD ME...
...SHE LOVES ME.

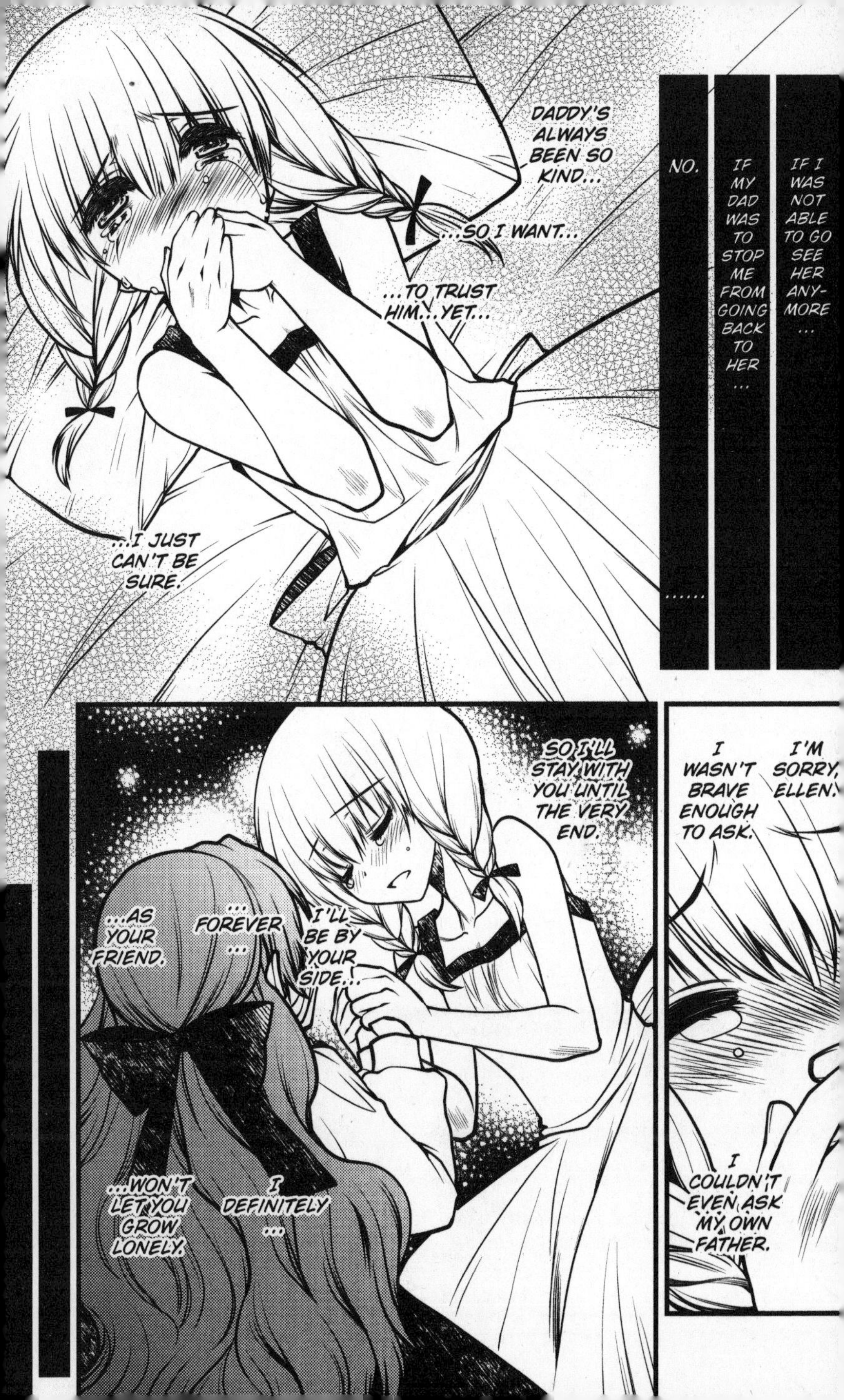
IF I WAS NOT ABLE TO GO SEE HER ANYMORE…
IF MY DAD WAS TO STOP ME FROM GOING BACK TO HER…
NO.
……
DADDY'S ALWAYS BEEN SO KIND…
…SO I WANT…
…TO TRUST HIM…YET…
…I JUST CAN'T BE SURE.
I'M SORRY, ELLEN.
I WASN'T BRAVE ENOUGH TO ASK.
I COULDN'T EVEN ASK MY OWN FATHER.
SO I'LL STAY WITH YOU UNTIL THE VERY END.
I'LL BE BY YOUR SIDE…
…FOREVER…
…AS YOUR FRIEND.
I DEFINITELY…
…WON'T LET YOU GROW LONELY.

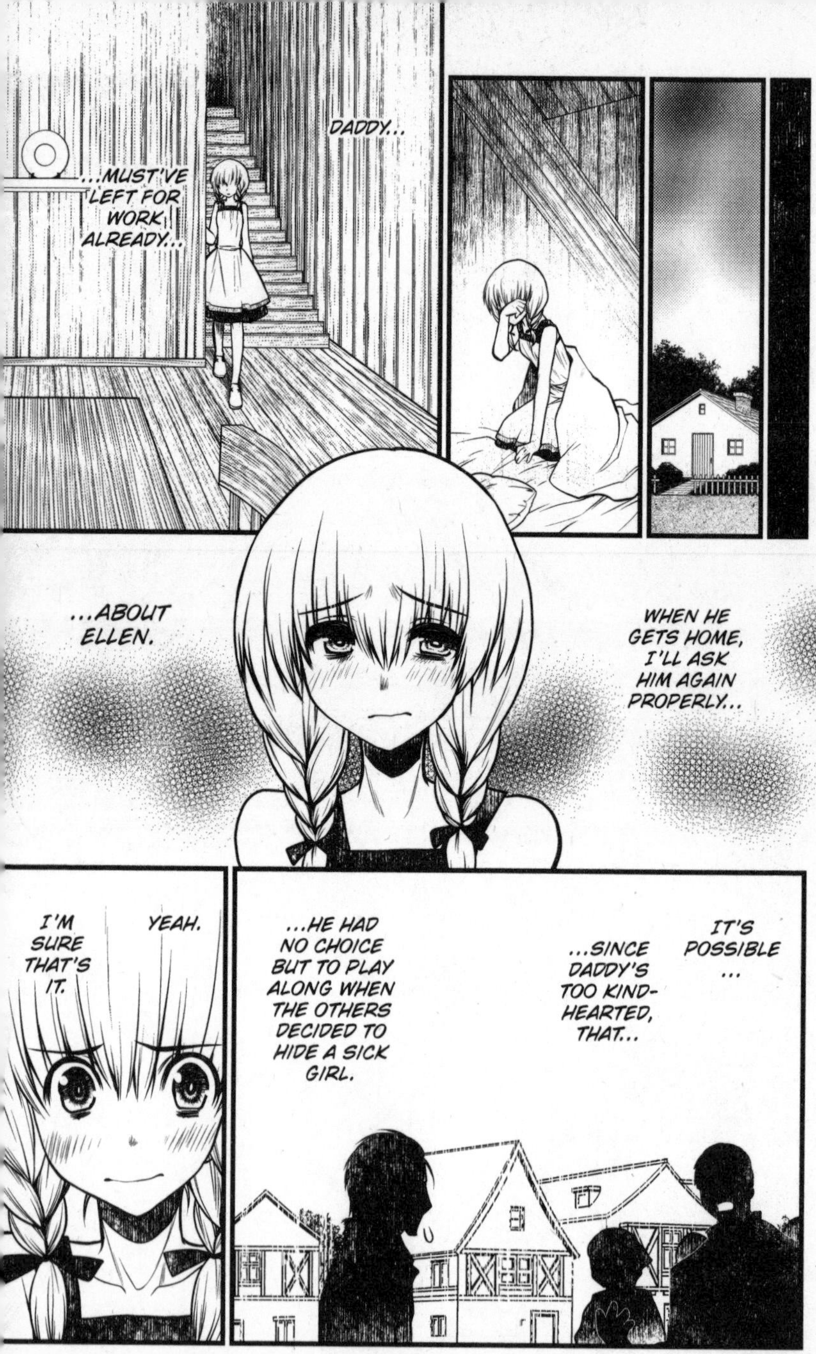
DADDY...
...MUST'VE LEFT FOR WORK ALREADY...
WHEN HE GETS HOME, I'LL ASK HIM AGAIN PROPERLY...
...ABOUT ELLEN.
IT'S POSSIBLE ...
...SINCE DADDY'S TOO KIND-HEARTED, THAT...
...HE HAD NO CHOICE BUT TO PLAY ALONG WHEN THE OTHERS DECIDED TO HIDE A SICK GIRL.
YEAH.
I'M SURE THAT'S IT.

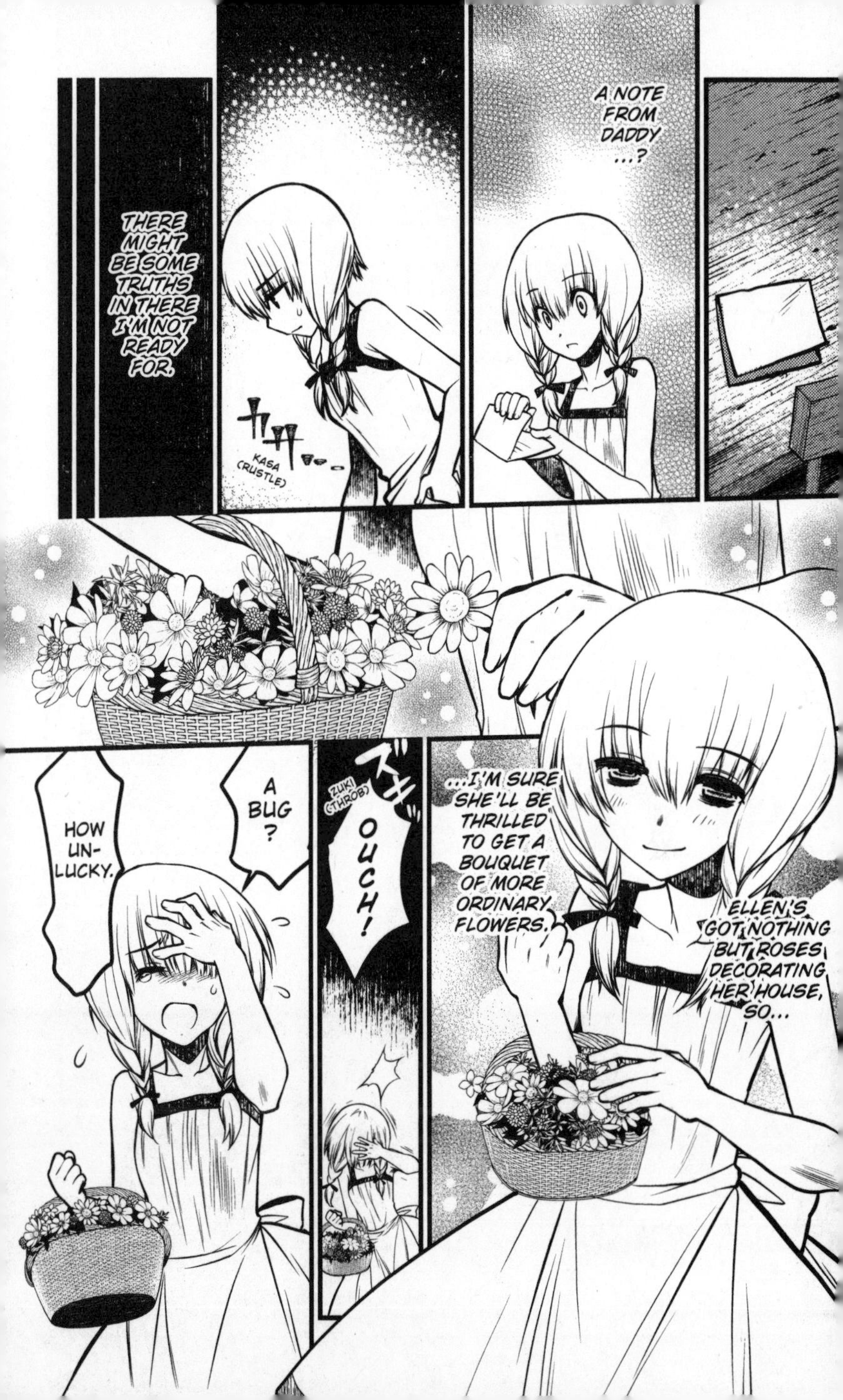
A NOTE FROM DADDY ...?
KASA (RUSTLE)
THERE MIGHT BE SOME TRUTHS IN THERE I'M NOT READY FOR.
ELLEN'S GOT NOTHING BUT ROSES DECORATING HER HOUSE, SO...
...I'M SURE SHE'LL BE THRILLED TO GET A BOUQUET OF MORE ORDINARY FLOWERS.
ZUKI (THROB)
OUCH!
A BUG?
HOW UN-LUCKY.

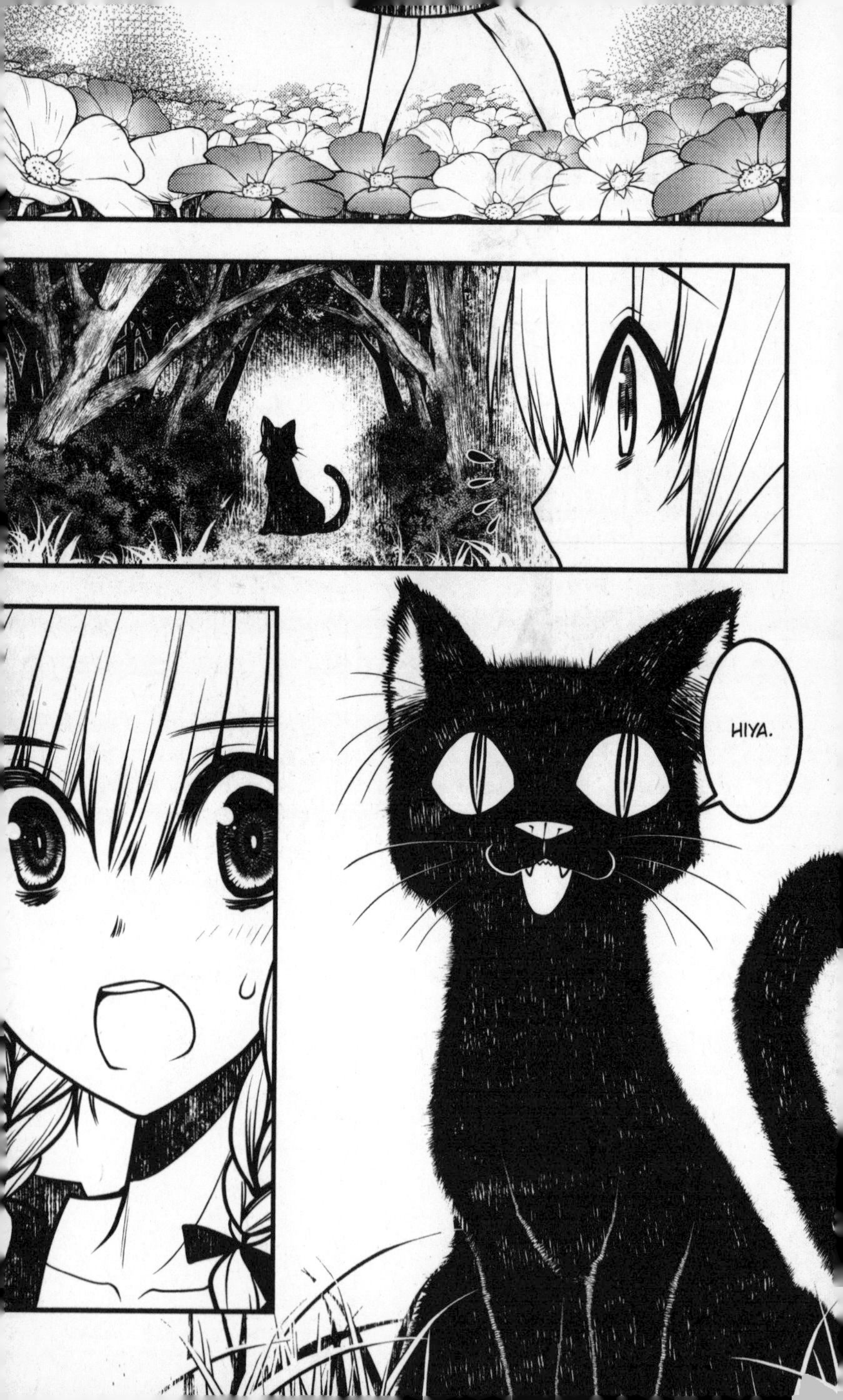
HIYA.

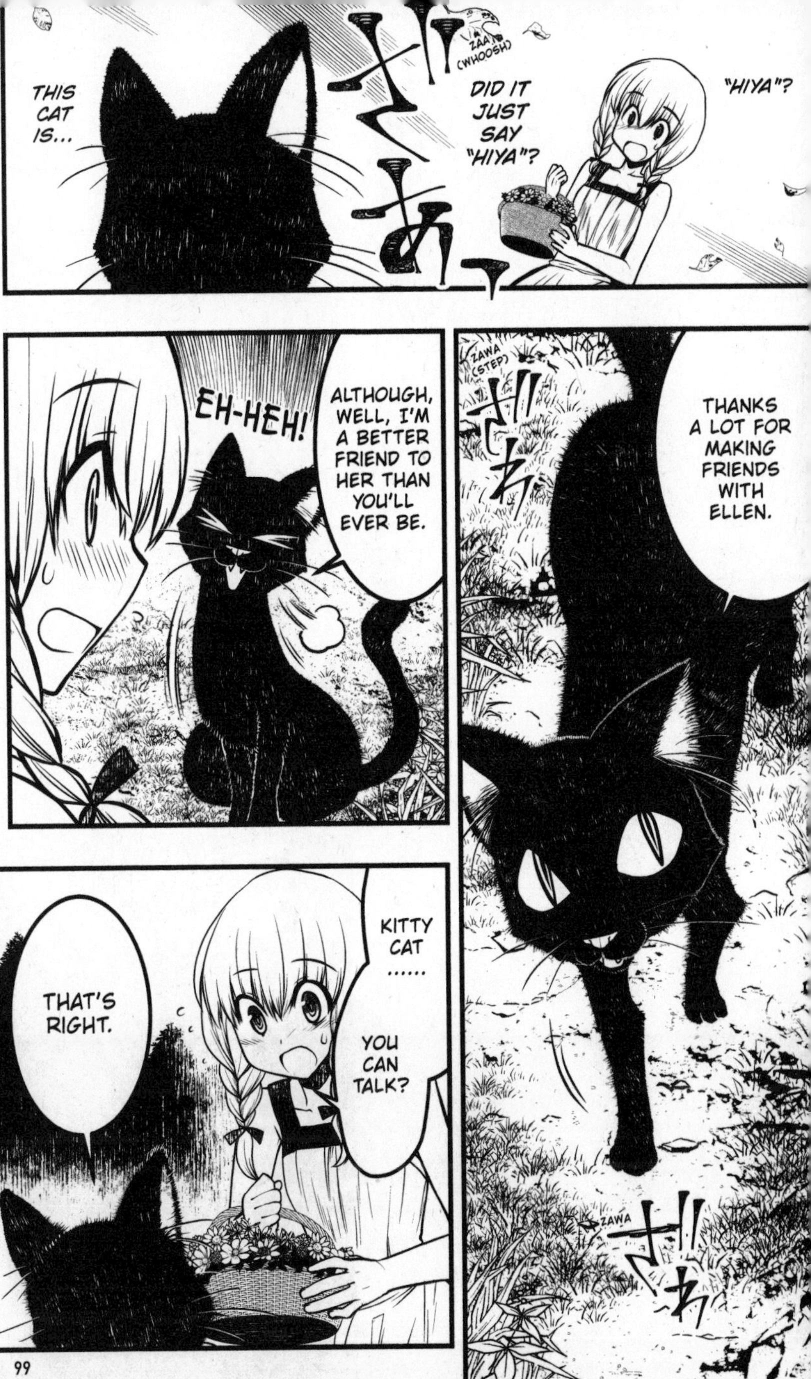
"HIYA"?
DID IT JUST SAY "HIYA"?
ZAA (WHOOSH)
THIS CAT IS...
ZAWA (STEP)
THANKS A LOT FOR MAKING FRIENDS WITH ELLEN.
ZAWA
ALTHOUGH, WELL, I'M A BETTER FRIEND TO HER THAN YOU'LL EVER BE.
EH-HEH!
KITTY CAT ......
YOU CAN TALK?
THAT'S RIGHT.

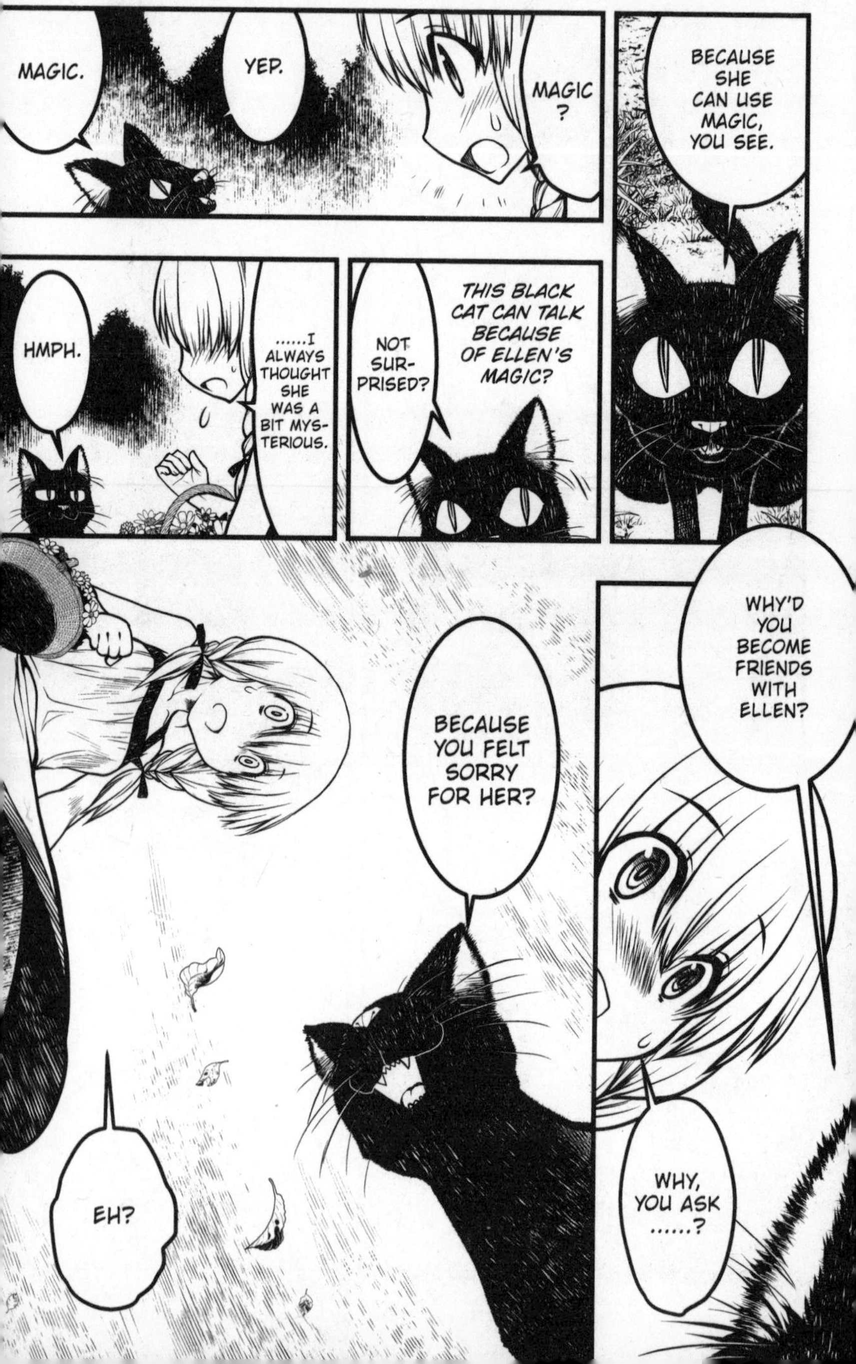
BECAUSE SHE CAN USE MAGIC, YOU SEE.
MAGIC?
YEP.
MAGIC.
THIS BLACK CAT CAN TALK BECAUSE OF ELLEN'S MAGIC?
NOT SURPRISED?
......I ALWAYS THOUGHT SHE WAS A BIT MYSTERIOUS.
HMPH.
WHY'D YOU BECOME FRIENDS WITH ELLEN?
WHY, YOU ASK ......?
BECAUSE YOU FELT SORRY FOR HER?
EH?

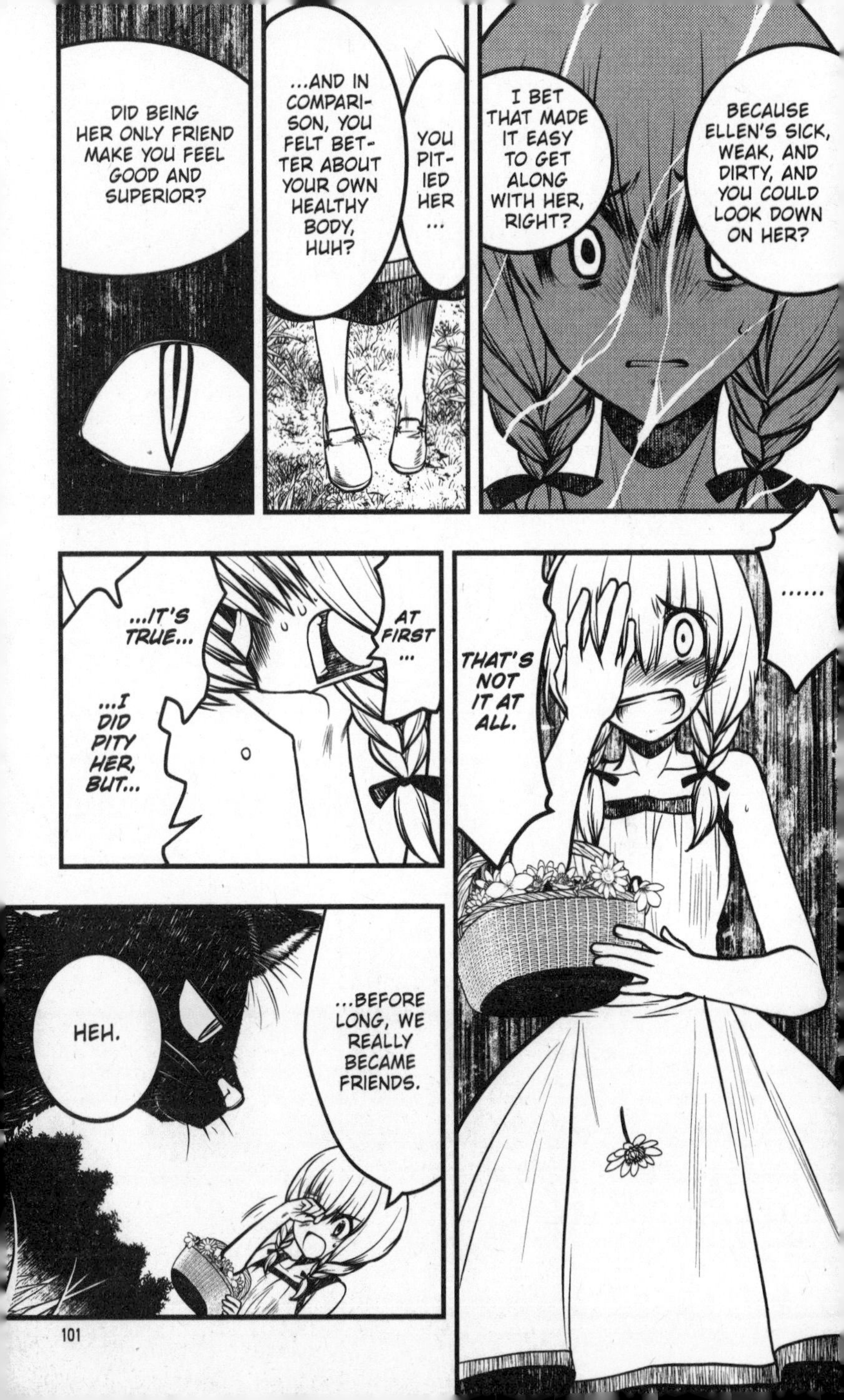
BECAUSE ELLEN'S SICK, WEAK, AND DIRTY, AND YOU COULD LOOK DOWN ON HER?
I BET THAT MADE IT EASY TO GET ALONG WITH HER, RIGHT?
YOU PITIED HER...
...AND IN COMPARISON, YOU FELT BETTER ABOUT YOUR OWN HEALTHY BODY, HUH?
DID BEING HER ONLY FRIEND MAKE YOU FEEL GOOD AND SUPERIOR?
......
THAT'S NOT IT AT ALL.
AT FIRST...
...IT'S TRUE...
...I DID PITY HER, BUT...
...BEFORE LONG, WE REALLY BECAME FRIENDS.
HEH.

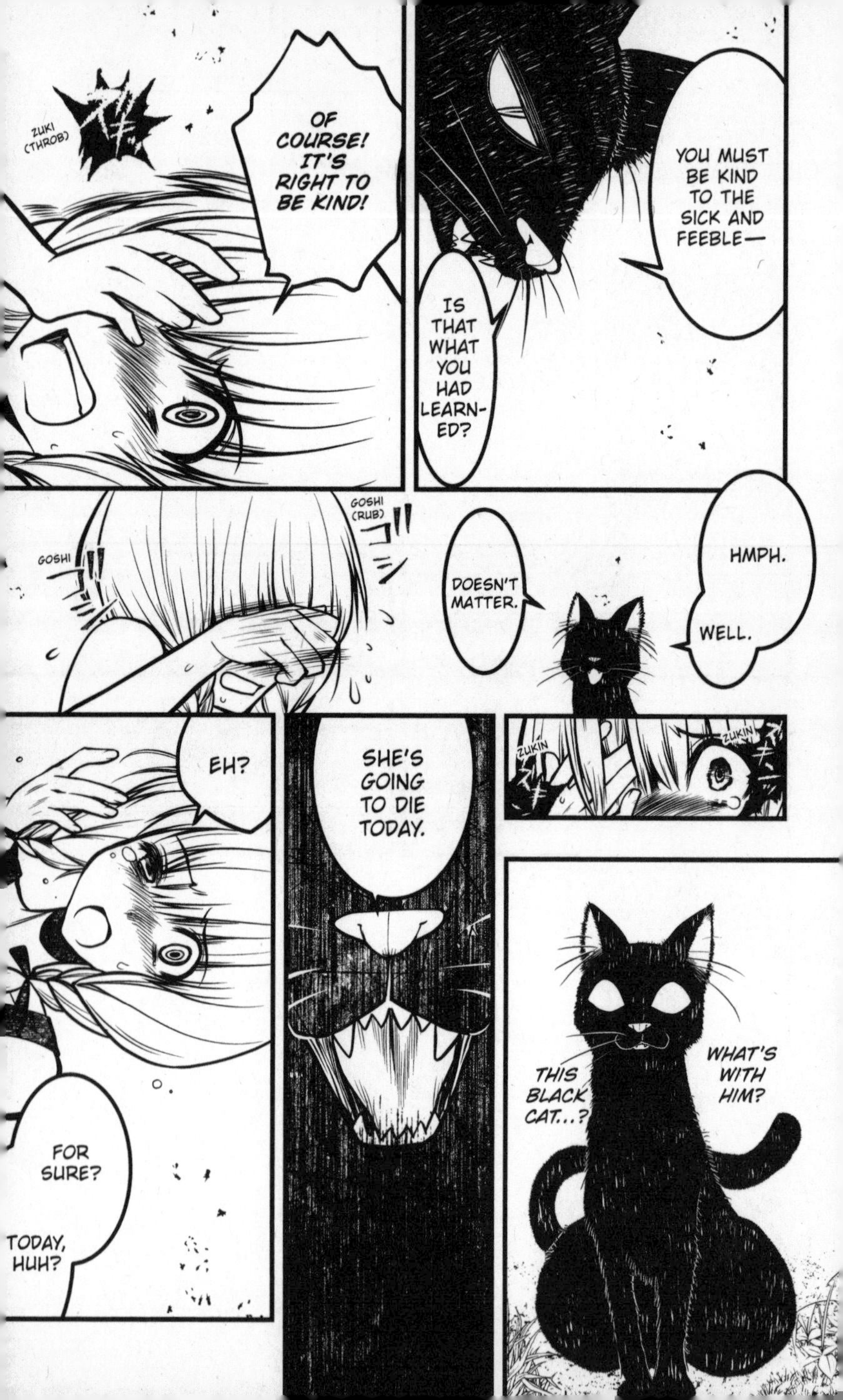
YOU MUST BE KIND TO THE SICK AND FEEBLE—
IS THAT WHAT YOU HAD LEARNED?
OF COURSE! IT'S RIGHT TO BE KIND!
ZUKI (THROB)
HMPH. WELL.
DOESN'T MATTER.
GOSHI (RUB)
GOSHI
ZUKIN
ZUKIN
WHAT'S WITH HIM?
THIS BLACK CAT...?
SHE'S GOING TO DIE TODAY.
EH?
FOR SURE?
TODAY, HUH?

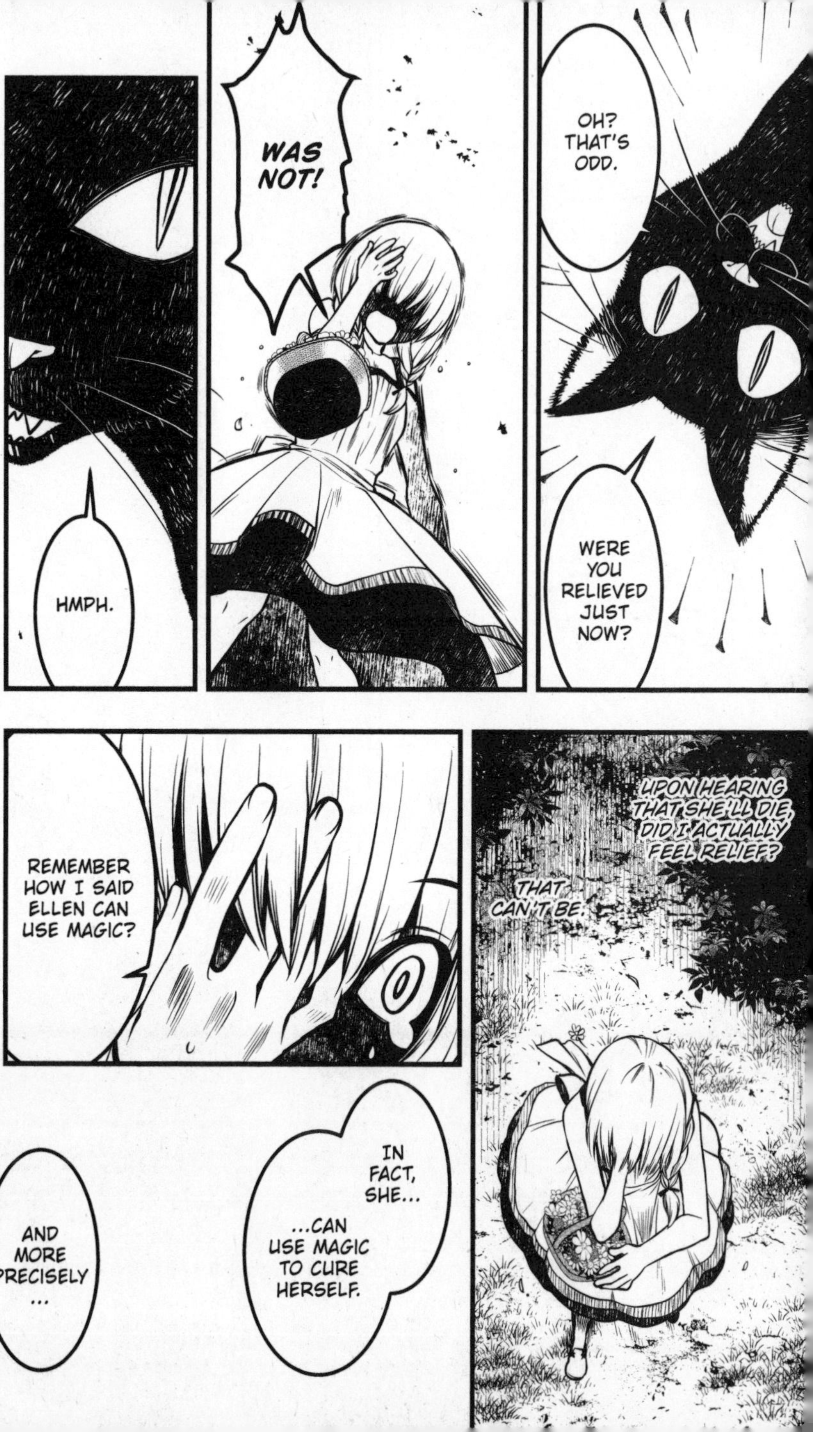
OH? THAT'S ODD.
WERE YOU RELIEVED JUST NOW?
WAS NOT!
HMPH.
UPON HEARING THAT SHE'LL DIE, DID I ACTUALLY FEEL RELIEF?
THAT CAN'T BE.
REMEMBER HOW I SAID ELLEN CAN USE MAGIC?
IN FACT, SHE...
...CAN USE MAGIC TO CURE HERSELF.
AND MORE PRECISELY ...

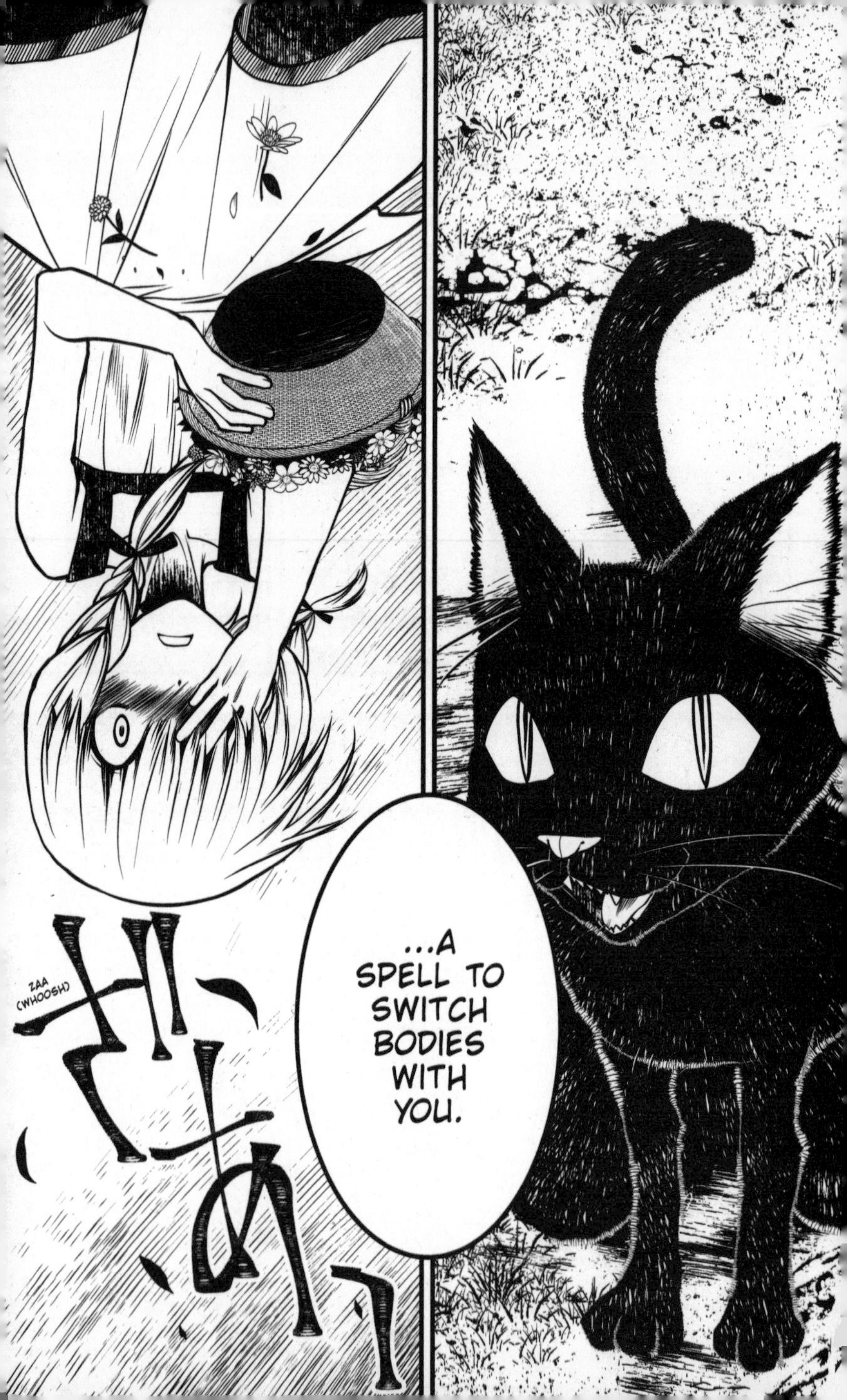
...A SPELL TO SWITCH BODIES WITH YOU.
ZAA (WHOOSH)

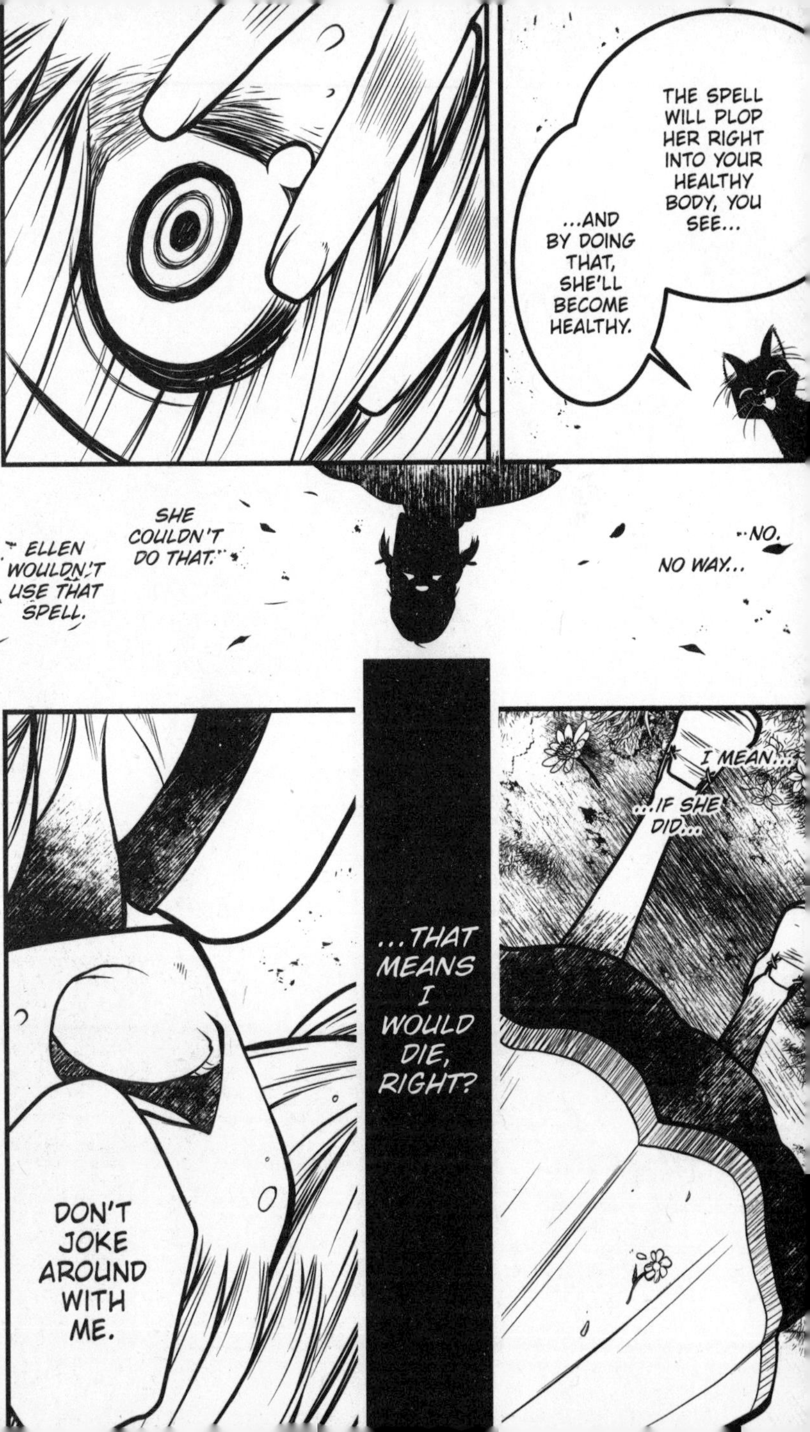
THE SPELL WILL PLOP HER RIGHT INTO YOUR HEALTHY BODY, YOU SEE...
...AND BY DOING THAT, SHE'LL BECOME HEALTHY.
...NO.
NO WAY...
SHE COULDN'T DO THAT.
ELLEN WOULDN'T USE THAT SPELL.
I MEAN...
...IF SHE DID...
...THAT MEANS I WOULD DIE, RIGHT?
DON'T JOKE AROUND WITH ME.

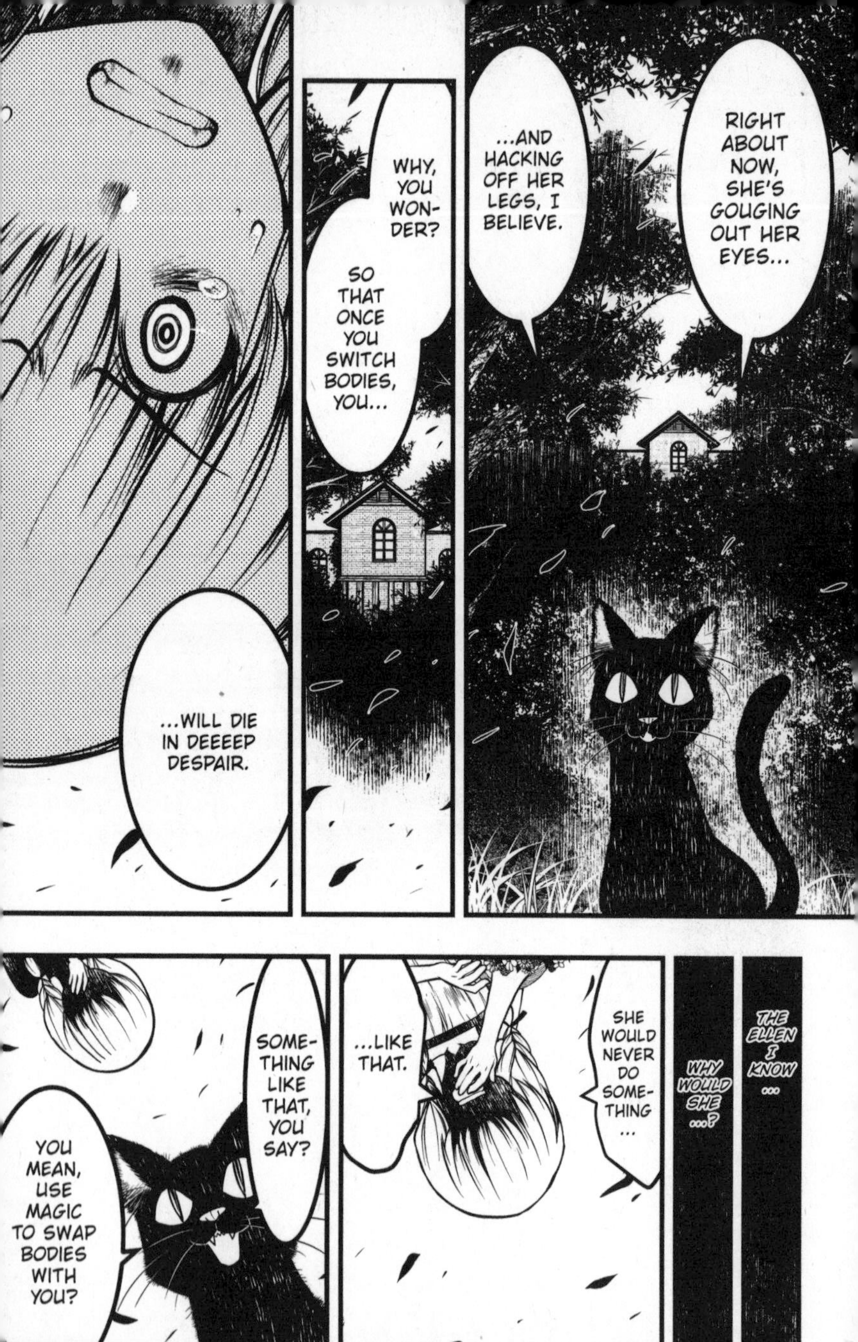
RIGHT ABOUT NOW, SHE'S GOUGING OUT HER EYES...
...AND HACKING OFF HER LEGS, I BELIEVE.
WHY, YOU WON-DER?
SO THAT ONCE YOU SWITCH BODIES, YOU...
...WILL DIE IN DEEEEP DESPAIR.
THE ELLEN I KNOW...
WHY WOULD SHE...?
SHE WOULD NEVER DO SOME-THING...
...LIKE THAT.
SOME-THING LIKE THAT, YOU SAY?
YOU MEAN, USE MAGIC TO SWAP BODIES WITH YOU?

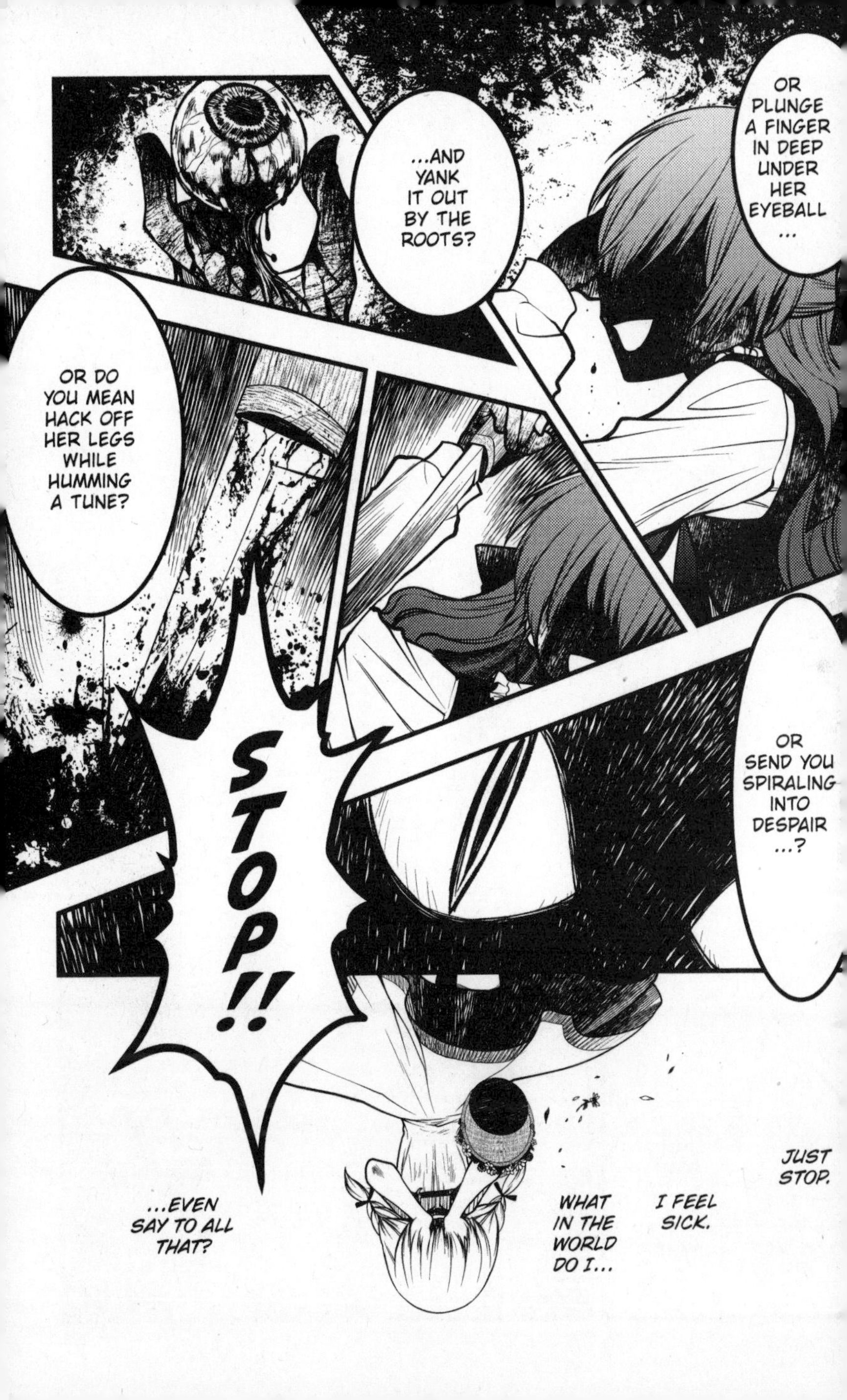
OR PLUNGE A FINGER IN DEEP UNDER HER EYEBALL...
...AND YANK IT OUT BY THE ROOTS?
OR DO YOU MEAN HACK OFF HER LEGS WHILE HUMMING A TUNE?
OR SEND YOU SPIRALING INTO DESPAIR...?
STOP!!
JUST STOP.
I FEEL SICK.
WHAT IN THE WORLD DO I...
...EVEN SAY TO ALL THAT?

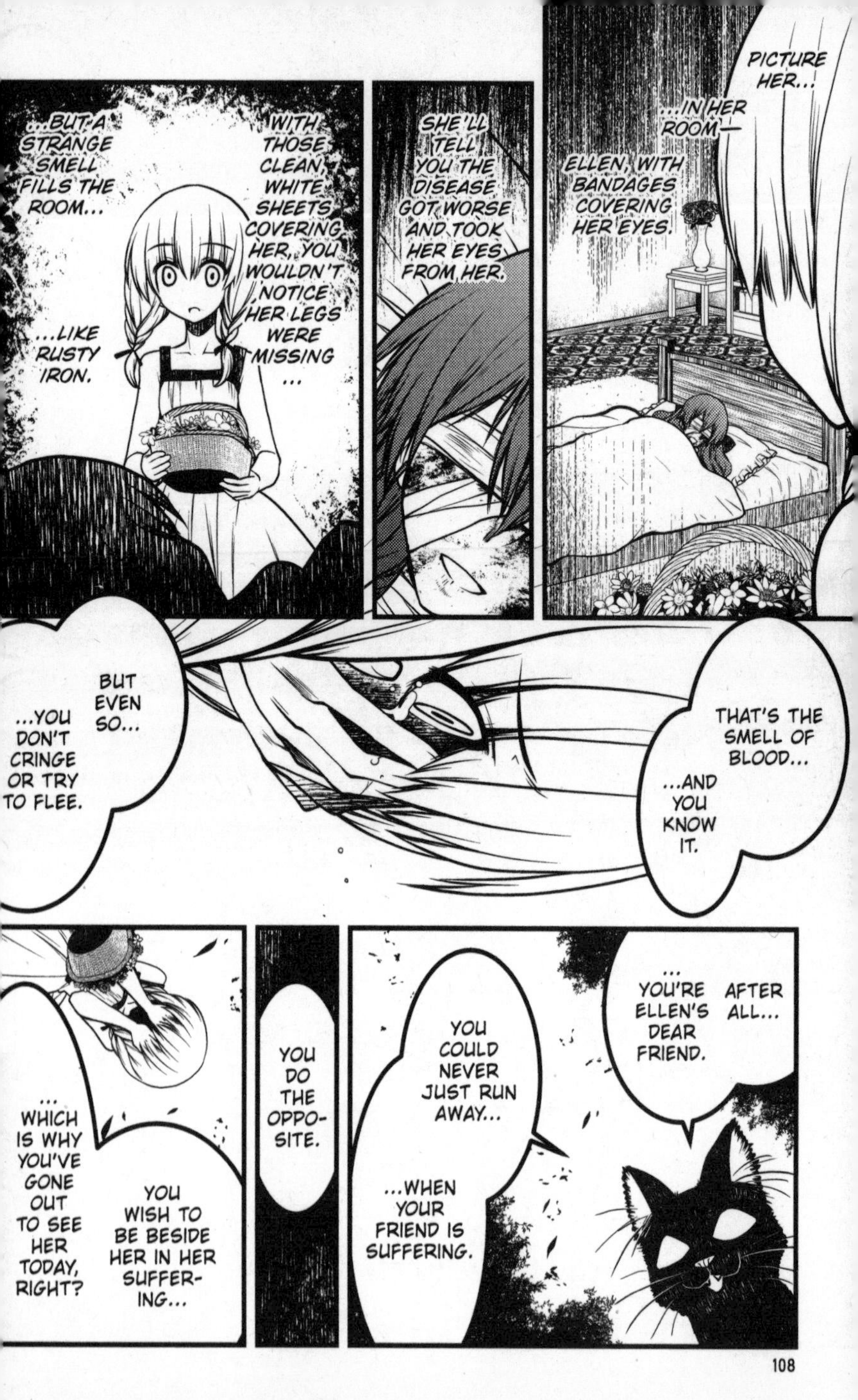
PICTURE HER...
...IN HER ROOM—
ELLEN, WITH BANDAGES COVERING HER EYES.
SHE'LL TELL YOU THE DISEASE GOT WORSE AND TOOK HER EYES FROM HER.
WITH THOSE CLEAN, WHITE SHEETS COVERING HER, YOU WOULDN'T NOTICE HER LEGS WERE MISSING...
...BUT A STRANGE SMELL FILLS THE ROOM...
...LIKE RUSTY IRON.
THAT'S THE SMELL OF BLOOD...
...AND YOU KNOW IT.
BUT EVEN SO...
...YOU DON'T CRINGE OR TRY TO FLEE.
AFTER ALL...
...YOU'RE ELLEN'S DEAR FRIEND.
YOU COULD NEVER JUST RUN AWAY...
...WHEN YOUR FRIEND IS SUFFERING.
YOU DO THE OPPOSITE.
YOU WISH TO BE BESIDE HER IN HER SUFFERING...
...WHICH IS WHY YOU'VE GONE OUT TO SEE HER TODAY, RIGHT?

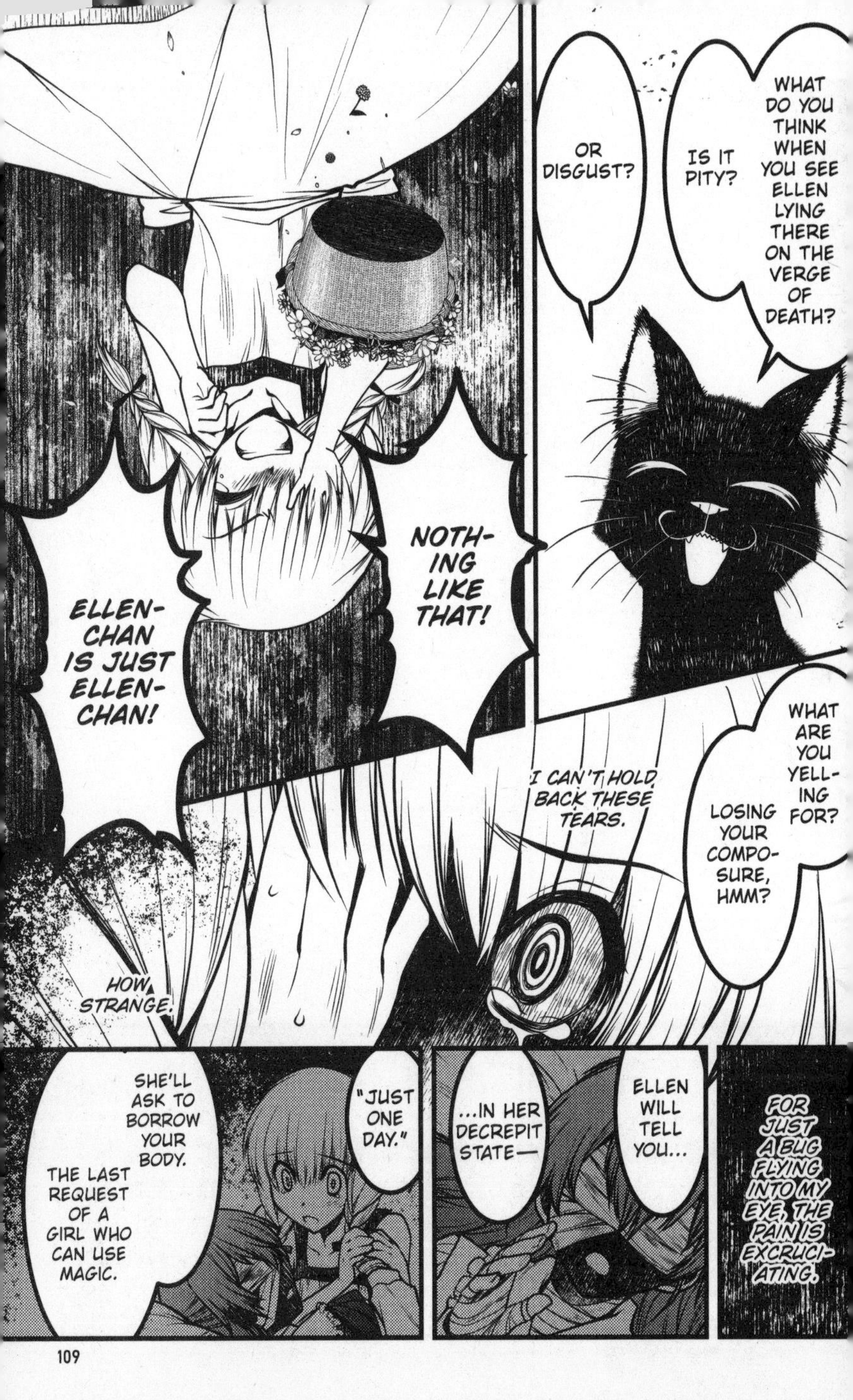
WHAT DO YOU THINK WHEN YOU SEE ELLEN LYING THERE ON THE VERGE OF DEATH?
IS IT PITY?
OR DISGUST?
NOTHING LIKE THAT!
ELLEN-CHAN IS JUST ELLEN-CHAN!
WHAT ARE YOU YELLING FOR?
LOSING YOUR COMPOSURE, HMM?
I CAN'T HOLD BACK THESE TEARS.
HOW STRANGE.
FOR JUST A BUG FLYING INTO MY EYE, THE PAIN IS EXCRUCIATING.
ELLEN WILL TELL YOU...
...IN HER DECREPIT STATE—
"JUST ONE DAY."
SHE'LL ASK TO BORROW YOUR BODY.
THE LAST REQUEST OF A GIRL WHO CAN USE MAGIC.

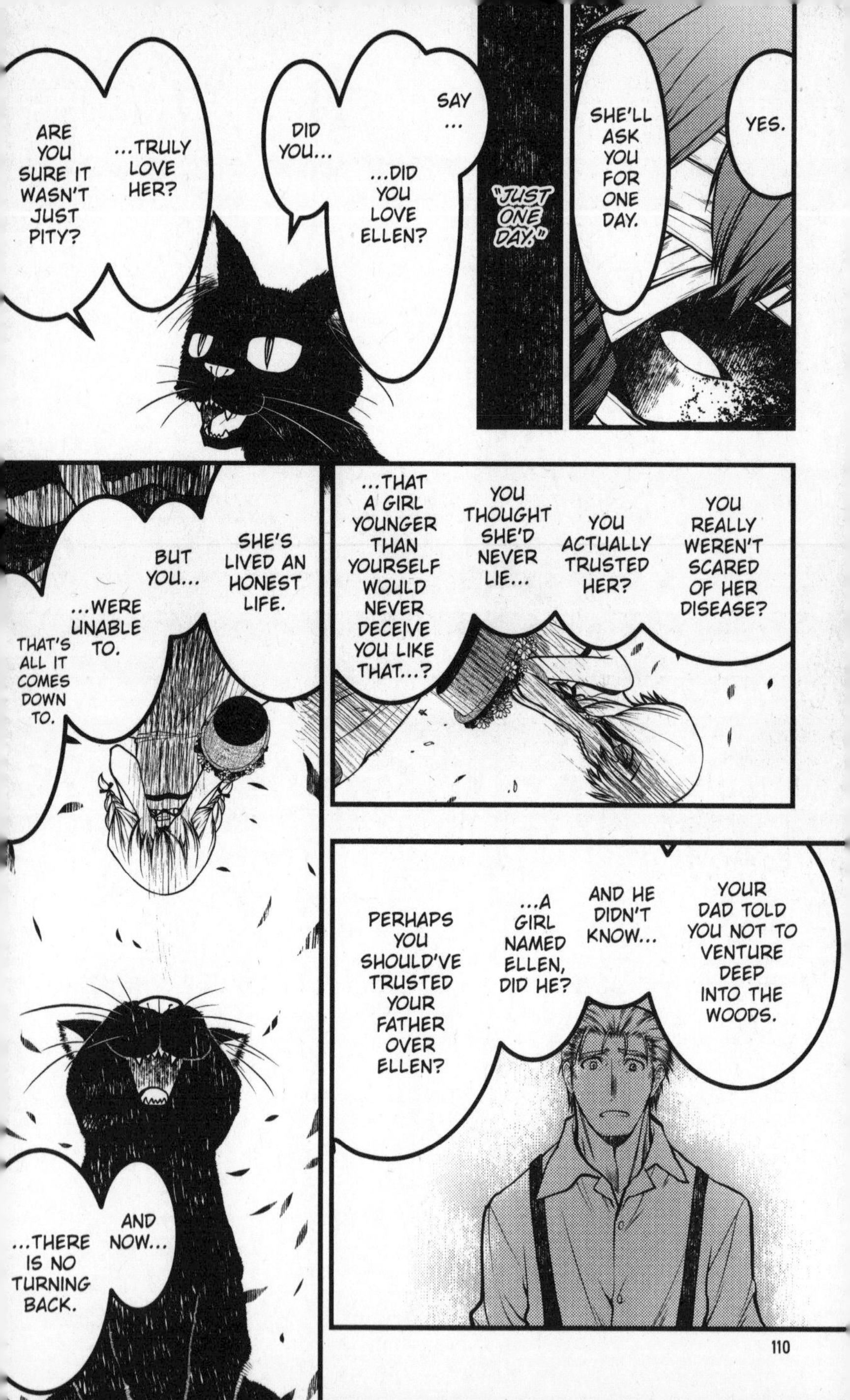
YES.
SHE'LL ASK YOU FOR ONE DAY.
"JUST ONE DAY."
SAY…
DID YOU…
…DID YOU LOVE ELLEN?
…TRULY LOVE HER?
ARE YOU SURE IT WASN'T JUST PITY?
YOU REALLY WEREN'T SCARED OF HER DISEASE?
YOU ACTUALLY TRUSTED HER?
YOU THOUGHT SHE'D NEVER LIE…
…THAT A GIRL YOUNGER THAN YOURSELF WOULD NEVER DECEIVE YOU LIKE THAT…?
YOUR DAD TOLD YOU NOT TO VENTURE DEEP INTO THE WOODS.
AND HE DIDN'T KNOW…
…A GIRL NAMED ELLEN, DID HE?
PERHAPS YOU SHOULD'VE TRUSTED YOUR FATHER OVER ELLEN?
SHE'S LIVED AN HONEST LIFE.
BUT YOU…
…WERE UNABLE TO.
THAT'S ALL IT COMES DOWN TO.
AND NOW…
…THERE IS NO TURNING BACK.

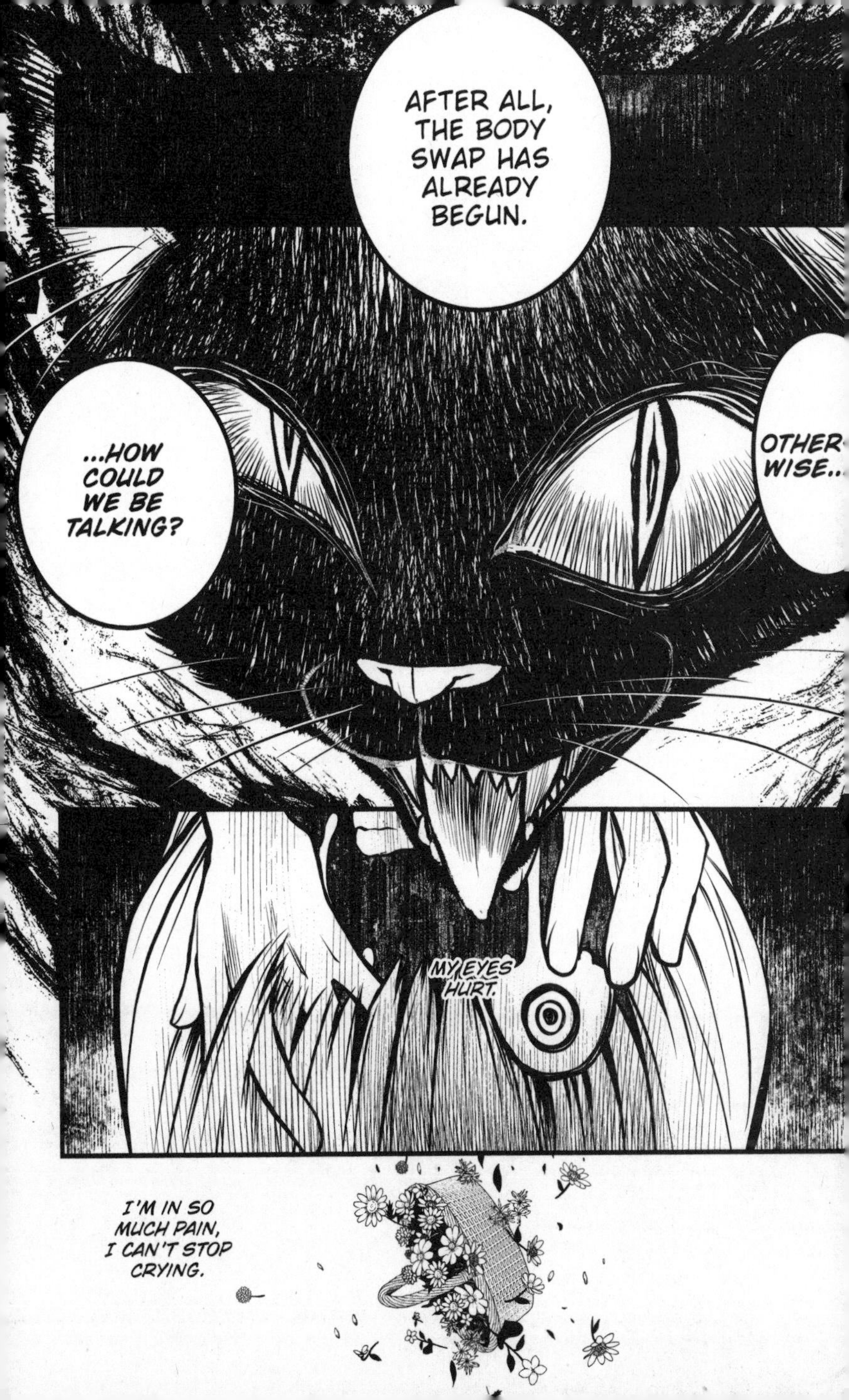
AFTER ALL, THE BODY SWAP HAS ALREADY BEGUN.
OTHERWISE...
...HOW COULD WE BE TALKING?
MY EYES HURT.
I'M IN SO MUCH PAIN, I CAN'T STOP CRYING.

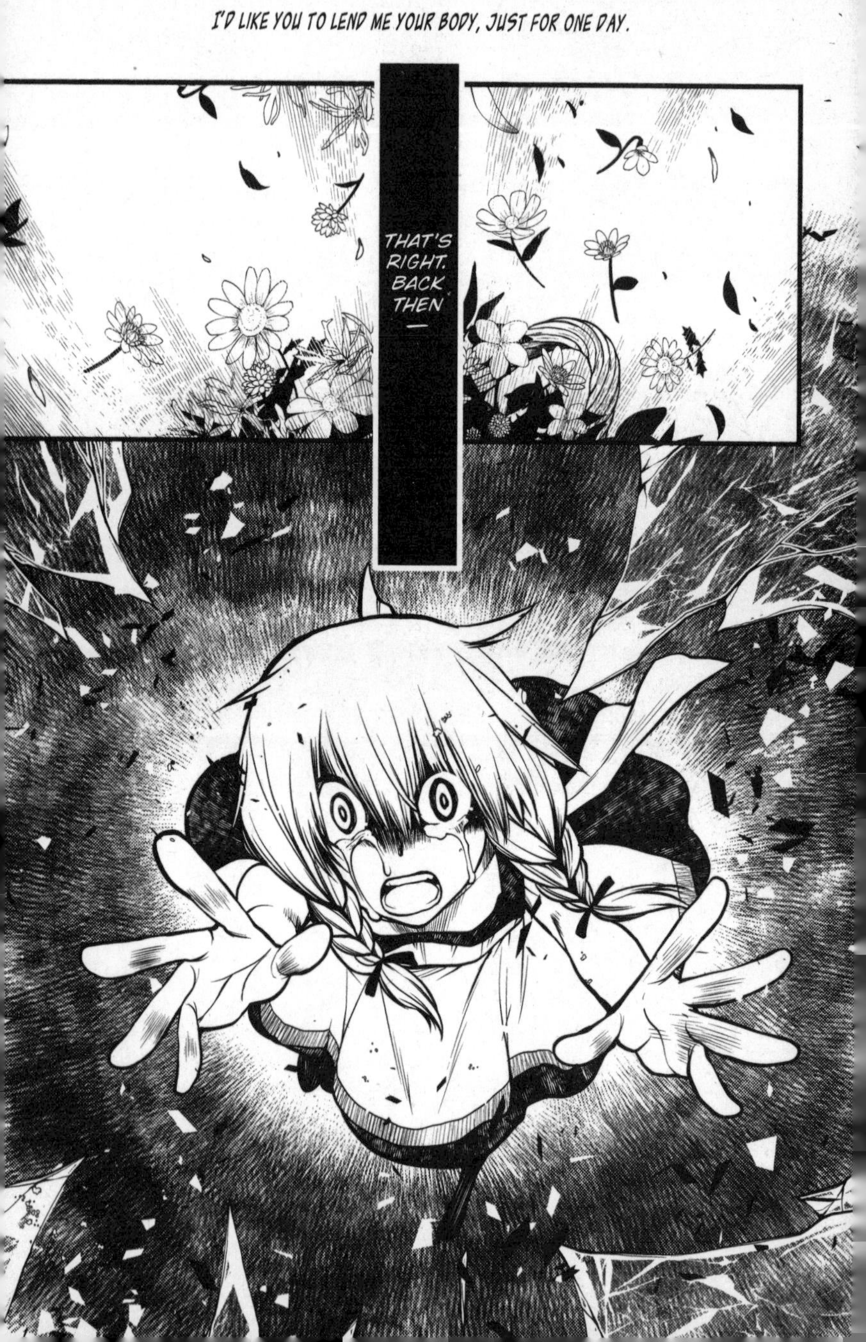
I'D LIKE YOU TO LEND ME YOUR BODY, JUST FOR ONE DAY.
THAT'S RIGHT. BACK THEN—

THE WITCH'S HOUSE

The Diary of Ellen

THE
WITCH'S
HOUSE

The Diary of Ellen

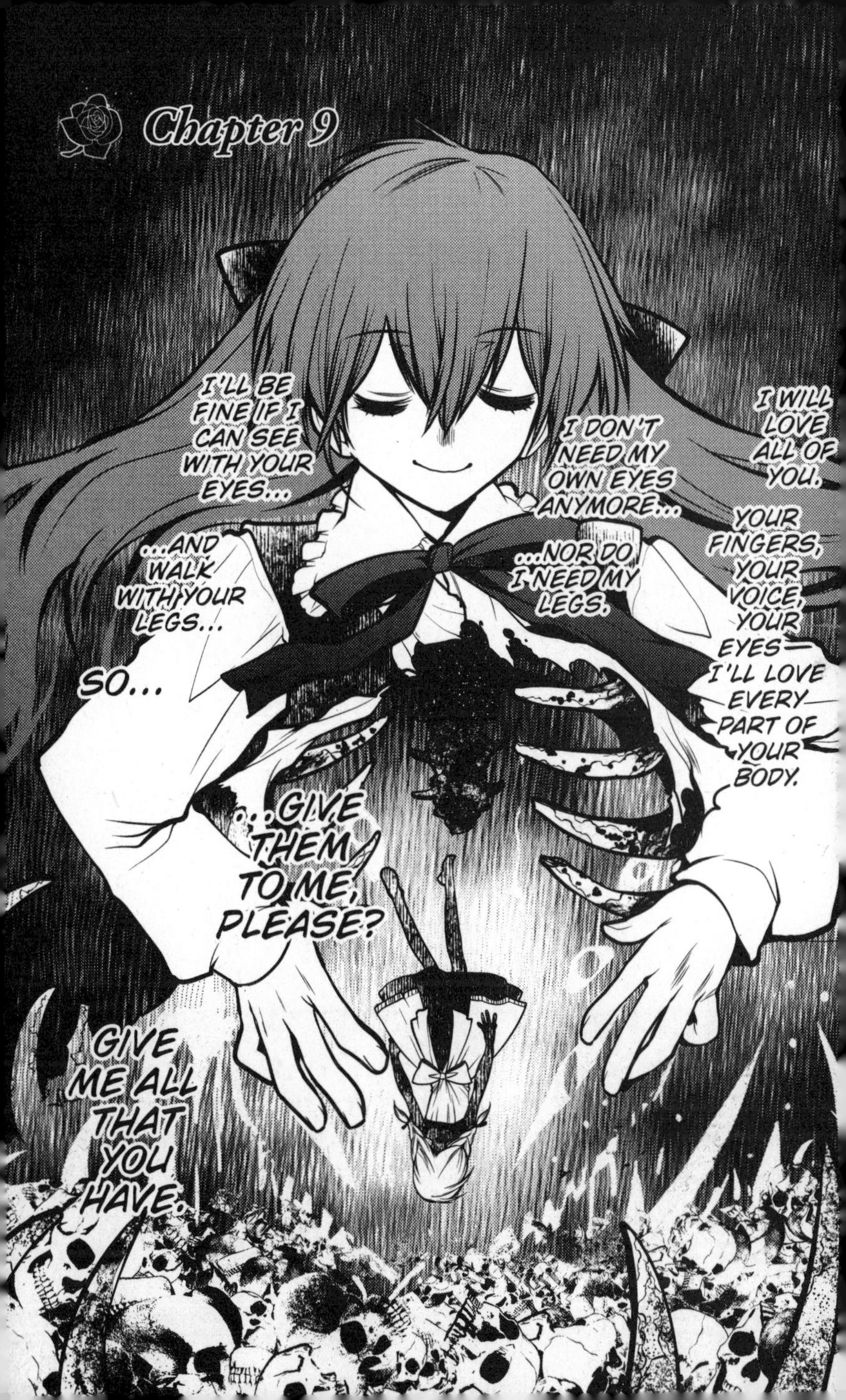
Chapter 9
I WILL LOVE ALL OF YOU.
YOUR FINGERS, YOUR VOICE, YOUR EYES— I'LL LOVE EVERY PART OF YOUR BODY.
I DON'T NEED MY OWN EYES ANYMORE...
...NOR DO I NEED MY LEGS.
I'LL BE FINE IF I CAN SEE WITH YOUR EYES...
...AND WALK WITH YOUR LEGS...
SO...
...GIVE THEM TO ME, PLEASE?
GIVE ME ALL THAT YOU HAVE.

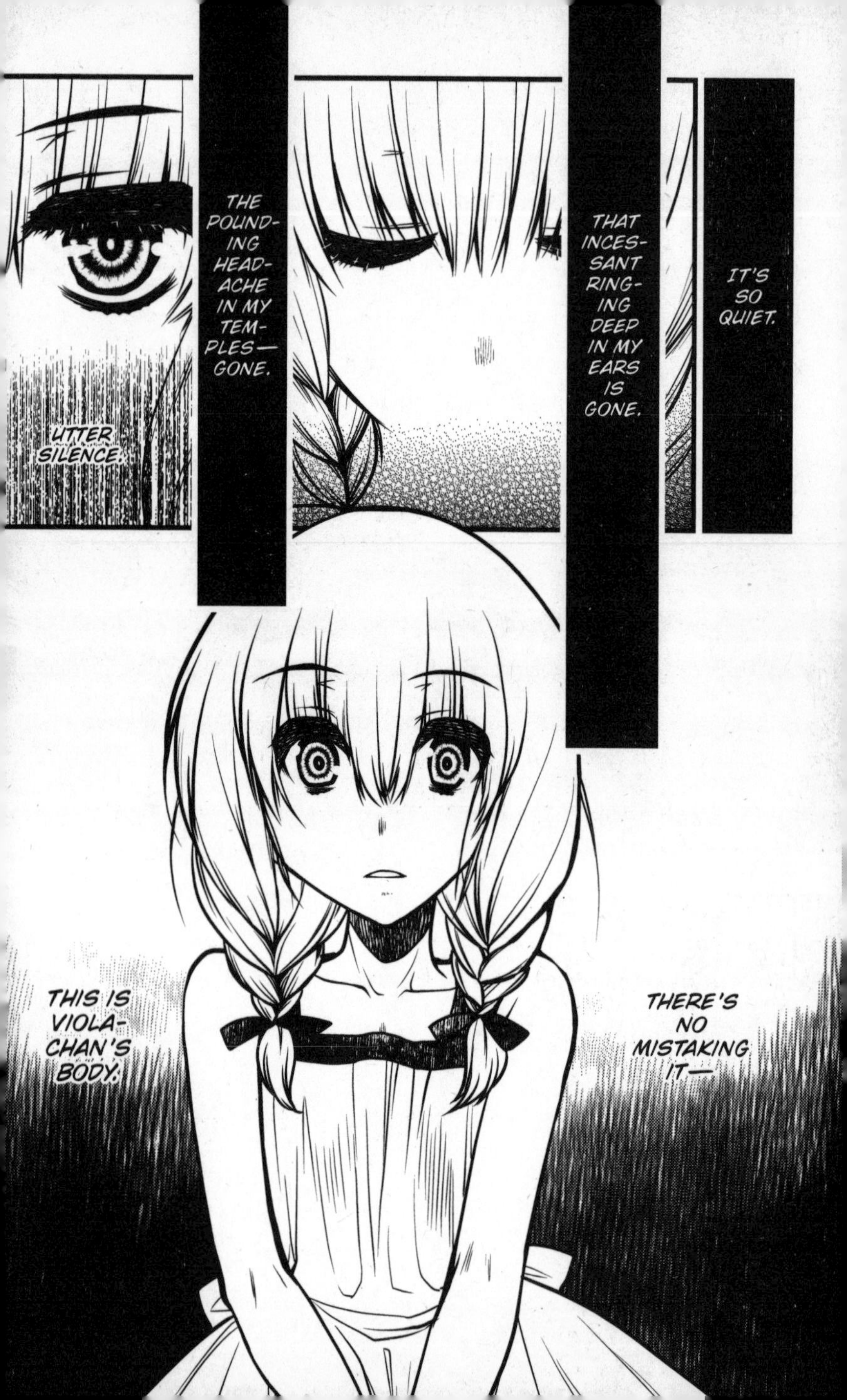
IT'S SO QUIET.
THAT INCESSANT RINGING DEEP IN MY EARS IS GONE.
THE POUNDING HEADACHE IN MY TEMPLES—GONE.
UTTER SILENCE.
THERE'S NO MISTAKING IT—
THIS IS VIOLA-CHAN'S BODY.

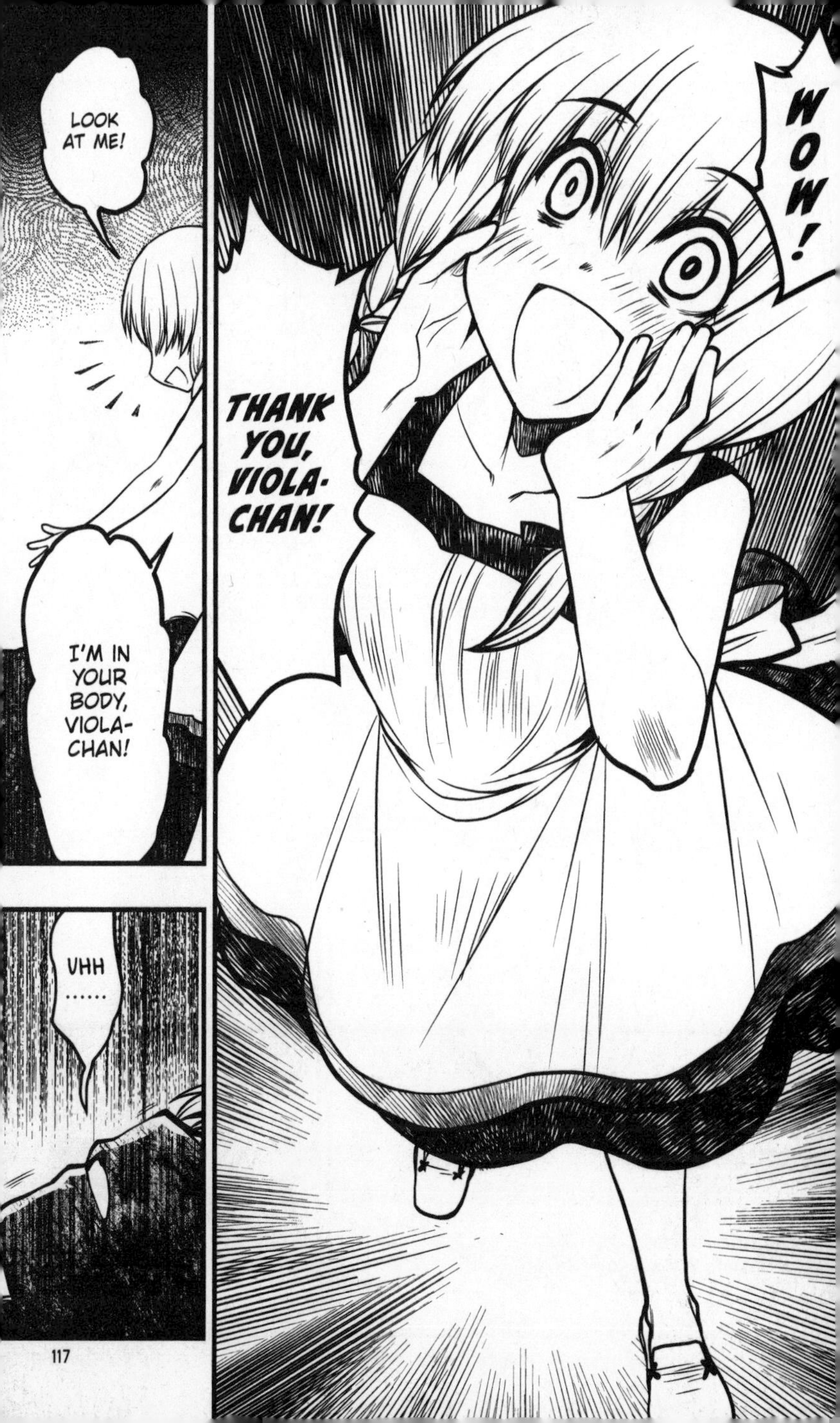
WOW!
THANK YOU, VIOLA-CHAN!
LOOK AT ME!
I'M IN YOUR BODY, VIOLA-CHAN!
UHH ....

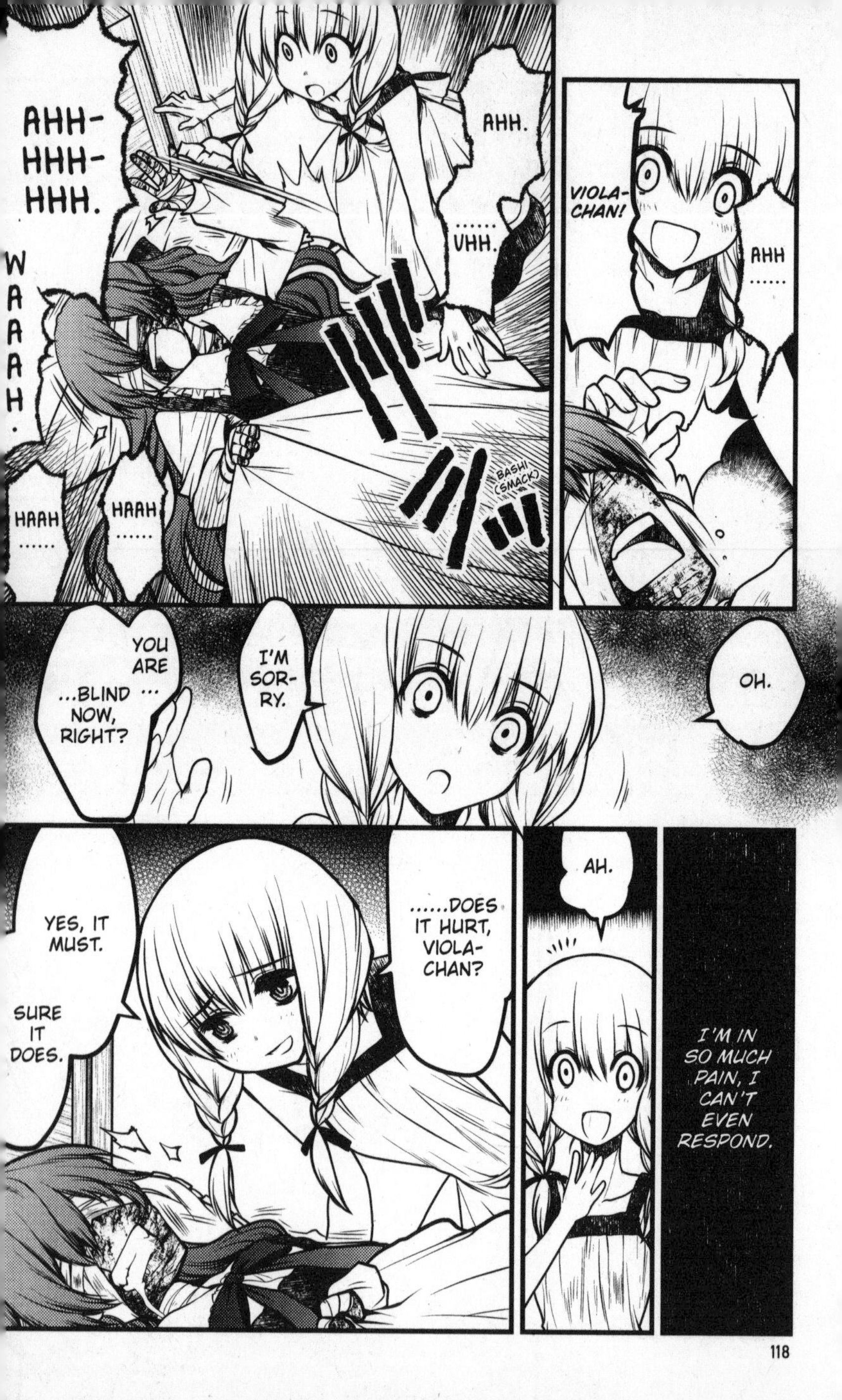
AHH ......
VIOLA-CHAN!
AHH.
...... UHH.
BASHI (SMACK)
AHH-HHH-HHH.
WAAAAH.
HAAH ......
HAAH ......
OH.
I'M SOR-RY.
YOU ARE ... ...BLIND NOW, RIGHT?
I'M IN SO MUCH PAIN, I CAN'T EVEN RESPOND.
AH.
......DOES IT HURT, VIOLA-CHAN?
YES, IT MUST.
SURE IT DOES.

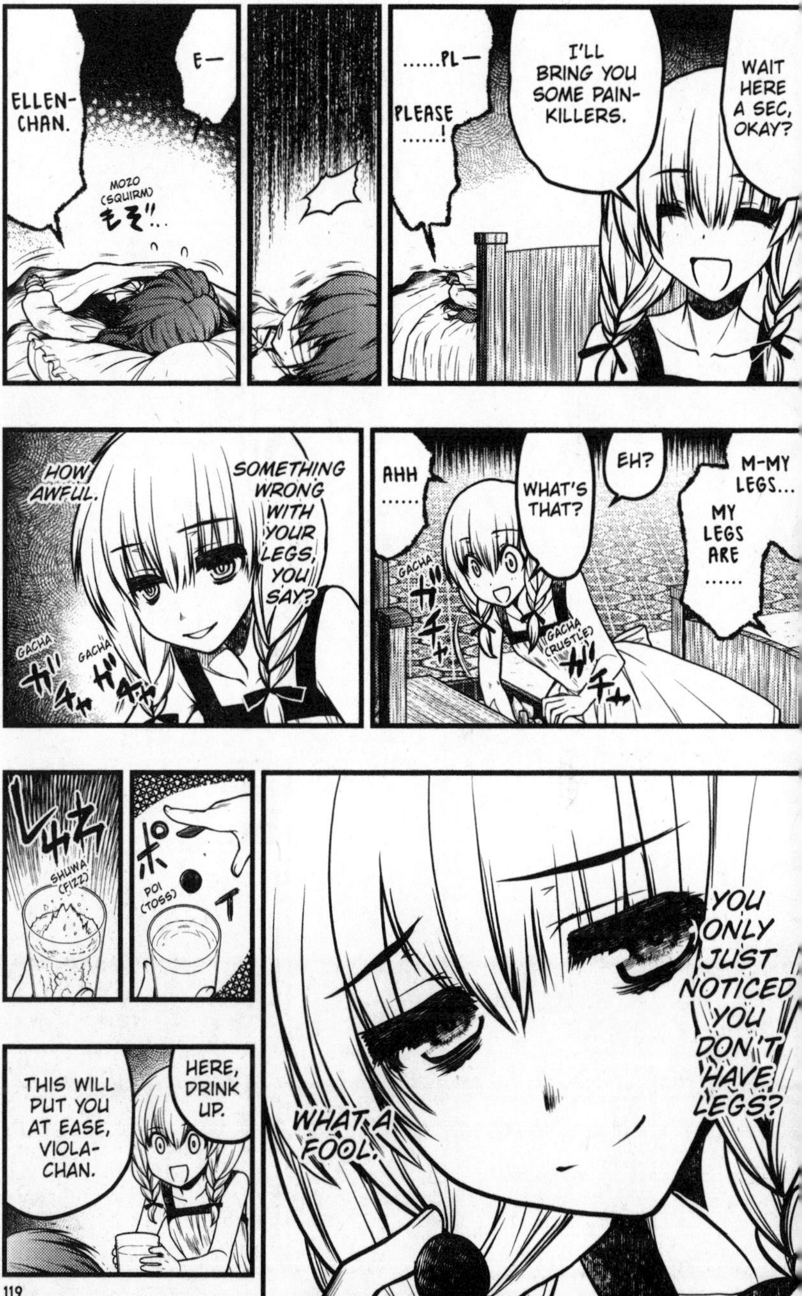

WAIT HERE A SEC, OKAY?
I'LL BRING YOU SOME PAIN-KILLERS.
......PL—
PLEASE ......!
E—
ELLEN-CHAN.
MOZO (SQUIRM)
もぞ‼...
M-MY LEGS...
MY LEGS ARE ......
EH?
WHAT'S THAT?
AHH ......
GACHA
GACHA (RUSTLE)
SOMETHING WRONG WITH YOUR LEGS, YOU SAY?
HOW AWFUL.
GACHA
GACHA
YOU ONLY JUST NOTICED YOU DON'T HAVE LEGS?
WHAT A FOOL.
POI (TOSS)
ポイ
SHUWA (FIZZ)
しゅわ
HERE, DRINK UP.
THIS WILL PUT YOU AT EASE, VIOLA-CHAN.

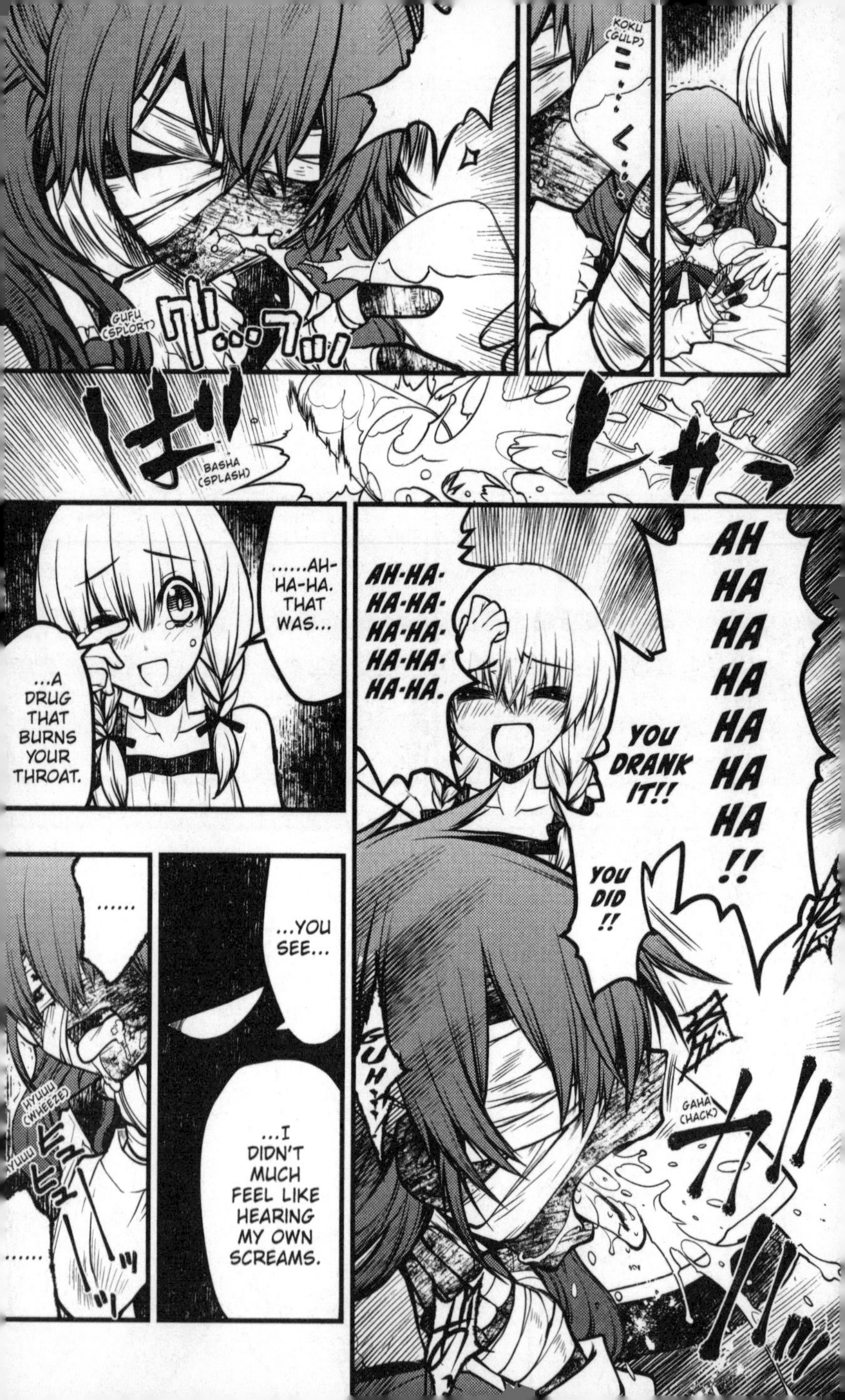
KOKU (GULP)
GUFU (SPLORT)
BASHA (SPLASH)
AH HA HA HA HA HA HA HA HA HA!!
YOU DRANK IT!!
AH-HA-HA-HA-HA-HA-HA-HA-HA-HA-HA.
YOU DID!!
GAHA (HACK)
......AH-HA-HA. THAT WAS...
...A DRUG THAT BURNS YOUR THROAT.
...YOU SEE...
...I DIDN'T MUCH FEEL LIKE HEARING MY OWN SCREAMS.
......
HYUUU (WHEEZE)
......

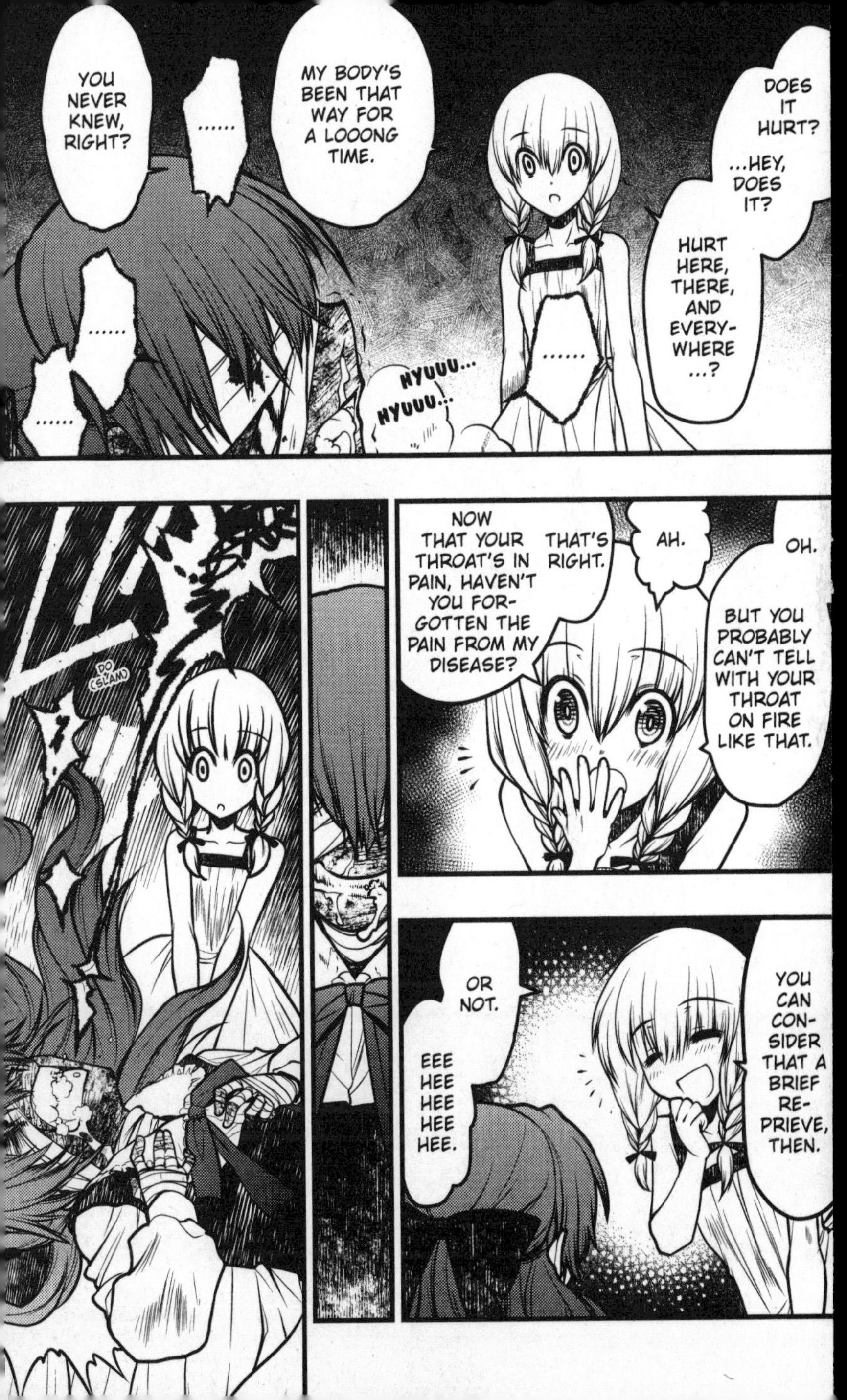
DOES IT HURT?
...HEY, DOES IT?
HURT HERE, THERE, AND EVERY-WHERE ...?
......
HYUUU... HYUUU...
MY BODY'S BEEN THAT WAY FOR A LOOONG TIME.
......
YOU NEVER KNEW, RIGHT?
......
......
OH.
BUT YOU PROBABLY CAN'T TELL WITH YOUR THROAT ON FIRE LIKE THAT.
AH.
THAT'S RIGHT.
NOW THAT YOUR THROAT'S IN PAIN, HAVEN'T YOU FOR-GOTTEN THE PAIN FROM MY DISEASE?
YOU CAN CON-SIDER THAT A BRIEF RE-PRIEVE, THEN.
OR NOT.
EEE HEE HEE HEE HEE.
DO (SLAM)

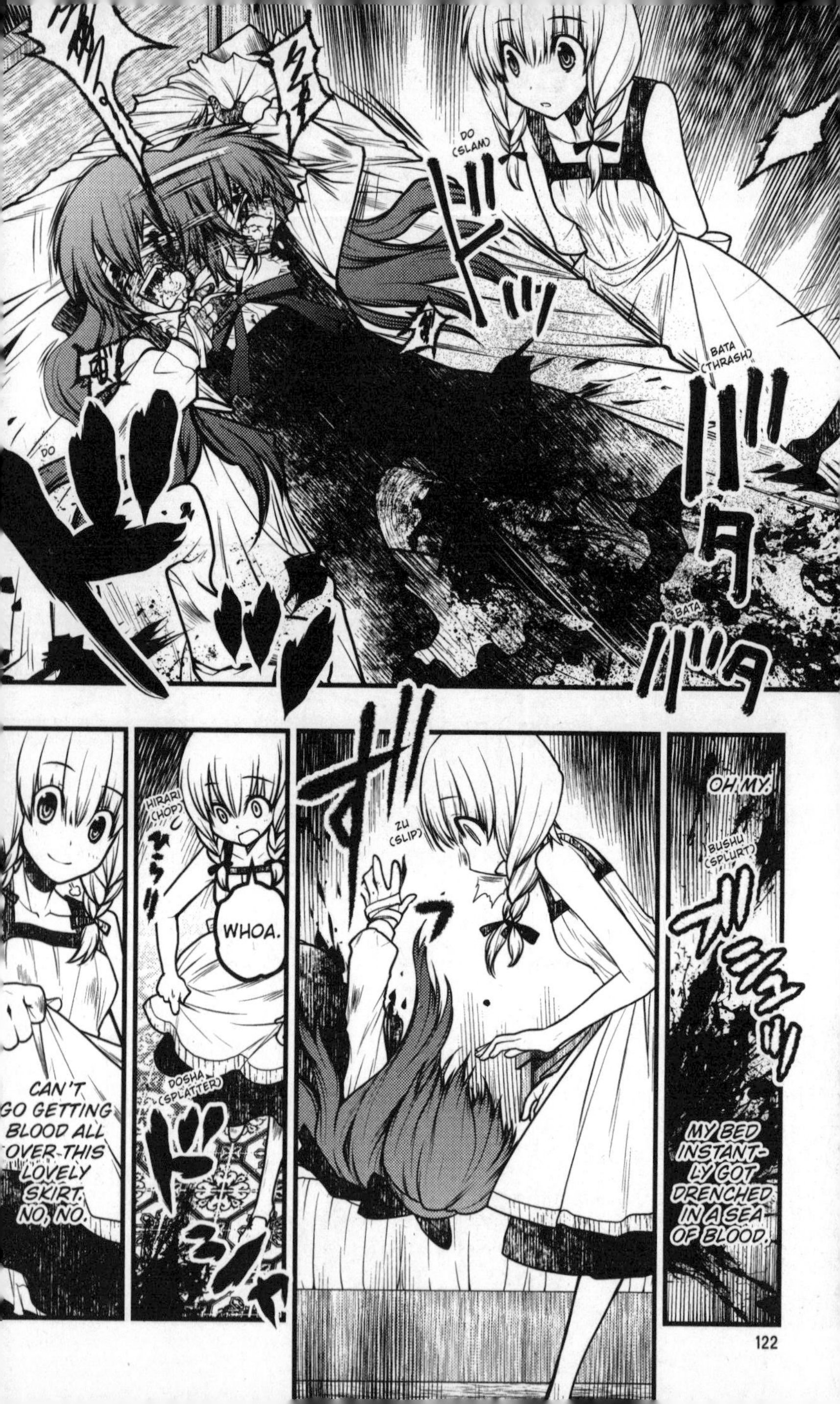
DO (SLAM)
BATA (THRASH)
BATA
DO
OH MY.
BUSHU (SPLURT)
MY BED INSTANT-LY GOT DRENCHED IN A SEA OF BLOOD.
ZU (SLIP)
HIRARI (HOP)
WHOA.
DOSHA (SPLATTER)
CAN'T GO GETTING BLOOD ALL OVER THIS LOVELY SKIRT. NO, NO.

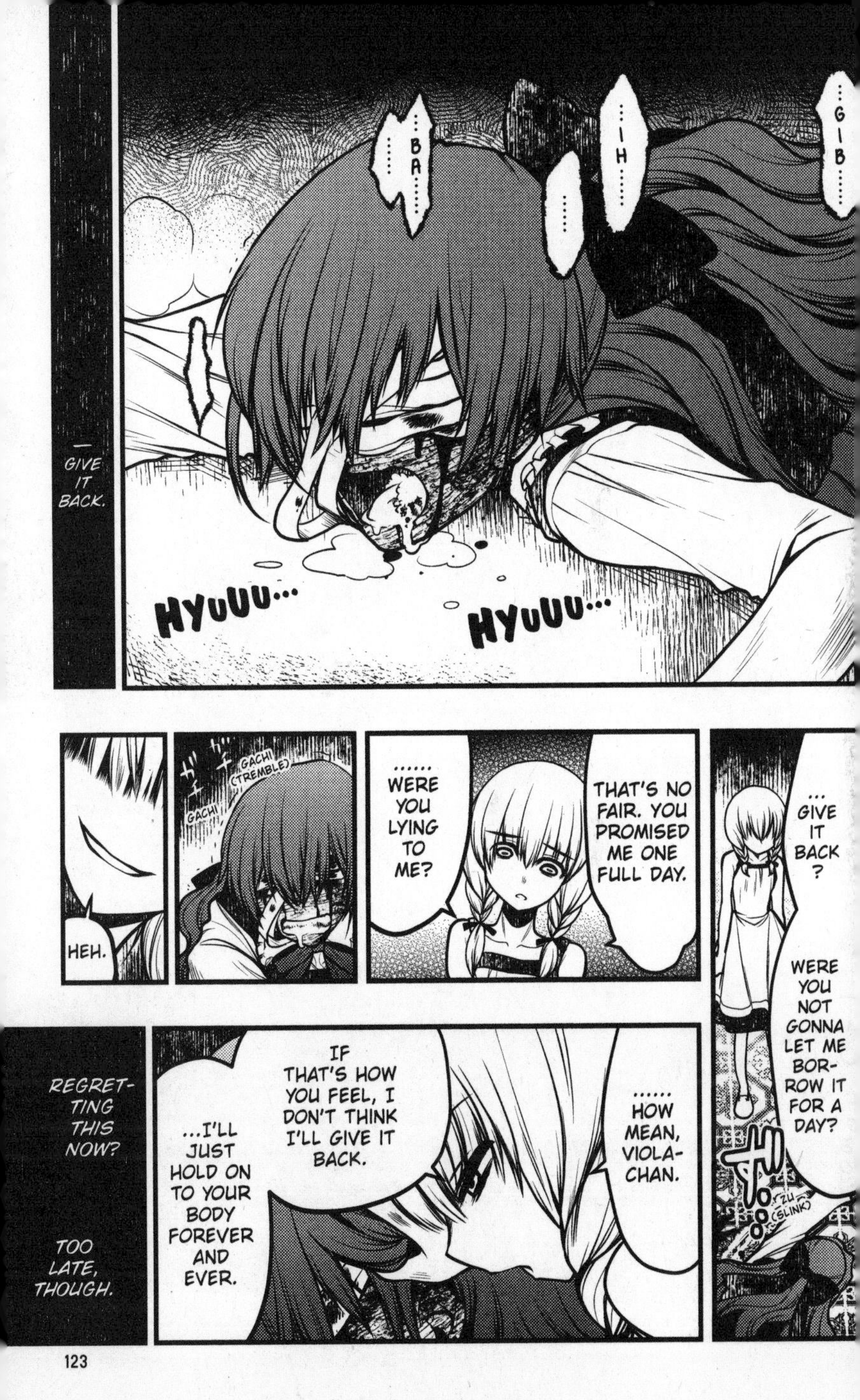
...GIB......
...IH......
......
......BA......
—GIVE IT BACK.
HYUUU...
HYUUU...
...GIVE IT BACK?
WERE YOU NOT GONNA LET ME BORROW IT FOR A DAY?
ZU (SLINK)
THAT'S NO FAIR. YOU PROMISED ME ONE FULL DAY.
......WERE YOU LYING TO ME?
GACHI
GACHI (TREMBLE)
HEH.
......HOW MEAN, VIOLA-CHAN.
IF THAT'S HOW YOU FEEL, I DON'T THINK I'LL GIVE IT BACK.
...I'LL JUST HOLD ON TO YOUR BODY FOREVER AND EVER.
REGRETTING THIS NOW?
TOO LATE, THOUGH.

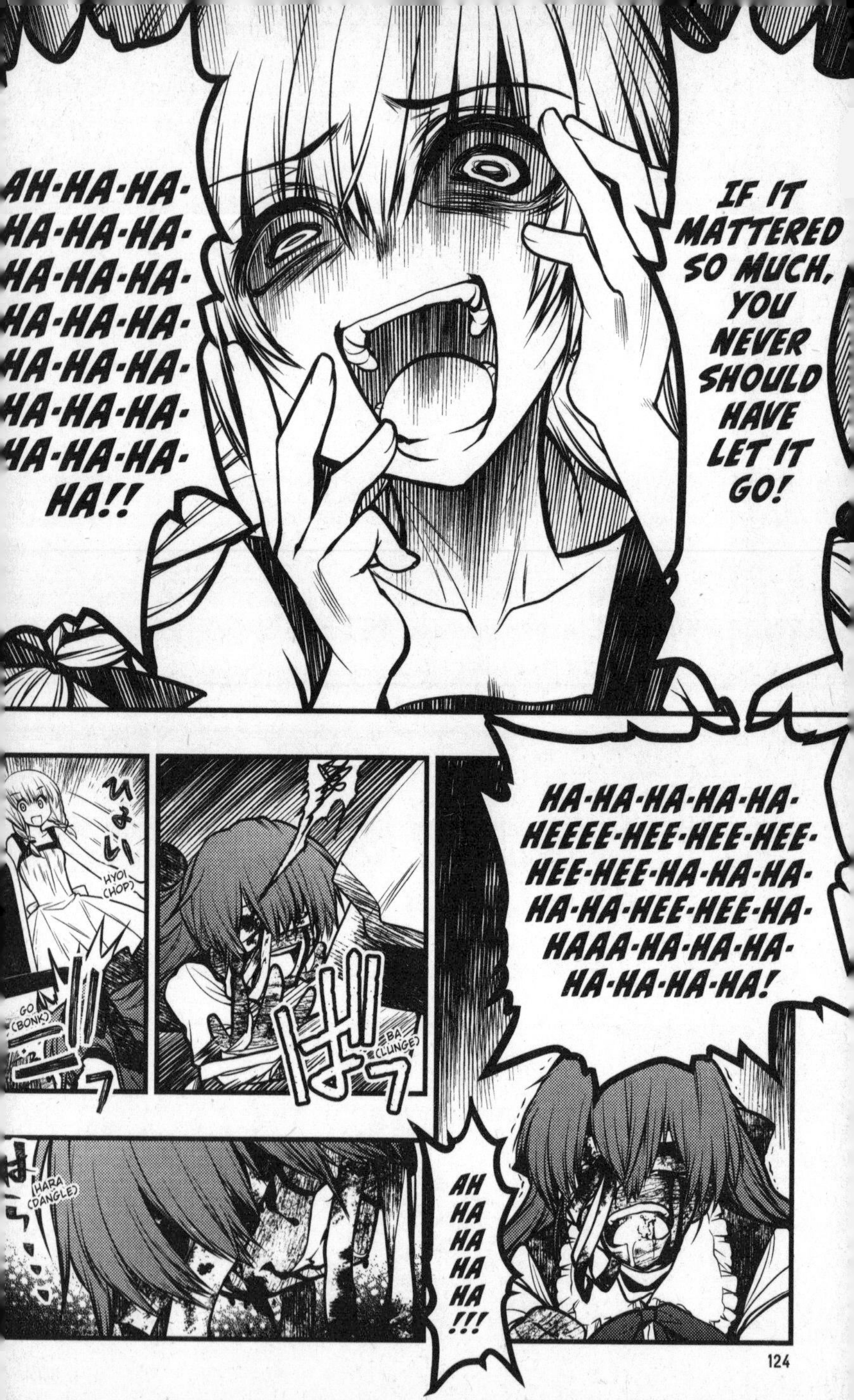
IF IT MATTERED SO MUCH, YOU NEVER SHOULD HAVE LET IT GO!
AH-HA-HA-HA-HA-HA-HA-HA-HA-HA-HA-HA-HA-HA-HA-HA-HA-HA-HA-HA-HA-HA!!
HA-HA-HA-HA-HA-HEEEE-HEE-HEE-HEE-HEE-HEE-HA-HA-HA-HA-HA-HEE-HEE-HA-HAAA-HA-HA-HA-HA-HA-HA-HA!
BA (LUNGE)
HYOI (HOP)
GO (BONK)
AH HA HA HA HA HA !!!
HARA (DANGLE)

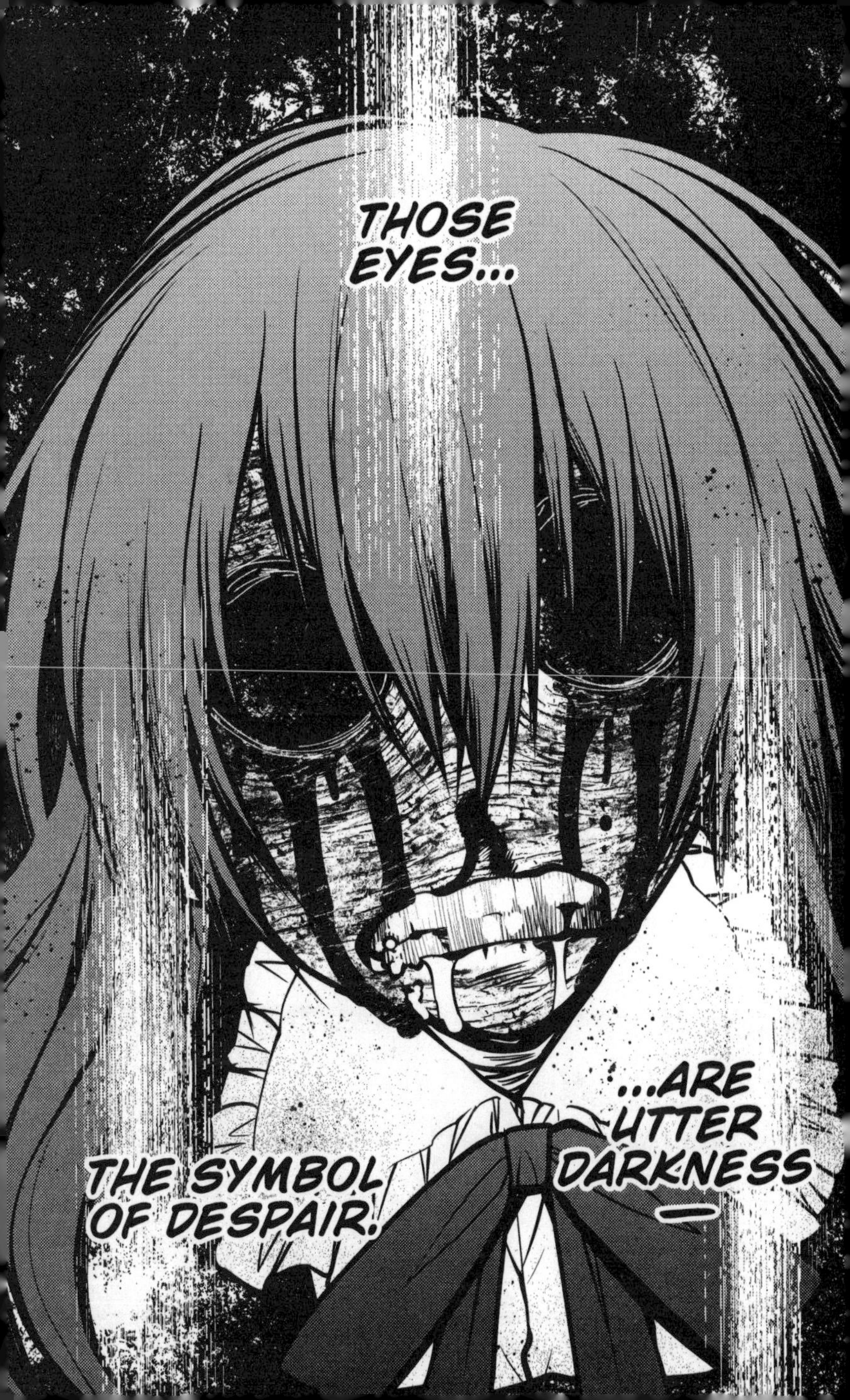
THOSE EYES...
...ARE UTTER DARKNESS —
THE SYMBOL OF DESPAIR!

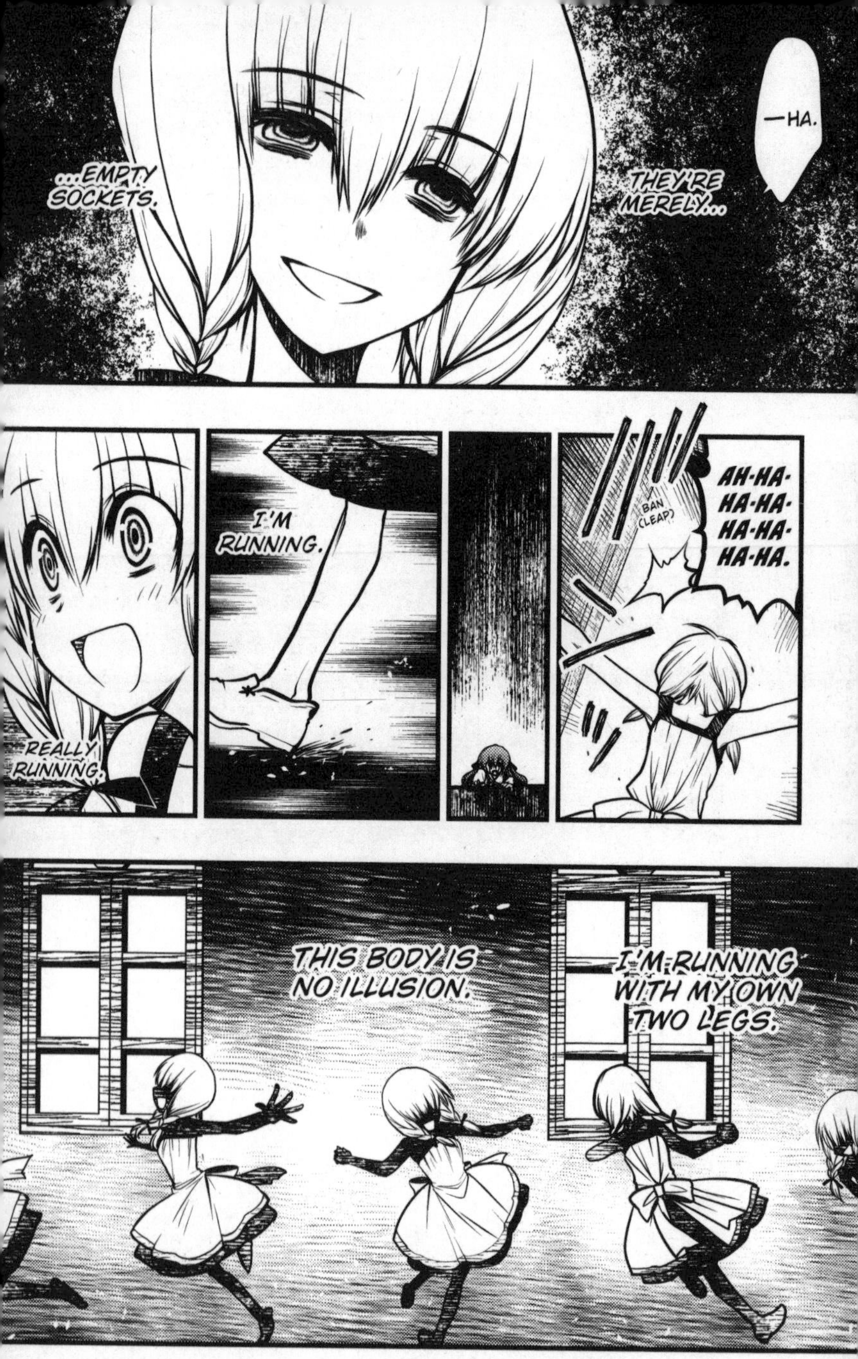
—HA.
THEY'RE MERELY...
...EMPTY SOCKETS.
AH-HA-HA-HA-HA-HA-HA-HA.
BAN (LEAP)
I'M RUNNING.
REALLY RUNNING.
I'M RUNNING WITH MY OWN TWO LEGS.
THIS BODY IS NO ILLUSION.

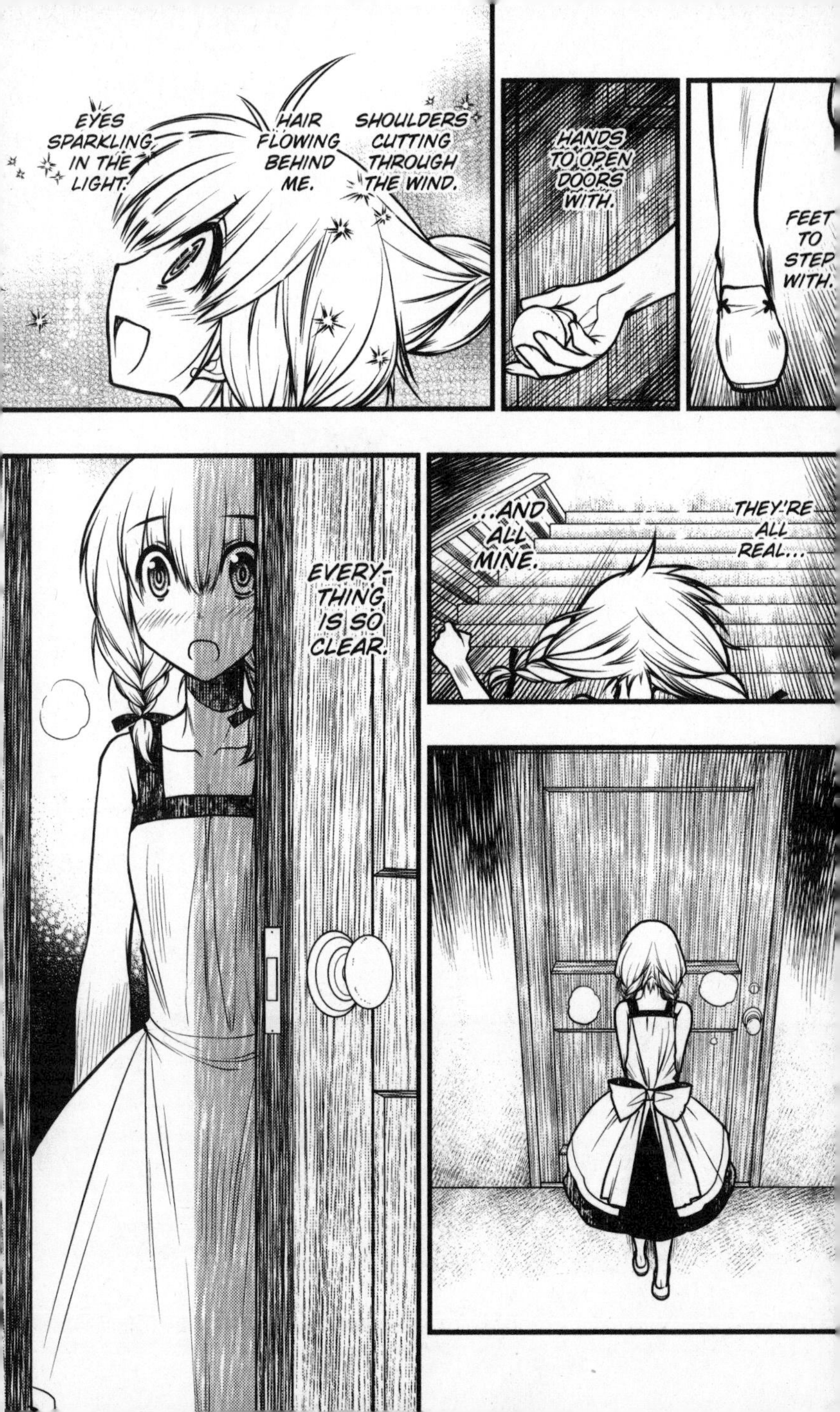
FEET TO STEP WITH.
HANDS TO OPEN DOORS WITH.
SHOULDERS CUTTING THROUGH THE WIND.
HAIR FLOWING BEHIND ME.
EYES SPARKLING IN THE LIGHT.
THEY'RE ALL REAL...
...AND ALL MINE.
EVERY-THING IS SO CLEAR.

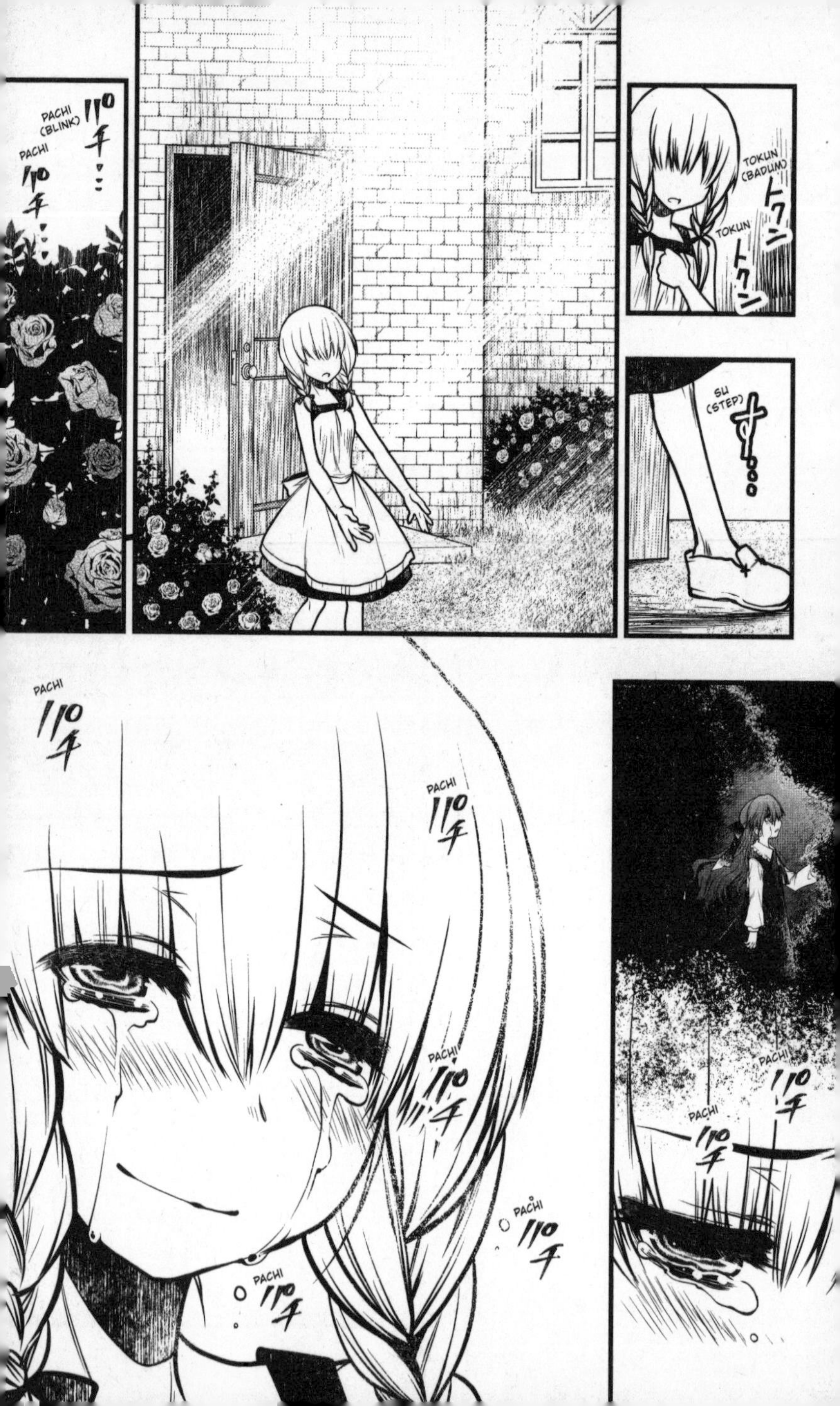
TOKUN (BADUM)
トクン
TOKUN
トクン
SU (STEP)
PACHI (BLINK)
PACHI
PACHI
PACHI
PACHI
PACHI
PACHI
PACHI
PACHI

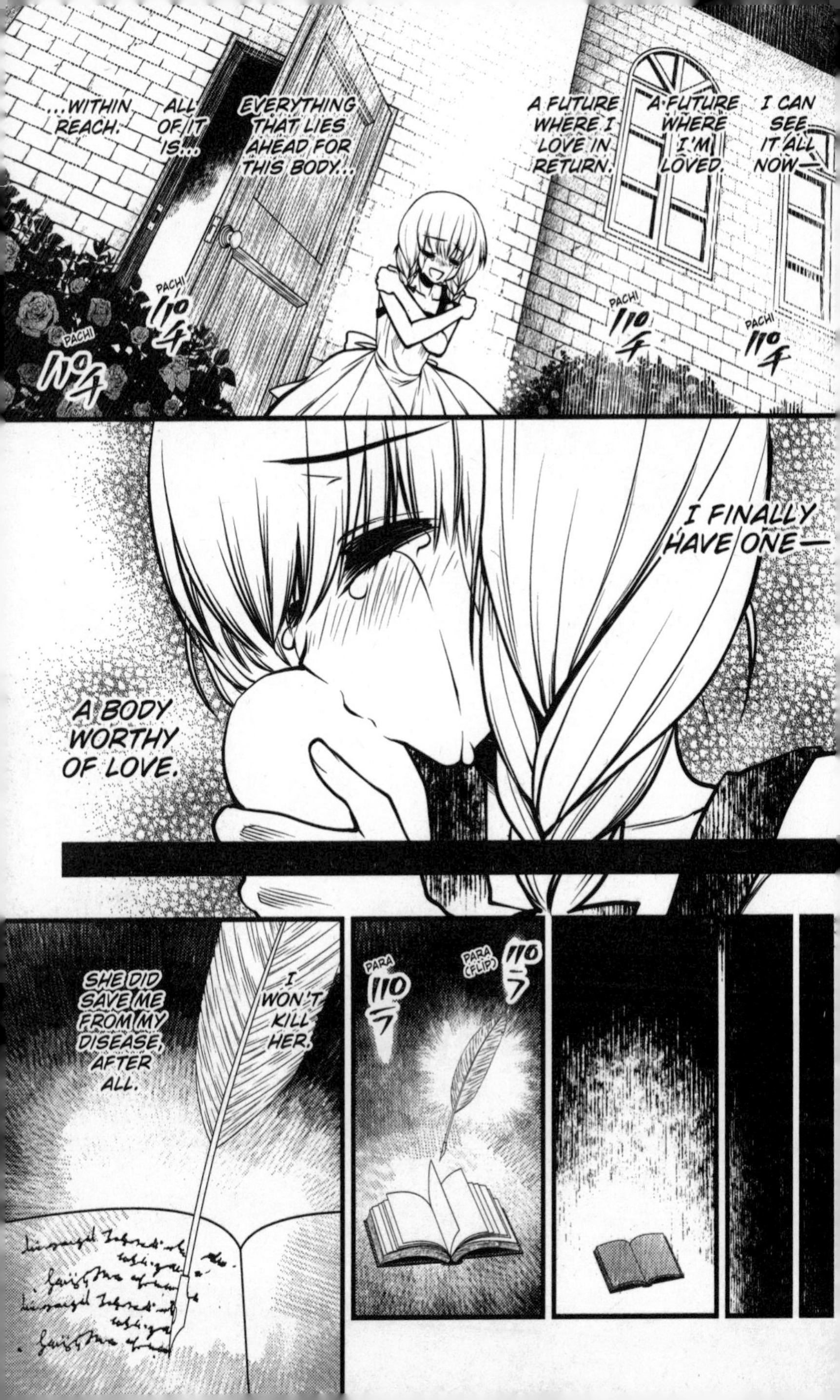
I CAN SEE IT ALL NOW—
A FUTURE WHERE I'M LOVED.
A FUTURE WHERE I LOVE IN RETURN.
EVERYTHING THAT LIES AHEAD FOR THIS BODY...
ALL OF IT IS...
...WITHIN REACH.
PACHI
PACHI
PACHI
PACHI
I FINALLY HAVE ONE—
A BODY WORTHY OF LOVE.
PARA (FLIP)
PARA
I WON'T KILL HER.
SHE DID SAVE ME FROM MY DISEASE, AFTER ALL.

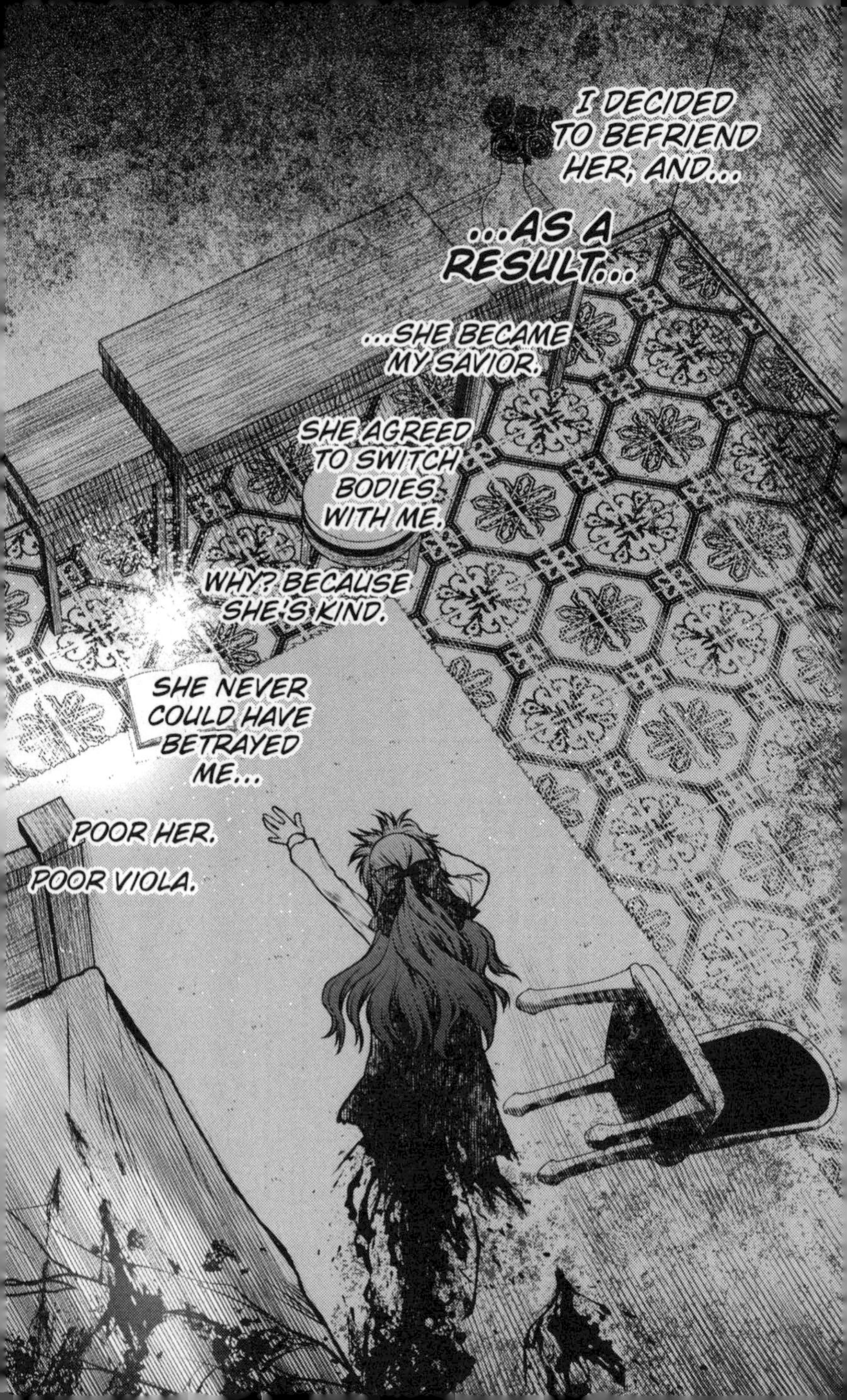
I DECIDED TO BEFRIEND HER, AND...
...AS A RESULT...
...SHE BECAME MY SAVIOR.
SHE AGREED TO SWITCH BODIES WITH ME.
WHY? BECAUSE SHE'S KIND.
SHE NEVER COULD HAVE BETRAYED ME...
POOR HER.
POOR VIOLA.

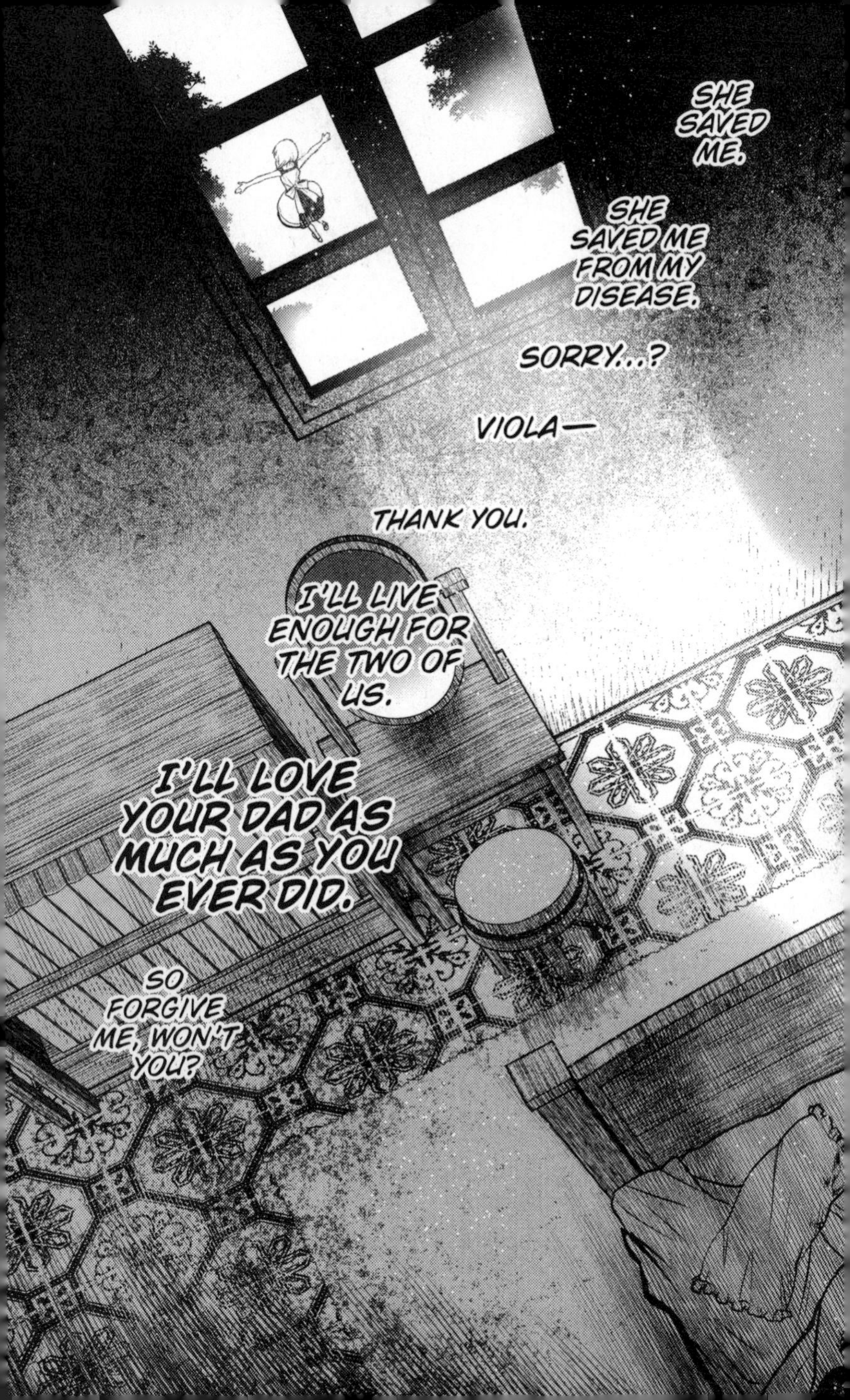
SHE SAVED ME.
SHE SAVED ME FROM MY DISEASE.
SORRY...?
VIOLA—
THANK YOU.
I'LL LIVE ENOUGH FOR THE TWO OF US.
I'LL LOVE YOUR DAD AS MUCH AS YOU EVER DID.
SO FORGIVE ME, WON'T YOU?

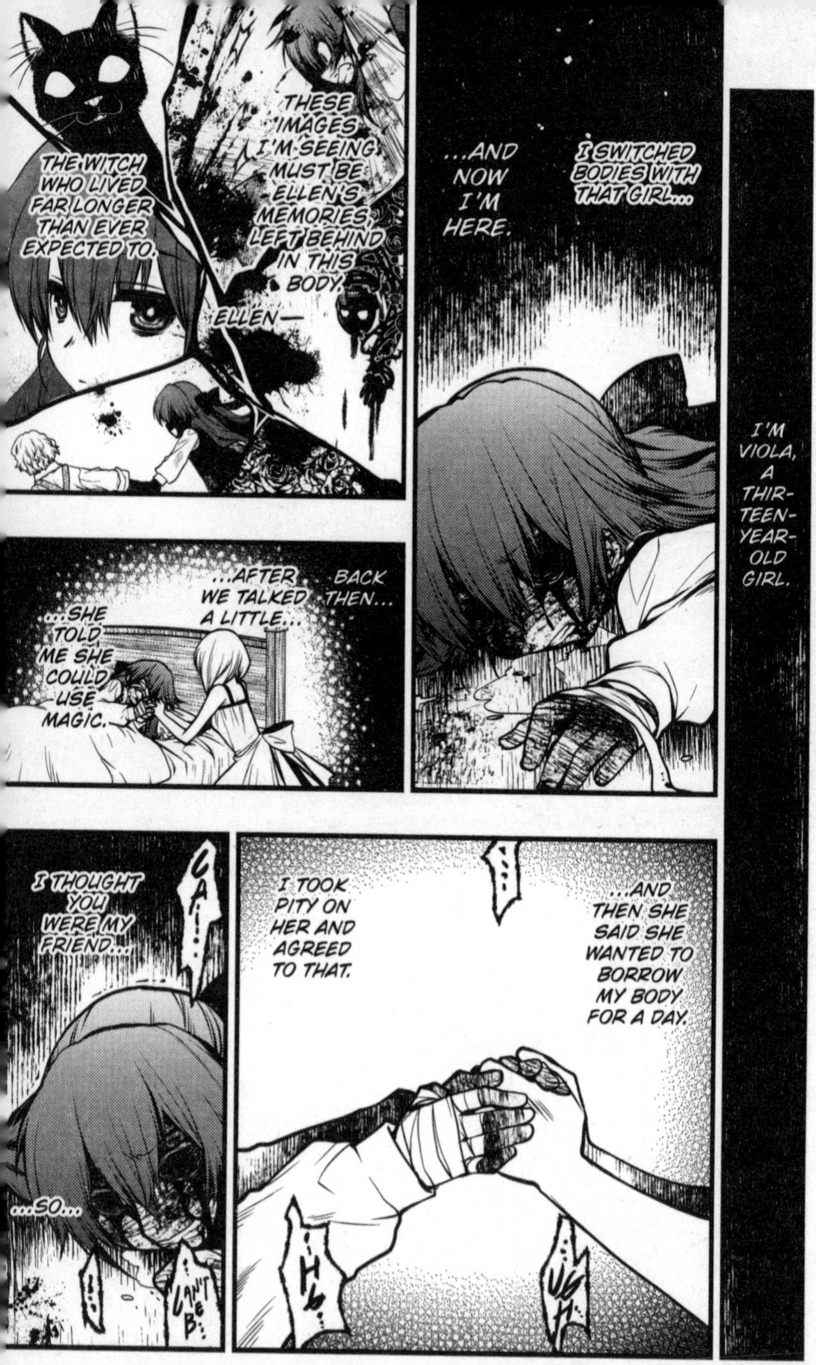
I'M VIOLA, A THIRTEEN-YEAR-OLD GIRL.
I SWITCHED BODIES WITH THAT GIRL...
...AND NOW I'M HERE.
THESE IMAGES I'M SEEING MUST BE ELLEN'S MEMORIES, LEFT BEHIND IN THIS BODY.
THE WITCH WHO LIVED FAR LONGER THAN EVER EXPECTED TO.
ELLEN—
BACK THEN...
...AFTER WE TALKED A LITTLE...
...SHE TOLD ME SHE COULD USE MAGIC.
...AND THEN SHE SAID SHE WANTED TO BORROW MY BODY FOR A DAY.
I TOOK PITY ON HER AND AGREED TO THAT.
...UGH...
...HK...
CA...!
I THOUGHT YOU WERE MY FRIEND...
...SO...
...CAN'T BE...

ズキ
(THROB)

WHY, YOU ASK?

YOU'RE STILL WONDERING ABOUT THAT, REALLY?

GE (THROB)

GE (HACK) GOHO (COUGH)

GEHO

ゴッ

YOU KNEW, DEEP DOWN.

I KNEW.

AH.

AH.

THIS'LL CONTINUE UNTIL YOU TELL THE TRUTH.

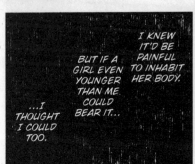

I KNEW IT'D BE PAINFUL TO INHABIT HER BODY.

BUT IF A GIRL EVEN YOUNGER THAN ME COULD BEAR IT...

...I THOUGHT I COULD TOO.

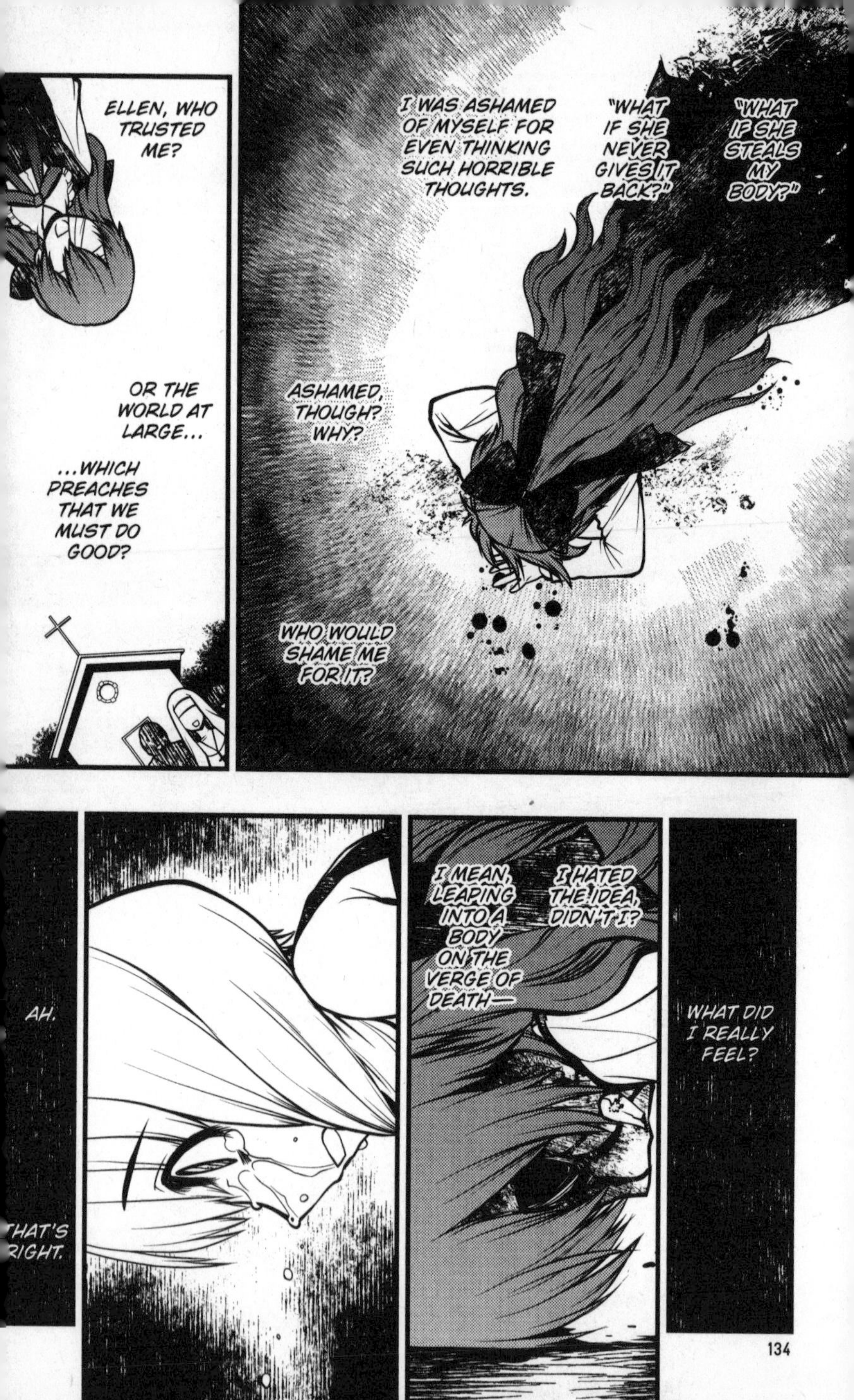
"WHAT IF SHE STEALS MY BODY?"
"WHAT IF SHE NEVER GIVES IT BACK?"
I WAS ASHAMED OF MYSELF FOR EVEN THINKING SUCH HORRIBLE THOUGHTS.
ASHAMED, THOUGH? WHY?
WHO WOULD SHAME ME FOR IT?
ELLEN, WHO TRUSTED ME?
OR THE WORLD AT LARGE...
...WHICH PREACHES THAT WE MUST DO GOOD?
WHAT DID I REALLY FEEL?
I HATED THE IDEA, DIDN'T I?
I MEAN, LEAPING INTO A BODY ON THE VERGE OF DEATH—
AH.
THAT'S RIGHT.

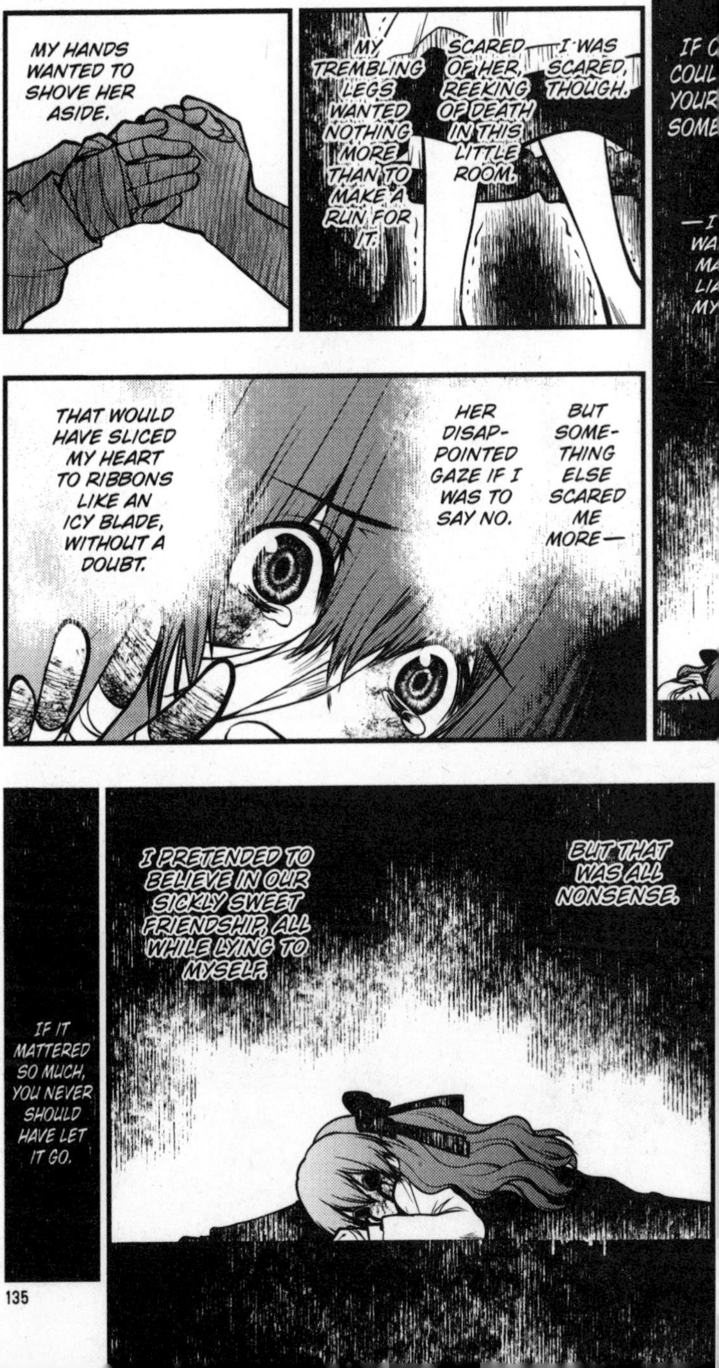
I WAS SCARED, THOUGH.
SCARED OF HER, REEKING OF DEATH IN THIS LITTLE ROOM.
MY TREMBLING LEGS WANTED NOTHING MORE THAN TO MAKE A RUN FOR IT.
MY HANDS WANTED TO SHOVE HER ASIDE.
BUT SOME-THING ELSE SCARED ME MORE—
HER DISAP-POINTED GAZE IF I WAS TO SAY NO.
THAT WOULD HAVE SLICED MY HEART TO RIBBONS LIKE AN ICY BLADE, WITHOUT A DOUBT.
BUT THAT WAS ALL NONSENSE.
I PRETENDED TO BELIEVE IN OUR SICKLY SWEET FRIENDSHIP, ALL WHILE LYING TO MYSELF.
IF IT MATTERED SO MUCH, YOU NEVER SHOULD HAVE LET IT GO.

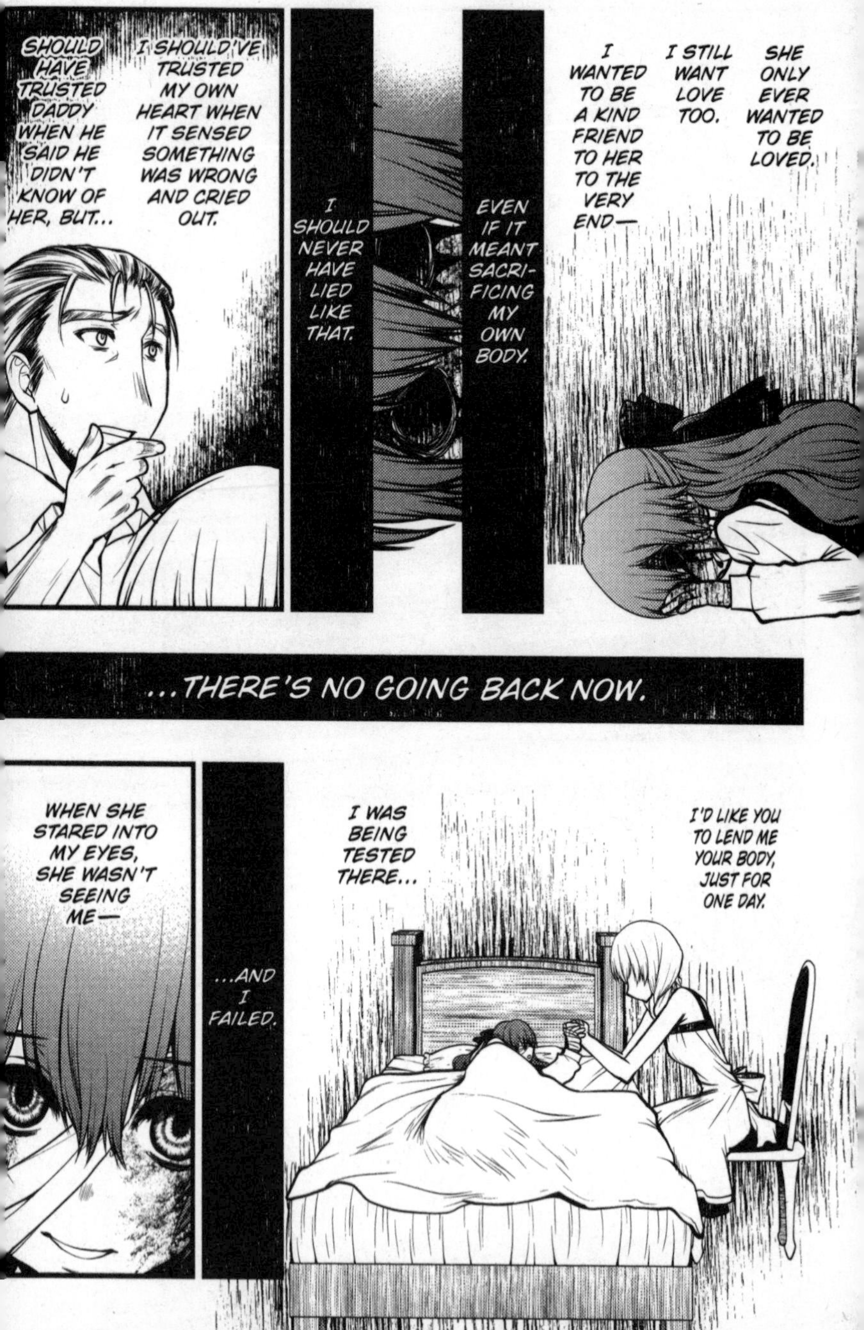

SHE ONLY EVER WANTED TO BE LOVED.
I STILL WANT LOVE TOO.
I WANTED TO BE A KIND FRIEND TO HER TO THE VERY END—
EVEN IF IT MEANT SACRIFICING MY OWN BODY.
I SHOULD NEVER HAVE LIED LIKE THAT.
I SHOULD'VE TRUSTED MY OWN HEART WHEN IT SENSED SOMETHING WAS WRONG AND CRIED OUT.
SHOULD HAVE TRUSTED DADDY WHEN HE SAID HE DIDN'T KNOW OF HER, BUT...
...THERE'S NO GOING BACK NOW.
I'D LIKE YOU TO LEND ME YOUR BODY, JUST FOR ONE DAY.
I WAS BEING TESTED THERE...
...AND I FAILED.
WHEN SHE STARED INTO MY EYES, SHE WASN'T SEEING ME—

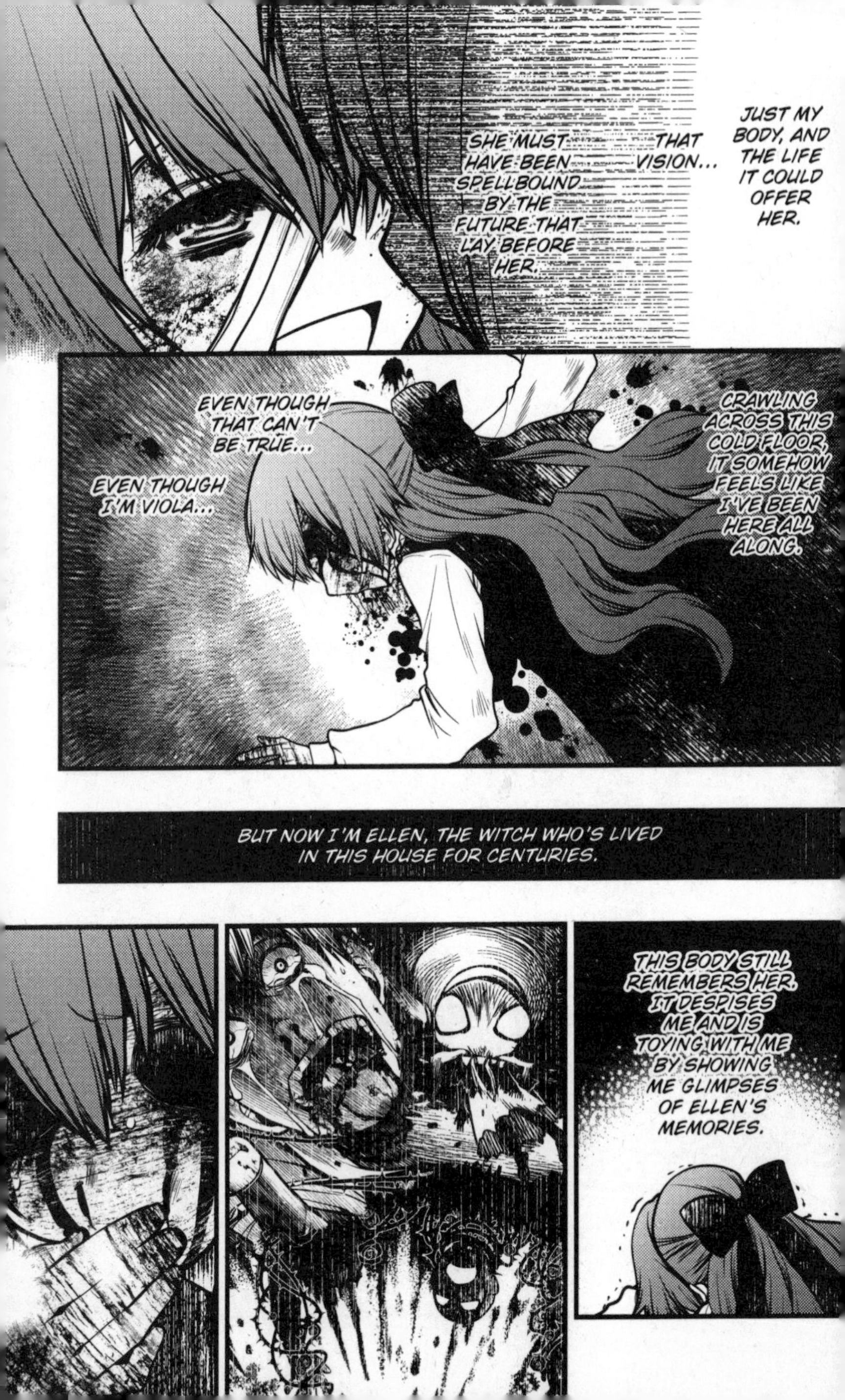
JUST MY BODY, AND THE LIFE IT COULD OFFER HER.
THAT VISION...
SHE MUST HAVE BEEN SPELLBOUND BY THE FUTURE THAT LAY BEFORE HER.
CRAWLING ACROSS THIS COLD FLOOR, IT SOMEHOW FEELS LIKE I'VE BEEN HERE ALL ALONG.
EVEN THOUGH THAT CAN'T BE TRUE...
EVEN THOUGH I'M VIOLA...
BUT NOW I'M ELLEN, THE WITCH WHO'S LIVED IN THIS HOUSE FOR CENTURIES.
THIS BODY STILL REMEMBERS HER. IT DESPISES ME AND IS TOYING WITH ME BY SHOWING ME GLIMPSES OF ELLEN'S MEMORIES.

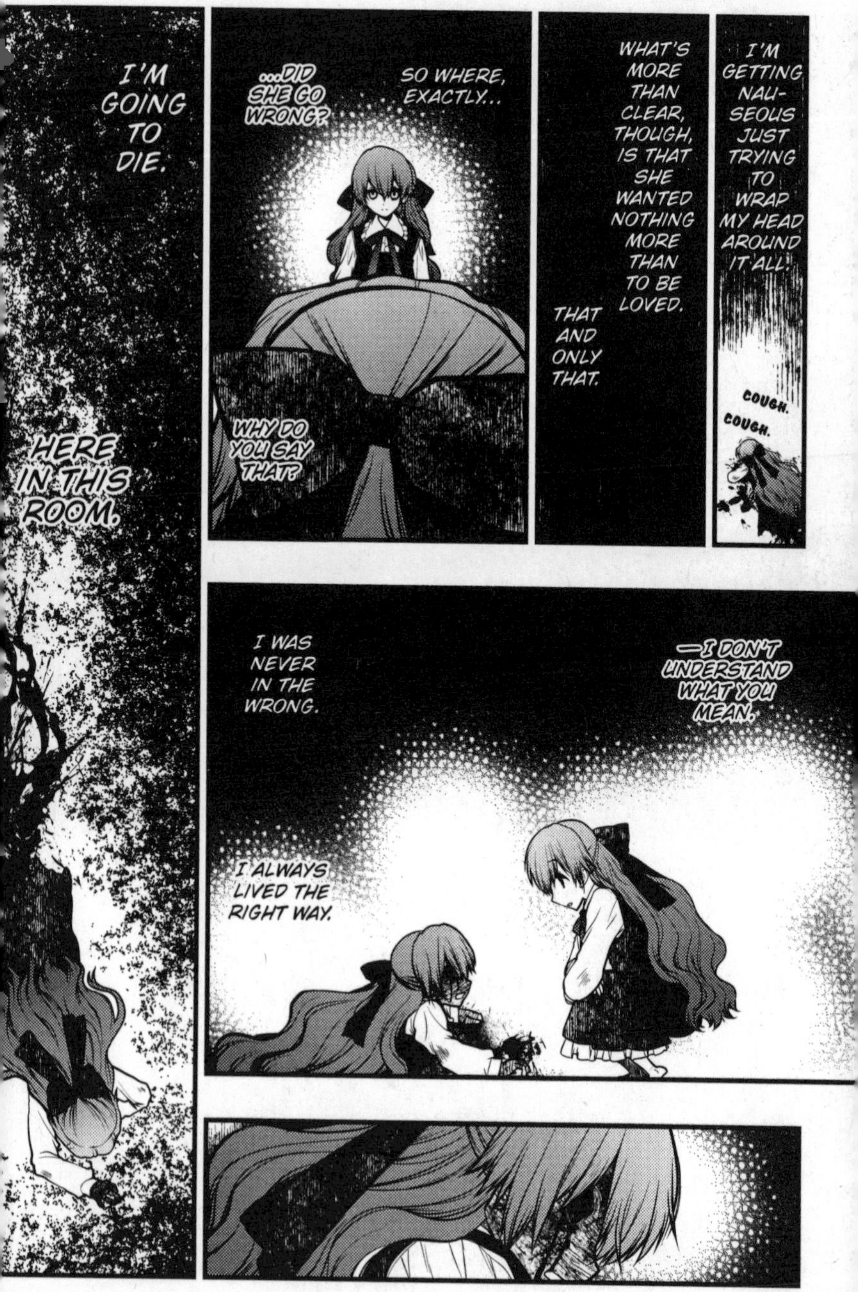
I'M GETTING NAUSEOUS JUST TRYING TO WRAP MY HEAD AROUND IT ALL.
COUGH.
COUGH.
WHAT'S MORE THAN CLEAR, THOUGH, IS THAT SHE WANTED NOTHING MORE THAN TO BE LOVED.
THAT AND ONLY THAT.
SO WHERE, EXACTLY...
...DID SHE GO WRONG?
WHY DO YOU SAY THAT?
—I DON'T UNDERSTAND WHAT YOU MEAN.
I WAS NEVER IN THE WRONG.
I ALWAYS LIVED THE RIGHT WAY.
I'M GOING TO DIE.
HERE IN THIS ROOM.

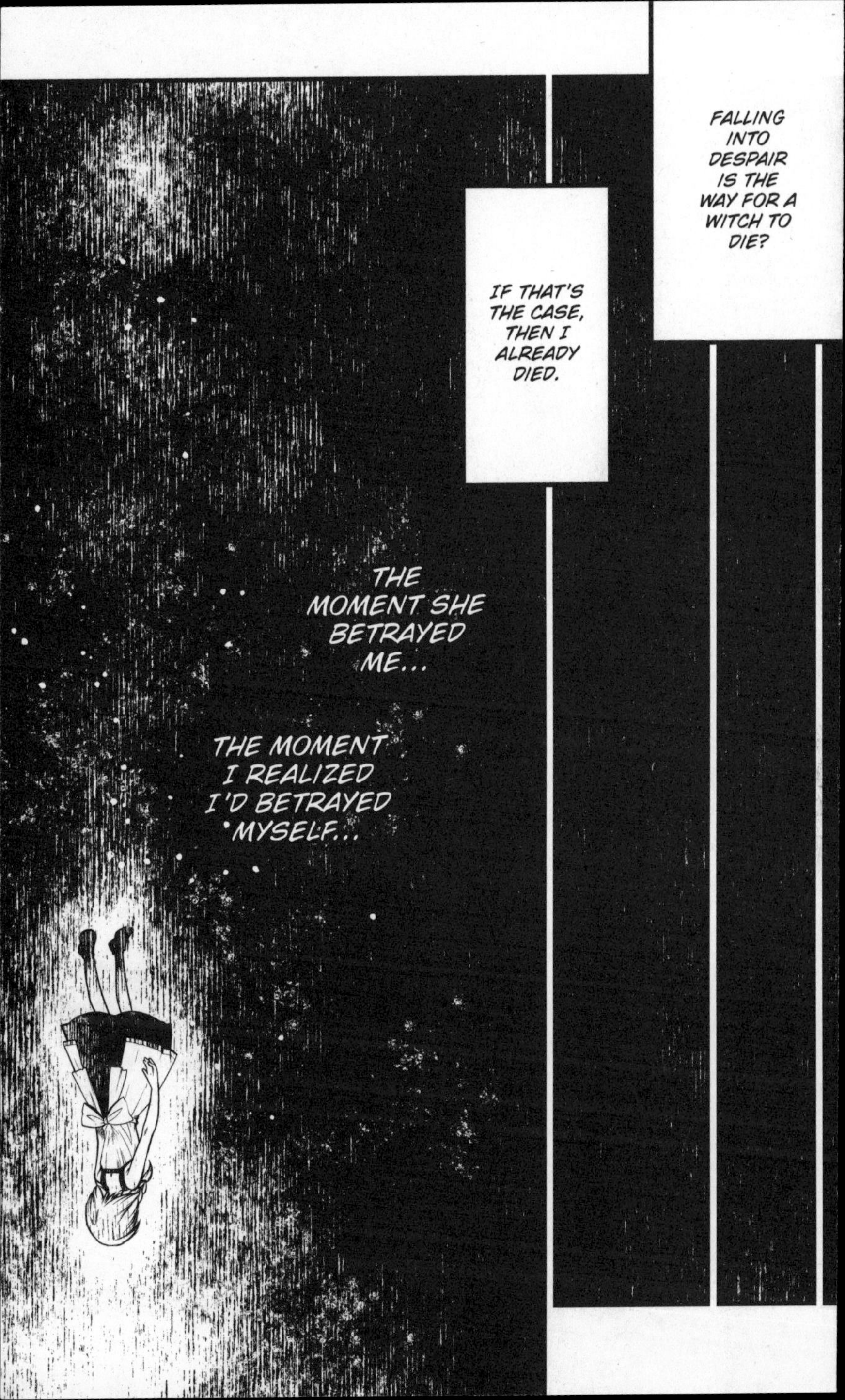

FALLING INTO DESPAIR IS THE WAY FOR A WITCH TO DIE?
IF THAT'S THE CASE, THEN I ALREADY DIED.
THE MOMENT SHE BETRAYED ME...
THE MOMENT I REALIZED I'D BETRAYED MYSELF...

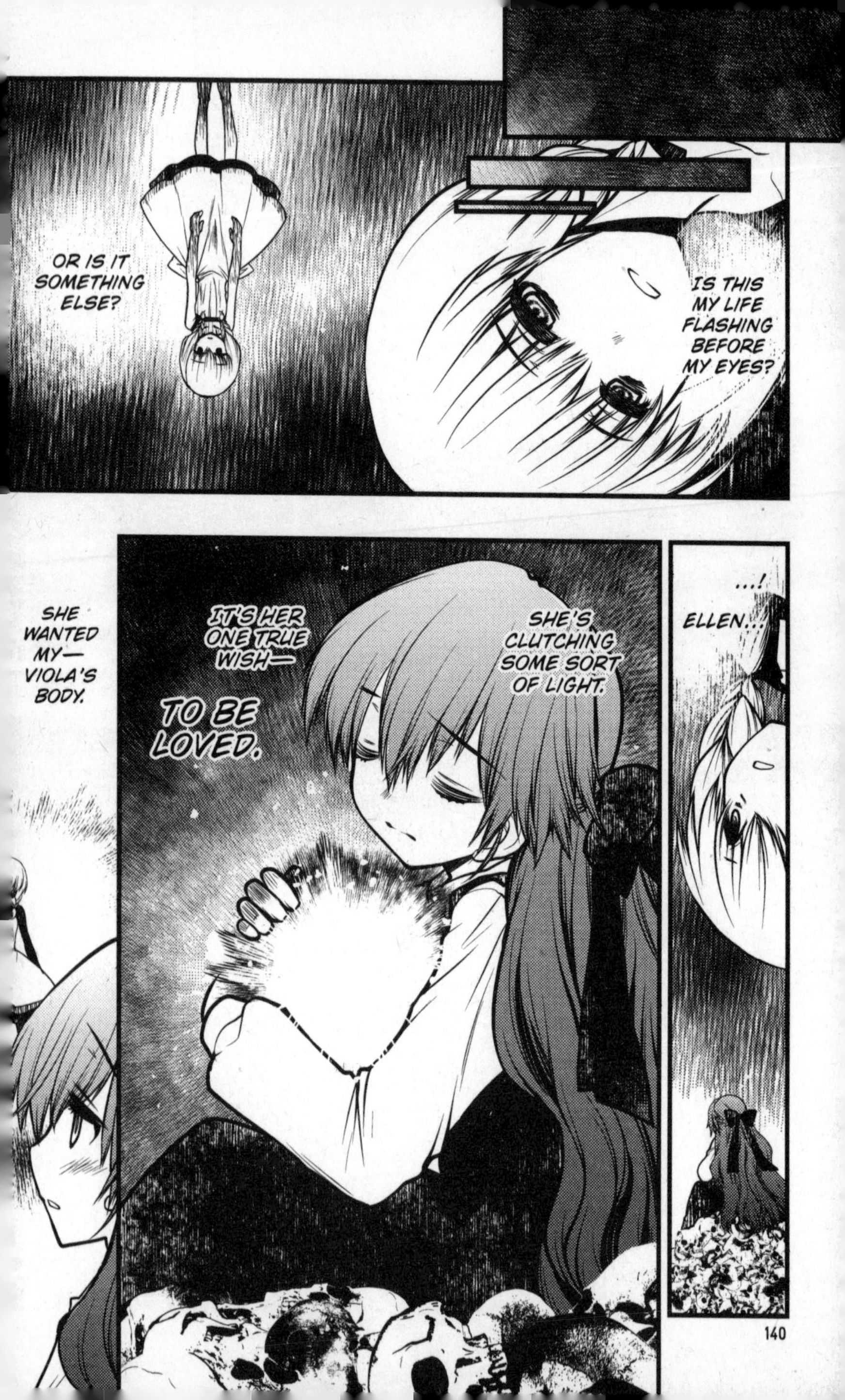
IS THIS MY LIFE FLASHING BEFORE MY EYES?
OR IS IT SOMETHING ELSE?
...!
ELLEN...
SHE'S CLUTCHING SOME SORT OF LIGHT.
IT'S HER ONE TRUE WISH—
TO BE LOVED.
SHE WANTED MY— VIOLA'S BODY.

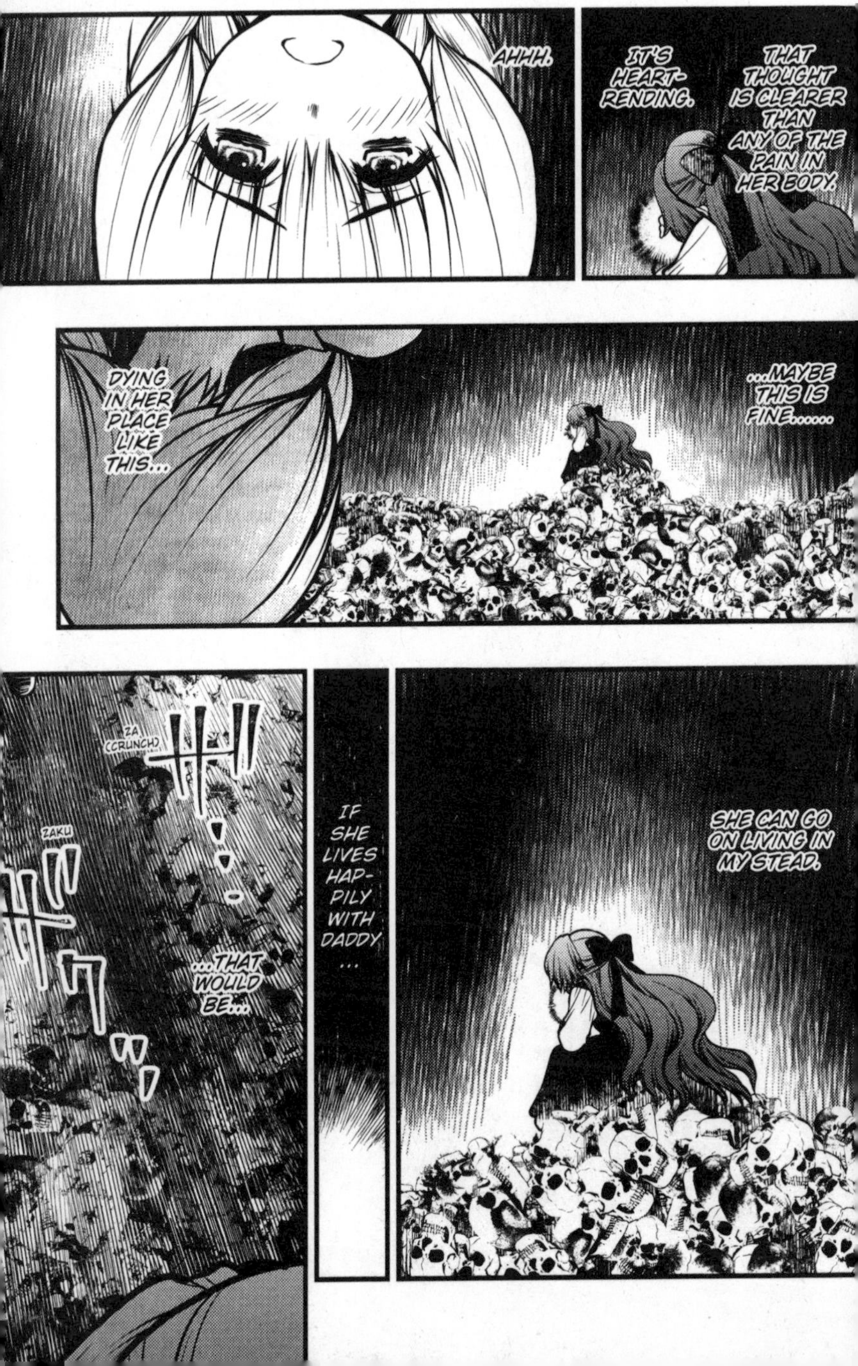
THAT THOUGHT IS CLEARER THAN ANY OF THE PAIN IN HER BODY.
IT'S HEART-RENDING.
AHHH.
...MAYBE THIS IS FINE......
DYING IN HER PLACE LIKE THIS...
SHE CAN GO ON LIVING IN MY STEAD.
IF SHE LIVES HAP-PILY WITH DADDY...
ZA (CRUNCH)
ZAKU
...THAT WOULD BE...

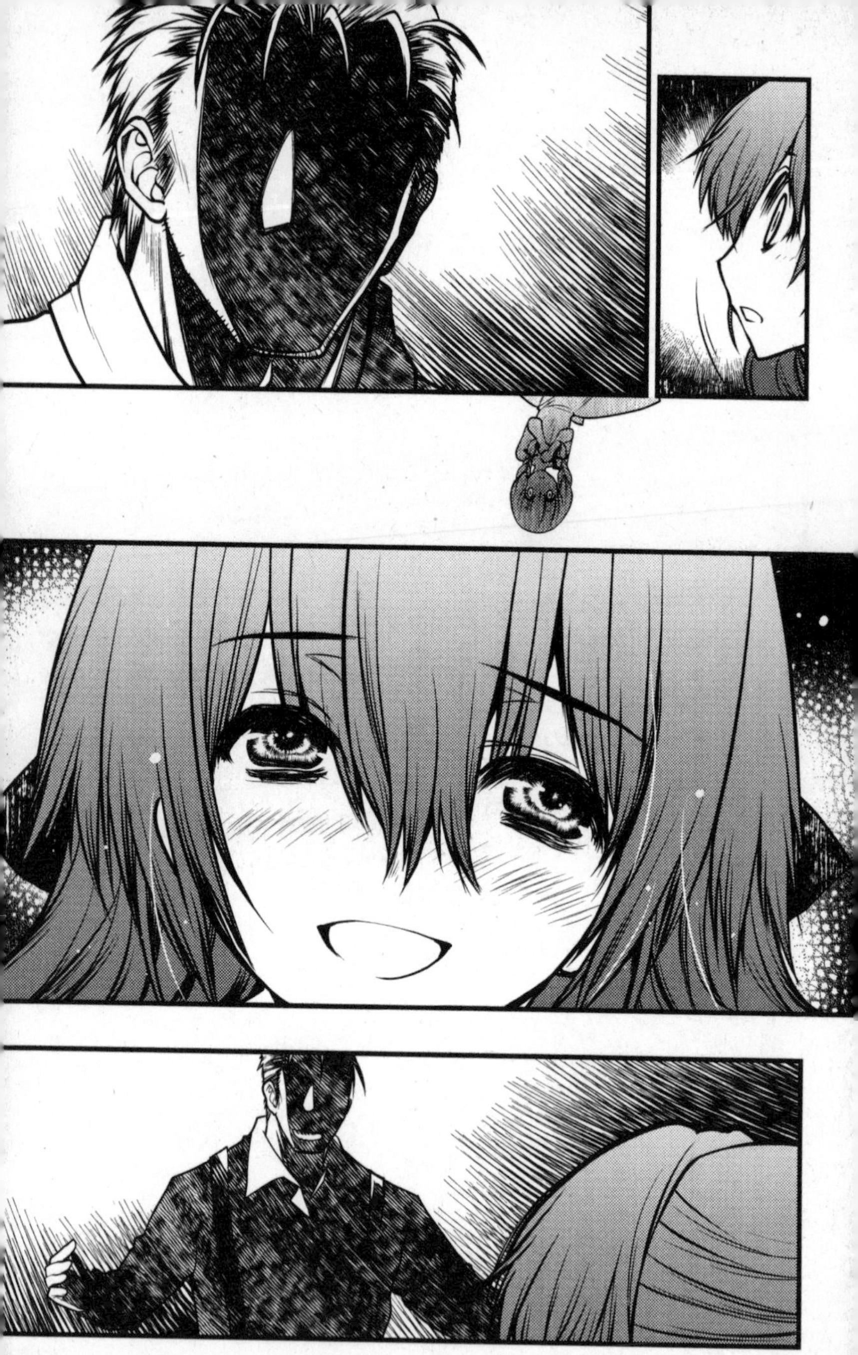

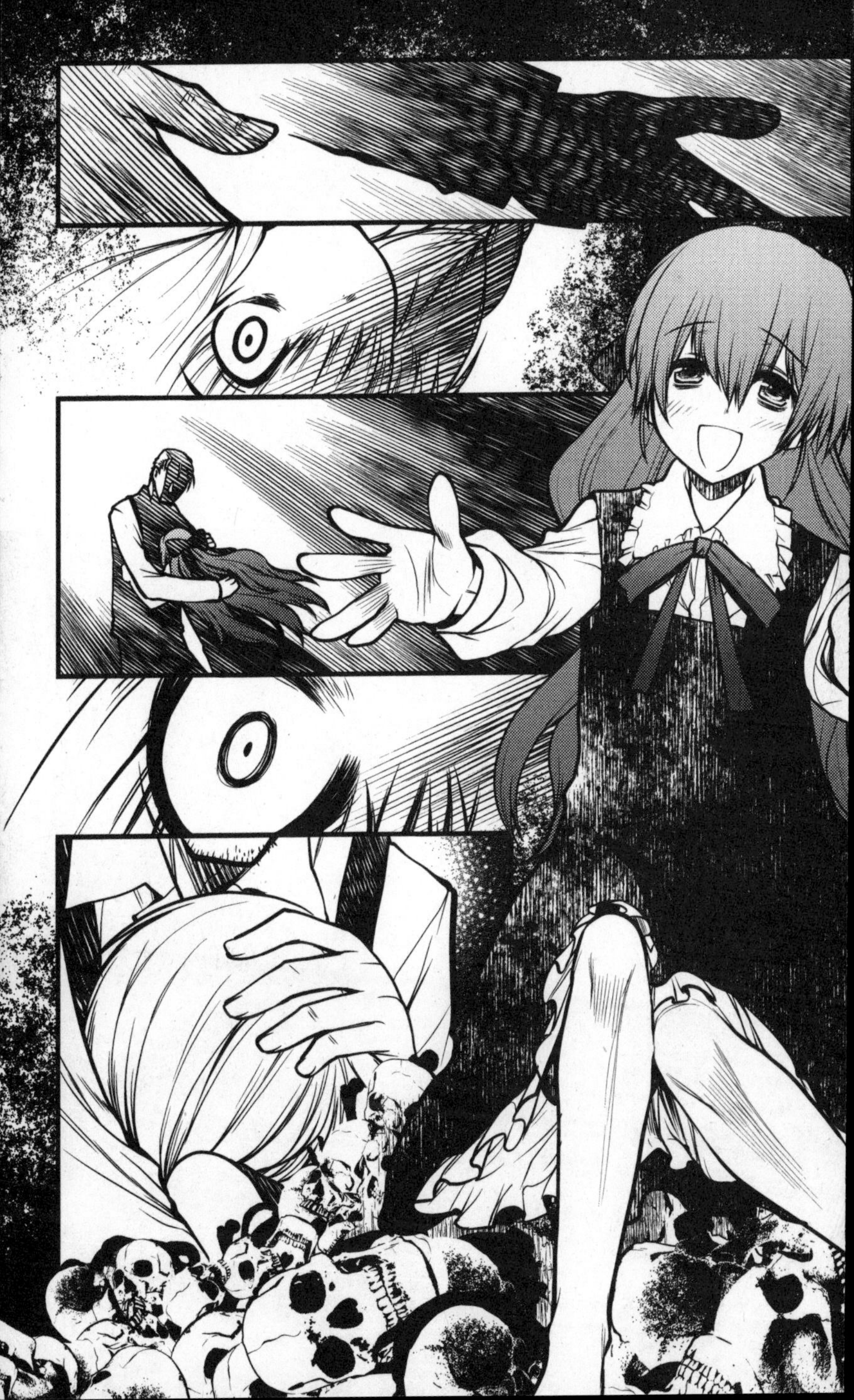

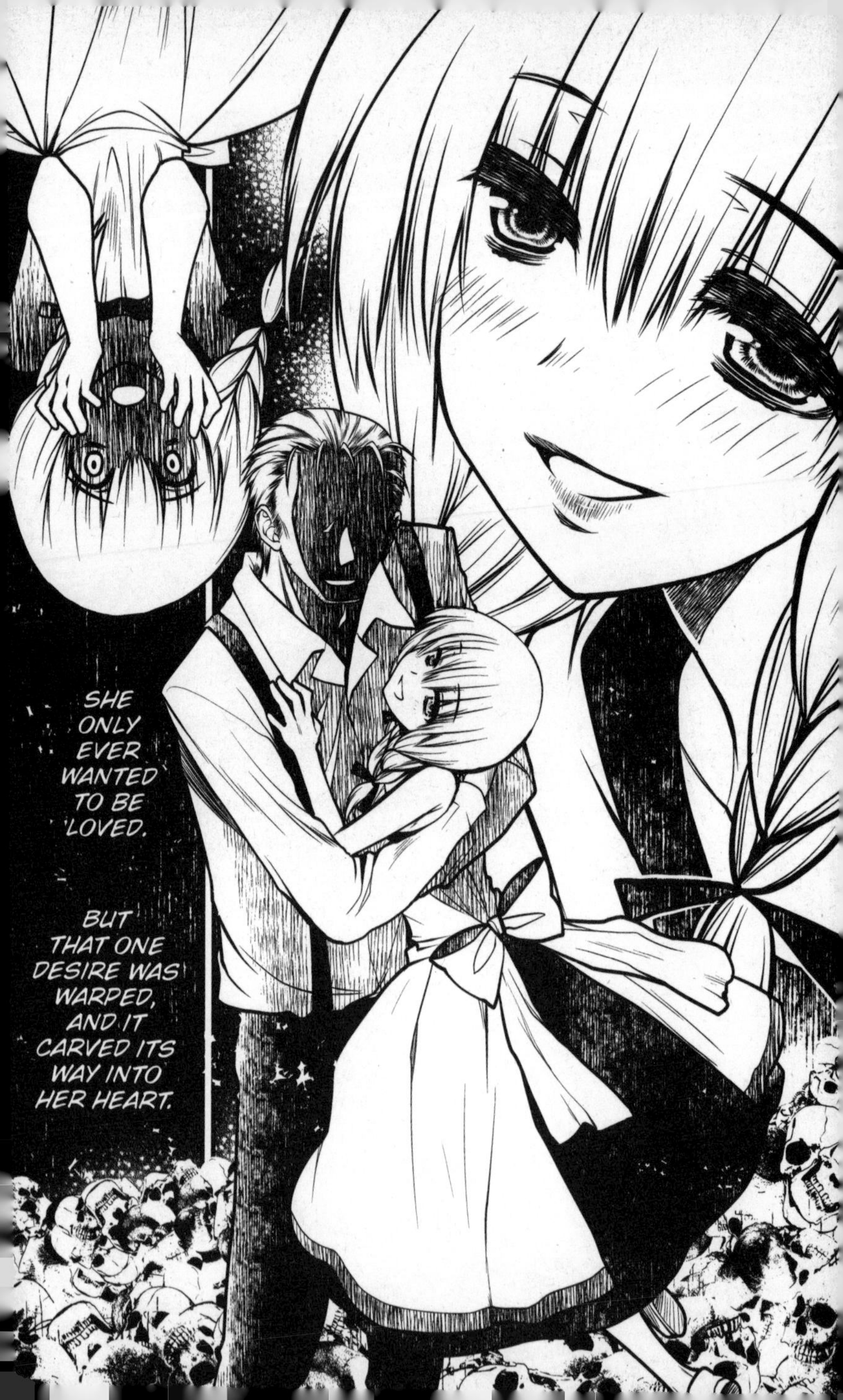
SHE ONLY EVER WANTED TO BE LOVED.
BUT THAT ONE DESIRE WAS WARPED, AND IT CARVED ITS WAY INTO HER HEART.

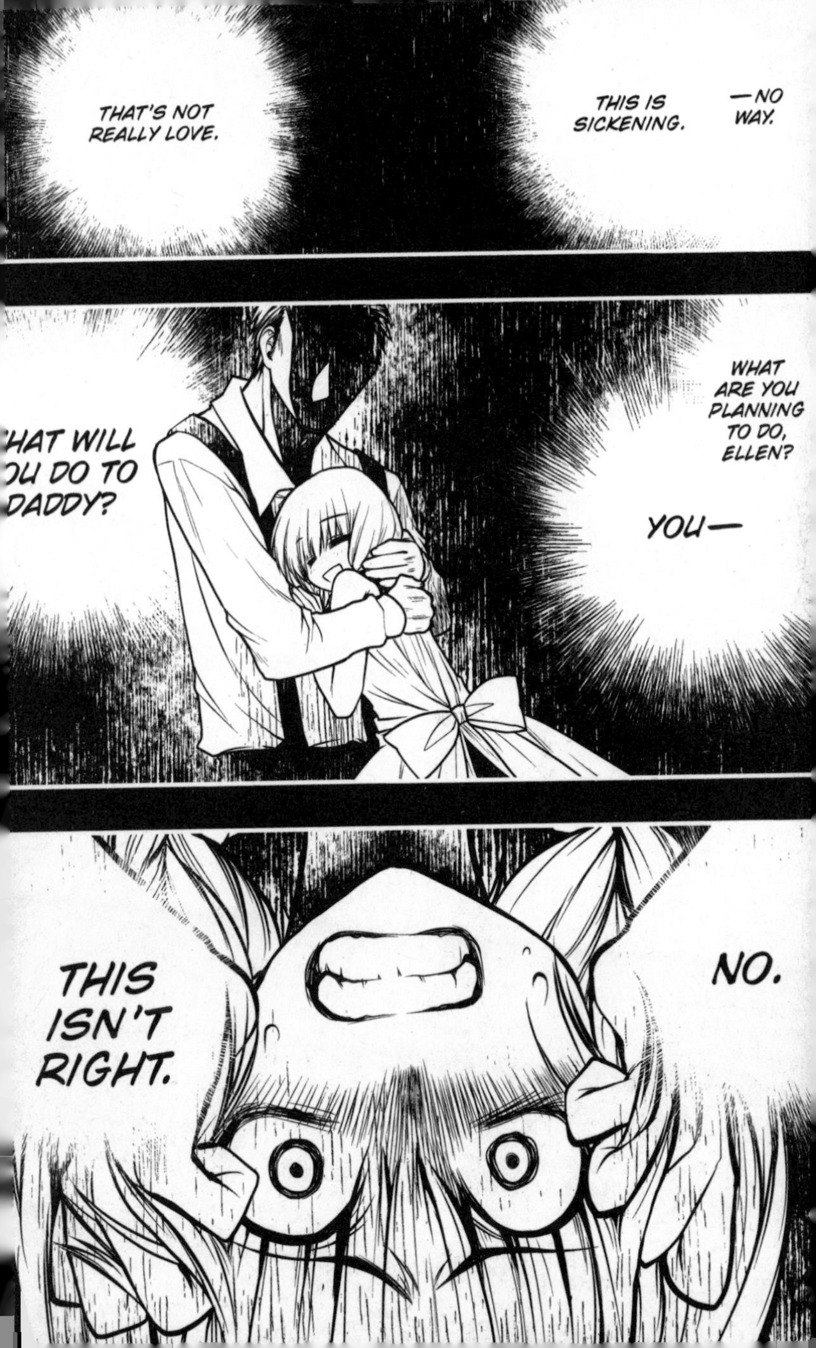
—NO WAY.
THIS IS SICKENING.
THAT'S NOT REALLY LOVE.
WHAT ARE YOU PLANNING TO DO, ELLEN?
YOU—
HAT WILL OU DO TO DADDY?
NO.
THIS ISN'T RIGHT.

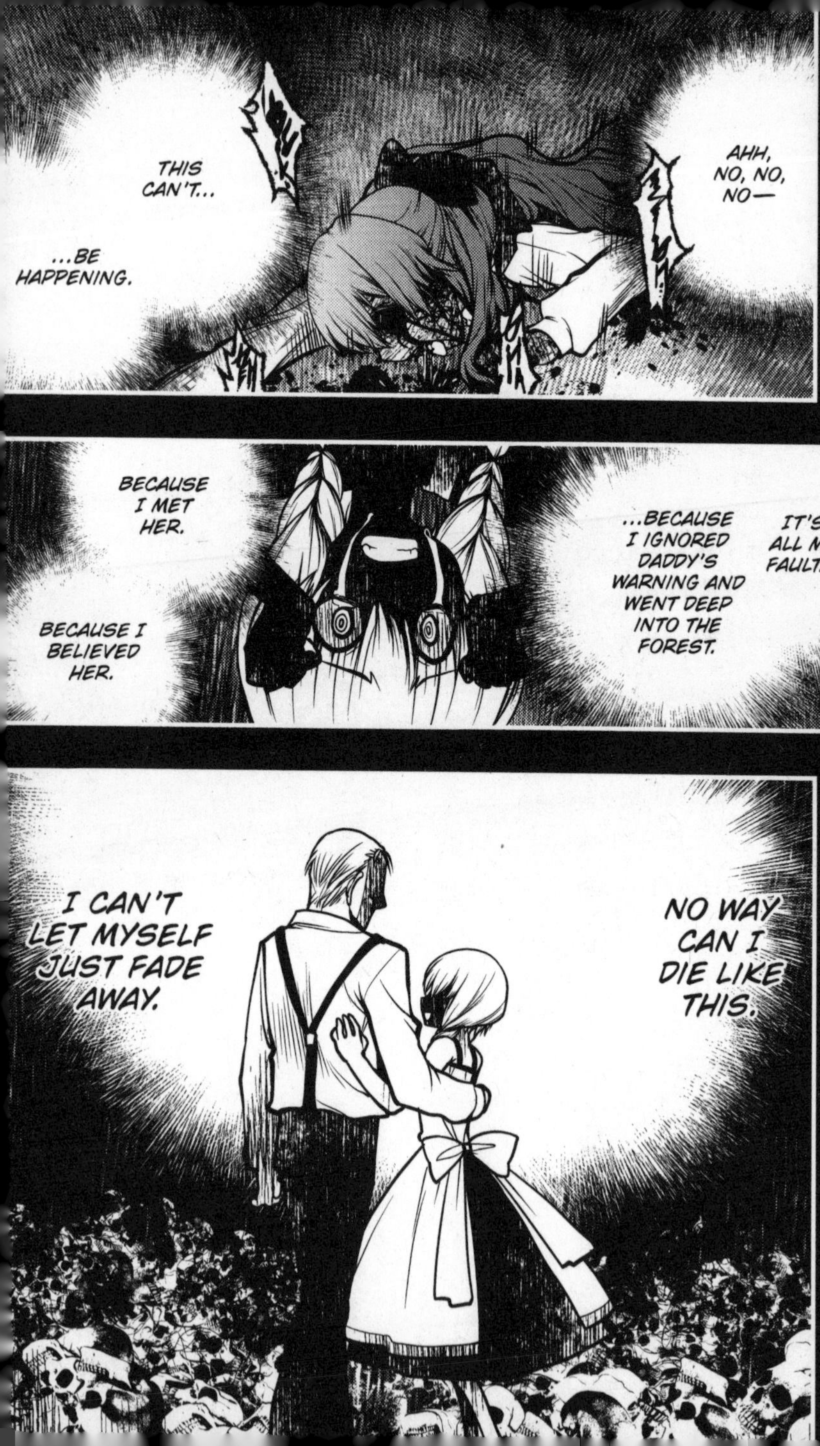
AHH, NO, NO, NO—
THIS CAN'T...
...BE HAPPENING.
IT'S ALL MY FAULT...
...BECAUSE I IGNORED DADDY'S WARNING AND WENT DEEP INTO THE FOREST.
BECAUSE I MET HER.
BECAUSE I BELIEVED HER.
NO WAY CAN I DIE LIKE THIS.
I CAN'T LET MYSELF JUST FADE AWAY.

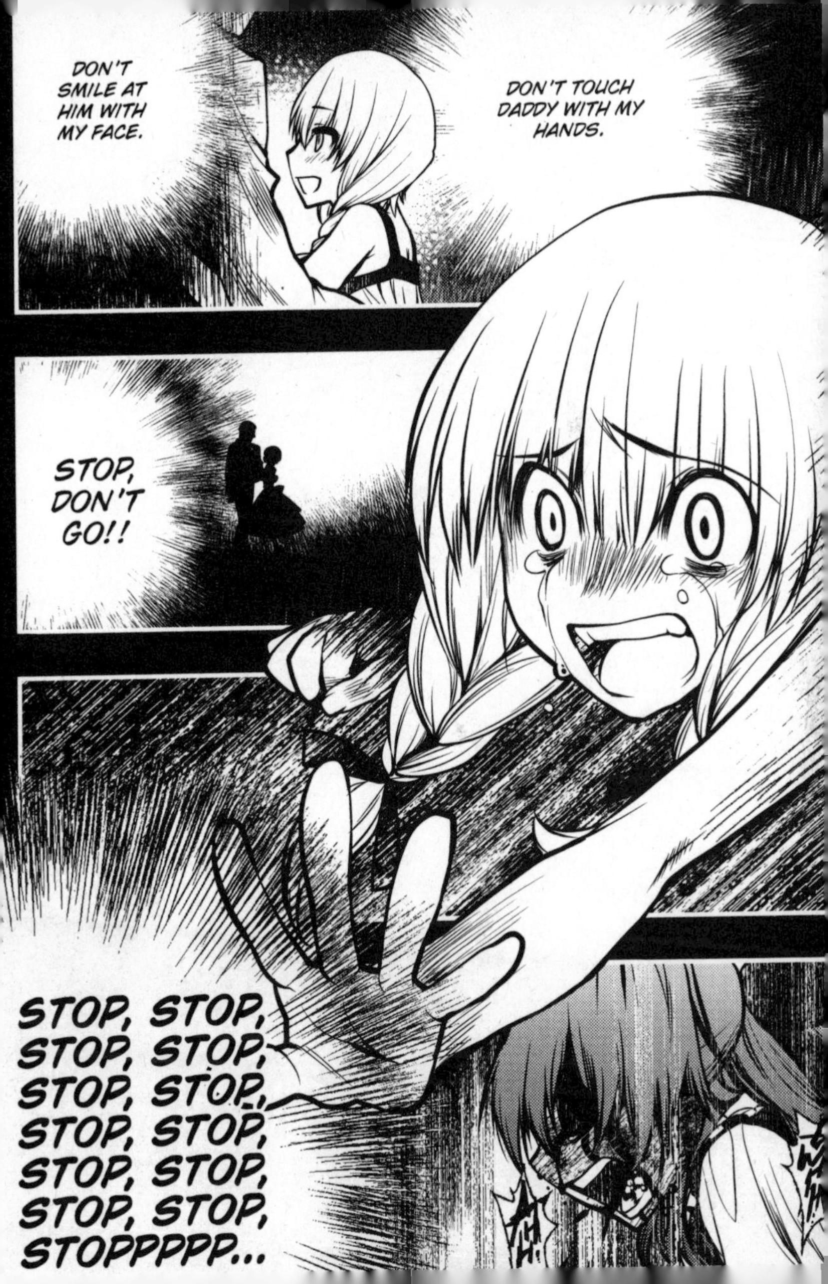
DON'T TOUCH DADDY WITH MY HANDS.
DON'T SMILE AT HIM WITH MY FACE.
STOP, DON'T GO!!
STOP, STOP, STOP, STOP, STOP, STOP, STOP, STOP, STOP, STOP, STOP, STOP, STOPPPPP...

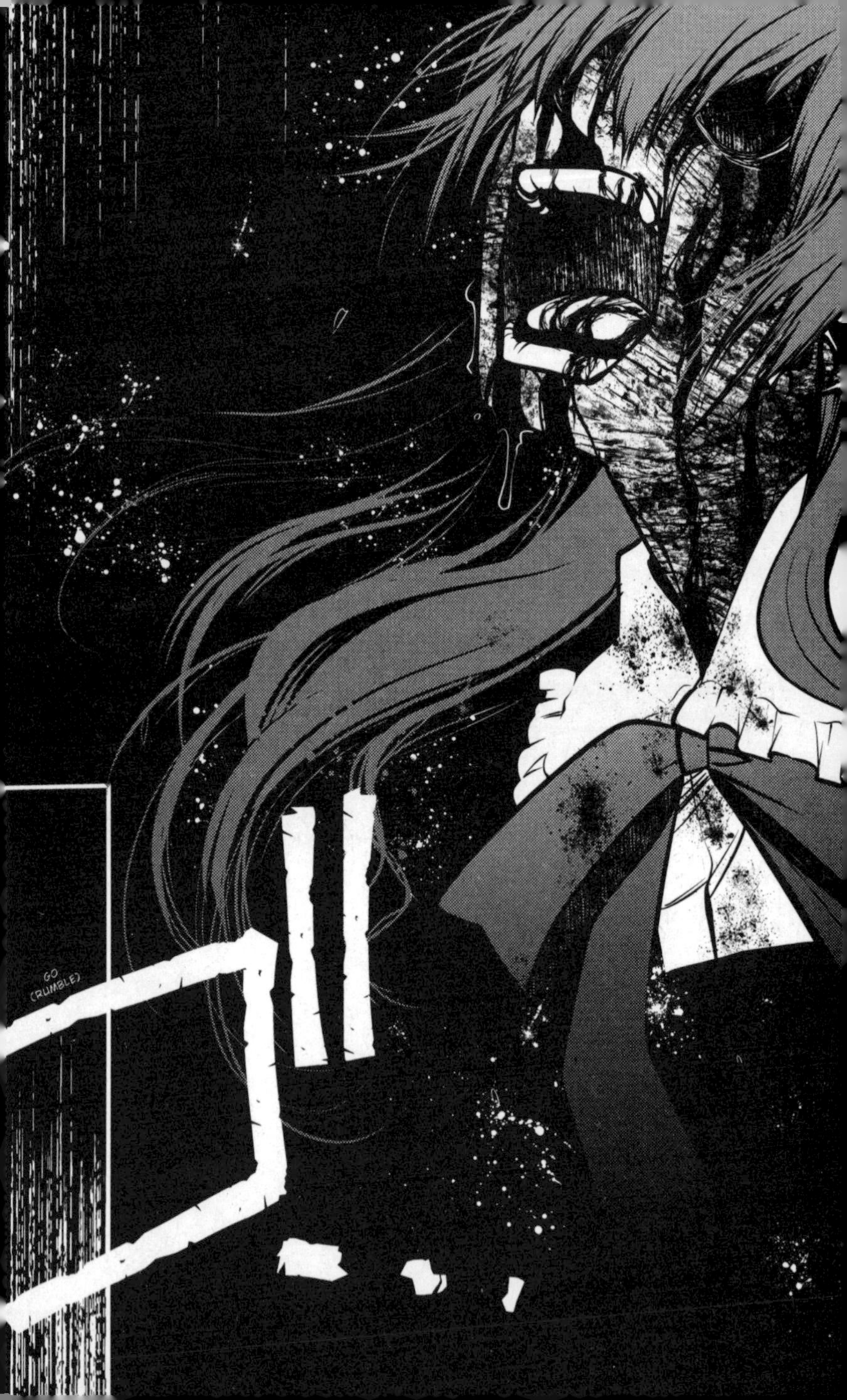
GO
(RUMBLE)

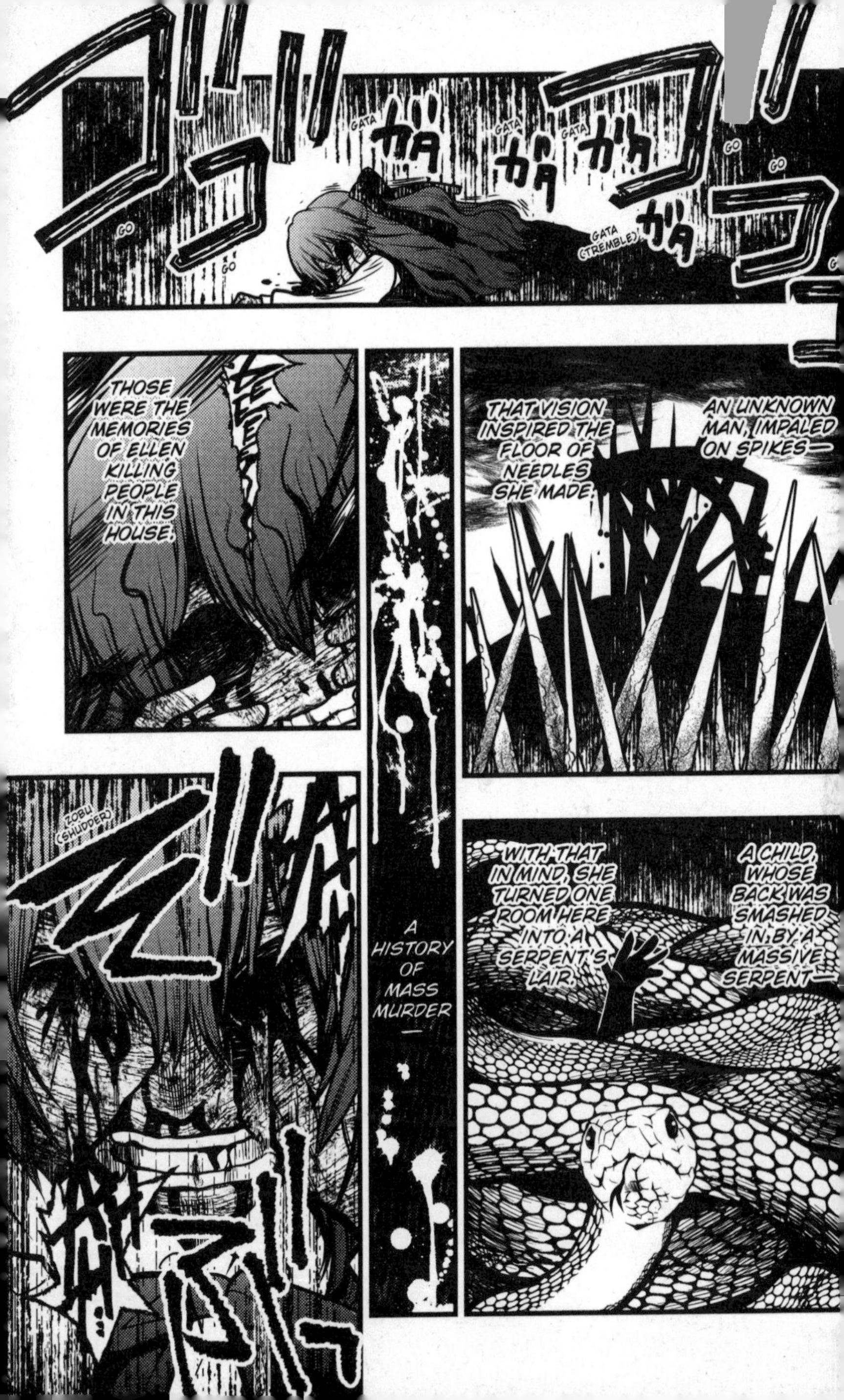
GO
GO
GATA
GATA
GATA
GATA (TREMBLE)
GO
GO
AN UNKNOWN MAN, IMPALED ON SPIKES—
THAT VISION INSPIRED THE FLOOR OF NEEDLES SHE MADE.
A CHILD, WHOSE BACK WAS SMASHED IN BY A MASSIVE SERPENT—
WITH THAT IN MIND, SHE TURNED ONE ROOM HERE INTO A SERPENT'S LAIR.
A HISTORY OF MASS MURDER—
THOSE WERE THE MEMORIES OF ELLEN KILLING PEOPLE IN THIS HOUSE.
ZOBU (SHUDDER)

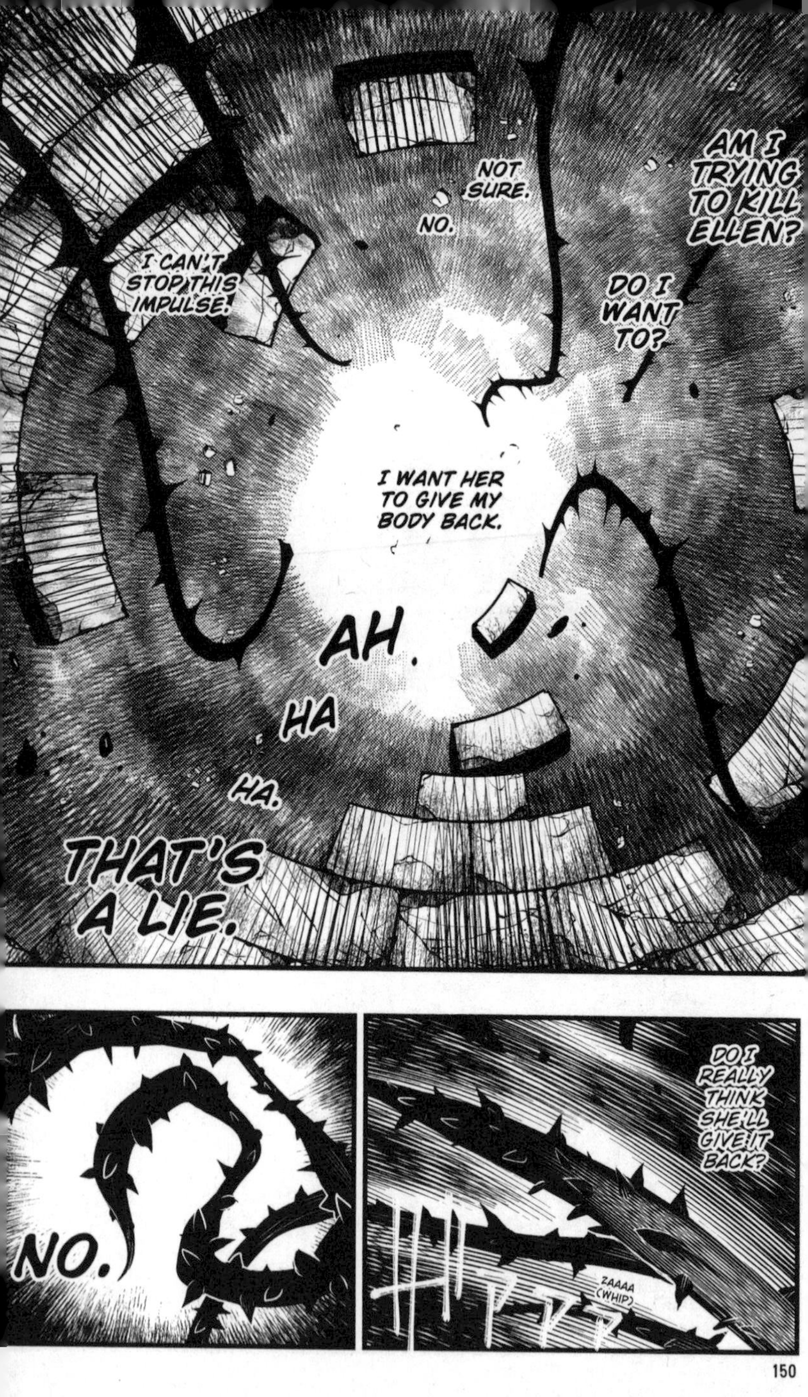
AM I TRYING TO KILL ELLEN?
DO I WANT TO?
NOT SURE.
NO.
I CAN'T STOP THIS IMPULSE!
I WANT HER TO GIVE MY BODY BACK.
AH. HA HA.
THAT'S A LIE.
DO I REALLY THINK SHE'LL GIVE IT BACK?
ZAAAA (WHIP)
NO.

I—

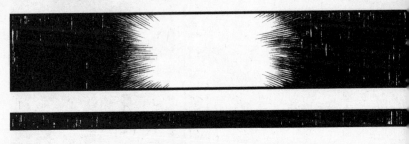

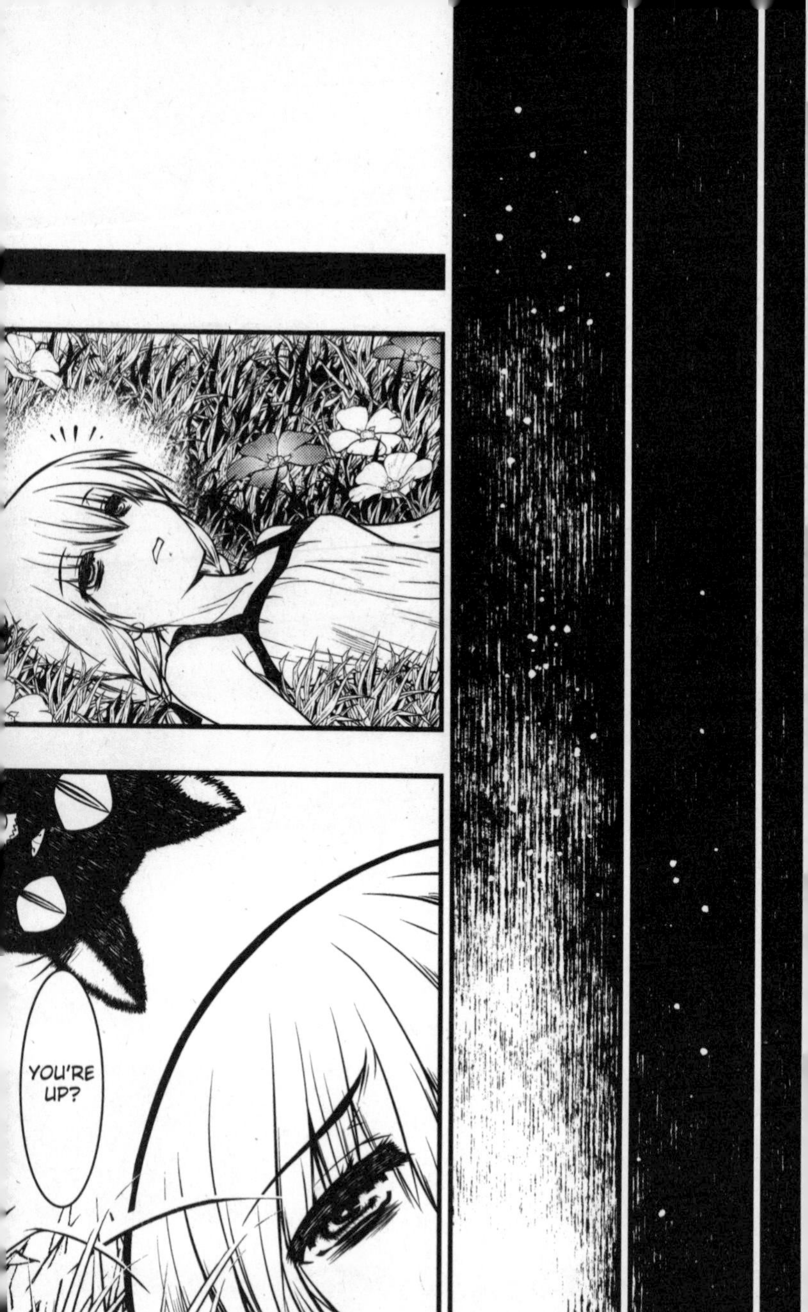
YOU'RE UP?

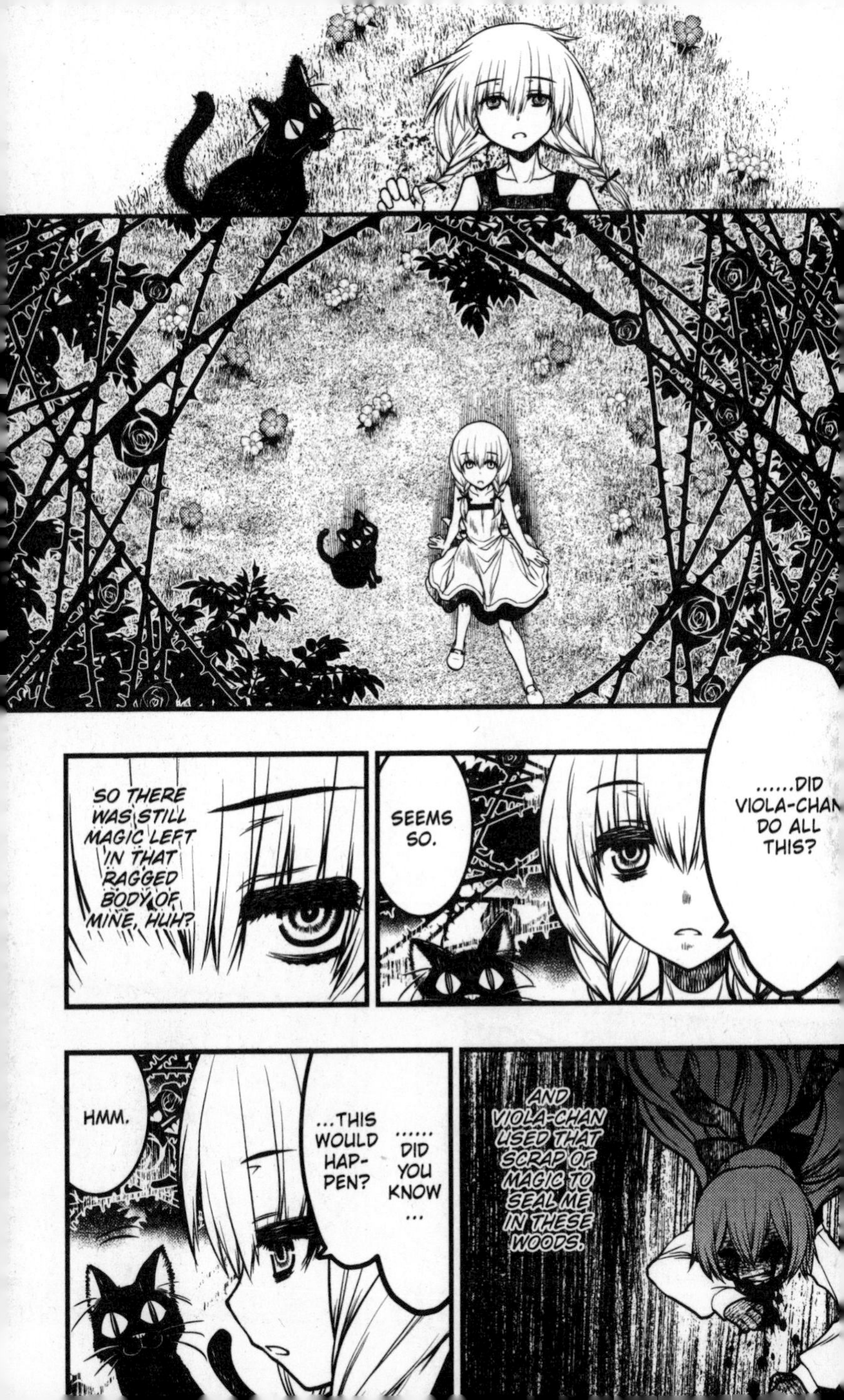
......DID VIOLA-CHAN DO ALL THIS?
SEEMS SO.
SO THERE WAS STILL MAGIC LEFT IN THAT RAGGED BODY OF MINE, HUH?
AND VIOLA-CHAN USED THAT SCRAP OF MAGIC TO SEAL ME IN THESE WOODS.
......DID YOU KNOW...
...THIS WOULD HAP-PEN?
HMM.

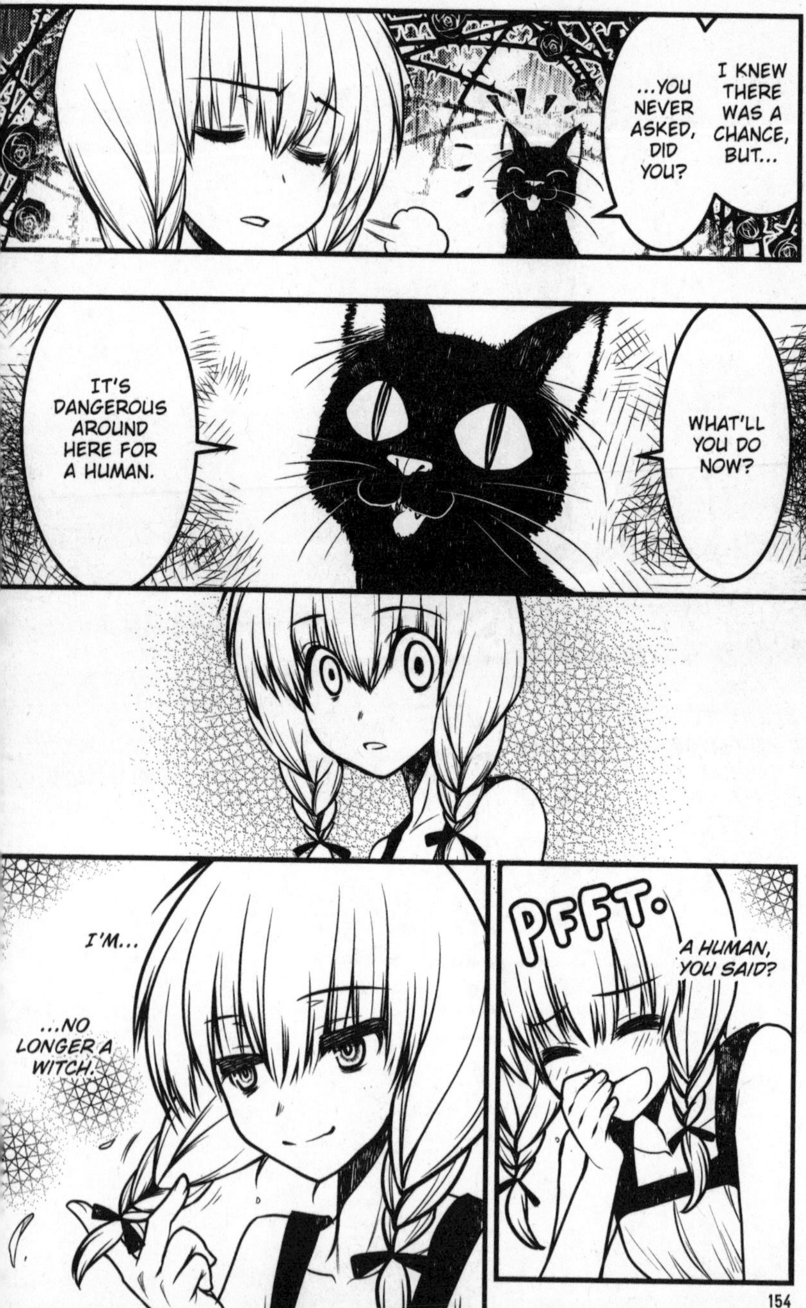
I KNEW THERE WAS A CHANCE, BUT...
...YOU NEVER ASKED, DID YOU?
WHAT'LL YOU DO NOW?
IT'S DANGEROUS AROUND HERE FOR A HUMAN.
PFFT.
A HUMAN, YOU SAID?
I'M...
...NO LONGER A WITCH.

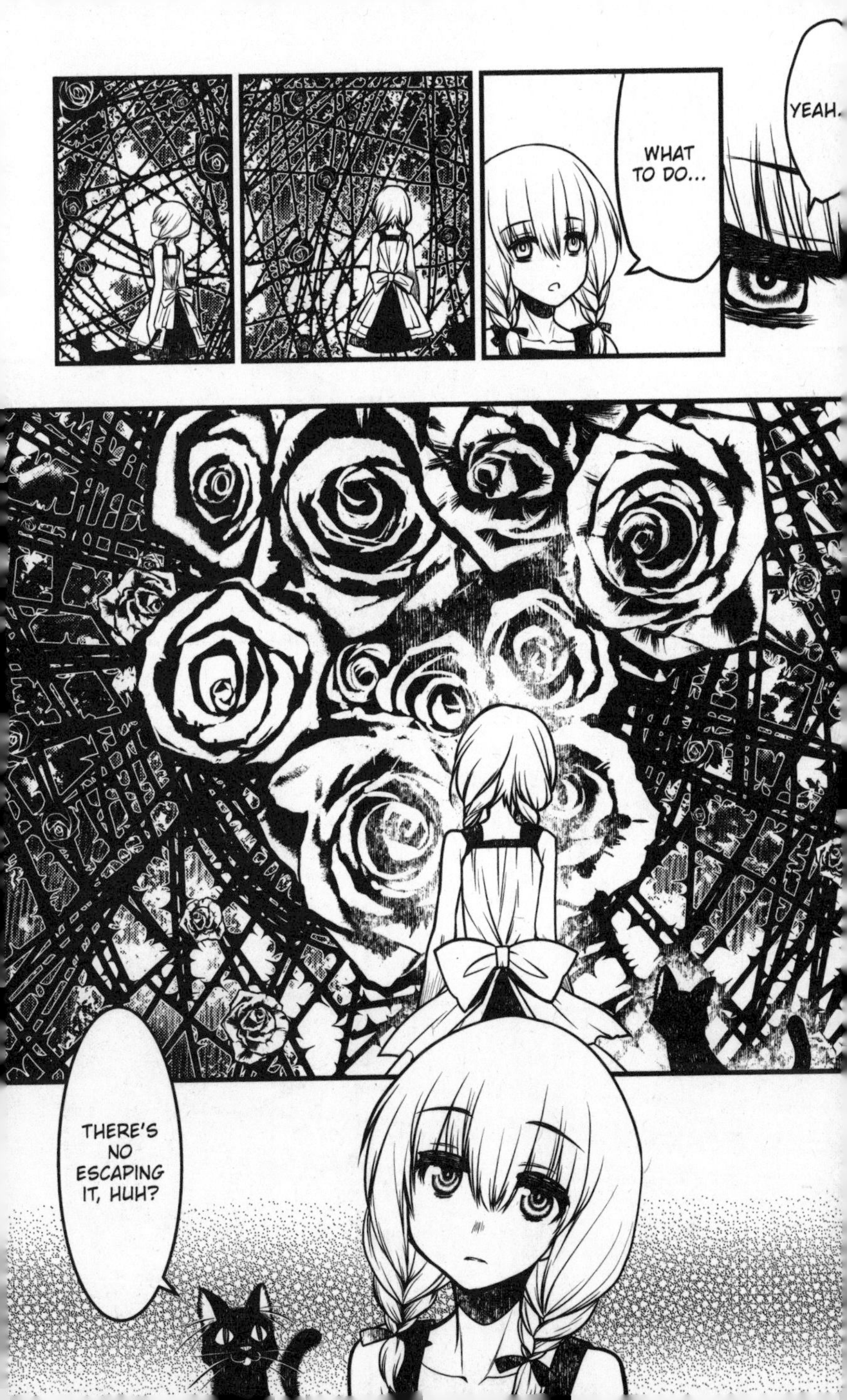
YEAH.
WHAT TO DO...
THERE'S NO ESCAPING IT, HUH?

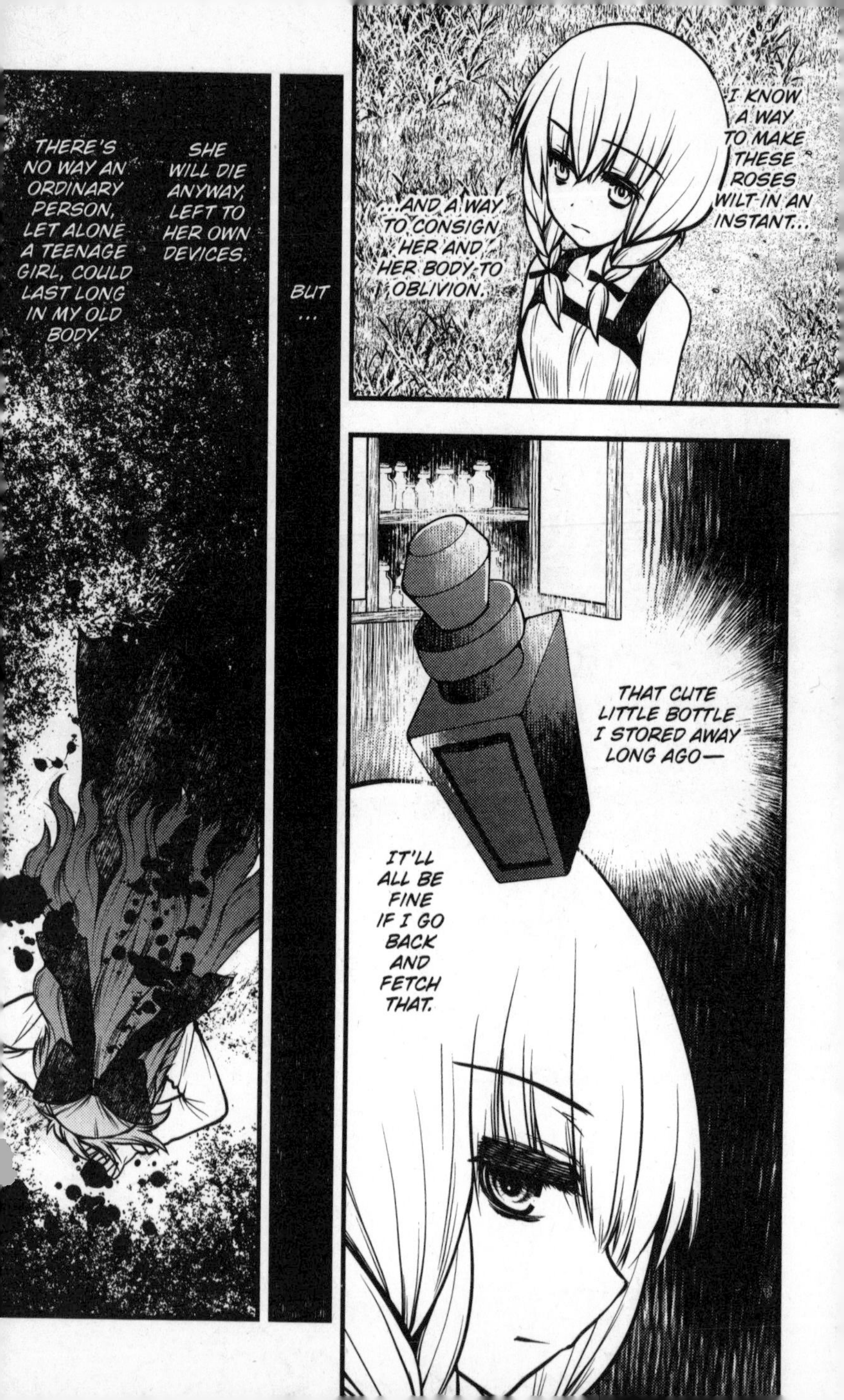
I KNOW A WAY TO MAKE THESE ROSES WILT IN AN INSTANT...
...AND A WAY TO CONSIGN HER AND HER BODY TO OBLIVION.
THAT CUTE LITTLE BOTTLE I STORED AWAY LONG AGO—
IT'LL ALL BE FINE IF I GO BACK AND FETCH THAT.
BUT...
SHE WILL DIE ANYWAY, LEFT TO HER OWN DEVICES.
THERE'S NO WAY AN ORDINARY PERSON, LET ALONE A TEENAGE GIRL, COULD LAST LONG IN MY OLD BODY.

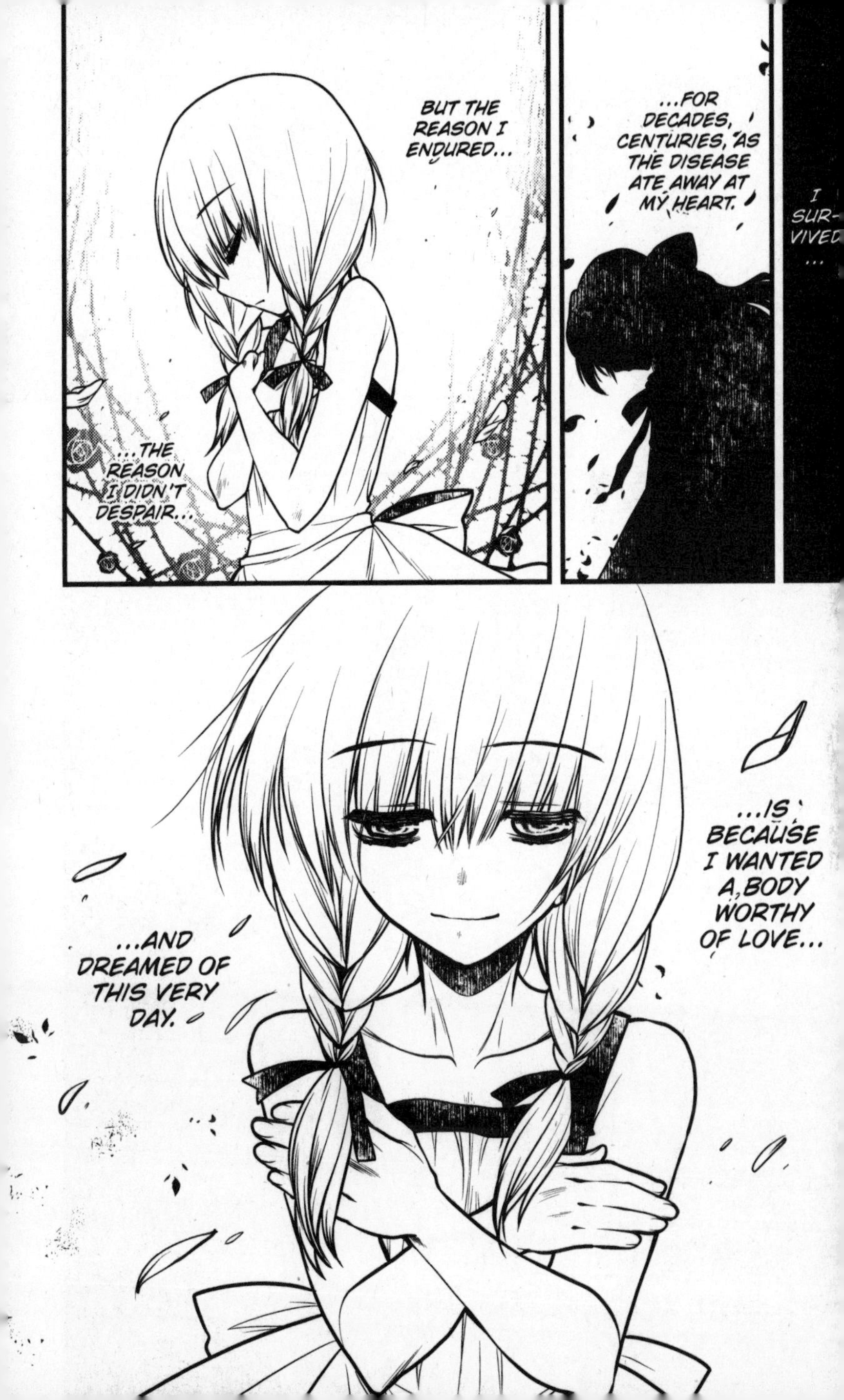
I SURVIVED...
...FOR DECADES, CENTURIES, AS THE DISEASE ATE AWAY AT MY HEART.
BUT THE REASON I ENDURED...
...THE REASON I DIDN'T DESPAIR...
...IS BECAUSE I WANTED A BODY WORTHY OF LOVE...
...AND DREAMED OF THIS VERY DAY.

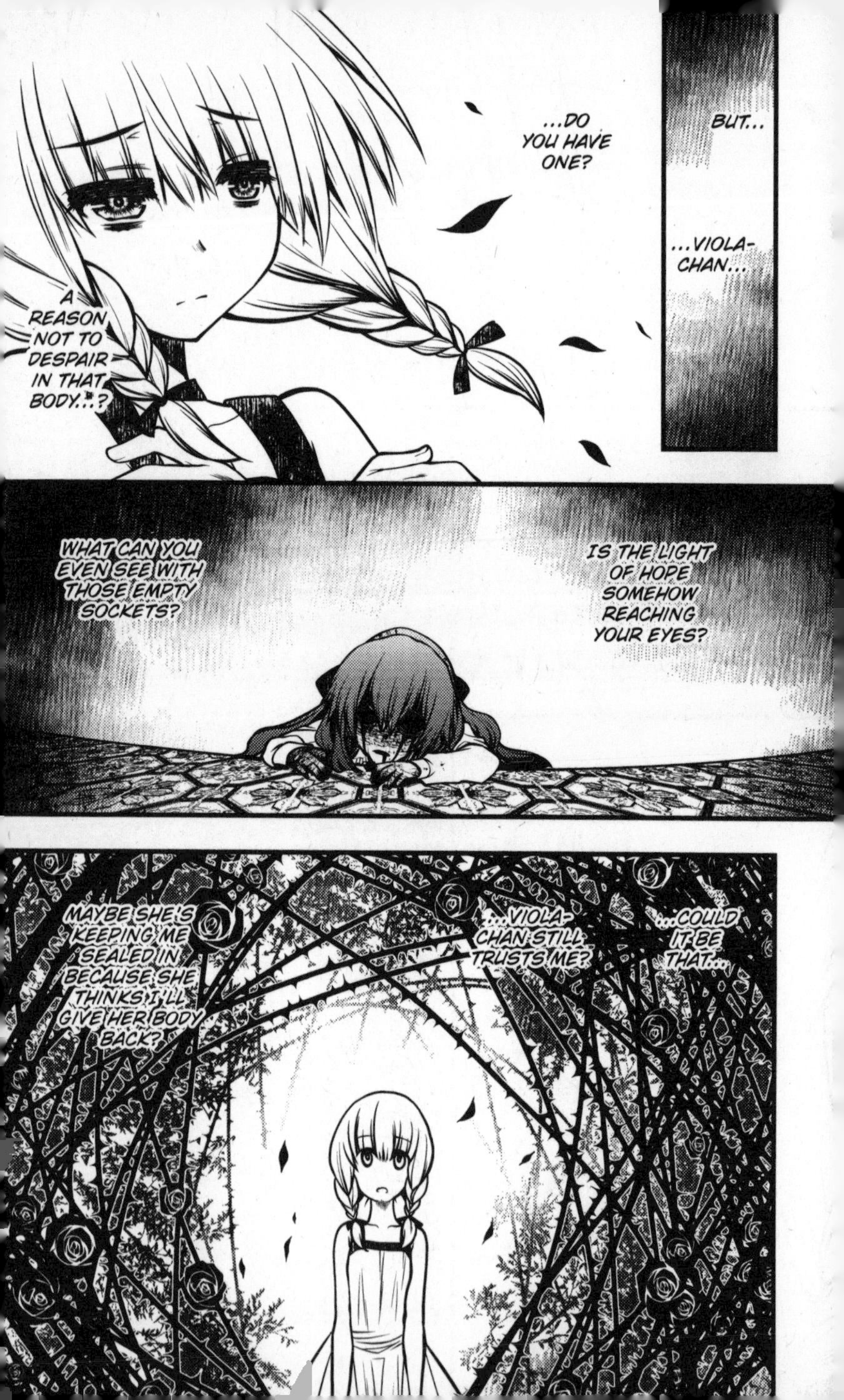
BUT...
...VIOLA-CHAN...
...DO YOU HAVE ONE?
A REASON NOT TO DESPAIR IN THAT BODY...?
IS THE LIGHT OF HOPE SOMEHOW REACHING YOUR EYES?
WHAT CAN YOU EVEN SEE WITH THOSE EMPTY SOCKETS?
...COULD IT BE THAT...
...VIOLA-CHAN STILL TRUSTS ME?
MAYBE SHE'S KEEPING ME SEALED IN BECAUSE SHE THINKS I'LL GIVE HER BODY BACK?

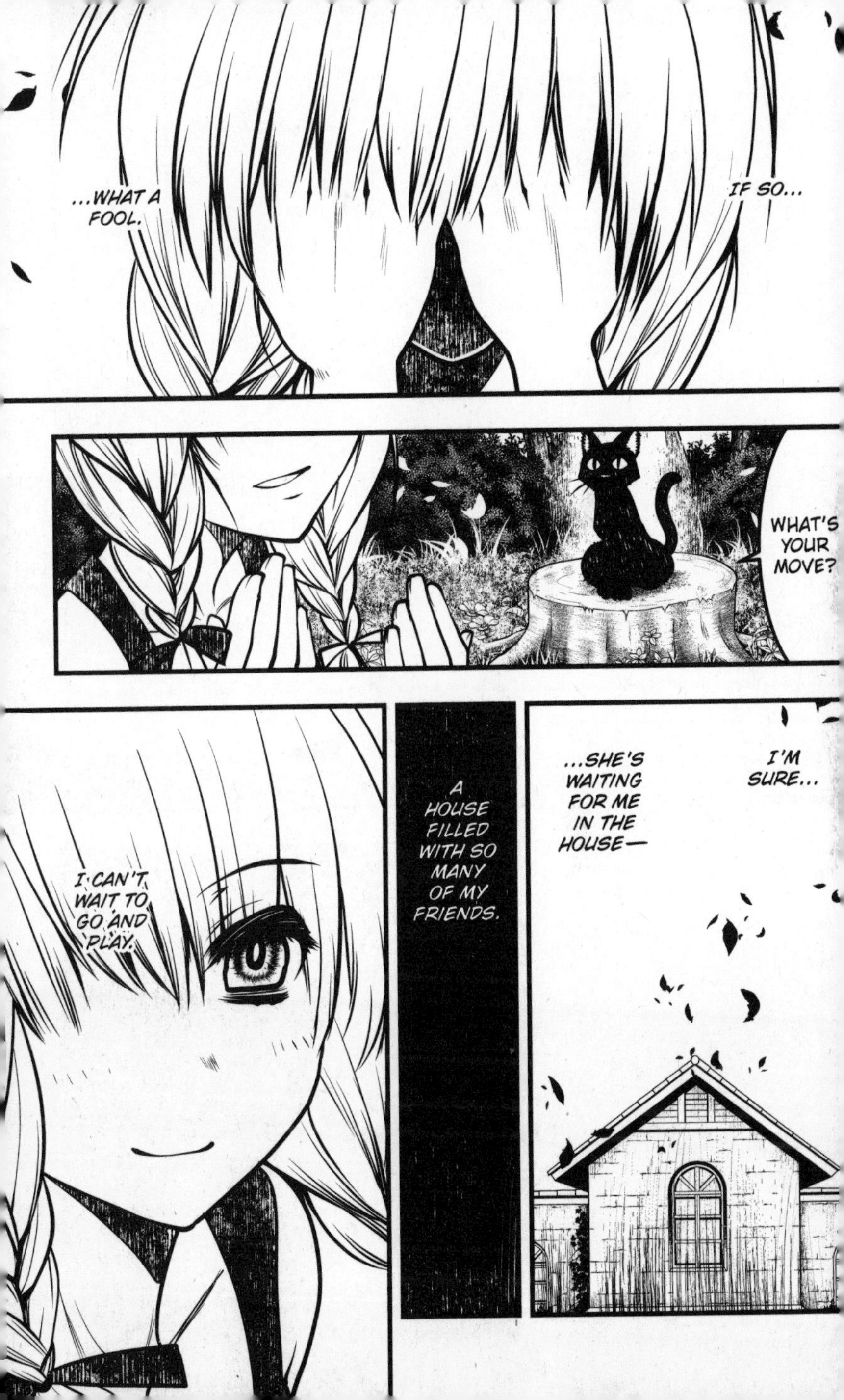
IF SO...
...WHAT A FOOL.
WHAT'S YOUR MOVE?
I'M SURE...
...SHE'S WAITING FOR ME IN THE HOUSE—
A HOUSE FILLED WITH SO MANY OF MY FRIENDS.
I CAN'T WAIT TO GO AND PLAY.

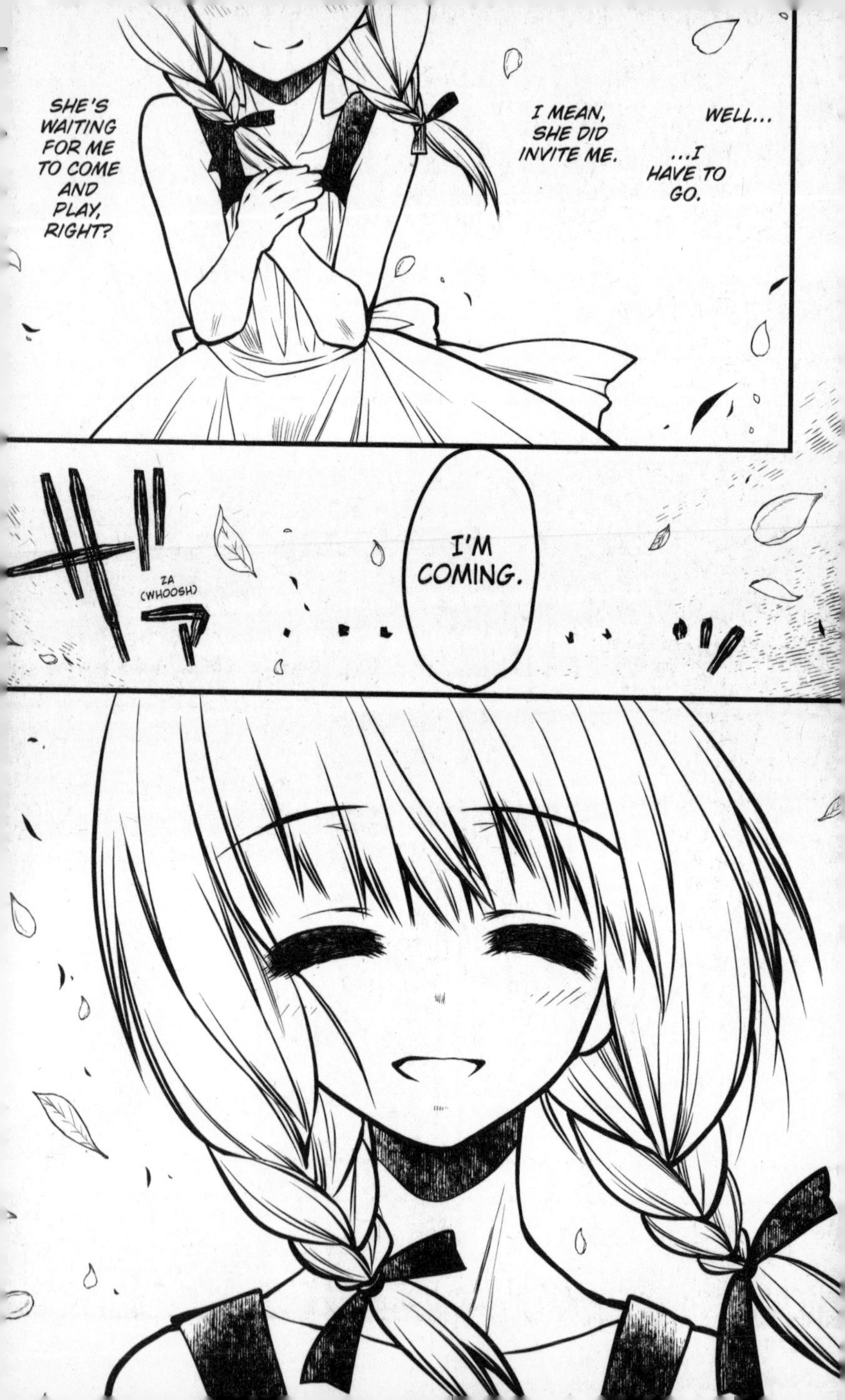
WELL...
...I HAVE TO GO.
I MEAN, SHE DID INVITE ME.
SHE'S WAITING FOR ME TO COME AND PLAY, RIGHT?
I'M COMING.
ZA (WHOOSH)

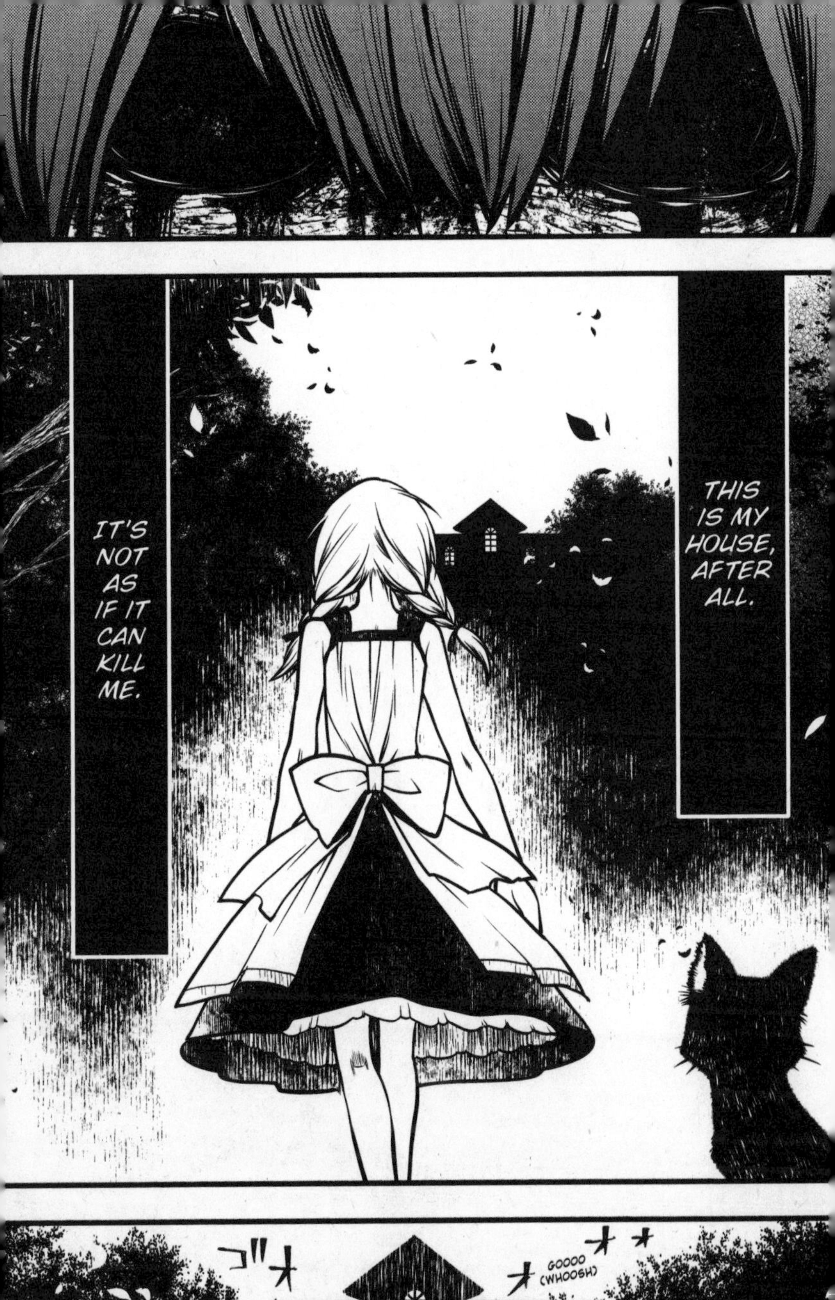
THIS IS MY HOUSE, AFTER ALL.
IT'S NOT AS IF IT CAN KILL ME.
ゴオオオ
GOOOO (WHOOSH)

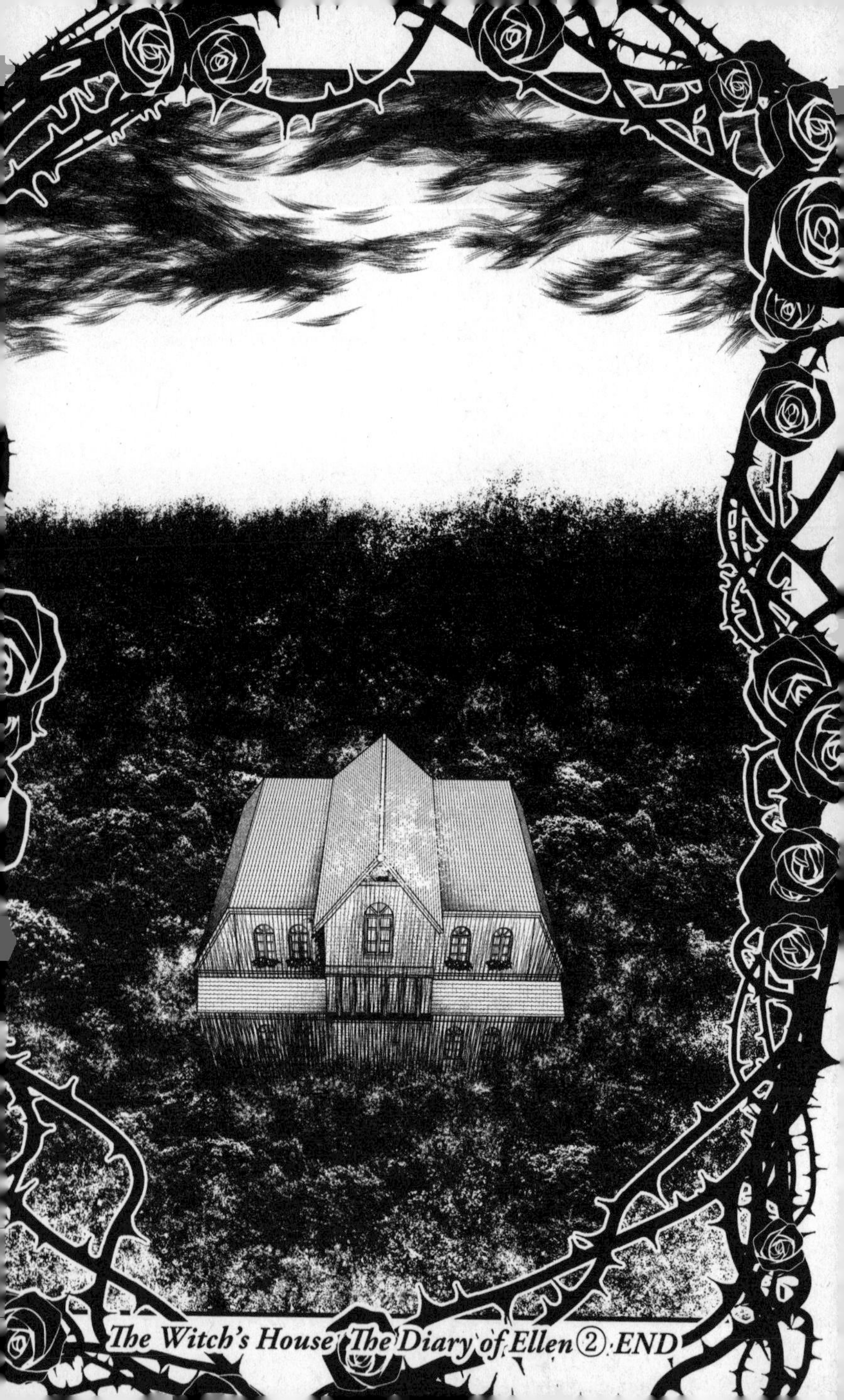
The Witch's House The Diary of Ellen ② END

THE WITCH'S HOUSE

HOUSE

The Diary of Ellen

THE WITCH'S HOUSE

The Diary of Ellen

ORIGINAL STORY:
Fummy

ART:
Yuna Kagesaki

TRANSLATION: CALEB D. COOK
LETTERING: ROCHELLE GANCIO

THE WITCH'S HOUSE THE DIARY OF ELLEN Volume 2
© Yuna Kagesaki 2018
© Fummy 2018
First published in Japan in 2018 by KADOKAWA CORPORATION, Tokyo.
English translation rights arranged with KADOKAWA CORPORATION, Tokyo
through TUTTLE-MORI AGENCY, INC., Tokyo.

English translation © 2019 by Yen Press, LLC

Yen Press
1290 Avenue of the Americas
New York, NY 10104

Visit us at yenpress.com
facebook.com/yenpress
twitter.com/yenpress

yenpress.tumblr.com
instagram.com/yenpress

First Yen Press Edition: June 2019
The chapters in this volume were originally published as ebooks by Yen Press.

Yen Press is an imprint of Yen Press, LLC.
The Yen Press name and logo are trademarks of Yen Press, LLC.

Library of Congress Control Number: 2018958638

ISBNs: 978-1-9753-5759-7 (paperback)
978-1-9753-8465-4 (ebook)

10 9 8 7 6 5 4 3 2 1

WOR

Printed in the United States of America